Exploring
Social Psychology

McGraw-Hill Series in Social Psychology

CONSULTING EDITOR Philip G. Zimbardo

Exploring Social Psychology

❖

David G. Myers
Hope College
Holland, Michigan

McGraw-Hill, Inc.

New York   St. Louis   San Francisco   Auckland   Bogotá   Caracas
Lisbon   London   Madrid   Mexico City   Milan   Montreal   New Delhi
San Juan   Singapore   Sydney   Tokyo   Toronto

EXPLORING SOCIAL PSYCHOLOGY

 This book is printed on recycled, acid-free paper containing 10% postconsumer waste.

2 3 4 5 6 7 8 9 0 DOC DOC 9 0 9 8 7 6 5 4

ISBN 0-07-044296-7

This book was set in Palatino by Better Graphics, Inc.
The editors were Christopher Rogers and James R. Belser;
the production supervisor was Leroy A. Young.
The cover was designed by Wanda Siedlecka.
R. R. Donnelley & Sons Company was printer and binder.

Library of Congress Cataloging-in-Publication Data

Myers, David G.
    Exploring social psychology / David G. Myers.
        p.   cm.—(McGraw-Hill series in social psychology)
    Includes bibliographical references and index.
    ISBN 0-07-044296-7
    1. Social psychology   I. Title   II. Series.
HM251.M894   1994
    302—dc20   93-17347

About the Author

———— ❖ ————

David G. Myers is the John Dirk Werkman Professor of Psychology at Michigan's Hope College, where students have voted him "Outstanding Professor." Myers' love of teaching psychology is manifest in his writings for the lay public. His articles have appeared in two dozen magazines, and he has authored or coauthored 10 books, most recently *The Pursuit of Happiness: Who Is Happy—and Why* (William Morrow, 1992).

Also an award-winning researcher, Myers received the Gordon Allport Prize from Division 9 of the American Psychological Association for his work on group polarization. His scientific articles have appeared in more than two dozen journals, including *Science, American Scientist,* and *Psychological Bulletin.* He has served his discipline as consulting editor to the *Journal of Experimental Social Psychology* and the *Journal of Personality and Social Psychology.*

In his spare time he has chaired his city's Human Relations Commission, helped found a community action agency which assists impoverished families, and given talks to dozens of collegiate and religious groups. David and Carol Myers are parents of two sons and a daughter.

Contents

❖

Foreword

❖

Whch social psychology works best, it touches the soul of society and the heartbeat of its individuals. Of course, it is an academic discipline with its own history, heroes, theories, methodologies, and jargon. As such, in recent years it has gradually moved to a central position within the field of psychology. In earlier days, it was looked upon as a peripheral curiosity, more akin to cultural anthropology than hard-nosed brass instrument and animal psychology that dominated a psychology proudly branded "Made in the U.S.A.," at least until the 1960s. As cognitive psychology has restored the mind and tongue to behaving organisms, social psychology has put them into a meaningful and lively social context. And as other domains of psychology have come to recognize the importance of the social setting and interpersonal dynamics in understanding the whys of human thought, feeling, and action, they too have added a social dimension to their studies. So we now have social-cognition, social-learning, social-developmental, social-personality, and many other hyphenated alliances that enrich the study of the individual. That person, though usually taken alone as the unit of psychology's research focus, is more fascinating when seen as part of the complex social fabric from which human nature is woven.

But what is unique among social psychologists is that their concern for experimental rigor and creativity in the laboratory equals their concerns for real-world relevance and viable interventions that may improve the quality of our lives. Virtually all of the most significant areas of application and extensions of psychology out of academia into the everyday life of ordinary people have come from, and are continuing to be energized by, social psychologists. What are those realms of social–psychologically inspired contributions to the human condition? Let us count but a few: health psychology, psychology and law, organizational behavior, environmental psychology, political psychology, peace psychology, and sports psychology. When a former president of the American Psychological Association urged his colleagues to "give psychology away" to the public, it was primarily the social psychologists who took his message to heart and went to work in the field of everyday little hassles and big-time troubles. So while some of us are proud to uncover a significant statistical effect in a laboratory test of key hypotheses derived from a theory, others are deriving joy from showing politicians how to negotiate more effectively, companies how to structure energy conservation programs, or the elderly how to take more control and personal responsibility over their lives.

We all recall the admonition of our inspirational leader, Kurt Lewin, who told us that there is nothing so practical as a good theory. But we now add to that intellectual call to arms that there is nothing as valuable as theoretically inspired practical applications. Furthermore, there is no reason not to embrace all of it— the abstract theory that unifies our singular observations and points us in new directions, the ingenious experimental test, the convincing demonstration of a social phenomenon, or the perceptive application of what we know to solving social problems facing our society and the world.

Despite this range of interests among social psychologists, most would agree on the basic "lessons" of social psychology that emerge from a variety of sources. Five principles can be identified. First, the power of the situation influences individual and group behavior more than we recognize in our individualistic, dispositionally oriented, culture. The second principle concerns the subjective construction of social reality, by which we mean that the social situation is a shared construal of a reality that does not exist "out there," but is created in our minds and passed on in gossip, rumors, ritual, folklore, school lessons, and racist tracts, among other sources of social communication. The third lesson is about the irrationality of some human behavior and the concurrent fallibility of human intuition—even among the best and brightest of us. Because we have shown that the presence of others, whether in groups of friends or coworkers, or in unstructured settings of strangers, influences the decisions and actions of individuals, our fourth lesson centers on group dynamism. Finally, social psychologists add the principle that it is possible to study complex social situations and generate practical solutions to some emerging problems, as well as apply what we already know to improve personal and societal functioning.

But such lessons are not merely the stuff of textbooks, they are the stuffing, or stories of life itself. Let me share a personal tale with you about the first two lessons, which, now that I think of it, also slips over into the rest of them.

Growing up in a South Bronx ghetto as a poor, sickly kid, I somehow learned the tactics and strategies of survival, known collectively as "street smarts." At first they were put to use to avoid being beaten up by the big tough guys through righteous utilization of ingratiation tactics and sensitivity to nonphysical sources of power. Then they worked to make me popular with the girls at school, which in turn enhanced my status with the less verbal neighboring big shots. By the time I got to junior high school, I was being chosen as class president, captain of this or that, and was generally looked to for advice and leadership. However, a strange thing happened along the path through adolescence. In 1948 my family moved to North Hollywood, California, for my junior year of high school. The initial wonder at being in this western paradise soon became a living nightmare. I was unable to make a single friend during the entire year, not one date. Nobody would even sit near me in the cafeteria! I was totally confused, bewildered, and of course very lonely. So much so that I became asthmatic. I became so with such intensity that my family used this newfound sickness as the excuse it needed to leave the polluted palms and general disillusionment we all felt to return to the dirty but comprehensible reality of the Bronx. Still more remarkable, within six months I was elected as the most popular boy in the senior class, "Jimmy Monroe" or James Monroe High School!

I was talking about this double transformation to my friend in homeroom class 12-H-3, Stanley Milgram, and we acknowledged that it wasn't me that had changed but the situation in which I was being judged by my peers, either as an alien New York Italian stereotype or a charming, reliable friend. We wondered how far someone could be changed by such divergent situations, and what was the stable constant in personality. "Just how much of what we see in others is in the eye of the beholder and the mouth of the judges?" Stanley wrote the senior class squibs for the Year Book and helped me to reclaim my California-lost ego by penning, "Phil's our vice president, tall and thin, with his blue eyes all the girls he'll win." So my Bronx street smarts were still working, at least sometimes, in some situations, for some people. Naturally, thereafter we both were heard to repeat loud and clear whenever asked about our predictions of what someone was like or might do: "It all depends on the situation."

Stanley went on to study conformity with Solomon Asch, a major contributor to early social psychology. At Yale, where we were on the faculty together for a short while, Milgram then conducted a series of now-classic studies on obedience to authority that have become the most cited experiments in our field because of their definitive demonstration of the power of the situation to corrupt good people into evil deeds. My way was not too divergent, since I studied how anonymity can lower restraints against antisocial acts and how putting normal, healthy young men in a mock prison ended up with their behaving in abnormal, pathological ways.

The irrationality lesson? It was the prejudice toward me created by applying an ill-fitting stereotype of being Mafia-like because of my ethnic identity and urban origins—by otherwise nice, intelligent white kids. The influence of the group prevented individual students from breaking through the constraints imposed by prejudiced thinking and group norms, even when their personal experience diverged from the hostile base rate. As a student at Brooklyn College I studied prejudice between allegedly liberal Whites and Blacks in their self-segregated seating patterns in the school cafeteria and also Black versus Puerto Rican prejudices in my neighborhood. Then when I became president of my White-Christian fraternity, I arranged to have it opened to Jews, Blacks, Puerto Ricans, and whoever made the new grade as a "good brother"—a first step in putting personal principles into social action.

You can see now why I feel that social psychology is not merely about the social life of the individual; for me, it is at the core of our lives. People are always crucial to the plot development of our most important personal stories.

The *McGraw-Hill Series in Social Psychology* has become a celebration of that basic theme. We have gathered some of the best researchers, theorists, teachers, and social change agents to write their stories about some aspect of our exciting field which they know best. They are encouraged to do so not just for their colleagues, as they do often in professional journals and monographs, but rather for intelligent undergraduates. With that youthful audience in mind, we all have tried to tap into their natural curiosity about human nature, to trigger their critical thinking, to touch their concerns for understanding the complexity of social life all about them, and to inspire them toward socially responsible utilization of their knowledge.

No one achieves those lofty goals better than the author of this text, David Myers. David writes with a clarity, precision of style, and graceful eloquence unmatched in all of psychology. He is the author of the best-selling introductory psychology textbook and also the best-selling social psychology text, a rare feat of effective writing and mind-boggling focused energy. What sets him apart from his talented peers is David's clear vision of his audience, to whom he talks as if they were welcomed guests at his dining table. We see him sharing his wealth of knowledge of psychology and of literature, posing just the right questions to peak their interest, or calling up the apt metaphor that clarifies a complex thought, and always integrating it all within a compelling story. In designing this newest addition to our Social Psychology Series, the psychology editor, Christopher Rogers (a rare jewel in almost any setting), and I wanted to free David from the traditional constraints of generic chapters of prescribed lengths and standard structures. David Myers has succeeded beyond our most ambitious expectations in bursting free to write 31 stories, or modules, that together form *Exploring Social Psychology*. Each one is a treat to read, and all gain from rereading, even for jaded old-timers like me. These 30-odd "magical modules," as I have come to think of them, offer both new and experienced readers of social psychology a feast—not in its overwhelming opulence but in a thoughtful series of compact, beautifully organized presentations of single flavors or themes. Whole sets of research are skillfully summarized, the right questions are posed, the perceptive conclusions extracted, and the meaningful implications adroitly drawn. Part of the task of a consulting editor is typically to recommend where text can be deleted, chapters chopped down, or the whole shortened in any way possible. This is the first time that I have had to insist that an author write more, because it was evident that David Myers had more tales to tell, and this was the place for his rhetoric to flow.

Popular magazine writers are cautioned against writing "puff pieces" extolling only virtues of their featured subjects; so I too must recognize that principle of not seeming undiscriminating in being so bullish on Myers' *Exploring Social Psychology*. The book does have a flaw. Its major flaw is that it is not the first social psychology book that I read as an undergraduate. Had it been, I would have known instantly and with absolute certainty that there is no more exciting adventure than to become one of them, a social psychologist with stories to learn from others and stories to pass on to all who are willing to listen at our feast of knowledge. Just as Allan Funt has shown us with his *Candid Camera Classics* that it is possible to learn while laughing, David Myers demonstrates the corollary: That it is possible to be entertained while becoming educated. So read and enjoy this master of the trade who offers you his best ever table setting, replete with wonderful tales accompanying every course.

PHILIP G. ZIMBARDO
Series Consulting Editor

Preface

———— ❖ ————

This is a book I have secretly wanted to write. I have long believed that what is wrong with all psychology textbooks (including those which I have written) is their overlong chapters. Few can read a 40-page chapter in a single sitting without their eyes glazing and their mind wandering. So why not organize the discipline into digestible chunks—say, forty 15-page chapters rather than fifteen 40-page chapters—that a student *could* read in a sitting, before laying the book down with a sense of completion?

Thus when McGraw-Hill psychology editor Chris Rogers first suggested over bowls of New England clam chowder that I abbreviate and restructure my 15-chapter 600-page *Social Psychology* into a series of crisply written 10-page modules, I said Eureka! At last a publisher willing to break convention by packaging the material in a form ideally suited to students' attention spans. By presenting concepts and findings in smaller bites, we also hoped not to overload students' capacities to absorb new information. And by keeping *Exploring Social Psychology* slim and economical, we sought to enable instructors to supplement it with other reading suitable for their teaching of introductory or social psychology.

As the playful module titles suggest, I have also broken with convention by introducing social psychology in an essay format. Each module is written in the spirit of Thoreau's admonition that "anything living is easily and naturally expressed in popular language." My aim in the parent *Social Psychology*, and even more so here, is to write in a voice that is both solidly scientific and warmly human, factually rigorous and intellectually provocative. I hope to reveal social psychology as an investigative reporter might, by providing a current summary of important social phenomena, by showing how social psychologists uncover and explain such phenomena, and by reflecting on their human significance.

In selecting material I have represented social psychology's scope, highlighting its scientific study of how we *think about, influence,* and *relate* to one another. I also emphasize material that casts social psychology in the intellectual tradition of the liberal arts. By the teaching of great literature, philosophy, and science, liberal education seeks to expand our thinking and awareness and to liberate us from the confines of the present. Social psychology can contribute to these goals. Many undergraduate social psychology students are not psychology majors; virtually all will enter other professions. By focusing on humanly significant issues such as belief and illusion, independence and interdependence, love and hate, one can present social psychology in ways that inform and stimulate all students.

A comprehensive teaching package accompanies *Exploring Social Psychology*. Martin Bolt has adapted his acclaimed *Teacher's Resource Manual* and Ann Weber's fine test-item file to fit this brief book. In collaboration with Allen Funt and Philip Zimbardo, McGraw-Hill has developed *Candid Camera Classics in Social Psychology*, a videodisc (also available on videotape) of 15 three- to five-minute clips from the original "Candid Camera" shows.

*A*cknowledgments

I remain indebted to the community of scholars who have guided and critiqued the evolution of this material through four editions of *Social Psychology*. These caring colleagues, acknowledged individually there, have enabled a better book than I, alone, could have created.

Special credit for this new book goes, of course, to psychology editor Christopher Rogers, whose brainchild it is. My thanks to Chris for his creativity and confidence and to series editor Philip Zimbardo for his encouragement. As my friendship with Phil has grown, I have come to admire his gifts as one of psychology's premier communicators.

As in all five of my published social psychology books with McGraw-Hill, I again pay tribute to three significant people. Were it not for the invitation of McGraw-Hill's Nelson Black, it surely never would have occurred to me to try my hand at text writing. James Belser has patiently guided the process of converting all my McGraw-Hill books from manuscript into finished text. Finally, poet Jack Ridl, my Hope College colleague and writing coach, helped shape the voice you will hear in these pages.

To all in this supporting cast, I am indebted. Working with all these people has made my work a stimulating, gratifying experience.

DAVID G. MYERS

Exploring
Social Psychology

Introducing
Social
Psychology

1

Doing Social Psychology

❖

‖❝O‖ur lives are connected by a thousand invisible threads," said the novelist Herman Melville. Social psychology—the science that studies our human connections—aims to illuminate those threads. It does so by asking questions, questions that you, too, may wonder about:

- How and what do people *think* of one another? How reasonable are the ideas we form of ourselves? of our friends? of strangers? How tight are the links between what we think and what we do?
- How, and how much, do people *influence* one another? How strong are the invisible threads that pull us? Are we creatures of our gender roles? our groups? our cultures? How can we resist social pressure, even sway the majority?
- What shapes the way we *relate* to one another? What leads people sometimes to hurt and sometimes to help? What kindles social conflict? And how might we transform the closed fists of aggression into the open arms of compassion?

Some common threads run through these questions: They all deal with how we view and affect one another. And that is what social psychology is all about. Social psychologists explore such questions using the scientific method. They study attitudes and beliefs, conformity and independence, love and hate. To put it formally, **social psychology** is *the scientific study of how people think about, influence, and relate to one another.*

3

Unlike other scientific disciplines, social psychology has 5.5 billion amateur practitioners. Few of us have firsthand experience in nuclear physics, but we are the very subject matter of social psychology. As we observe people, we form ideas about how human beings think about, influence, and relate to one another. Professional social psychologists do the same, only more painstakingly, often with experiments that create miniature social dramas that pin down cause and effect.

Most of what you will learn about social-psychological research methods you will absorb as you read later modules. But let us go backstage now and take a brief look at how social psychology is done. This glimpse behind the scenes will be just enough, I trust, for you to appreciate findings discussed later.

Social-psychological research varies by location. It can take place in the laboratory (a controlled situation) or in the **field** (everyday situations outside the laboratory). And it varies by method—being either **correlational** (asking whether two factors are naturally associated) or **experimental** (manipulating some factor to see its effect on another). If you want to be a critical reader of popularly reported psychological research, it will pay you to understand the difference between correlational and experimental research.

To illustrate the advantages and disadvantages of correlational and experimental procedures, consider a practical question: Is college a good financial investment? Surely you have heard the claims about the economic benefits of going to college. Are they something more than a sales pitch? How might we separate fact from falsehood in assessing the impact of college upon lifetime earnings?

CORRELATIONAL RESEARCH: DETECTING NATURAL ASSOCIATIONS

First, we might discern whether any relation—or *correlation*, as we say— exists between educational level and earnings. If college is a good financial investment, then college graduates should, on average, earn more than those who don't attend. Sure enough, Figure 1–1 shows that college graduates have a whopping income advantage. So can we now agree with college recruiters that higher education is the gateway to economic success?

Before we answer yes, let's take a closer look. We know that formal education correlates with earnings; that's beyond question. But does this necessarily mean that education *causes* higher incomes? Perhaps you can identify factors other than education that might explain the education-earnings correlation. (We call these factors *variables* because people will vary on them.) What about family social status? What about intellectual

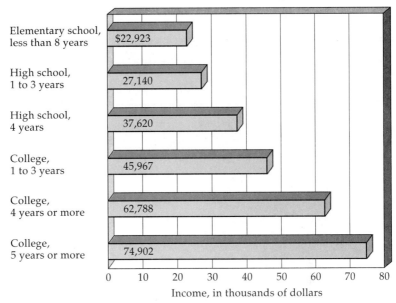

FIGURE 1–1
Income of families, by education of head of household.

ability and achievement drive? Might these not already be higher in those who go to college? Perhaps the higher earnings come from some combination of these variables, and not the college degree. Or perhaps education and earnings correlate because those who have money can most easily afford college in the first place.

Correlation versus Causation

The education-earnings question illustrates the most irresistible thinking error made by both amateur and professional social psychologists. When two factors like education and earnings go together, it is terribly tempting to conclude that one is causing the other.

Consider two examples of the correlation-causation issue in psychology. If a particular style of child rearing correlates with the personality traits of children exposed to it, what does this tell us? If parents who often spank or even abuse their children often have unruly children, what does this tell us? With every correlation, there are three possible explanations (Figure 1–2). The effect of the parents on the child ($x{\rightarrow}y$) is one. Perhaps physically punitive parents are more likely to have aggressive children because the parents' own example teaches such behavior. You might, however, be surprised at the strength of the evidence for children affect-

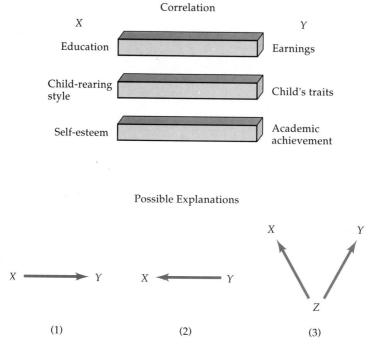

FIGURE 1–2
When two variables correlate, any combination of three explanations is possible.

ing their parents (*x*←*y*) (Bell & Chapman, 1986). Unruly children may elicit punishment from exasperated parents. Or maybe, as explanation 3 in Figure 1–2 suggests, there is a common source (*z*) for both the child-rearing style and the child's traits. Perhaps the characteristics of both parent and child are rooted in shared genes. Perhaps the punitive parent and the aggressive child both mirror the influence of violent TV programs and movies watched in the home. Or perhaps all of these things are true at once.

Consider another very real correlation—between self-esteem and academic achievement. Children with high self-esteem tend also to have high academic achievement. (As with any correlation, we can also state this the other way around: High achievers tend to have high self-esteem.) Why do you suppose this is?

Some people believe that a "healthy self-concept" contributes to achievement. Thus, boosting a child's self-image may also boost the child's school achievement. Others argue that high achievement produces a favorable self-image. As a recent study of 635 Norwegian school-children confirms, a string of gold stars by one's name on the spelling chart and constant praise from an admiring teacher can boost a child's self-esteem (Skaalvik & Hagtvet, 1990). But in other studies—one a nationwide sample of 1600 young American men, another of 715 Minnesota youngsters—self-esteem and achievement were *not* causally related (Bachman & O'Malley, 1977; Maruyama & others, 1981). Rather, they correlated because both were linked to intelligence and family social status. When the researchers statistically removed the effect of intelligence and family status, the correlation between self-esteem and achievement evaporated. Similarly, John McCarthy and Dean Hoge (1984) dispute the idea that the correlation between low self-esteem and delinquency means that low self-esteem causes delinquency; rather, their study of 1658 teenagers suggests, delinquent acts lower self-esteem. Breaking rules leads to condemnation leads to lowered self-esteem, suggest the researchers.

These studies can *suggest* cause-effect relations in correlational research by pulling apart obviously related factors (like education, family status, and aptitude) to isolate the predictive power of each. Such studies can also consider the sequence of events (for example, by detecting whether changes in achievement more often precede or follow changes in self-esteem). Yet the moral of the story remains: Correlational research allows us to *predict* but cannot tell us whether changing one variable (such as education) will *cause* changes in another (such as income).

Thus, the advantage of correlational research: it tends to occur in real-world settings where we can examine factors like race, sex, and education that we cannot manipulate in the laboratory. And its disadvantage: its results are often misinterpreted. Knowing that two variables change together enables us to *predict* one when we know the other. But discerning cause and effect is trickier.

*E*XPERIMENTAL RESEARCH: SEARCHING FOR CAUSE AND EFFECT

The near impossibility of discerning cause and effect among naturally correlated events prompts most social psychologists to create laboratory simulations of everyday processes whenever this is feasible and ethical. These simulations are similar to how aeronautical engineers work. They don't begin by observing how flying objects perform in a wide variety of natural environments. The variations in both atmospheric conditions and flying objects are so complex that they would surely find it difficult to organize and use such data to design better aircraft. Instead, they construct a simulated reality that is under their control—a wind tunnel. Now they can manipulate wind conditions and ascertain the precise effect of particular wind conditions on particular wing structures.

Control: Manipulating Variables

Like aeronautical engineers, social psychologists experiment by constructing social situations that simulate important features of our daily lives. By varying just one or two factors at a time—called **independent variables**—the experimenter pinpoints how changes in these one or two things affect us. As the wind tunnel helps the aeronautical engineer discover principles of aerodynamics, so the experiment enables the social psychologist to discover principles of social thinking, social influence, and social relations. As the ultimate aim of wind tunnel simulations is to understand and predict the flying characteristics of complex aircraft, so social psychologists experiment to understand and predict human behavior.

Social psychologists have used the experimental method in about three-fourths of their research studies (Higbee & others, 1982), and in two out of three studies the setting has been a research laboratory (Adair & others, 1985). To illustrate the laboratory experiment, consider an issue we will explore in a later chapter: television's effects on children's attitudes and behavior. Children who watch many violent television programs tend to be more aggressive than those who watch few. This suggests that children might be learning from what they see on the screen. But, as I hope you now recognize, this is a correlational finding. Figure 1–2 reminds us that there are two other cause-effect interpretations which do not implicate television as the cause of the children's aggression. (What are they?)

Social psychologists have therefore brought television viewing into the laboratory, where they control the amount of violence the children see. By exposing children to violent and nonviolent programs, researchers can observe how the amount of violence affects behavior. Robert Liebert and Robert Baron (1972) showed young Ohio boys and girls a violent excerpt from a gangster television show or an excerpt from an exciting track race. The children who viewed the violence were subsequently most likely to press vigorously a special red button which supposedly would heat a rod, causing a burning pain to another child. This measure of behavior we call the **dependent variable**. (Actually, there was no other child, so no one was really harmed.) Such experiments indicate that television *can* be one cause of children's aggressive behavior.

So far we have seen that the logic of experimentation is simple: By creating and controlling a miniature reality, we can vary one factor and then another and discover how these factors, separately or in combination, affect people. Now let's go a little deeper and see how an experiment is done.

Every social-psychological experiment includes two essential ingredients. One we have just considered—*control*. We manipulate one or two independent variables while trying to hold everything else constant. The other ingredient is *random assignment*.

Random Assignment: The Great Equalizer

Recall that we were reluctant to credit having gone to college with the higher incomes of college graduates, who may benefit not only from their education but also from their social backgrounds and aptitudes. A survey researcher might measure each of these likely other factors and then note the income advantage enjoyed by college graduates above and beyond what these other factors predict. Such statistical gymnastics are well and good. But the researcher can never adjust for all the factors that might distinguish graduates from nonattenders. The alternative explanations for the income difference are limitless—perhaps ethnic heritage, or sociability, or good looks, or any of hundreds of other factors the researcher hasn't considered.

So, for the moment, let's give free reign to our imaginations and see how all these complicating factors might be equalized in one maneuver. Suppose someone gave us the power to take a group of high school graduates and **randomly assign** some to college and some to other endeavors (Figure 1–3). Each person would have an equal chance of being assigned to either the college or noncollege condition. Thus the people in both groups would, in every conceivable way—family status, looks, aptitude—average about the same. Random assignment would roughly equalize all these previously complicating factors. Any later income difference between these two groups could therefore not be caused by any of

FIGURE 1–3
Randomly assigning people either to a condition which receives the experimental treatment or to a control condition which does not gives the researcher confidence that any later difference is somehow caused by the treatment.

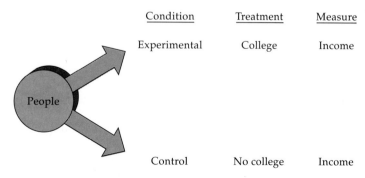

	Condition	Treatment	Measure
	Experimental	College	Income
People			
	Control	No college	Income

these factors. Rather, it would almost surely have *something* to do with the variable we manipulated. Similarly, if an experiment on malaria in Central America revealed that only people assigned to sleeping rooms with-unscreened windows catch it, this would not mean that unscreened windows *cause* malaria, but it would indicate that the cause has something to do with the lack of screens (which keep out insects).

The Ethics of Experimentation

Our college example also illustrates why some experiments are neither feasible nor ethical. Social psychologists would never manipulate people's lives in this way. In such cases we rely upon the correlational method and squeeze from it all the information we can.

In other cases, such as the issue of how television affects children, we briefly alter people's social experience and note the effects. Sometimes the experimental treatment is a harmless, perhaps even enjoyable experience to which people give their knowing consent. Sometimes, however, researchers find themselves operating in that gray area between the harmless and the risky.

Social psychologists often venture into that ethical gray area when they design experiments which really engage people's thoughts and emotions. Experiments need not have what Elliot Aronson, Marilyn Brewer, and Merrill Carlsmith (1985) call **mundane realism**. That is, laboratory behavior (for example, delivering electric shocks as part of an experiment on aggression) need not be literally the same as everyday behavior. For many researchers, that sort of realism is indeed mundane—not too important. But the experiment *should* have **experimental realism**: it should absorb and involve the participants. Experimenters do not want their people consciously playacting or ho-humming it; they want to engage real psychological processes. Forcing people to choose whether to give intense or mild electric shock to someone else can, for example, be a realistic measure of aggression. It functionally simulates real aggression.

Achieving experimental realism often requires deceiving people. If the person in the next room is actually not receiving the shocks, the experimenter does not want the participants to know this. That would destroy the experimental realism. Thus, about one-third of social-psychological studies (though a decreasing number) have temporarily deceived their participants (Vitelli, 1988).

Experimenters also seek to hide their predictions lest the participants, in their eagerness to be "good subjects," merely do what's expected—or, in an ornery mood, do the opposite. In subtle ways, the experimenter's words, tone of voice, and gestures may nevertheless call forth desired responses. To minimize such **demand characteristics**—cues that seem to "demand" certain behavior—experimenters typically standardize their instructions or even write or tape-record them.

Researchers often walk a tightrope in designing experiments that will be involving yet ethical. To believe that you are hurting someone, or to be subjected to strong social pressure to see if it will change your opinion or behavior, may be temporarily uncomfortable. Such experiments raise the age-old question of whether ends justify means. Do the insights gained justify deceiving and sometimes distressing people?

Thanks to researchers' increased concern for the dignity of their "subjects," university ethics committees now review social-psychological research to ensure that it will treat people humanely. Ethical principles developed by the American Psychological Association (1981, 1992) and the British Psychological Society (1991) urge investigators to:

- Tell potential participants enough about the experiment to enable their **informed consent**.
- Be truthful. Use deception only if justified by a significant purpose and if there is no alternative.
- Protect people from harm and significant discomfort.
- Treat information about the individual participants confidentially.
- Fully explain the experiment afterward, including any deception. The only exception to this rule is when the feedback would be distressing, say by making people realize they have been stupid or cruel.

The experimenter should be sufficiently informative *and* considerate that people leave feeling at least as good about themselves as when they came in. Better yet, the participants should be repaid by having learned something about the nature of psychological inquiry. When treated in a courteous, nonmanipulative way, few participants mind being deceived (Christensen, 1988). Indeed, say social psychology's defenders, we provoke far greater anxiety and distress by giving and returning course exams than we now do in our experiments.

E XPLAINING AND PREDICTING: USING THEORIES

Although basic research often produces practical benefits, application isn't our only reason for doing social psychology. Many of us are in the profession because we have a hard time thinking of anything more fascinating than our own human existence. If, as Socrates counseled, "the unexamined life is not worth living," then simply "knowing thyself" seems a worthy enough goal.

As we wrestle with human nature to pin down its secrets, we organize our ideas and findings into theories. A **theory** is an integrated set of principles that explain and predict phenomena. Some people wonder why social psychologists are so preoccupied with theories: Why don't they just gather facts? Our aeronautical engineering analogy is again useful. The engineers would soon be overwhelmed if, without any guiding principles, they tried by trial and error to create an exhaustive catalog of how different wind conditions affect different wing structures. So, they formulate broad concepts or theories about how air movements interact with wing structures and use the wind tunnel to test predictions derived from these concepts. Theories are a scientific shorthand.

In everyday conversation, "theory" often means "less than fact"—a middle rung on a confidence ladder going down from fact to theory to guess. But to any kind of scientist, facts and theories are different things, not different points on a continuum. Facts are agreed-upon statements about what we observe. Theories are *ideas* that summarize and explain facts. "Science is built up with facts, as a house is with stones," said Jules-Henri Poincaré, "but a collection of facts is no more a science than a heap of stones is a house."

Theories not only summarize but also imply testable predictions, called **hypotheses.** Hypotheses serve several purposes. First, they allow us to *test* the theories on which they are based. By making specific predictions, a theory puts its money where its mouth is. Second, predictions give *direction* to research. Any scientific field will mature more rapidly if its researchers have a sense of direction. Theoretical predictions suggest new areas for research; they send investigators looking for things they might never have thought of. Third, the predictive feature of good theories can also make them very *practical* as well. What, for example, would be of greater practical value today than a theory of aggression that would predict when to expect it and show how to control it? As Kurt Lewin, one of modern social psychology's founders, declared, "There is nothing so practical as a good theory."

Consider how this works. Say we observe that people sometimes explode violently when in crowds. We might therefore theorize that the presence of other people makes individuals feel anonymous and lowers their inhibitions. Let's let our minds play with this idea for a moment. Perhaps we could test it by constructing a laboratory experiment similar to execution by electric chair. What if we asked individuals in groups to administer punishing shocks to a hapless victim without knowing which one of the group was actually shocking the victim? Would these individuals administer stronger shock than individuals acting alone, as our theory predicts?

We might also manipulate anonymity: Would people hiding behind masks deliver stronger shocks because they could not be identified? If the results confirm our hypothesis, they might suggest some practical applications. Perhaps police brutality could be reduced by having officers wear large name tags and drive cars identified with large numbers or by videotaping their arrests.

But how do we conclude that one theory is better than another? A good theory does all its functions well: (1) It effectively summarizes a wide range of observations; (2) and it makes clear predictions that we can use to (a) confirm or modify the theory, (b) generate new exploration, and (c) suggest practical application. When we discard theories, usually it's not because they have been proved false. Rather, like an old car, they get replaced by newer, better models.

GENERALIZING FROM LABORATORY TO LIFE

As the TV experiment illustrates, social psychology mixes everyday experience and laboratory analysis. Throughout this book we will do the same by drawing our data mostly from the laboratory and our illustrations mostly from life. Social psychology displays a healthy interplay between laboratory research and everyday life. Hunches gained from everyday experience often inspire laboratory research, which deepens our understanding of our experience. What we see around us we can explore in experiments, the results of which we may then apply to social problems. This interplay appears in the research on children's television. What people saw in everyday life suggested experiments. Network and government policymakers are now well aware of the results (although economics and politics constrain their policies).

However, we must generalize from laboratory to life cautiously. Although the laboratory uncovers basic secrets of human existence, it is still a simplified, controlled reality. It tells us what effect to expect of variable x, all other things being equal—which in real life they never are. Moreover, as you will see, the participants in many social-psychological experiments are college students. While this may help you identify with them, college students are hardly a random sample of all humanity. Would we get similar results with people of different ages, educational levels, and cultures? This is always an open question. But experience teaches us to distinguish between the *content* of people's thinking and acting (their attitudes, for example) and the *process* by which they think and act (for example, how attitudes affect actions and vice versa). From culture to culture the content varies more than the process: People of different cultures may hold different opinions, yet form them in similar ways. Likewise, college students in Puerto Rico report greater loneliness than collegians on the U.S. mainland. Yet in both cultures the ingredients of loneliness are much the same—shyness, uncertain purpose in life, low self-esteem (Jones & others, 1985).

Correlations, experiments, research ethics, theory testing, generalizing to everyday life—with our methodological tool kit in hand, let the fun begin.

CONCEPTS TO REMEMBER

Social psychology   The scientific study of how people think about, influence, and relate to one another.

Field research   Research done in natural, real-life settings outside the laboratory.

Correlational research   The study of the naturally occurring relationships among variables.

Independent variable   The experimental factor that a researcher manipulates (the predictor variable).

Dependent variable   The variable being predicted and measured, so-called because it may *depend* on manipulations of the independent variable.

Experimental research   Studies which seek clues to cause-effect relationships by manipulating one or more factors (independent variables) while controlling others (holding them constant).

Random assignment   The process of assigning participants to the conditions of an experiment such that all persons have the same chance of being in a given condition. Random *assignment* in experiments differs from random **sampling** in surveys. Random assignment helps us infer cause and effect. Random sampling helps us generalize to a population.

Mundane realism   Degree to which an experiment is superficially similar to everyday situations.

Experimental realism   Degree to which an experiment absorbs and involves its participants.

Demand characteristics   Cues in an experiment that tell the participant what behavior is expected.

Informed consent   An ethical principle requiring that research participants be told enough to enable them to choose whether they wish to participate.

Theory   An integrated set of principles that explain and predict observed events.

Hypothesis   A testable proposition that describes a relationship that may exist between events.

2

Did You Know It All Along?

❖

Anything seems commonplace, once explained.
Dr. Watson to Sherlock Holmes

D o social psychology's theories provide *new* insight into the human condition? Or do they only describe the obvious? Many of the conclusions presented in this book will probably have already occurred to you, for social psychology is all around you. Every day we observe people thinking about, influencing, and relating to one another. For centuries, philosophers, novelists, and poets have observed and commented upon social behavior, often with keen insight. As English philosopher Alfred North Whitehead noted, "Everything important has been said before."

Might it therefore also be said that social psychology is only common sense in different words? Social psychology faces two contradictory criticisms: One is that it is trivial because it documents the obvious; the other is that it is dangerous because its findings could be used to manipulate people. Is the first objection valid: does social psychology simply formalize what any good amateur social psychologist already knows intuitively?

Cullen Murphy (1990), editor of *The Atlantic*, thinks so. So far as he can detect, the social sciences turn up "no ideas or conclusions that can't be found in [any] encyclopedia of quotations. . . . Day after day social scientists go out into the world. Day after day they discover that people's behavior is pretty much what you'd expect." Nearly a half century earlier, historian Arthur Schlesinger, Jr., (1949) reacted similarly to social scientists' studies of American World War II soldiers as reported in the two volumes of *The American Soldier*—"ponderous demonstrations" of common sense knowledge, he said.

What were the findings? Another reviewer, Paul Lazarsfeld (1949), offered a sample with interpretive comments, a few of which I paraphrase:

1. Better educated soldiers suffered more adjustment problems than less educated soldiers. (Intellectuals were less prepared for battle stresses than street-smart people.)
2. Southern soldiers coped better with the hot South Sea Island climate than Northern soldiers. (Southerners are more accustomed to hot weather.)
3. White privates were more eager to be promoted to noncommissioned officers than Black privates. (Years of oppression take a toll on achievement motivation.)
4. Southern Blacks preferred Southern to Northern White officers (because Southern officers were more experienced and skilled in interacting with Blacks).
5. As long as the fighting continued, soldiers were more eager to return home than after the war ended. (During the fighting, soldiers knew they were in mortal danger.)

One problem with common sense, however, is that we invoke it *after* we know the facts. Events are far more "obvious" and predictable in hindsight than beforehand. Baruch Fischhoff and others (Slovic & Fischhoff, 1977) have repeatedly demonstrated that when people learn the outcome of an experiment, that outcome suddenly seems unsurprising—certainly less surprising than it is to people who are simply told about the experimental procedure and the possible outcomes. People overestimate their ability to have foreseen the result. This happens especially when the result seems determined and not a mere product of chance (Hawkins & Hastie, 1990).

Daphna Baratz (1983) tested college students' sense of the obvious. She gave them pairs of supposed social findings, one true (for example, "In prosperous times people spend a larger proportion of their income than during a recession" or "People who go to church regularly tend to have more children than people who go to church infrequently"), the other its opposite. Her finding: Whether given the truth or its opposite, most students rated a supposed finding as something "I would have predicted."

You perhaps experienced this phenomenon when reading Lazarsfeld's summary of findings from *The American Soldier*. For actually, Lazarsfeld went on to say, *"every one of these statements is the direct opposite of what was actually found."* In reality, the book reported that poorly educated soldiers adapted more poorly. Southerners were *not* more likely than Northerners to adjust to a tropical climate. Blacks were *more* eager than Whites for promotion, and so forth. "If we had mentioned the actual results of the investigation first [as Schlesinger experienced], the reader would have labelled these 'obvious' also. Obviously something is wrong with the entire argument of obviousness. . . . Since every kind of human reaction is conceivable, it is of great importance to know which reactions actually occur most frequently and under what conditions."

Likewise, in everyday life we often do not expect something to happen until it does. We *then* suddenly see clearly the forces that brought it to be and feel unsurprised. After Ronald Reagan's presidential victory over Jimmy Carter in 1980, commentators—forgetting that the election had been "too close to call" until the campaign's final few days—found the Reagan landslide unsurprising and easily understandable. When, the day before the election, Mark Leary (1982) asked people what percentage of votes they thought each candidate would receive, the average person, too, foresaw only a slim Reagan victory. The day after the election Leary asked other people what result they *would have predicted* the day before the election; most indicated a Reagan vote that was closer to the Reagan landslide.

Jack Powell (1988) found a similar knew-it-all-along effect after the 1984 Reagan triumph over Walter Mondale. Finding out that something had happened made it seem more inevitable. As the Danish philosopher-theologian Sören Kierkegaard put it, "Life is lived forwards, but understood backwards."

If this **hindsight bias** (also called the I-knew-it-all-along phenomenon) is pervasive, you may now be feeling that you already knew about it. Indeed, almost any conceivable result of a psychological experiment can seem like common sense—*after* you know the result. You can demonstrate the phenomenon by asking half a group to predict the outcome of some current event, such as an upcoming election. Ask the other half, a week after the outcome is known, what they would have predicted. For example, when Martin Bolt and John Brink (1991) invited Calvin College students to predict the U.S. Senate vote on controversial Supreme Court nominee Clarence Thomas, 58 percent predicted his approval. A week after his confirmation, Bolt asked other students to recall what they would have predicted. "I thought he would be approved," said 78 percent.

Or give half a group one psychological finding and the other half the opposite result. For example, tell half:

> Social psychologists have found that, whether choosing friends or falling in love, we are most attracted to people whose traits are different from our own. There seems to be wisdom in the old saying, "Opposites attract."

Tell the other half the truth:

> Social psychologists have found that, whether choosing friends or falling in love, we are most attracted to people whose traits are similar to our own. There seems to be wisdom in the old saying, "Birds of a feather flock together."

Ask the people first to explain the result. Then ask them to say whether it is "surprising" or "not surprising." Virtually all will find whichever result they were given "not surprising."

As these examples show, we can draw upon the stockpile of ancient proverbs to make almost any result seem to make sense. Because nearly every possible outcome is conceivable, there are proverbs for various occasions. Shall we say with John Donne, "No man is an island," or with Thomas Wolfe, "Every man is an island"? If a social psychologist reports that separation intensifies romantic attraction, Joe Public responds, "You get paid for this? Everybody knows that 'absence makes the heart grow fonder.' " Should it turn out that separation weakens attraction, Judy Public may say, "My grandmother could have told you, 'Out of sight, out of mind.' " No matter what happens, there will be someone who knew it would.

Karl Teigen (1986) must have had a few chuckles when asking University of Leicester (England) students to evaluate actual proverbs and their opposites. When given the actual proverb "Fear is stronger than love," most rated it as true. But so did students who were given its reversed form, "Love is stronger than fear." Likewise, the genuine proverb "He that is fallen cannot help him who is down" was rated highly; but so, too, was "He that is fallen can help him who is down." My favorites, however, were the two highly rated proverbs: "Wise men make proverbs and fools repeat them" (authentic) and its made-up counterpart, "Fools make proverbs and wise men repeat them."

The hindsight bias creates a problem for many psychology students. When you read the results of experiments in your textbooks, the material often seems easy, even obvious. When you later take a multiple-choice test on which you must choose among several plausible conclusions, the task may become surprisingly difficult. "I don't know what happened," the befuddled student later moans. "I thought I knew the material." (A word to the wise: Beware of the phenomenon when studying for exams, lest you fool yourself into thinking that you know the material better than you do.)

The I-knew-it-all-along phenomenon not only can make social science findings seem like common sense but also can have unhealthy consequences. It is conducive to arrogance—an overestimation of our own intellectual powers. After the invention and acceptance of the type-writer, people said it was a machine that demanded invention and that, once invented, had to be a success. But to Christopher Latham Sholes, creator of the Remington, its success was not so obvious beforehand. In an 1872 letter he confided: "My apprehension is [that] it will have its brief day and be thrown aside."

Moreover, because outcomes seem as if they should have been fore-seeable, we are more likely to blame decision makers for what are in retrospect "obvious" bad choices than to praise them for good choices, which also seem "obvious." *After* the 1991 Persian Gulf War, it seemed obvious that the overwhelming air superiority of the United States and its allies would rout the Iraqi military, though that was hardly clear to most politicians and pundits beforehand. After Japan's attack on Pearl Harbor, hints of the impending attack seemed similarly obvious to Monday morn-ing historians, who chastised the U.S. military leadership for not having anticipated what happened.

Likewise, we sometimes chastise ourselves for "stupid mistakes"— perhaps for not having handled a situation or a person better. Looking back, we see how we should have handled it. Realizing the culprit at the end of a mystery movie, we—like Dr. Watson in the Sherlock Holmes novels—chide ourselves for missing the clues that now seem obvious. But sometimes we are too hard on ourselves. We forget that what is obvious to us *now* was not nearly so obvious at the time. Physicians told both a patient's symptoms and the cause of death (as determined by autopsy) sometimes wonder how an incorrect diagnosis could have been made. Other physicians, given only the symptoms, don't find the diag-nosis nearly so obvious (Dawson & others, 1988). (Would juries be slower to assume malpractice if they were forced to take a foresight rather than a hindsight perspective?)

So what shall we conclude—that common sense is usually wrong? Sometimes it is. Until science dethroned the common sense view, cen-turies of daily experience assured people that the sun revolved around the earth. Medical experience assured doctors that bleeding was an effec-tive treatment for typhoid fever, until someone in the middle of the last century bothered to experiment—to divide patients into two groups, one bled, the other given mere bed rest (which proved not less effective). Often, though, there are conditions under which conventional wisdom is right. Other times, there are sages supporting both sides of an issue: Does happiness come from knowing the truth, or preserving illusions? From being with others, or living in peaceful solitude? From living a virtuous life, or getting away with evil? Opinions are a dime a dozen; no matter what we find, there will be someone who foresaw it. But which of the many competing ideas best fit reality?

So, the point is not that common sense is predictably wrong. Rather, common sense usually is right *after the fact*; it describes events more easily than it predicts them. We therefore easily deceive ourselves into thinking that we know and knew more than we do and did.

CONCEPTS TO REMEMBER

Hindsight bias   The tendency to exaggerate, *after* learning an outcome, one's ability to have foreseen how something turned out. Also known as the *I-knew-it-all-along phenomenon*.

Social Thinking

Intuition: The Power and Limits of Our Inner Knowing

❖

W hat are our powers of intuition—of immediately knowing something without reasoning or analysis? Advocates of "intuitive management" believe we should tune into our hunches. When judging others, we should plug into the nonlogical smarts of our "right brain." When hiring, firing, and investing, we should listen to our premonitions. In making judgments, we should follow the example of *Star Wars'* Luke Skywalker by switching off our computer guidance systems and trusting the force within.

Are the intuitionists correct that important information is immediately available apart from our conscious analysis? Or are the skeptics right in jesting that intuition is "our knowing we are right, whether we are or not"?

THE POWERS OF OUR INNER KNOWING

"The heart has its reasons which reason does not know," observed seventeenth-century philosopher-mathematician Blaise Pascal. Three centuries later, scientists have proved Pascal correct. We know more than we know we know.

Studies of our unconscious information processing confirm our limited access to what's going on in our minds (Greenwald, 1992; Uleman & Bargh, 1989). Our thinking is partly controlled (deliberate and conscious) and—more than most of

us once supposed—partly *automatic* (effortless and without our awareness). Automatic thinking occurs not "on screen" but off screen, out of
sight, where reason does not know. Consider:

- *Schemas*—mental templates—automatically, intuitively, guide our
  perceptions and interpretations of our experience. Whether we
  hear someone speaking of religious *sects* or *sex* depends not only on
  the word spoken but on how we automatically interpret the sound.
  As an old Chinese proverb says, "Two-thirds of what we see is
  behind our eyes."

- Some *emotional reactions* are nearly instantaneous, before there is
  time for deliberate thinking. Simple likes, dislikes, and fears typically involve little reasoned analysis. Although our intuitive reactions sometimes defy logic, they may still be adaptive. Our
  ancestors who intuitively feared a sound in the bushes were usually fearing nothing, but they were more likely to survive to pass
  their genes down to us than their more deliberative cousins.

- Given sufficient *expertise*, people may intuitively know the answer
  to a problem. The situation cues information stored in their memory. Without knowing quite how we do it, we recognize our
  friend's voice after the first spoken word of a phone conversation.
  Master chess players intuitively recognize meaningful patterns
  that novices miss.

- Some things—facts, names, and past experiences—we remember
  explicitly (consciously). But other things—skills and conditioned
  dispositions—we remember *implicitly*, without consciously knowing and declaring that we know. It's true of us all, but most
  strikingly evident in brain-damaged persons who cannot form new
  explicit memories. Thus, having learned how to solve a block-
  stacking puzzle or play golf, they will deny ever having experienced the task. Yet (surprisingly to themselves) they perform like
  practiced experts. If repeatedly shown the word "perfume," they
  won't recall having seen it. But if asked to guess a word you have in
  mind beginning with "per," they surprise themselves by intuitively knowing the answer.

- Equally dramatic are the cases of *blindsight*. Having lost a portion of
  the visual cortex to surgery or stroke, people may be functionally
  blind in part of their field of vision. Shown a series of sticks in the
  blind field, the patients report seeing nothing. After correctly
  guessing whether the sticks are vertical or horizontal, the patients
  are astounded when told, "You got them all right." Again, the
  patients know more than they know they know. There are, it
  seems, little minds—parallel processing units—operating unseen.

- *Prosopagnosia* patients suffer damage to a brain area involved in face
  recognition. They can see familiar people but are unable to recog-

nize them as their spouses or children. Yet, shown pictures of such people, their heart knows them; its rate increases as their body shows signs of unconscious recognition.

- For that matter, consider your own taken-for-granted capacity to intuitively recognize a face. As you look at a photo, your brain breaks the visual information into subdimensions such as color, depth, movement, and form and works on each aspect simultaneously before reassembling the components. Finally, somehow, your brain compares the perceived image with previously stored images. Voilà! Instantly and effortlessly, you recognize your grandmother. If intuition is immediately knowing something without reasoned analysis, perceiving is intuition par excellence.

- Although below our threshold for conscious awareness, *subliminal* stimuli may nevertheless have intriguing effects. Shown certain geometric figures for less than 0.01 second each, people will deny having seen anything more than a flash of light. Yet they will later express a preference for the forms they saw. Sometimes we intuitively feel what we cannot explain. Likewise, invisible flashed words can *prime* or predispose our responses to later questions. If the word "bread" is flashed too briefly to recognize, we may then detect a flashed, related word such as "butter" more easily than an unrelated word such as "bottle."

To repeat, many routine cognitive functions occur automatically, unintentionally, without awareness. Our minds function rather like big corporations. Our CEO—our controlled consciousness—attends to the most important or novel issues and assigns routine affairs to subordinates. This delegation of attentional resources enables us to react to many situations quickly, efficiently, *intuitively*, without taking limited time to reason and analyze.

THE LIMITS OF OUR INNER KNOWING

Although researchers affirm that unconscious information processing can produce flashes of intuition, they have their doubts about its brilliance. Elizabeth Loftus and Mark Klinger (1992) speak for today's cognitive scientists in reporting "a general consensus that the unconscious may not be as smart as previously believed." For example, although subliminal stimuli can trigger a weak, fleeting response—enough to evoke a feeling if not conscious awareness—there is no evidence that commercial subliminal tapes can powerfully "reprogram your unconscious mind" for success. [Indeed, a mass of new evidence indicates that they can't (Greenwald & others, 1991).]

Moreover, our intuitive judgments err often enough to understand why poet T. S. Eliot would describe "The hollow man . . . Headpiece filled with straw." Social psychologists have explored our error-prone hindsight judgments (our intuitive sense, after the fact, that we knew-it-all-along). Other domains of psychology have explored our capacity for illusion—perceptual misinterpretations, fantasies, and constructed beliefs. Michael Gazzaniga and other brain researchers have discovered that patients whose brain hemispheres have been surgically separated will instantly fabricate—and believe—explanations of puzzling behaviors. If the patient gets up and takes a few steps after the experimenter flashes the instruction "walk" to the patient's nonverbal right hemisphere, the verbal left hemisphere will instantly invent a plausible explanation ("I felt like getting a drink").

Illusory thinking also appears in the vast new literature on how we take in, store, and retrieve social information. As perception researchers study visual illusions for what they reveal about our normal perceptual mechanisms, social psychologists study illusory thinking for what it reveals about normal information processing. These researchers want to give us a map of everyday social thinking, with the hazards clearly marked. As we examine some of these efficient thinking patterns, remember this: Demonstrations of how people create counterfeit beliefs do not prove that all beliefs are counterfeit. Still, to recognize counterfeiting, it helps to know how it's done. So let's explore how efficient information processing can go awry, beginning with our self-knowledge.

WE OFTEN DO NOT KNOW WHY WE DO WHAT WE DO

"There is one thing, and only one in the whole universe which we know more about than we could learn from external observation," noted C. S. Lewis (1960, pp. 18–19). "That one thing is [ourselves]. We have, so to speak, inside information; we are in the know."

Indeed. Yet sometimes we *think* we know, but our inside information is wrong. This is the unavoidable conclusion of some fascinating recent research.

Explaining Our Behavior

Why did you choose your college? Why did you lash out at your roommate? Why did you fall in love with that special person? Sometimes we know. Sometimes we don't know. Asked why we have felt or acted as we have, we produce plausible answers. Yet, when causes and determinants are not obvious, our self-explanations often err. Factors that have big effects we sometimes report as innocuous. Factors that have little effect we sometimes perceive as influential.

Richard Nisbett and Stanley Schachter (1966) demonstrated this by asking Columbia University students to take a series of electric shocks of steadily increasing intensity. Beforehand, some took a fake pill which, they were told, would produce heart palpitations, breathing irregularities, and butterflies in the stomach—the very symptoms that usually accompany being shocked. Nisbett and Schachter anticipated that people would attribute the symptoms of shock to the pill rather than to the shock. Thus they, more than people not given the pill, should tolerate shock. Indeed, the effect was enormous: people given the fake pill took four times as much shock.

When informed that they had taken more shock than average and asked why, their answers did not mention the pill. When pressed (even after the experimenter explained the experiment's hypotheses in detail), they denied the pill's influence. They would usually say that the pill probably did affect some people, but not them. A typical reply was "I didn't even think about the pill."

Sometimes people think they *have* been affected by something that has had no effect. Nisbett and Timothy Wilson (1977) had University of Michigan students rate a documentary film. While some of them watched, a power saw roared outside the room. Most people felt that this distracting noise affected their ratings. But it didn't; their ratings were similar to those of control subjects who viewed the film without distraction.

Even more thought provoking are studies in which people recorded their own moods every day for two or three months (Stone & others, 1985; Weiss & Brown, 1976; Wilson & others, 1982). They also recorded factors that might affect their moods—the day of the week, the weather, the amount they slept, and so forth. At the end of each study, the people judged how much each factor had affected their moods. Remarkably (given that their attention was being drawn to their daily moods) there was little relationship between their perceptions of how important a factor was and how well the factor actually predicted their mood. In fact, their estimates of how well the weather or the day of the week had predicted their mood were no better than estimates made by strangers. These findings raise a disconcerting question: How much insight do we really have into what makes us happy or unhappy?

Predicting Our Behavior

Finally, we often err in predicting our own behavior. Asked whether they would obey demands to deliver severe electric shocks or would hesitate to help a victim if several other people were present, people overwhelmingly deny their vulnerability to such influences. But as we will see, experiments have shown that many of us are vulnerable. Moreover, consider what Sidney Shrauger (1983) discovered when he had college students predict the likelihood of their experiencing dozens of different events during the ensuing two months (becoming romantically involved, being sick, and so forth): Their self-predictions were hardly more accurate than predictions based on the average person's experience. The surest thing we can say about your individual future is that it's hard for even you to predict. The best advice is to look at your past behavior in similar situations (Osberg & Shrauger, 1986).

CONSTRUCTING MEMORIES

Do you agree or disagree with this statement?

> Memory can be likened to a storage chest in the brain into which we deposit material and from which we can withdraw it later if needed. Occasionally, something is lost from the "chest," and then we say we have forgotten.

About 85 percent of college students agree (Lamal, 1979). As a 1988 ad in *Psychology Today* put it, "Science has proven the accumulated experience of a lifetime is preserved perfectly in your mind."

Actually, psychological research has proved the opposite. Memories are not copies of experiences that remain on deposit in a memory bank. Rather, we construct our memories at the time of withdrawal. Memory involves backward reasoning. It infers what must have been, given what we now believe or know. Like a paleontologist inferring the appearance of a dinosaur from bone fragments, we reconstruct our distant past by combining fragments of information using our current expectations (Hirt, 1990). Thus we may unconsciously revise our memories to suit our current knowledge. When one of my sons complained, "The June issue of *Cricket* never came," and was shown where it was, he delightedly responded, "Oh good, I knew I'd gotten it."

Reconstructing Past Attitudes

Five years ago, how did you feel about nuclear power? about George Bush or John Major? about your parents? If your attitudes have changed, do you know how much?

Experimenters have tried to answer such questions. The results have been unnerving: People whose attitudes have changed often insist that they have always felt much as they now feel. Daryl Bem and Keith McConnell (1970) took a survey among Carnegie-Mellon University students. Buried in it was a question concerning student control over the university curriculum. A week later the students agreed to write an essay opposing student control. After doing so, their attitudes shifted toward greater opposition to student control. When asked to recall how they had answered the question before writing the essay, they "remembered" holding the opinion that they *now* held and denied that the experiment had affected them. After observing Clark University students similarly denying their former attitudes, researchers D. R. Wixon and James Laird (1976) commented: "The speed, magnitude, and certainty" with which the students revised their own histories "was striking."

In 1973, University of Michigan researchers interviewed a national sample of high school seniors and then reinterviewed them in 1982 (Markus, 1986). When recalling their 1973 attitudes on issues such as aid to minorities, the legalization of marijuana, and equality for women, people's reports were much closer to their 1982 attitudes than to those they actually expressed in 1973. Studies that follow children's lives through time reveal a similarly shocking conclusion: Teens' recollections of their early childhood bear no relation to their actual early childhood experiences. Instead, their current adjustment determines their recollections. Healthy, positive teens have positive recollections of their past; maladjusted teens have negative recollections (Lewis & Feiring, 1992). As George Vaillant (1977, p. 197) noted after following adults for a period of time: "It is all too common for caterpillars to become butterflies and then to maintain that in their youth they had been little butterflies. Maturation makes liars of us all."

Cathy McFarland and Michael Ross (1985) found that we even revise our recalled views of other people as our relationships with them change. They had university students rate their steady dating partners. Two months later, they rated them again. Students who were more in love than ever had a tendency to recall love at first sight. Those who had broken up were more likely to recall having recognized the partner as somewhat selfish and ill-tempered.

Diane Holmberg and John Holmes (in press) discovered the same phenomenon among 373 newlywed couples, most of whom reported being very happy. When resurveyed two years later, those whose marriages had soured recalled that things had always been bad. The results are "frightening," say Holmberg and Holmes: "Such biases can lead to a dangerous downward spiral. The worse your current view of your partner is, the worse your memories are, which only further confirms your negative attitudes." Passions exaggerate.

It's not that we are totally unaware of how we used to feel; it's just that when memories are hazy, current feelings guide our recall. Parents of every generation bemoan the values of the next generation, partly because they misrecall their youthful values as being closer to their current values.

Reconstructing Past Behavior

Memory construction enables us to revise our own histories. Michael Ross, Cathy McFarland, and Garth Fletcher (1981) exposed some University of Waterloo students to a message convincing them of the desirability of toothbrushing. Later, in a supposedly different experiment, these students recalled brushing their teeth more often during the preceding two weeks than did students who had not heard the message. Likewise, when representative samples of Americans are asked about their cigarette smoking and their reports are projected to the nation as a whole, at least a third of the 600 billion cigarettes sold annually are unaccounted for (Hall, 1985). Noting the similarity of such findings to happenings in George Orwell's *Nineteen Eighty-Four*—where it was "necessary to remember that events happened in the desired manner"—social psychologist Anthony Greenwald (1980) surmised that we all have "totalitarian egos" that revise the past to suit our present views.

Sometimes our present view is that we've improved—in which case we may misrecall our past as more *un*like the present than it actually was. This tendency resolves a puzzling pair of consistent findings: Those who participate in self-improvement programs (weight-control programs, antismoking programs, exercise programs, psychotherapy) show only modest improvement on average. Yet they often claim considerable benefit (Myers, 1992). Michael Conway and Michael Ross (1985) explain why. Having expended so much time, effort, and money on self-improvement, people may conveniently think, "I may not be perfect now, but I was worse before; this did me a lot of good."

"Know thyself," urged the ancient Greek philosopher Thales. We try. But to a striking extent, we are often wrong about what has influenced us and what we will feel and do. Our intuitive self-knowledge errs.

This fact of life has two practical implications. The first is for psychological inquiry. Although the intuitions of clients or research subjects may provide useful clues to their psychological processes, *self-reports are often untrustworthy.* Errors in self-understanding limit the scientific usefulness of subjective personal reports.

The second implication is for our everyday lives. The sincerity with which people report and interpret their experiences is no guarantee of the validity of these reports. Personal testimonies are powerfully persuasive, but they may also convey unwitting error. Keeping this potential for error in mind can help us feel less intimidated by others and to be less gullible.

4

Reasons for Unreason

❖

What good fortune for those in power that people do not think.
Adolf Hitler

The mixed picture of our intuitive self-knowledge (the module on intuition) is paralleled by the mixed picture of our rationality. On the one hand, what species better deserves the name *homo sapiens*—wise humans? Our cognitive powers outstrip the smartest computers in recognizing patterns, handling language, and processing abstract information. Our information processing is also wonderfully efficient. With such precious little time to process so much information, we specialize in mental shortcuts. Scientists marvel at the speed and ease with which we form impressions, judgments, and explanations. In many situations, our snap generalizations—"That's dangerous!"—are adaptive. They promote our survival.

But our adaptive efficiency has a trade-off; snap generalizations sometimes err. Our helpful strategies for simplifying complex information can lead us astray. To enhance our own powers of critical thinking, let's consider five reasons for unreason—common ways in which people form or sustain false beliefs.

1. OUR PRECONCEPTIONS CONTROL OUR INTERPRETATIONS

We earlier noted a significant fact about the human mind: Our preconceptions influence our constructed memories, even our recall for our own previous attitudes and experiences. Preconceptions also affect the way people perceive and interpret information. This was tragically demonstrated in 1988 when the crew of the *USS Vincennes* perceived an Iranian airliner to be an F-14 fighter plane and then proceeded to shoot it down. As social psychologist Richard Nisbett (1988)

31

noted in a congressional hearing on the incident, "The effects of expectations on generating and sustaining mistaken hypotheses can be dramatic." There is more to perception than meets the eye.

The same is true of social perception. An experiment by Robert Vallone, Lee Ross, and Mark Lepper (1985) revealed how powerful preconceptions can be. They showed pro-Israeli and pro-Arab students six network news segments describing the 1982 killing of civilian refugees at two camps in Lebanon. As Figure 4–1 illustrates, each group perceived the networks as hostile to its side. The phenomenon is commonplace: Presidential candidates and their supporters nearly always view the news media as unsympathetic to their cause. Sports fans perceive referees as partial to the other side. People in conflict (married couples, labor and management, opposing racial groups) see impartial mediators as biased against them.

Our assumptions can also make ambiguous evidence seem supportive. For example, Ross and Lepper assisted Charles Lord (1979) in showing Stanford University students the results of two supposed new research studies. Half the students favored capital punishment, and half opposed it. One study confirmed and the other disconfirmed the students' beliefs about the deterrence effect of the death penalty. Both proponents and opponents of capital punishment readily accepted evidence that confirmed their belief but were sharply critical of disconfirming evidence. Showing the two groups an *identical* body of mixed evidence had therefore not narrowed their disagreement but *increased* it. Each side perceived the evidence as supporting its belief and now believed even more strongly.

FIGURE 4–1
Pro-Israeli and pro-Arab students who viewed network news descriptions of the "Beirut massacre" believed that the coverage was biased against their point of view.   (Data from Vallone, Ross, & Lepper, 1985.)

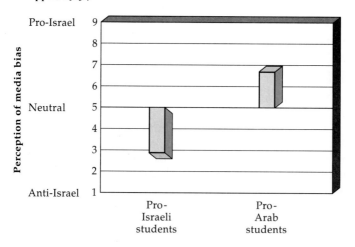

Is this why, in politics, religion, and science, ambiguous information often fuels conflict? Presidential TV debates in the United States have mostly reinforced predebate opinions. By nearly a 10 to 1 margin, those who already favored one candidate or the other in the 1960, 1976, and 1980 debates perceived their candidate as having won (Kinder & Sears, 1985).

Some experiments manipulate preconceptions, with astonishing effects. Myron Rothbart and Pamela Birrell (1977) had University of Oregon students assess the facial expression of the man shown in Figure 4-2. Students told he was a Gestapo leader responsible for barbaric medical experiments on concentration camp inmates during World War II judged his expression as cruel. (Can you see that barely suppressed sneer?) Those told he was a leader in the anti-Nazi underground movement whose courage saved thousands of Jewish lives judged his facial expression as warm and kindly. (On second thought, look at those caring eyes and that almost smiling mouth.) As filmmakers know, an ambiguous expression can seem sad, thoughtful, or happy, depending on the context.

FIGURE 4-2
"Kurt Walden," as shown by Myron Rothbart and Pamela Birrell. Judge for yourself: Is he cruel or kindly?

2. WE OVERESTIMATE THE ACCURACY OF OUR JUDGMENTS

The intellectual conceit evident in our judgments of our past knowledge ("I knew it all along") extends to estimates of our current knowledge. Daniel Kahneman and Amos Tversky (1979) gave people factual questions and asked them to fill in the blanks, as in: "I feel 98 percent certain that the air distance between New Delhi and Beijing is more than _____ miles but less than _____ miles."

Most subjects were overconfident: About 30 percent of the time, the correct answers lay outside the range they felt 98 percent confident about. Baruch Fischhoff and his colleagues (1977) discovered the same **overconfidence phenomenon** when people rated their certainty about their answers to multiple-choice questions, such as: "Which is longer: (a) the Panama Canal or (b) the Suez Canal?" If people 60 percent of the time answer such a question correctly, they will typically *feel* about 75 percent sure. (Answers: The Suez Canal is twice as long as the Panama Canal. New Delhi is 2500 miles from Beijing.)

To find out whether overconfidence extends to social judgments, David Dunning and his associates (1990) created a little game show. They asked students to guess a stranger's answers to a series of questions, such as, "Would you prepare for a difficult exam alone or with others?" and "Would you rate your lecture notes as neat or messy?" Knowing the type of questions, but not the actual questions, the subjects first interviewed their target person about background, hobbies, academic interests, aspirations, astrological sign—anything they thought might be helpful. Then while the target persons answered 20 of the two-choice questions, the interviewers predicted their target's answers and rated their own confidence.

The interviewers guessed right 63 percent of the time, beating chance by 13 percent. But, on average, they *felt* 75 percent sure of their predictions. When guessing their own roommates' responses, they were 68 percent correct and 78 percent confident. Moreover, the most confident people were most likely to be *over*confident.

Do people better predict their own behavior? To find out, Robert Vallone and his colleagues (1990) had college students predict in September whether they would drop a course, declare a major, elect to live off campus next year, and so forth. Although the students felt 84 percent sure of these self-predictions, on average, they erred nearly twice as often (29 percent of the time) as they expected. Even when feeling 100 percent sure of their predictions, they erred 15 percent of the time.

Overconfidence also permeates everyday decision making. Investment experts market their services with the confident presumption that they can beat the stock market average, forgetting that for every stockbroker or buyer saying "Sell!" at a given price there is another saying

"Buy!" A stock's price is the balance point between these mutually confident judgments. Thus, incredible as it may seem, economist Burton Malkiel (1985) reports that mutual fund portfolios selected by investment analysts do *not* outperform randomly selected stocks.

What constructive lessons can we draw from research on overconfidence? One might be to downplay other people's dogmatic statements. Even when people seem sure that they are right, they may be wrong. So don't let cocky people intimidate you.

Two techniques have successfully reduced the overconfidence bias. One is prompt feedback on the accuracy of their judgments (Lichtenstein & Fischhoff, 1980). In everyday life, weather forecasters and those who set the odds in horse racing both receive clear, daily feedback. Experts in both groups therefore do quite well at estimating their probable accuracy (Fischhoff, 1982).

When people think about why an idea *might* be true, it begins to seem true (Koehler, 1991). Thus, another way to reduce overconfidence is to get people to think of one good reason *why their judgments might be wrong*, forcing them to consider why opposing ideas might be right (Koriat & others, 1980). Managers might foster more realistic judgments by insisting that all proposals and recommendations include reasons why they might not work.

Still, we should be careful not to undermine people's self-confidence to a point where they spend too much time in self-analysis or where self-doubts begin to cripple their decisiveness. In times when their wisdom is needed, those lacking self-confidence may shrink from speaking up or making tough decisions. *Over*confidence can cost us, but realistic self-confidence is adaptive.

3. WE OFTEN ARE SWAYED MORE BY ANECDOTES THAN STATISTICAL FACTS

Anecdotal information is persuasive. Researchers Richard Nisbett and Eugene Borgida (Nisbett & others, 1976) explored the tendency to overuse anecdotal information by showing University of Michigan students videotaped interviews of people who supposedly had participated in an experiment in which most subjects failed to assist a seizure victim. Learning how *most* subjects acted had little effect upon people's predictions of how the individual they observed acted. The apparent niceness of this individual was more vivid and compelling than the general truth about how most subjects really acted: "Ted seems so pleasant that I can't imagine him being unresponsive to another's plight." This illustrates the **base-rate fallacy**: Focusing upon the specific individual can push into the background useful information about the population the person came from.

There is, of course, a positive side to viewing people as individuals and not merely as statistical units. The problem arises when we formulate our beliefs about people in general from our observations of particular persons. Focusing on individuals distorts our perception of what is generally true. Our impressions of a group, for example, tend to be overly influenced by its extreme members. One man's attempt to assassinate President Reagan caused people to bemoan, "It's not safe to walk the streets anymore," and to conclude, "There's a sickness in the American soul." As psychologist Gordon Allport put it, "Given a thimbleful of facts we rush to make generalizations as large as a tub."

Indeed, people are remarkably quick to infer general truth from a vivid instance. One University of Michigan study presented students with a vivid welfare case—a magazine article about a supposedly ne'er-do-well Puerto Rican woman who had a succession of unruly children sired by a succession of common-law husbands. This case was set against factual statistics about welfare cases—indicating that, contrary to this case, 90 percent of welfare recipients in her age bracket "are off the welfare rolls by the end of four years." Nevertheless, the facts affected people's decreased opinion of most welfare recipients less than the single vivid case (Hamill & others, 1980). No wonder that after hearing and reading countless instances of rapes, robberies, and beatings, 9 out of 10 Canadians overestimate—usually by a considerable margin—the percentage of crimes that involve violence (Doob & Roberts, 1988).

Sometimes the vivid example is a personal experience. Before buying a new car several years ago, I consulted the *Consumer Reports* survey of car owners and found the repair record of the Dodge Colt to be quite good. A short while later, I mentioned my interest in the Colt to a student. "Oh no," he moaned, "don't buy a Colt. I worked in a garage last summer and serviced two Dodge Colts that kept falling apart and were brought in for one thing after another." How did I use this information—and the glowing testimonies from two friends who owned Hondas, which I was also considering? Did I simply increment the *Consumer Reports* surveys of Colt and Honda owners by two more people each? Logically, that is what I should have done. But it was nearly impossible to downplay my consciousness of those vivid accounts. I bought the Honda.

Relying on the Availability Heuristic

Consider: Does the letter "k" appear more often as a word's first letter or as its third? Do more people live in Thailand or Iraq?

You probably answered in terms of how readily instances of each category came to mind. If examples are readily *available* in our memory—as words beginning with "K" and as Iraqis tend to be—then we presume that the event is commonplace. Usually it is, so we are often well served by this cognitive rule of thumb, called the **availability heuristic**. But sometimes the rule deludes us. (Actually, "K" occurs three times as often as the third letter, and Thailand's 55 million people more than triple Iraq's 18 million.)

The availability heuristic explains why vivid anecdotes are more compelling than base-rate statistical information, and why, therefore, perceived risk is often so badly out of joint with the real risks of things (Allison & others, 1992). News footage of airplane crashes is a readily available memory for most of us. This misleads people to suppose that they are more at risk traveling in a commercial airplane than in a car. Actually, U.S. travelers during the 1980s were 26 times more likely to die in a car crash than on a commercial flight covering the same distance (National Safety Council, 1991).

Or consider this: Three jumbo jets full of passengers crashing every day would not equal tobacco's deadly effects. If the deaths caused by tobacco occurred in horrible accidents, the resulting uproar would long ago have eliminated cigarettes. Because, instead, the deaths are disguised as "cancer" and "heart disease" and diffused on obituary pages, we hardly notice. Thus, rather than eliminating the hazard, the U.S. government continues to subsidize the tobacco industry's program for quietly killing its customers. The point: Dramatic events stick in our minds, and we use ease of recall—the availability heuristic—when predicting the likelihood of something happening.

4. WE MISPERCEIVE CORRELATION AND CONTROL

Another influence on everyday thinking is our search for order in random events, a tendency that can lead us down all sorts of wrong paths.

Illusory Correlation

It's easy to see a correlation—an **illusory correlation**—where none exists. As part of their research with the Bell Telephone Laboratories, William Ward and Herbert Jenkins (1965) showed people the results of a hypothetical 50-day cloud-seeding experiment. They told their subjects which of the 50 days the clouds had been seeded and which days it rained. This information was nothing more than a random mix of results: Sometimes it rained after seeding; sometimes it didn't. People nevertheless became convinced—in conformity with their supposition about the effects of cloud seeding—that they really had observed a relationship between cloud seeding and rain.

If we believe a correlation exists, we are more likely to notice and recall confirming instances. If we believe that premonitions correlate with events, we notice and remember the joint occurrence of the premonition and the later occurrence of that event. We seldom notice or remember all the times unusual events do not coincide. If, after we think about a friend, the friend calls us, we notice and remember this coincidence more than all the times we think of a friend without any ensuing call, or receive a call from a friend about whom we've not been thinking. Thus, we easily overestimate the frequency with which these strange things happen.

One familiar example of perceived correlation is the presumption that women's moods correlate with their menstrual cycle. To find out whether they do, several researchers have had women make daily ratings of their moods. When Cathy McFarland and her colleagues (1989) did this with Ontario women, they obtained typical results. The women's self-rated negative emotions (whether they were experiencing irritability, loneliness, depression, and so forth) did not increase during their premenstrual and menstrual phases. Yet the women later *perceived* a correlation between negative mood and menstruation (Figure 4–3).

Pamela Kato and Diane Ruble (1992) say this is typical: Although many women recall mood changes over their cycle, their day-to-day experiences reveal few such changes. Moreover, cycle-related hormonal changes have no known emotional effects that would lead us to expect mood changes. So why do so many women believe they experience premenstrual tension or menstrual irritability? Because, say Kato and Ruble, their implicit theories of menstruation lead them to notice and

FIGURE 4–3
Menstruation, actual mood, and perceived mood. Ontario women's daily mood reports did not vary across their menstrual cycle. Yet they perceived that their moods were generally worse just before and during menstruation and better at other times of the cycle.   (Data from C. McFarland & others, 1989.)

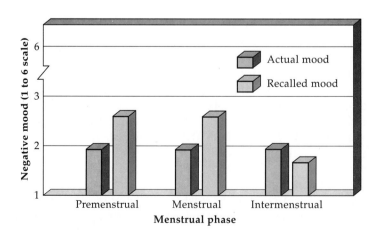

remember the joint appearances of negative moods and the onset of menstruation, but not to notice and remember bad moods two weeks later.

Infertile couples who adopt, it is popularly theorized, finally relax—and conceive. But no such theory is necessary, because it isn't so. Although researchers have found no correlation between adoption and conception, our attention is drawn to couples who have conceived after adopting (rather than to those who conceive before adopting or who don't conceive after adopting). Thus we easily misperceive random events as confirming our hunches.

Illusion of Control

Our tendency to perceive random events as related feeds an **illusion of control**—the idea that chance events are subject to our influence. This is what keeps gamblers going, and what makes the rest of us do all sorts of silly things. During the 1988 summer drought, for example, retired farmer Elmer Carlson arranged a rain dance by 16 Hopi in Audubon, Iowa. The next day it rained 1 inch. "The miracles are still here, we just have to ask for them," explained Carlson (Associated Press, 1988).

Gambling

Ellen Langer (1977) demonstrated the illusion of control with experiments on gambling. People readily believed they could beat chance. Compared to those given an assigned lottery number, people who chose their own lottery number demanded four times as much money when asked for how much they would sell their ticket. When playing a game of chance against an awkward and nervous person, they bet significantly more than when playing against a dapper, confident opponent. Given some unusual early successes in a chance situation, they often discounted later failures. In these and other ways, Langer consistently found people acting as if they could control chance events.

Real-life gamblers also exhibit an illusion of control. Dice players may throw softly for low numbers and hard for high numbers (Henslin, 1967). The gambling industry thrives on gamblers' illusions. Gamblers' hopes that they can beat the laws of chance sustain their gambling. Gamblers attribute wins to their skill and foresight. Losses become "near misses" or "flukes"—perhaps (for the sports gambler) a bad call by the referee or a freakish bounce of the ball (Gilovich & Douglas, 1986).

Regression toward the Average

Tversky and Kahneman (1974) noted another way by which an illusion of control may arise: We fail to recognize the statistical phenomenon of **regression toward the average**. Because exam scores fluctuate partly by chance, most students who get extremely high scores on an exam will get lower scores on the next exam. Because their first score is at the ceiling, their second score is more likely to fall back ("regress") toward their own average than to push the ceiling even higher. (This is why a student who does consistently good work, even if never the best, will sometimes end a course at the top of the class.) Conversely, the lowest-scoring students on the first exam are likely to improve. If those who scored lowest go for tutoring after the first exam, the tutors are likely to feel effective when the student improves, even if the tutoring had no effect.

Indeed, anything can seem effective, whether it actually had an effect or not. When things reach a low point, we will try anything, and whatever we try—going to a psychotherapist, starting a new diet-exercise plan, reading a self-help book—is more likely to be followed by improvement than by further deterioration. (When we're extremely high or low, we tend to fall back toward our normal average.)

Sometimes we recognize that events are not likely to continue at an unusually good or bad extreme. Experience has taught us that when everything is going great, something will go wrong, and that when life is dealing us terrible blows, we can usually look forward to things getting better. Often, though, we fail to recognize this regression effect. We puzzle at why baseball's rookie-of-the-year often has a more ordinary second year: did he become overconfident? self-conscious? We forget that exceptional performance tends to regress toward normality.

Imagine a volleyball coach who rewards her team with lavish praise and a light practice after their best match of the season and harasses them after an exceptionally bad match. But she fails to understand that because performance is not perfectly reliable, unusual performances tend to fall back toward the usual. She then wrongly concludes that rewards lead to poorer performance in the next game, while punishments improve performance. Parents and teachers may reach the same wrong conclusion after reacting to unusually good or bad behavior.

Thus, note Tversky and Kahneman, nature operates in such a way that we often *feel* punished for rewarding others and rewarded for punishing them. In actuality, as every student of psychology knows, positive reinforcement for doing things right is usually more effective and has fewer negative side effects.

5. OUR BELIEFS MAY GENERATE THEIR OWN CONFIRMATION

There's one additional reason why our intuitive beliefs resist reality: They sometimes lead us to act in ways that produce their apparent confirmation. Our beliefs about other people can therefore become **self-fulfilling prophecies**.

In his well-known studies of "experimenter bias," Robert Rosenthal (1985) found that research subjects sometimes live up to what is expected of them. In one study experimenters asked subjects to judge the successfulness of people in various photographs. The experimenters read the same instructions to all their subjects and showed them the same photos. Nevertheless, experimenters led to expect high ratings obtained higher ratings than those who expected their subjects to see the photographed people as failures. Even more startling—and controversial—are reports that teachers' beliefs about their students similarly serve as self-fulfilling prophecies.

Do Teacher Expectations Affect Student Performance?

Teachers do have higher expectations for some students than for others. Perhaps you have detected this after having a brother or sister precede you in school, after receiving a label such as "gifted" or "learning disabled," or after being tracked with the "high-ability" or "average-ability" students. Or perhaps the conversation in the teachers' lounge sent your reputation ahead of you, or your new teacher scrutinized your school file or discovered your family's social status. Teacher expectations correlate with student achievement, but that's mostly because students' achievements affect their teachers' expectations (Jussim & Eccles, 1993). But do expectations also affect performance? Often they don't. But in 39 percent of the 448 published experiments they do (Rosenthal, 1991).

Why? Rosenthal and other investigators report that teachers look, smile, and nod more at "high-potential students." In one study, Elisha Babad, Frank Bernieri, and Rosenthal (1991) videotaped teachers talking to, or about, unseen students for whom they held high or low expectations. A random 10-second clip of either the teacher's voice or face was enough to tell viewers—both children and adults—whether this was a good or poor student and how much the teacher liked the student. Although teachers may think they can conceal their feelings, students are acutely sensitive to teachers' facial expressions and body movements. Teachers also may teach more to their "gifted" students, set higher goals for them, call on them more, and give them more time to answer (Cooper, 1983; Harris & Rosenthal, 1985, 1986; Jussim, 1986).

Reading the experiments on teacher expectations makes me wonder about the effect of *students'* expectations upon their teachers. You no doubt begin many of your courses having heard that "Professor Smith is interesting" and "Professor Jones is a bore." To see whether such effects might also occur in actual classrooms, a research team led by David Jamieson (1987) experimented with four Ontario high school classes taught by a newly transferred teacher. During individual interviews they told students in two of the classes that both other students and the research team rated the teacher very highly. Moreover, the teacher herself was very enthusiastic about the class. Compared to the control classes, whose expectations they did not raise, the students given positive expectations paid better attention during class. At the end of the teaching unit, they also got better grades and rated the teacher as clearer in her teaching. The attitudes that a class has toward its teacher are as important, it seems, as the teacher's attitude toward the students.

Do We Get What We Expect from Others?

So, the expectations of experimenters and teachers are occasionally self-fulfilling prophecies. How general is this effect? Do we get from others what we expect of them? There are times when negative expectations of someone lead us to be extra nice to that person, which induces them to be nice in return—thus *dis*confirming our expectations. But the most common finding in studies of social interaction is that, yes, we do tend to get what we expect (Miller & Turnbull, 1986).

In laboratory games, hostility nearly always begets hostility: People who *perceive* their opponents as noncooperative will readily induce them to *be* noncooperative (Kelley & Stahelski, 1970). Self-confirming beliefs abound when there is conflict. Each party's perception of the other as aggressive, resentful, and vindictive induces the other to display these behaviors in self-defense, thus creating a vicious self-perpetuating circle. Whether I expect my wife to be in a bad mood or in a warm, loving mood may affect how I relate to her, thereby inducing her to confirm my belief.

Several experiments conducted by Mark Snyder (1984) at the University of Minnesota show how, once formed, erroneous beliefs about the social world can induce others to confirm those beliefs, a phenomenon called **behavioral confirmation**. In one study, Snyder, Elizabeth Tanke, and Ellen Berscheid (1977) had men students talk on the telephone with women they thought (from having been shown a picture) were either attractive or unattractive. Analysis of just the women's comments during the conversations revealed that the supposedly attractive women spoke more warmly than the supposedly unattractive women. The men's erroneous beliefs had become a self-fulfilling prophecy, by leading them to act in a way that influenced the women to fulfill their stereotype that beautiful people are desirable people.

Expectations influence children's behavior too. After observing the amount of litter in three classrooms, Richard Miller and his colleagues (1975) had the teacher and others repeatedly tell one class that they should be neat and tidy. This persuasion increased the amount of litter placed in wastebaskets from 15 to 45 percent, but only temporarily. Another class, which also had been placing only 15 percent of its litter in wastebaskets, was repeatedly congratulated for being so neat and tidy.

After eight days of hearing this, and still two weeks later, these children were fulfilling the expectation by putting more than 80 percent of their litter in wastebaskets. Repeatedly tell children they are hardworking and kind (rather than lazy and mean), and they may live up to their label.

These experiments help us understand how social beliefs, such as stereotypes about disabled people or about people of a particular race or sex, may be self-confirming. We help construct our own social realities. How others treat us reflects how we and others have treated them.

CONCLUSIONS

We could extend our list of reasons for unreason, but surely this has been a sufficient glimpse at how people come to believe what may be untrue. We can't easily dismiss these experiments: Most of the participants were intelligent people, mostly students at leading universities. Moreover, these distortions and biases occurred even when payment for right answers motivated people to think optimally. As one researcher concluded, the illusions "have a persistent quality not unlike that of perceptual illusions" (Slovic, 1972).

Research in cognitive social psychology thus mirrors the mixed review given humanity in literature, philosophy, and religion. Many research psychologists have spent lifetimes exploring the awesome capacities of the human mind (Manis, 1977). We are smart enough to have cracked our own genetic code, to have invented talking computers, to have sent people to the moon. Moreover, our intuitive hunches—our efficient mental shortcuts—generally are adaptive. "The mind works in the overwhelmingly large part to do or die, not to reason or to know why," notes Robert Ornstein (1991). "There has never been, nor will there ever be, enough time to be truly rational." Three cheers for intuition.

Well, two cheers—because the mind's priority on efficiency makes our intuition more vulnerable to error than we suspect. With remarkable ease, we form and sustain false beliefs. Led by our preconceptions, overconfident of our judgments, persuaded by vivid anecdotes, perceiving correlations and control where none exists, we construct our idea of the social world around us, and then influence that world to confirm our beliefs. "The naked intellect," observed novelist Madeleine L'Engle, "is an extraordinarily inaccurate instrument."

CONCEPTS TO REMEMBER

Overconfidence phenomenon   The tendency to be more confident than correct —to overestimate the accuracy of one's beliefs.

Base-rate fallacy   The tendency to ignore or underuse base-rate information (information that describes most people) and instead to be influenced by distinctive features of the case being judged.

Availability heuristic   An efficient but fallible rule of thumb that judges the likelihood of things in terms of their availability in memory. If instances of something come readily to mind, we presume it to be commonplace.

Illusory correlation   Perception of a relationship where none exists, or perception of a stronger relationship than actually exists.

Illusion of control   Perception of uncontrollable events as subject to one's control or as more controllable than they are.

Regression toward the average   The statistical tendency for extreme scores or extreme behavior to return toward one's average.

Self-fulfilling prophecy   The tendency for one's expectations to evoke behavior that confirms the expectations.

Behavioral confirmation   A type of self-fulfilling prophecy whereby people's social expectations lead them to act in ways that cause others to confirm their expectations.

Clinical Intuition: The Perils of Psychologizing

————— ❖ —————

Clinical psychologists—psychologists who study, assess, and treat people with psychological difficulties—struggle to make accurate judgments, recommendations, and predictions in any number of real situations: Is Susan suicidal? Should John be committed to a mental hospital? If released, will Tom be a homicide risk?

Professional clinical judgment is a form of social judgment. Like all social judgments it therefore is efficient yet vulnerable to biases such as illusory correlations, overconfidence bred by hindsight, and self-confirming diagnoses.

ILLUSORY CORRELATIONS

Consider the following court transcript in which a seemingly confident psychologist (PSY) is being questioned by an attorney (ATT):

ATT: You asked the defendant to draw a human figure?
PSY: Yes.
ATT: And this is the figure he drew for you? What does it indicate to you about his personality?
PSY: You will note this is a rear view of a male. This is very rare, statistically. It indicates hiding guilt feelings, or turning away from reality.

ATT: And this drawing of a female figure, does it indicate anything to you; and, if so, what?

PSY: It indicates hostility toward women on the part of the subject. The pose, the hands on the hips, the hard-looking face, the stern expression.

ATT: Anything else?

PSY: The size of the ears indicates a paranoid outlook, or hallucinations. Also, the absence of feet indicates feelings of insecurity. (Jeffery, 1964)

The assumption here, as in so many clinical judgments, is that test results reveal something important. Do they? There is a simple way to decide. Have one clinician administer and interpret the test. Have another clinician assess the same person's symptoms. And repeat this process over many people. The proof is in the pudding: Are test outcomes indeed correlated with reported symptoms? Some tests are indeed predictive. With other tests, such as the Draw-a-Person test above, the correlation is far weaker than its users suppose. Why, then, do clinicians continue to express confidence in such uninformative tests?

Pioneering experiments by Loren Chapman and Jean Chapman (1969, 1971) help us see why. They invited both college students and professional clinicians to study patients' test performances and diagnoses. If the students or clinicians expected a particular association, they generally were able to perceive it, regardless of whether the data were supportive. For example, clinicians who believed that suspicious people draw peculiar eyes on the Draw-a-Person test perceived such a relationship—even when shown cases in which suspicious people drew peculiar eyes *less* often than nonsuspicious people. Believing that a relationship existed between two things, they were more likely to notice confirming than disconfirming instances.

But let's not single out clinicians. Illusory thinking also occurs among political analysts, historians, sportscasters, personnel directors, stockbrokers, and many other professionals, including the research psychologists who point them out. Indeed, people in any profession that involves social judgment will often perceive what they expect. To believe is to see.

HINDSIGHT BIAS

If someone we know commits suicide, how do we react? One common reaction is to think that we, or those close to the person, should have been able to predict and therefore to prevent the suicide. In hindsight, we can see the suicidal signs and the pleas for help: "We should have known." Indeed, people given a summary of a case and told that the person committed suicide more often say they "would have expected" the suicide than do those given the *same* case information without the suicide being mentioned (Goggin & Range, 1985). Moreover, if told of the suicide, people's reactions to the victim's family were more negative: "They should have foreseen and averted the suicide." After such tragedy, an I-should-have-known-it-all-along phenomenon can also leave family, friends, and therapists feeling guilty. When a client becomes violent, a therapist may, in retrospect, seem negligent for not having foreseen the danger and taken appropriate measures. Perhaps if this phenomenon was more widely understood, people could be more accepting of themselves and others in such times.

Hindsight bias also afflicts professionals' judgments, as Hal Arkes and his colleagues (1988) discovered when they asked neuropsychologists to diagnose a man described as suffering a tremor and deteriorating memory. For each of three groups, one of three possible diagnoses was said to be correct. Given a supposed diagnosis, nearly half the neuropsychologists thought they, too, would have made the same diagnosis. They look back and interpret early symptoms in light of the diagnosis, which then makes the diagnosis seem more obvious than it was. Arkes found a way to minimize hindsight bias (similar to how one can reduce the I-knew-it-all-along hindsight effect): Ask the professionals to give a reason why one of the other diagnoses *might* have been correct.

Stanford psychologist David Rosenhan (1973) and his associates provided a striking example of potential error in after-the-fact explanations. To test mental health workers' clinical insights, they each made an appointment with a different mental hospital admissions office and complained of "hearing voices." Apart from giving false names and vocations, they reported their life histories and emotional states honestly and exhibited no further symptoms. Most got diagnosed as schizophrenic and remained hospitalized for two to three weeks. The clinicians then searched for incidents in the pseudo patients' life histories and hospital behavior that "confirmed" and "explained" the diagnosis. Rosenhan tells of one pseudo patient who truthfully explained to the interviewer that he

> . . . had a close relationship with his mother but was rather remote from his father during his early childhood. During adolescence and beyond, however, his father became a close friend, while his relationship with his mother cooled. His present relationship with his wife was characteristically close and warm. Apart from occasional angry exchanges, friction was minimal. The children had rarely been spanked.

The interviewer, "knowing" the person suffered from schizophrenia, explained the problem this way:

> This white 39-year-old male . . . manifests a long history of considerable ambivalence in close relationships, which begins in early childhood. A warm relationship with his mother cools during his adolescence. A distant relation-

ship to his father is described as becoming very intense. Affective stability is absent. His attempts to control emotionality with his wife and children are punctuated by angry outbursts and, in the case of the children, spankings. And while he says that he has several good friends, one senses considerable ambivalence embedded in those relationships also.

Rosenhan later told some mental hospital staff members (who had heard about his controversial experiment but doubted such mistakes could occur in their hospital) that during the next three months one or more pseudo patients would seek admission to their hospital. After the three months, he asked the staff to guess which of the 193 patients admitted during that time were really pseudo patients. Of the 193 new patients, 41 were accused by at least one staff member of being normal. Actually, there were none.

SELF-CONFIRMING DIAGNOSES

So far we've seen that mental health workers sometimes perceive illusory correlations and offer questionable hindsight explanations. A third problem with clinical judgment is that people may also supply information that fulfills clinicians' expectations. In a clever series of experiments at the University of Minnesota, Mark Snyder (1984), in collaboration with William Swann and others, gave interviewers some hypotheses to test concerning individuals' traits. To get a feel for their experiments, imagine yourself on a blind date with someone who has been told that you are an uninhibited, outgoing person. To see whether this is true, your date slips questions into the conversation, such as, "Have you ever done anything crazy in front of other people?" As you answer such questions, will your date meet a different "you" than if you were probed for instances when you were shy and retiring?

Snyder and Swann found that people often test for a trait by looking for information that will confirm it. If they are trying to find out if someone is an extravert, they often solicit instances of extraversion ("What would you do if you wanted to liven things up at a party?"). Testing for introversion, they are more likely to ask, "What factors make it hard for you to really open up to people?" Such questioning led those being tested for extraversion to behave more sociably and those being tested for introversion to appear more shy and reserved. We help create the people we expect to meet.

At Indiana University, Russell Fazio and his colleagues (1981) reproduced this finding and also discovered that those asked the "extraverted questions" later perceived themselves as actually more outgoing than those asked the introverted questions. Moreover, they really became noticeably more outgoing. An accomplice of the experimenter later met each subject in a waiting room and 70 percent of the time correctly guessed from the subject's outgoingness which condition the subject had come from. When given the structured list of questions to choose from, even experienced psychotherapists prefer the extraverted questions when testing for extraversion and unwittingly trigger extraverted behavior among their interviewees (Dallas & Baron, 1985; Snyder & Thomsen, 1988). Here, then, is more evidence that our beliefs may generate their own confirmation.

In later experiments, Snyder and his colleagues (1982) tried to get people to search for behaviors that would *disconfirm* the trait they were testing. In one experiment, they told the interviewers that "it is relevant and informative to find out ways in which the person . . . may not be like the stereotype." In another experiment Snyder (1981) offered "$25 to the person who develops the set of questions that tell the most about . . . the interviewee." Regardless, people still resisted choosing "introverted" questions when testing for extraversion.

This illustrates **confirmation bias**. When testing our beliefs, we seek information that will verify them before we seek disconfirming information. P. C. Wason (1960) demonstrated this, as you can, by giving people a sequence of three numbers—2, 4, 6—which conformed to a rule he had in mind (the rule was simply *any three ascending numbers*). To enable the people to discover the rule, Wason invited each person to generate sets of three numbers. Each time Wason told the person whether the set did or didn't conform to his rule. When they were sure they had discovered the rule, the people were to stop and announce it. The result? Seldom right but never in doubt: 23 of the 29 people convinced themselves of a wrong rule. They typically formed some erroneous belief about the rule (for example, counting by twos) and then searched for *confirming* evidence (for example, by testing 8, 10, 12) rather than attempting to *disconfirm* their hunches.

Snyder's demonstrations of self-confirming diagnoses prompted follow-up studies that revealed their limits. When ordinary people or psychotherapists are invited to make up *their own* questions to test for extraversion, they are less likely to display the confirmation bias (Dallas & Baron, 1985; Trope & others, 1984). Many of their questions seem quite appropriate for distinguishing extraverted from introverted people. Nevertheless, when interviewers have very definite ideas of their own, these ideas *will* influence the questions they ask (Lalljee & others, 1984; Leyens, 1989; Swann & Giuliano, 1987).

Thus, say researchers, though our primary goal is to ask informative questions, our questions are often slanted by a secondary desire to get a yes answer that will confirm our hypotheses (Devine & others, 1990; Slowiaczek & others, 1991).

On the basis of Snyder's experiments, can you see why the behaviors of psychotherapy clients come to fit the theories of their therapists (Whitman & others, 1963)? When a psychologist and a psychiatrist, Harold Renaud and Floyd Estess (1961), conducted life history interviews of 100 healthy, successful adult men, they were startled to discover that their subjects' childhood experiences were loaded with "traumatic events," tense relations with certain people, and bad decisions by their parents—the very factors usually used to explain psychiatric problems. When Freudian therapists go fishing for traumas in early childhood experiences, they will often find their hunches confirmed. Thus, surmises Snyder (1981):

> The psychiatrist who believes (erroneously) that adult gay males had bad childhood relationships with their mothers may meticulously probe for recalled (or fabricated) signs of tension between their gay clients and their mothers, but neglect to so carefully interrogate their heterosexual clients about their maternal relationships. No doubt, any individual could recall some friction with his or her mother, however minor or isolated the incidents.

The nineteenth-century poet Robert Browning anticipated Snyder's conclusion:

> As is your sort of mind,
> So is your sort of search:
> You'll find
> What you desire.

CLINICAL VERSUS STATISTICAL PREDICTION

Given these hindsight- and diagnosis-confirming tendencies, it will come as no surprise that most clinicians and interviewers express more confidence in their intuitive assessments than in statistical data. Yet when researchers pit statistical prediction (as when predicting graduate school success using a formula that includes grades and aptitude scores) against intuitive prediction, the former usually wins. Statistical predictions aren't terribly accurate, but human intuition—even expert intuition—is even less so (Dawes & others, 1989; Faust & Ziskin, 1988; Meehl, 1954).

Three decades after demonstrating the superiority of statistical over intuitive prediction, Paul Meehl (1986) said the evidence was stronger than ever:

> There is no controversy in social science which shows [so many] studies coming out so uniformly in the same direction as this one. . . . When you are pushing 90 investigations, predicting everything from the outcome of football games to the diagnosis of liver disease and when you can hardly come up with a half dozen studies showing even a weak tendency in favor of the clinician, it is time to draw a practical conclusion. . . .
> Surely we all know that the human brain is poor at weighing and computing. When you check out at a supermarket, you don't eyeball the heap of purchases and say to the clerk, "Well it looks to me as if it's about $17.00 worth; what do you think?"

So, why do so many clinicians continue to interpret Rorschach ink-blot tests and offer intuitive predictions about parolees, suicide risks, and likelihood of child abuse? Partly out of sheer ignorance, says Meehl, but also partly out of "mistaken conceptions of ethics":

> If I try to forecast something important about a college student, or a criminal, or a depressed patient by inefficient rather than efficient means, meanwhile charging this person or the taxpayer 10 times as much money as I would need to achieve greater predictive accuracy that is not a sound ethical practice. That it feels better, warmer, and cuddlier to me as predictor is a shabby excuse indeed.

Such words are shocking. Do Meehl and the other researchers under-estimate professional intuition? To see why such findings are apparently true, consider the assessment of human potential by graduate admissions interviewers. Researcher Robyn Dawes (1976) illustrates why statistical prediction is so often superior to an interviewer's intuition when pre-dicting outcomes such as graduate school success:

> What makes us think that we can do a better job of selection by interviewing (students) for a half hour, than we can by adding together relevant (stan-dardized) variables, such as undergraduate GPA, GRE score, and perhaps ratings of letters of recommendation. The most reasonable explanation to me lies in our overevaluation of our cognitive capacity. And it is really cognitive conceit. Consider, for example, what goes into a GPA. Because for most graduate applicants it is based on at least 3^1/$_2$ years of undergraduate study, it is a composite measure arising from a minimum of 28 courses and possibly, with the popularity of the quarter system, as many as 50. . . . Yet you and I, looking at a folder or interviewing someone for a half hour, are supposed to be able to form a better impression than one based on 3^1/$_2$ years of the cumulative evaluations of 20–40 different professors. . . . Finally, if we do wish to ignore GPA, it appears that the only reason for doing so is believing that the candidate is particularly brilliant even though his or her record may not show it. What better evidence for such brilliance can we have than a score on a carefully devised aptitude test? Do we really think we are better equipped to assess such aptitude than is the Educational Testing Service, whatever its faults?

IMPLICATIONS

So when making professional judgments, clinical psychologists are like the rest of us—vulnerable to normal cognitive pitfalls. Thus they

- Can easily convince clients of worthless diagnoses
- Are frequently the victims of illusory correlation
- Are too readily convinced of their own after-the-fact analyses
- Often fail to appreciate how erroneous diagnoses can be self-confirming

The practical implications for mental health workers are more easily stated than practiced: Be mindful that clients' verbal agreement with what you say does not prove its validity. Beware of the tendency to see relationships that you expect to see or that are supported by striking examples readily available in your memory. Recognize that hindsight is seductive: It can lead you to feel overconfident and sometimes to judge yourself too harshly for not having foreseen outcomes. Guard against the tendency to ask questions that assume your preconceptions are correct; consider opposing ideas and test them too.

This module's research on illusory thinking has implications not only for mental health workers but for all psychologists. What physician Lewis Thomas (1978) has said of biology may as justly be said of psychology:

> The solidest piece of scientific truth I know of, the one thing about which I feel totally confident, is that we are profoundly ignorant about nature. Indeed, I regard this as the major discovery of the past 100 years of biology. . . . It is this sudden confrontation with the depth and scope of ignorance that represents the most significant contribution of 20th century science to the human intellect. We are, at last, facing up to it. In earlier times, we either pretended to understand how things worked or ignored the problem, or simply made up stories to fill the gaps.

Psychology has crept only a little way across the edge of insight into our human condition. Ignorant of their ignorance, some psychologists invent theories to fill the gaps in understanding. Intuitive observation seems to support these theories, even if they are mutually contradictory. Research on illusory thinking therefore leads us to a new humility concerning the truth of our unchecked speculation. It reminds research psychologists why they must test their preconceptions before propounding them as truth. To seek the hard facts, even if they threaten cherished illusions, is the goal of every science.

I am *not* arguing that the scientific method can answer all human questions. There are questions which it cannot address and ways of knowing which it cannot capture. But science *is* one means for examining claims about nature, human nature included. Propositions that imply observable results are best evaluated by systematic observation and experiment—which is the whole point of social psychology. We also need creative genius, or we test only trivialities. But whatever unique and enduring insights psychology can offer will be hammered out by research psychologists sorting through competing claims. Science always involves an interplay between intuition and rigorous check, between creative hunch and skepticism, between professional hunch and humble testing.

CONCEPTS TO REMEMBER

Confirmation bias   A tendency to search for information that confirms one's preconceptions.

MODULE

6

The Fundamental Attribution Error

❖

A s later modules will reveal, social psychology's most important lesson concerns how much we are affected by our social environment. At any moment, our internal state, and therefore what we say and do, depends on the situation, as well as on what we bring to the situation. In experiments, a slight difference between two situations sometimes greatly affects how people respond. I see this when I teach classes at both 8:30 A.M. and 7:00 P.M. Silent stares greet me at 8:30; at 7:00 I have to break up a party. In each situation some individuals are more talkative than others, but the difference between the two situations exceeds the individual differences.

Researchers who study our **attributions**—how we explain our own and others' behavior—report that we often fail to appreciate this important lesson. When explaining someone's behavior, we underestimate the impact of the situation and overestimate the extent to which it reflects the individual's traits and attitudes. Thus, even knowing the effect of the time of day on classroom conversation, I find it terribly tempting to assume that the people in the 7:00 P.M. class are more extraverted than the "silent types" who come at 8:30 A.M.

This discounting of the situation, dubbed by Lee Ross (1977) the **fundamental attribution error**, appears in many experiments. In the first such study, Edward Jones and Victor Harris (1967) had Duke University students read debaters' speeches supporting or attacking Cuba's leader, Fidel Castro. When the position taken was said to have been chosen by the debater, the students logically enough assumed it reflected the person's own attitude. But what happened when the students were told that the debate coach had assigned the position? Debaters write stronger statements than you'd expect from those feigning a position they

53

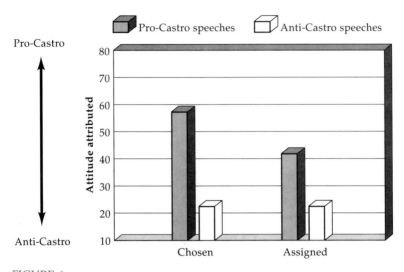

FIGURE 6-1
The fundamental attribution error. When people read a debate speech supporting or attacking Fidel Castro, they attribute corresponding attitudes to the speech writer, even when the debate coach assigned the writer's position.   (Data from Jones & Harris, 1967.)

don't hold (Miller & others, 1990). Thus, even knowing that the debater had been told to take a pro-Castro position did not prevent their inferring that the debater in fact had some pro-Castro leanings (Figure 6-1).

We commit the fundamental attribution error when explaining *other people's* behavior. We often explain our own behavior in terms of the situation while holding others responsible for their behavior. John might attribute his behavior to the situation ("I was angry because everything was going wrong"), but others might think, "John was hostile because he is an angry person." When referring to ourselves, we typically use verbs that describe our actions and reactions ("I get annoyed when . . ."). Referring to someone else, we more often describe what that person *is* ("He is nasty") (Fiedler & others, 1991; McGuire & McGuire, 1986; White & Younger, 1988).

*T*HE FUNDAMENTAL ATTRIBUTION ERROR OCCURS IN EVERYDAY LIFE

If we know that the checkout cashier is programmed to say, "Thank you and have a nice day," do we nevertheless automatically conclude that the cashier is a friendly, grateful person? We certainly know how to discount behavior that we attribute to ulterior motives (Fein & others, 1990). Yet consider what happened when Williams College students talked with a supposed clinical psychology graduate student who acted either warm and friendly or aloof and critical. Researchers David Napolitan and George Goethals (1979) told half the students beforehand that her behavior would be spontaneous. They told the other half that for purposes of the experiment she had been instructed to feign friendly (or unfriendly) behavior. The effect of the information? None. If she acted friendly, they assumed she was really a friendly person; if she acted unfriendly, they assumed she was an unfriendly person. As when viewing a dummy on the ventriloquist's lap or a movie actor playing a "good-guy" or "bad-guy" role, we find it difficult to escape the illusion that the programmed behavior reflects an inner disposition. Perhaps this is why Leonard Nimoy, who played Mr. Spock on the original *Star Trek*, entitled his book *I Am Not Spock*.

The discounting of social constraints was further revealed in a thought-provoking experiment by Lee Ross and his collaborators (Ross & others, 1977). The experiment re-created Ross's firsthand experience of moving from graduate student to professor. His doctoral oral exam had proved a humbling experience as his apparently brilliant professors quizzed him on topics they specialized in. Six months later, *Dr.* Ross was himself an examiner, now able to ask penetrating questions on *his* favorite topics. Ross's hapless student later confessed to feeling exactly as Ross had a half year before—dissatisfied with his ignorance and impressed with the apparent brilliance of the examiners.

In the experiment, with Teresa Amabile and Julia Steinmetz, Ross set up a simulated quiz game. He randomly assigned some Stanford University students to play the role of questioner, some to play the role of contestant, and others to observe. The researchers invited the questioners to make up difficult questions that would demonstrate their general wealth of knowledge. It's fun to imagine the questions: "Where is Bainbridge Island?" "What is the seventh book in the Old Testament?" "Which has the longer coastline, Europe or Africa?"

If even these few questions have you feeling a little uninformed, then you will appreciate the results of this experiment.[1] Everyone had to know that the questioner would have the advantage. Yet both contestants and observers came to the erroneous conclusion that the questioners *really were* more knowledgeable than the contestants (Figure 6–2). Follow-up research shows that the misimpressions are hardly a reflection of low social intelligence. If anything, intelligent and socially competent people are *more* likely to make the attribution error (Block & Funder, 1986).

In real life, those with social power usually initiate and control conversation, which often leads underlings to overestimate their knowledge

---

[1] Bainbridge Island is across Puget Sound from Seattle. The seventh Old Testament book is Judges. Although the African continent is more than double the area of Europe, Europe's coastline is longer. (It is more convoluted, with lots of harbors and inlets, a geographical fact that contributed to its role in the history of maritime trade.)

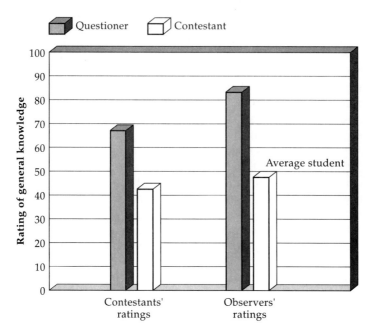

FIGURE 6–2

Both contestants and observers of a simulated quiz game assumed that a person who had been randomly assigned the role of questioner was actually far more knowledgeable than the contestant. This failure to appreciate the extent to which the assigned roles of questioner and contestant simply made the questioner *seem* more knowledgeable illustrates the fundamental attribution error. (Data from Ross, Amabile, & Steinmetz, 1977.)

and intelligence.[2] Medical doctors, for example, are often presumed to be experts on all sorts of questions unrelated to medicine. Similarly, students often overestimate the brilliance of their teachers. (As in Ross's experiment, teachers are questioners on subjects of their special expertise.) When some of these students later become teachers, they are usually amazed to discover that teachers are not so brilliant after all.

Attributions of responsibility are at the heart of many judicial decisions (Fincham & Jaspars, 1980). In 1988, after Colonel Oliver North was indicted on charges of theft, fraud, and conspiracy, a controversy ensued: Was North accountable for illegal activity, and should he therefore be jailed? Or was North acting under orders in the line of duty? (In a 1991 book he maintained that even President Reagan knew of the orders he was following.) The case exemplifies many judicial controversies: The

---

[2] In unstructured mixed-sex discussions, men tend to dominate conversations (see Module 13). What implications might this have for men's and women's perceptions of each others' competence?

prosecution argues, "You are to blame, for you could have done otherwise": the defendant replies, "It wasn't my fault; I was a victim of the situation," or "Under the circumstance I did no wrong."

To illustrate the fundamental attribution error, most of us need look no further than our own experience. Determined to make some new friends, Bev plasters a smile on her face and anxiously plunges into a party. Everyone else seems quite relaxed and happy as they laugh and talk with one another. Bev wonders to herself, "Why is everyone always so at ease in groups like this while I'm feeling shy and tense?" Actually, everyone else is feeling nervous, too, and making the same attributional error in assuming that Bev and the others *are* as they *appear*—confidently sociable.

WHY DO WE MAKE THE ATTRIBUTION ERROR?

So far we have seen a bias in the way we explain other people's behavior: We often ignore powerful situational determinants. Why do we tend to underestimate the situational determinants of others' behavior but not our own?

Difference in Perspective

Attribution theorists point out that we have a different perspective when observing than when acting (Jones & Nisbett, 1971; Jones, 1976). When we act, the environment commands our attention. When we watch another person act, that *person* occupies the center of our attention. To use the perceptual analogy of figure and ground, the person is the figure that stands out from the surrounding environmental ground. So the person seems to cause whatever happens. If this is true, what might we expect if the perspectives were reversed? What if we could see ourselves as others see us and if we saw the world through their eyes? Shouldn't this eliminate or reverse the typical attribution error?

See if you can predict the result of a clever experiment conducted by Michael Storms (1973). Put on your thinking cap, and picture yourself as a subject in Storms' experiment. You are seated facing another student with whom you are to talk for a few minutes. Beside you is a TV camera that shares your view of the other student. Facing you from alongside the other student are an observer and another TV camera. Afterward, both you and the observer judge whether your behavior was caused more by your personal characteristics or by the situation.

Question: Which of you—subject or observer—will attribute the least importance to the situation? Storms found it was the observer who most discounted the situation (another demonstration of the fundamental attribution tendency). What if we reverse points of view by having you and the observer each watch the videotape recorded from the other's perspective? (You now view yourself, while the observer views what you saw.) This reverses the attributions: The observer now attributes your behavior mostly to the situation you faced, while you now attribute it to your person. What matters then is our *focus of attention*. If it's on the person, we make a personal attribution. *Remembering* our own experiences from an observer's perspective—by "seeing" ourselves from the outside—we therefore accept more responsibility for our own behavior (Frank & Gilovich, 1989). If we see things from the person's perspective, we see better the situation's influence.

In another experiment, people viewed a videotape of a suspect confessing during an interview by a police detective. If they viewed the confession through a camera focused on the suspect, they perceived the confession as genuine. If they viewed it through a camera focused on the detective, they perceived it as more coerced (Lassiter & Irvine, 1986). In courtrooms, most videotaped confessions focus on the confessor. As we might expect, note Daniel Lassiter and Kimberly Dudley (1991), such tapes yield a nearly 100 percent conviction rate when played by prosecutors. Perhaps, then, a more impartial videotape would show both interrogator and suspect.

Time can change observers' perspectives. As the once-salient person recedes in their memory, observers often give more and more credit to the situation. Immediately after hearing someone argue an assigned position, people assume that's how the person really felt. A week later they are much more likely to credit the situational constraints (Burger, 1991). The day after the 1988 presidential election, Jerry Burger and Julie Pavelich (1991) asked Santa Clara, California, voters why the election turned out as it did. Most attributed the outcome to the candidates' personal traits and positions (incumbent Bush was likeable; challenger Dukakis ran a poor campaign). When they asked other voters the same question a year later, only a third attributed the verdict to the candidates. More people now credited circumstances, such as the country's good mood and the robust economy.

Editorial reflections on the six U.S. presidential elections between 1964 and 1988 show the same growth in situational explanations with time, Burger and Pavelich report. Just after the 1978 election, editorial pundits focused on Ford's and Carter's campaigns and personalities. Two years later the situation loomed larger: "The shadows of Watergate . . . cleared the way for [Carter's] climb to the Presidency," noted one editorial in the *New York Times*. So one reason we underestimate situations is that we focus on the person rather than on the situation.

Seeing ourselves on closed-circuit television redirects our attention to ourselves. Seeing ourselves in a mirror, hearing our tape-recorded voices, having our pictures taken, filling out biographical questionnaires—such experiences similarly focus our attention inward, making us *self*-conscious instead of *situation*-conscious. Here then is one good reason for the attribution error: *We find causes where we look for them.*

To see this in your own experience, consider: Would you say your social psychology instructor is a quiet or a talkative person?

My guess is you inferred that he or she is fairly outgoing. But consider: Your attention focuses on your instructor while he or she behaves in a context that demands speaking. The instructor, on the other hand, observes his or her own behavior in many different situations—in the classroom, in meetings, at home. "Me talkative?" your instructor might say. "Well, it all depends on the situation. When I'm in class or with good friends, I'm rather outgoing. But at conventions and in unfamiliar situations I feel and act rather shy."

If we are acutely aware of how our behavior varies with the situation, we should also see ourselves as more variable than other people. And that is precisely what studies in the United States, Canada, and Germany have found (Baxter & Goldberg, 1987; Kammer, 1982; Sande & others, 1988). Moreover, the less opportunity we have to observe people's behavior in context, the more we attribute to their personalities. Thomas Gilovich (1987) explored this by showing people a videotape of someone and then having them describe the person's actions to other people. The secondhand impressions were more overgeneralized. Similarly, people's impressions of someone they have often heard about from a friend are typically more overgeneralized than their friend's firsthand impressions. The better you know someone, the less prone you are to overgeneralizing (Prager & Cutler, 1990). Those you know well you observe in differing contexts.

Cultural Differences

Cultures also influence the attribution error (Ickes, 1980; Watson, 1982). Our western world view predisposes us to assume that people, not situations, cause events. Jerald Jellison and Jane Green (1981) reported that among University of Southern California students internal explanations are more socially approved. "You can do it!" we are assured by the pop psychology of positive-thinking western culture.

This assumes that, with the right disposition and attitude, anyone can surmount almost any problem: You get what you deserve and deserve what you get. Thus we often explain bad behavior by labeling the person as "sick," "lazy," or "sadistic." As children grow up in western culture, they increasingly explain behavior in terms of the other's personal characteristics (Rholes & others, 1990; Ross, 1981). As a first grader, one of my sons brought home an example. He unscrambled the words "gate the sleeve caught Tom on his" into "The gate caught Tom on his sleeve." His teacher, applying the western cultural assumptions of the curriculum materials, marked this wrong. The "right" answer located the cause within Tom: "Tom caught his sleeve on the gate."

Some languages promote external attributions. Instead of "I was late," Spanish idiom allows one to say, "The clock caused me to be late." In less individualist cultures, people less often perceive others in terms of personal dispositions (Zebrowitz-McArthur, 1988). When told of someone's actions, Hindus in India are less likely than Americans to offer dispositional explanations ("She is kind") and more likely to offer situational explanations ("Her friends were with her") (Miller, 1984). College students in Japan are less likely than American students to answer the question, "Who am I?" with psychological traits ("I am sincere," "I am confident") and more likely to declare their social identities ("I am a Keio student") (Cousins, 1989).

HOW FUNDAMENTAL IS THE FUNDAMENTAL ATTRIBUTION ERROR?

Like most provocative ideas, the presumption that we're all prone to a fundamental attribution error has its critics. Granted, say some, there is an attribution *bias*. But in any given instance, this may or may not produce an "error," just as parents who are biased to believe their child does not use drugs may or may not be in error (Harvey & others, 1981). We can be biased to believe what is true. Moreover, some everyday circumstances, such as being in church or on a job interview, are like the experiments we have been considering: As actors realize better than observers, the circumstances involve clear constraints. Hence the attribution error. But in other settings—in one's room, at a park—people exhibit their individuality. In such settings, people may see their own behavior as *less* constrained than observers do (Monson & Snyder, 1977; Quattrone, 1982). So it's an overstatement to say that at all times and in all settings observers underestimate situational influences.

Nevertheless, experiments reveal that the bias occurs even when we are aware of the situational forces—when we know that an assigned debate position is not a good basis for inferring someone's real attitudes (Croxton & Morrow, 1984; Croxton & Miller, 1987; Reeder & others, 1989) or that the questioners' role in the quiz game gives them an advantage (Johnson & others, 1984). It is sobering to think that you and I can know about a social process that distorts our thinking and still be susceptible to it. Perhaps that's because it takes more mental effort to assess social effects on people's behavior than merely to attribute it to their disposition (Gilbert & others, 1988). It's as if the person thinks, "This isn't a very good basis for making a judgment, but it's easy and all I've got to go on."

The attribution error is *fundamental* because it colors our explanations in basic and important ways. Researchers in Britain, India, Australia, and the United States have found, for example, that people's attributions predict their attitudes toward the poor and unemployed (Feather, 1983a; Furnham, 1982; Pandey & others, 1982; Wagstaff, 1983). Those who attribute poverty and unemployment to personal dispositions ("They're just lazy and undeserving") tend to adopt political positions unsympathetic to such people. Their views differ from those who make external attributions ("If you or I were to have lived with the same overcrowding, poor education, and discrimination, would we be any better off?"). French investigators Jean-Leon Beauvois and Nicole Dubois (1988) report that "relatively privileged" middle-class people are more likely than less advantaged people to assume that people's behaviors have internal explanations. (Those who have made it tend to assume that you get what you deserve.)

How might we benefit from being aware of the bias? Perhaps being sensitive to it can help. Recently, I assisted with some interviews for a faculty position. One candidate was interviewed by six of us at once; each of us had the opportunity to ask two or three questions. I came away thinking, "What a stiff, awkward person he is." The second candidate I met privately over coffee, and we immediately discovered we had a close, mutual friend. As we talked, I became increasingly impressed by what a "warm, engaging, stimulating person she is." Only later did I remember the fundamental attribution error and reassess my analysis. I had attributed his stiffness and her warmth to their dispositions; in fact, I later realized, such behavior resulted partly from the formality versus informality of their interview situations. Had I viewed these interactions through their eyes, instead of my own, I might have come to different conclusions.

CONCEPTS TO REMEMBER

Attributions   How we explain behavior. Attribution theorists explore, for example, the influences upon our attributing someone's behavior to internal *dispositions* (enduring traits, motives, and attitudes) or to external *situations*.

Fundamental attribution error   The tendency for observers to underestimate situational influences and overestimate dispositional influences upon others' behavior. (Also called "correspondence bias," because more often than we should we see behavior as corresponding to a disposition.)

A New Look at Pride

❖

I t is widely believed that most of us suffer from low self-esteem. A generation ago, humanistic psychologist Carl Rogers (1958) concluded that most people he knew "despise themselves, regard themselves as worthless and unlovable." Many popularizers of humanistic psychology concur. "All of us have inferiority complexes," contends Father John Powell (1989). "Those who seem not to have such a complex are only pretending." As Groucho Marx lampooned, "I'd never join any club that would accept a person like me."

S ELF-SERVING BIAS: "HOW DO I LOVE ME? LET ME COUNT THE WAYS"

Actually, most of us have a good reputation with ourselves. In studies of self-esteem, even low-scoring people respond in the midrange of possible scores. (A "low" self-esteem person responds to such statements as "I have good ideas" with a qualifying adjective, such as "somewhat" or "sometimes.") Moreover, one of social psychology's most provocative yet firmly established conclusions concerns the potency of self-serving bias.

Attributions for Positive and Negative Events

Time and again, experimenters have found that people readily accept credit when told they have succeeded (attributing the success to their ability and effort), yet attribute failure to such external factors as bad luck or the problem's inherent "impossibility" (Whitley & Frieze, 1985). Similarly, in explaining their victories, athletes commonly credit themselves, but attribute losses to something else: bad breaks, bad referee calls, the other team's super effort (Grove & others, 1991; Mullen & Riordan, 1988). And how much responsibility do you suppose car drivers tend to accept for their accidents? On insurance forms, drivers have described their accidents in words such as these: "An invisible car came out of nowhere, struck my car and vanished." "As I reached an intersection, a hedge sprang up, obscuring my vision and I did not see the other car." "A pedestrian hit me and went under my car" (*Toronto News*, 1977).

In experiments that require two people to cooperate to make money, most individuals blame their partner for failure (Myers & Bach, 1976). This follows a tradition established in the most ancient example of self-serving bias, Adam's excuse: "The woman whom you gave to be with me, she gave me fruit from the tree, and I ate." Thus while managers usually blame poor performance on workers' lack of ability or effort, workers are more likely to blame something external—inadequate supplies, excessive work load, difficult co-workers, ambiguous assignments (Rice, 1985).

Michael Ross and Fiore Sicoly (1979) observed a marital version of self-serving bias. They found that young married Canadians usually felt they took more responsibility for such activities as cleaning the house and caring for the children than their spouses credited them for. In a more recent survey of Americans, 91 percent of the wives but only 76 percent of the husbands credited the wife with doing most of the food shopping (Burros, 1988). In another study, husbands estimated that they did more of the housework than their wives did; the wives, however, estimated that their own efforts were more than double their husbands'(Fiebert, 1990). Every night, my wife and I pitch our laundry at the foot of our bedroom clothes hamper. In the morning, one of us puts it in. When she suggested that I take more responsibility for this, I thought, "Huh? I already do it 75 percent of the time." So I asked her how often she thought she picked up the clothes. "Oh," she replied, "about 75 percent of the time." Small wonder that divorced people usually blame their partner for the breakup and view themselves as victim rather than villain (Gray & Silver, 1990).

Students also exhibit this **self-serving bias**. After receiving an exam grade, those who do well tend to accept personal credit. They judge the exam to be a valid measure of their competence (Arkin & Maruyama, 1979; Davis & Stephan, 1980; Gilmor & Reid, 1979; Griffin & others, 1983). Those who do poorly are much more likely to criticize the exam.

Reading about these experiments, I cannot resist a satisfied "knew-it-all-along" feeling. But college professors are not immune: Mary Glenn Wiley and her co-workers asked 230 scholars who had submitted articles to sociology journals why their papers had been accepted or rejected. The scholars attributed rejections mostly to factors beyond their control (for example, bad luck in the editor's choice of critic for the paper). As you can by now imagine, they did not attribute acceptances to *good* luck but rather to controllable factors, like the quality of their articles and the effort they put into them.

Can We All Be Better Than Average?

Self-serving bias also appears when people compare themselves with others. If the sixth-century B.C. Chinese philosopher Lao-tzu was right that "at no time in the world will a man who is sane over-reach himself, over-spend himself, over-rate himself," then most of us are a little insane. For on nearly any dimension that is both *subjective* and *socially desirable*, most people see themselves as better than average. Consider:

- Most businesspeople see themselves as more ethical than the average businessperson (Baumhart, 1968; Brenner & Molander, 1977). Ninety percent of all business managers rate their performance as superior to their average peer (French, 1968).
- In Australia, 86 percent of the people rate their job performance as above average, 1 percent as below average (Headey & Wearing, 1987).
- Most community residents see themselves as less prejudiced and as fairer than others in their communities (Fields & Schuman, 1976; Lenihan, 1965; Messick & others, 1985; O'Gorman & Garry, 1976).
- Most drivers—even most drivers who have been hospitalized for accidents—believe themselves to be safer and more skilled than the average driver (Svenson, 1981).
- Most Americans perceive themselves as more intelligent than their average peer (Wylie, 1979) and as better looking (*Public Opinion*, 1984).
- Most adults believe they support their aging parents more than their siblings do (Lerner & others, 1991).
- Few people anticipate dying earlier than average (Larwood, 1978; C. R. Snyder, 1978). Los Angeles residents view themselves as healthier than most of their neighbors. Most college students believe they will outlive their actuarially predicted age of death by about 10 years.

Every American community, it seems, is like Garrison Keillor's fictional Lake Wobegon, where "all the women are strong, all the men are good-looking, and all the children are above average." Perhaps one reason for this optimism is that although 12 percent of all Americans feel old for their age, many more—66 percent—think they are young for their age (*Public Opinion*, 1984). All of which calls to mind Freud's joke about the man who told his wife, "If one of us should die, I think I would go live in Paris."

Subjective dimensions (such as "disciplined") trigger greater self-serving bias than objective, behavioral dimensions (such as "punctual"). Students are more likely to rate themselves superior in "moral goodness" than in "intelligence" (Allison & others, 1989; Van Lange, 1991). This is partly because subjective qualities give us so much leeway in constructing our own definitions of success (Dunning & others, 1989, 1991). Rating my "athletic ability," I ponder my basketball play, not the agonizing weeks I spent as a Little League baseball player hiding in right field. Assessing my "leadership ability," I conjure up an image of a great leader whose style is similar to mine. By defining ambiguous criteria in our own terms, each of us can see ourselves as relatively successful. In one College Entrance Examination Board survey of 829,000 high school seniors taking its Scholastic Aptitude Test, 0 percent rated themselves below average in "ability to get along with others" (a subjective, desirable trait), 60 percent rated themselves in the top 10 percent, and 25 percent saw themselves among the top 1 percent!

We also support our self-image by assigning importance to the things we're good at. Over a semester, those who ace an introductory computer science course come to place a higher value on their identity as a computer-literate person in today's world. Those who do poorly are more likely to scorn the computer geeks and to exclude computer skills as pertinent to their self-image (Hill & others, 1989).

Other Self-Serving Tendencies

These tendencies toward self-serving attributions and self-congratulatory comparisons are not the only signs of favorably biased self-perceptions. In previous essays we saw that most of us overestimate how desirably we would act in a given situation. We also display a "cognitive conceit" by overestimating the accuracy of our beliefs and judgments. And we misremember our own past in self-enhancing ways.

Additional streams of evidence converge to form a river:

- If an undesirable act cannot be misremembered or undone, then, as we will see, we may justify it.
- The more favorably we perceive ourselves on some dimension (intelligence, persistence, sense of humor), the more we use that dimension as a basis for judging others (Lewicki, 1983).
- If a test or some other source of information—even a horoscope—flatters us, then we believe it, and we evaluate positively both the test and any evidence suggesting that the test is valid (Glick & others, 1989; Pyszczynski & others, 1985; Tesser & Paulhus, 1983).

- We tend to see ourselves as center stage, we overestimate the extent to which others' behavior is aimed at us, and we see ourselves as responsible for events in which we played only a small part (Fenigstein, 1984).
- Judging from photos, we not only guess that attractive people have desirable personalities but also guess that they, more than unattractive people, have personalities like our own (Marks & others, 1981).
- We like to associate ourselves with the glory of others' success. And if we find ourselves linked with (say, born on the same day as) some reprehensible person, we boost ourselves by softening our view of the rascal (Finch & Cialdini, 1989).

What is more, many of us have what researcher Neil Weinstein (1980, 1982) terms "an unrealistic optimism about future life events." At Rutgers University, for example, students perceive themselves as far more likely than their classmates to get a good job, draw a good salary, and own a home, and as far less likely to experience negative events, such as developing a drinking problem, having a heart attack before age 40, or being fired. In Dundee, Scotland, most late adolescents think they are much less likely than their peers to become infected by the AIDS virus (Abrams, 1991). After experiencing the 1989 earthquake, San Francisco Bay–area students did lose their optimism about being less vulnerable than their classmates to injury in a natural disaster, but within three months their illusory optimism had rebounded (Burger & Palmer, 1991).

Linda Perloff (1987) notes how illusory optimism increases our vulnerability. Believing ourselves immune to misfortune, we do not take sensible precautions. Most young Americans know that half of U.S. marriages end in divorce but persist in believing that *theirs* will not (Lehman & Nisbett, 1985). Sexually active undergraduate women perceive themselves, compared with other women at their university, as much *less* vulnerable to unwanted pregnancy, especially if they do *not* consistently use effective contraception (Burger & Burns, 1988). Even more astonishing is a recent finding by UCLA researchers (Taylor & others, 1992) that 238 gay men who had tested positive for the HIV virus were *more* optimistic about not developing AIDS than a comparison group of 312 gay men who were HIV negative![1] Those who cheerfully shun seat belts, deny the effects of smoking, and stumble into ill-fated relationships remind us that blind optimism, like pride, may, as the ancient proverb warns, go before a fall.

---

[1] The researchers wonder: "What will happen if these men go on to develop AIDS, as research suggests many, if not most of them, will." "Will they be shattered by their disconfirmed beliefs in their ability to overcome the virus, or will they be able to accommodate as well or better than the men who did not hold these unrealistically optimistic beliefs? At present, we have no answer to this question."

A dash of pessimism can save us from the perils of unrealistic optimism. Self-doubt can, for example, energize students, most of whom exhibit excess optimism about upcoming exams (Sparrell & Shrauger, 1984). Students who are overconfident tend to underprepare. Their equally able but more anxious peers, fearing that they are going to bomb the upcoming exam, study furiously and get higher grades (Goodhart, 1986; Norem & Cantor, 1986; Showers & Ruben, 1987). Success in school and beyond requires enough optimism to sustain hope and enough pessimism to motivate concern.

Finally, we have a curious tendency to enhance our self-image by overestimating or underestimating the extent to which others think and act as we do—a phenomenon called the **false consensus effect**. On matters of *opinion*, we find support for our positions by overestimating the extent to which others agree (Marks & Miller, 1987; Mullen & Goethals, 1990). When we behave badly or fail in a task, we reassure ourselves by thinking that such lapses are common. We guess that others think and act as we do: "I do it, but so does everyone else." If we favor Brian Mulroney for prime minister, cheat on our income taxes, or smoke, we are likely to overestimate the number of other people who do likewise. Lance Shotland and Jane Craig (1988) suspect that this helps explain why males are quicker than females to perceive friendly behavior as sexually motivated: Men have a lower threshold for sexual arousal and are likely to assume that women share similar feelings.

One might argue that false consensus occurs when we rationally generalize from a limited sample, which includes ourselves (Dawes, 1990). But on matters of *ability* or when we behave well or successfully, a **false uniqueness effect** more often occurs (Goethals & others, 1991). We serve our self-image by seeing our talents and behaviors as relatively unusual. Thus those who drink heavily but use seat belts will *over*estimate (false consensus) the number of other heavy drinkers and *under*estimate (false uniqueness) the commonality of seat belt use (Suls & others, 1988). Simply put, people see their failings as normal, their virtues as rare.

SELF-DISPARAGEMENT

Perhaps you have by now recalled times when someone was not self-praising but self-disparaging. But even put-downs can be self-serving, for often they elicit reassuring "strokes." A remark such as, "I wish I weren't so ugly," elicits at least a, "Come now. I know a couple of people who are uglier than you."

There is another reason people verbally disparage themselves and praise others. Think of the coach who, before the big game, extols the opponent's strength. Is the coach sincere? Robert Gould, Paul Brounstein, and Harold Sigall (1977) found that in a laboratory contest their

University of Maryland students similarly exalted their anticipated opponent, but only when the assessment was made publicly. Anonymously, they credited their future opponent with much less ability.

When coaches publicly exalt their opponents, they convey an image of modesty and good sportsmanship and set the stage for a favorable evaluation no matter what the outcome. A win becomes a praiseworthy achievement, a loss attributable to the opponent's "great defense." Modesty, said the seventeenth-century philosopher Francis Bacon, is but one of the "arts of ostentation."

Self-Handicapping

Sometimes people sabotage their chances for success by presenting themselves as shy, ill, or handicapped by past traumas. Far from being deliberately self-destructive, such behaviors typically have a self-protective aim (Arkin & others, 1986; Baumeister & Scher, 1988; Rhodewalt, 1987): "I'm not a failure—I'm okay except for this problem that handicaps me."

Can people handicap themselves with self-defeating behavior? Recall that we eagerly protect our self-images by attributing failures to external factors. Can you see why, *fearing failure*, people might handicap themselves by partying half the night before a job interview or by playing video games instead of studying before a big exam? When self-image is tied up with performance, it can be more self-deflating to try hard and fail than to have a ready excuse. If we fail while working under a handicap, we can cling to a sense of competence; if we succeed under such conditions, it can only boost our self-image. Handicaps protect self-esteem by allowing us to attribute failures to something temporary ("I was feeling sick"; "I was out too late the night before") rather than to inability.

This analysis of **self-handicapping**, proposed by Steven Berglas and Edward Jones (1978), has been confirmed. One experiment was said to concern "drugs and intellectual performance." Imagine yourself in the position of their Duke University subjects. You guess answers to some difficult aptitude questions and then are told, "Yours was one of the best scores seen to date!" Feeling incredibly lucky, you are then offered a choice between two drugs before answering more of these items. One drug will aid intellectual performance, and the other will inhibit it. Which drug do you want? Most students wanted the drug that would supposedly disrupt their thinking and thus provide a handy excuse for anticipated poorer performance.

Researchers have documented other ways in which people self-handicap. Fearing failure, people will:

- Reduce their preparation for important individual athletic events (Rhodewalt & others, 1984)

- Not try as hard as they could during a tough ego-involving task (Hormuth, 1986; Pyszczynski & Greenberg, 1983)
- Give their opponent an advantage (Shepperd & Arkin, 1991)
- Report feeling depressed (Baumgardner, 1991)
- Perform poorly at the beginning of a task in order not to create unreachable expectations (Baumgardner & Brownlee, 1987)

After losing to some younger rivals, tennis great Martina Navratilova confessed that she was "afraid to play my best. . . . I was scared to find out if they could beat me when I'm playing my best because if they can, then I am finished" (Frankel & Snyder, 1987).

WHY THE SELF-SERVING BIAS?

The self-serving bias has been explained in three ways: as an effort to *present* a positive image, as a by-product of how we *process information*, or as *motivated* by our desire to protect and enhance our self-esteem.

Self-Presentation

Self-presentation refers to our wanting to present a good image both to an external audience (other people) and to an internal audience (ourselves). Thus we work at managing the impressions we create. Intentionally or not, we deceive, excuse, justify, or apologize as necessary to shore up our self-esteem and verify our self-image (Schlenker & Weigold, 1992).

No wonder, say self-presentation researchers, that people will self-handicap when failure might make them look bad (Arkin & Baumgardner, 1985). No wonder people express more modesty when their self-flattery is vulnerable to being debunked or when experts will be scrutinizing their self-evaluations (Arkin & others, 1980; Riess & others, 1981; Weary & others, 1982). Professor Smith will express less confidence in the significance of her work when presenting it to professional colleagues than when presenting to students.

Presenting oneself in ways that create a good impression is a very delicate matter. People want to be seen as able but also as modest and honest (Carlston & Shovar, 1983). Modesty creates a good impression, and unsolicited boasting creates a bad impression (Forsyth & others, 1981; Holtgraves & Srull, 1989; Schlenker & Leary, 1982). Thus people often display *less* self-esteem than they privately feel (Miller & Schlenker, 1985). When explaining an important success, they are doubly likely to acknowledge others' help if their explanation is public (Baumeister & Ilko, 1991). But when we have obviously done extremely well, false disclaimers ("I did well, but it's no big deal") may come across as feigned humility. Self-handicapping, too, can make a bad impression (Smith & Strube, 1991). To make good impressions—as modest yet competent—requires social skill.

The tendency to self-present modesty is especially great in cultures that value self-restraint, such as those of China and Japan (Markus & Kitayama, 1991; Wu & Tseng, 1985). There, people's identity and feelings of success are linked more with their group's performance. But the self-serving bias is hardly restricted to North America. Self-serving perceptions have been noted among Dutch high school and university students, Belgian basketball players, Hindus in India, Japanese drivers, Australian students and workers, Chinese students, and French people of all ages (Codol, 1976; de Vries & van Knippenberg, 1987; Feather, 1983b; Hagiwara, 1983; Jain, 1990; Liebrand & others, 1986; Lefebvre, 1979; Murphy-Berman & Sharma, 1986; and Ruzzene & Noller, 1986, respectively).

Information Processing

Why do people across the world perceive (if not always present) themselves in self-enhancing ways? One explanation sees the self-serving bias as simply a by-product of how we process and remember information about ourselves.

Recall the study by Michael Ross and Fiore Sicoly (1979) in which married people gave themselves more credit for household work than their spouses. Might this not be due, as Ross and Sicoly believe, to our greater recall for what we've actively done and our lesser recall for what we've not done or merely observed others doing? I can easily picture myself picking up the laundry, but I have difficulty picturing myself absentmindedly overlooking it.

Self-Esteem Motivation

But are the biased perceptions simply a perceptual error, an unemotional bent in how we process information? Or are self-serving *motives* also involved? A third view presumes that we are motivated to protect and enhance our self-esteem (Tice, 1991).

Experiments confirm that a motivational engine powers our cognitive machinery (Kunda, 1990). For example, Abraham Tesser (1988) at the University of Georgia reports that a "self-esteem maintenance" motive predicts a variety of interesting findings, even friction among brothers and sisters. Do you have a sibling of the same sex who is close to you in age? If so, people probably compared the two of you as you grew up. Tesser presumes that people's perceiving one of you as more capable than the other will motivate the less able one to act in ways that maintain his or her self-esteem. (Tesser thinks the threat to self-esteem is greatest for an older child with a highly capable younger sibling.) Men with a brother of differing ability typically recall not getting along well with him; men with a brother of similar ability are more likely to recall very little friction. Self-esteem threats occur among friends and married partners, too. Although shared interests are healthy, *identical* career goals may produce tension or jealousy (Clark & Bennett, 1992).

REFLECTIONS ON THE SELF-SERVING BIAS

No doubt many readers are finding all this either depressing or contrary to their own occasional feelings of inadequacy. To be sure, those of us who exhibit the self-serving bias—and apparently that includes most of us—may still feel inferior to specific individuals, especially those who are a step or two higher on the ladder of success, attractiveness, or skill. And not everyone operates with a self-serving bias. (Like other social psychological findings, it describes most people most of the time.) Some people *do* suffer from low self-esteem. Do such people hunger for esteem and therefore often exhibit self-serving bias? Is self-serving bias just a cover-up? This is what some theorists, such as Erich Fromm, have proposed (Shrauger, 1975).

And it's true: When feeling good about ourselves, we are less defensive (Epstein & Feist, 1988). We are also less thin-skinned and judgmental—less likely to praise those who like us and berate those who don't (Baumgardner & others, 1989). In experiments, people whose self-esteem is temporarily bruised—say, by being told they did miserably on an intelligence test—are more likely to disparage others. More generally, people who are down on themselves tend also to be down on others (Wills, 1981). And those whose ego has recently been wounded are more prone to self-serving explanations of success or failure than those whose ego has recently received a boost (McCarrey & others, 1982). So, when feeling unaffirmed, people may offer self-affirming boasts, excuses, and put-downs of others. Mockery says as much about the mocker as the one mocked.

Nevertheless, those who score highest on self-esteem tests (who say nice things about themselves) also say nice things about themselves when explaining their successes and failures (Ickes & Layden, 1978; Levine & Uleman, 1979; Rosenfeld, 1979; Schlenker & others, 1990), when describing their own traits (Roth & others, 1986), when evaluating their group (Brown & others, 1988), and when comparing themselves to others (Brown, 1986). So, threats to self-esteem provoke self-serving defensiveness; yet in questionnaire studies, the trait of high self-esteem goes hand in hand with self-serving perceptions.

The Self-Serving Bias as Adaptive

Without the self-serving bias, and its accompanying excuses, people with low self-esteem are more vulnerable to anxiety and depression (Snyder & Higgins, 1988). Although most people excuse their failures on laboratory tasks or perceive themselves as being more in control than they are, depressed people's self-appraisals are more accurate: sadder but wiser.

And consider: Thanks to our reluctance to share negative impressions, most of us have difficulty gauging how strangers and casual acquaintances are really perceiving us (DePaulo & others, 1987; Kenny & Albright, 1987). Mildly depressed people are less prone to illusions; they generally see themselves *as* other people see them (Lewinsohn & others, 1980). This prompts the unsettling thought that Pascal may have been right: "I lay it down as a fact that, if all men knew what others say of them, there would not be four friends in the world."

As this new research on depression suggests, there may be some practical wisdom in self-serving perceptions. Cheaters give a more convincing display of honesty if they believe in their honesty. Belief in our superiority can also motivate us to achieve—creating a self-fulfilling prophecy—and can sustain a sense of hope in difficult times.

Self-Serving Bias as Maladaptive

The self-serving bias is not always adaptive. People who blame others for their social difficulties are often unhappier than people who can acknowledge their mistakes (C. A. Anderson & others, 1983; Newman & Langer, 1981; Peterson & others, 1981). Research by Barry Schlenker (1976; Schlenker & Miller, 1977a, 1977b) at the University of Florida has also shown how self-serving perceptions can poison a group. In nine experiments Schlenker had people work together on some task. He then falsely informed them that their group had done either well or poorly. In every one of these studies the members of successful groups claimed more responsibility for their group's performance than members of groups that supposedly failed at the task. Most presented themselves as contributing more than the others in their group when the group did well; few said they contributed less.

Such self-deception can lead individual group members to expect greater-than-average rewards when their organization does well and less-than-average blame when it does not. If most individuals in a group believe they are underpaid and underappreciated relative to their contributions, disharmony and envy are likely. College presidents and academic deans will readily recognize the phenomenon. Most college faculty members—94 percent in one survey at the University of Nebraska (Cross, 1977), 90 percent in a survey of the faculties of 24 institutions (Blackburn &

others, 1980)—rate themselves as superior to their average colleague. It is therefore inevitable that when merit salary raises are announced and half receive an average raise or less, many will feel themselves victims of injustice.

Biased self-assessments also distort managerial judgment. When groups are comparable, most people consider their own group superior (Codol, 1976; Taylor & Doria, 1981; Zander, 1969). Thus, most corporation presidents predict more growth for their own firms than for their competition (Larwood & Whittaker, 1977). And most production managers overpredict their production (Kidd & Morgan, 1969). As Laurie Larwood and William Whittaker (1977) noted, such overoptimism can produce disastrous consequences. If those who deal in the stock market or in real estate perceive their business intuition to be superior to that of their competitors, they may be in for severe disappointment. Even the seventeenth-century economist Adam Smith, a defender of human economic rationality, foresaw that people would overestimate their chances of gain. This "absurd presumption in their own good fortune," he said, arises from "the overweening conceit which the greater part of men have of their own abilities" (Spiegel, 1971, p. 243). Falsely imagining that we could have predicted the present (the hindsight bias) reinforces overoptimism about our ability to predict the future (Johnson & Sherman, 1990).

That people see and present themselves with a favorable bias is hardly new: the tragic flaw portrayed in ancient Greek drama was *hubris*, or pride. Like the subjects of our experiments, the Greek tragic figures were not self-consciously evil; they merely thought too highly of themselves. In literature, the pitfalls of pride are portrayed again and again. In religion, pride has long been first among the "seven deadly sins."

If pride is akin to the self-serving bias, then what is humility? Is it self-contempt? Or can we be self-affirming and self-accepting without a self-serving bias? To paraphrase the English scholar-writer C. S. Lewis, humility is not handsome people trying to believe they are ugly and clever people trying to believe they are fools. False modesty can actually be a cover for pride in one's better-than-average humility. (Perhaps some readers have by now congratulated themselves on being unusually free of self-serving bias.) True humility—a third alternative to self-serving bias and depressive realism—is more like self-forgetfulness than false modesty. It leaves people free to rejoice in their special talents and, with the same honesty, to recognize others' talents.

CONCEPTS TO REMEMBER

Self-serving bias The tendency to perceive oneself favorably.

False consensus effect The tendency to overestimate the commonality of one's opinions and one's undesirable or unsuccessful behaviors.

False uniqueness effect   The tendency to underestimate the commonality of one's abilities and one's desirable or successful behaviors.

Self-handicapping   Protecting one's self-image by creating a handy excuse for failure.

Self-presentation   The act of expressing oneself and behaving in ways designed to create a favorable impression or an impression that corresponds to one's ideals. (Self-presentation is a prime example of "impression management.")

MODULE

8

The Power of Positive Thinking

❖

We have considered two potent biases uncovered by social psychologists: a tendency to ignore situational forces when explaining others' behavior (the fundamental attribution error) and a tendency to perceive ourselves favorably (the self-serving bias). The first can dispose us to misunderstand others' problems (for example, by assuming that unemployed people are necessarily lazy or incompetent). The second can fuel conflict among people and nations when all see themselves as more moral and deserving than others.

Studies of the fundamental attribution error and the self-serving bias expose deep truths about human nature. But single truths are seldom sufficient, because the world is complex. Indeed, there is an important complement to these truths. High self-esteem—a sense of self-worth—is adaptive. Compared to those with low self-esteem, people with high self-esteem are happier, less neurotic, less troubled by ulcers and insomnia, and less prone to drug and alcohol addictions (Brockner & Hulton, 1978; Brown, 1991). Many clinical psychologists report that underneath much human despair is an impoverished self-acceptance.

Additional research on "locus of control," optimism, and "learned helplessness" confirms the benefits of seeing oneself as competent and effective. Albert Bandura (1986) merges much of this research into a concept called **self-efficacy**, a scholarly version of the wisdom behind the power of positive thinking. An optimistic belief in our own possibilities pays dividends. People with strong feelings of self-efficacy are more persistent, less anxious and depressed, and more academically successful (Gecas, 1989; Maddux, 1991; Scheier & Carver, 1992).

L OCUS OF CONTROL

Which do you more strongly believe?

In the long run people get the respect they deserve in this world.	or Unfortunately, people's worth often passes unrecognized no matter how hard they try.
What happens to me is my own doing.	or Sometimes I feel that I don't have enough control over the direction my life is taking.
The average person can have an influence in government decisions.	or This world is run by the few people in power, and there is not much the little guy can do about it.

Do your answers to such questions (from Rotter, 1973) indicate that you believe you control your own destiny (**internal locus of control**) or that chance or outside forces determine your fate (**external locus of control**)? Those who see themselves as internally controlled are more likely to do well in school, successfully stop smoking, wear seat belts, practice birth control, deal with marital problems directly, make lots of money, and delay instant gratification in order to achieve long-term goals (for example, Findley & Cooper, 1983; Lefcourt, 1982; Miller & others, 1986).

O PTIMISM

How competent and effective we feel also depends on how we explain negative events. Perhaps you have known students who blame poor grades on things beyond their control—their feelings of stupidity or their "poor" teachers, texts, or tests. If such students are coached to adopt a more hopeful attitude—to believe that effort, good study habits, and self-discipline can make a difference—their grades tend to go up (Noel & others, 1987; Peterson & Barrett, 1987).

Successful people are more likely to see setbacks as a fluke or to think "I need a new approach." New life insurance sales representatives who view failures as controllable ("It's difficult, but with persistence I'll get better") sell more policies. They are half as likely as their more pessimistic colleagues to quit during their first year (Seligman & Schulman, 1986). Among college swimming team members, those with an optimistic "explanatory style" are more likely than pessimists to perform beyond expectations (Seligman & others, 1990). As the Roman poet Virgil said in the Aeneid, "They can because they think they can."

Optimists also tend to be healthier. Several studies have confirmed that a pessimistic style of explaining bad events (saying, "It's my responsibility, it's going to last, and it's going to undermine everything") makes illness more likely. Christopher Peterson and Martin Seligman (1987) studied the press quotes of 94 members of baseball's Hall of Fame and gauged how often they offered pessimistic (stable, global, internal) explanations for bad events, such as losing big games. Those who routinely did so tended to die at somewhat younger ages. Optimists—who offered stable, global, and internal explanations for *good* events—usually outlived the pessimists.

Peterson, Seligman, and George Vaillant (1988) offer other findings: Harvard graduates who expressed the most optimism when interviewed in 1946 were healthiest when restudied in 1980. Virginia Tech introductory psychology students who offered optimistic (not stable and global) explanations for bad events suffered fewer colds, sore throats, and flus a year later. Michael Scheier and Charles Carver (1992) similarly report that optimists (who agree, for example, that "I usually expect the best") are less often bothered by various illnesses and recover faster from coronary bypass surgery.

Even cancer patients appear more likely to survive if their attitude is hopeful and determined rather than pessimistic and stoic (Levy & others, 1988; Pettingale & others, 1985). One study of 86 women undergoing breast cancer therapy found that those who participated in morale-boosting weekly support group sessions survived an average of 37 months, double the 19-month average survival time among the nonparticipants (Spiegel & others, 1989). Blood tests provide a reason, by linking the pessimistic explanatory style with weaker immune defenses (Kamen & others, 1988). Compared to UCLA cancer patients in a control group, those who participated in support groups became more upbeat, with an associated increase in immune cells (Cousins, 1989). Beliefs, it seems, can boost biology.

LEARNED HELPLESSNESS VERSUS SELF-DETERMINATION

The benefits of an optimistic sense of personal efficacy also appear in animal research. Dogs that learn a sense of helplessness (by being taught they cannot escape shocks) will later fail to take the initiative in another situation when they *could* escape the punishment. Dogs that learn personal control (by escaping their first shocks successfully) adapt easily to a new situation. Researcher Seligman (1975, 1991) notes similarities in human situations. Depressed or oppressed people, for example, become passive because they believe that their efforts have no effect. Helpless dogs and depressed people both suffer paralysis of the will, passive resignation, even motionless apathy.

Here is a clue to how institutions—whether malevolent, like concentration camps, or benevolent, like hospitals—can dehumanize people. In hospitals, "good patients" don't ring bells, don't ask questions, don't try to control what's happening (Taylor, 1979). Such passivity may be good for hospital efficiency, but it is bad for people. Feelings of efficacy, of an ability to control one's life, enhance health and survival. Losing control over what you do and what others do to you can make unpleasant events profoundly stressful (Pomerleau & Rodin, 1986). Several diseases are associated with feelings of helplessness and diminished choice. So is the rapidity of decline and death in concentration camps and nursing homes. Hospital patients who are trained to believe in their ability to control stress require fewer pain relievers, and nurses see them as exhibiting less anxiety (Langer & others, 1975). Clearly, people benefit from viewing themselves not as pawns of external forces but as free creatures.

Ellen Langer and Judith Rodin (1976) showed the importance of personal control by treating elderly patients in a highly-rated Connecticut nursing home in one of two ways. With one group the benevolent caregivers stressed "our responsibility to make this a home you can be proud of and happy in." They treated these patients as passive recipients of the normal, well-intentioned, sympathetic care. Three weeks later, most were rated by themselves, by interviewers, and by nurses as further debilitated. Langer and Rodin's other treatment promoted personal control—the *un*learning of helplessness. It stressed opportunities for choice, the possibilities for influencing nursing-home policy, and the person's responsibility "to make of your life whatever you want." These patients were given small decisions to make and responsibilities to fulfill. Over the ensuing three weeks, 93 percent of this group showed improved alertness, activity, and happiness.

The experience of the first group must have been similar to that of James MacKay (1980), an 87-year-old psychologist:

> I became a nonperson last summer. My wife had an arthritic knee which put her in a walker, and I chose that moment to break my leg. We went to a nursing home. It was all nursing and no home. The doctor and the head nurse made all decisions; we were merely animate objects. Thank heavens it was only two weeks. . . . The top man of the nursing home was very well trained and very compassionate; I considered it the best home in town. But we were nonpersons from the time we entered until we left.

A similar loss of control can exacerbate the stress of poverty. Well-being for most people stems less from *having* what they want than being able to *do* what they want—feeling empowered, in control of their lives. Matthew Dumont (1989), a community psychiatrist in Chelsea, which has Masschusetts' lowest per person income, reflects on the powerlessness of its distress-prone people:

What is poverty? It soon became evident to me that what is pathogenic about it is not merely the lack of money. The amount of money, the buying power, commanded by a welfare recipient in Chelsea would have been like a king's ransom to any member of a thriving hunter-gatherer tribe in the Kalahari. Yet the life of the welfare recipient appears terribly impoverished in contrast to that of the tribe member. A closer observation of life in Chelsea resolves the paradox. Chelsea residents possess material things unknown to the hunter but, despite this (meager) purchasing power, they experience little control over the circumstances of their lives. The efforts of the Kalahari hunters, on the other hand, had a direct effect on the shape of their lives and the possibilities of their existence.

Mindful of self-defeating resignation, Jesse Jackson has carried a take-control-of-your-life message to urban youth, a message summed up in his speech to the 1983 civil rights march on Washington: "If my mind can conceive it and my heart can believe it, I know I can achieve it." Advocates of "cognitive behavior therapy" harness the power of positive thinking. Their therapy aims to reverse the negative, self-defeating thinking that underlies difficulties such as depression. It trains people to see how their negative interpretations make them depressed and to reverse their negative self-talk.

Studies confirm that systems of governing or managing people that promote self-efficacy will indeed promote health and happiness (Deci & Ryan, 1987). Prisoners given some control over their environments—by being able to move chairs, control TV sets, and switch the lights—experience less stress, exhibit fewer health problems, and commit less vandalism (Ruback & others, 1986; Wener & others, 1987). Workers given leeway in carrying out tasks and participating in decision making experience improved morale (Miller & Monge, 1986). Institutionalized residents allowed choice in such matters as what to eat for breakfast, when to go to a movie, and whether to sleep late or get up early may live longer and certainly are happier (Timko & Moos, 1989).

REFLECTIONS ON SELF-EFFICACY

Although research on self-efficacy is new, the emphasis on taking charge of one's life and realizing one's potential is not. The you-can-do-it theme of Horatio Alger's rags-to-riches books is an enduring American idea. We find it in Norman Vincent Peale's 1950s best-seller, *The Power of Positive Thinking* ("If you think in positive terms you will get positive results. That is the simple fact."). We find it in self-help books and videos that urge people to succeed through positive mental attitudes.

Research on self-efficacy gives us greater confidence in traditional virtues such as perseverance and hope. Yet Bandura believes that self-efficacy grows not primarily by self-persuasion ("I think I can, I think I can") or by puffing people up like hot-air balloons ("You're terrific. You are somebody. You are beautiful."). Its chief source is undertaking challenging yet realistic tasks and succeeding. After learning to conquer an animal phobia, people become less timid and more self-directed and venturesome in other areas of their life. After mastering the physical skills needed to repel a sexual assault, women feel less vulnerable, less anxious, and more in control (Ozer & Bandura, 1990). After experiencing academic success, students develop higher appraisals of their academic ability, which in turn often stimulates them to work harder and achieve more (Felson, 1984). To do one's best and achieve is to feel more confident and empowered.

So there is a power to positive thinking. But let us remember the point at which we began our consideration of self-efficacy: Any truth, separated from its complementary truth, is a half-truth. The truth embodied in the concept of self-efficacy may encourage us not to resign ourselves to bad situations, to persist despite initial failures, to exert effort without being overly distracted by self-doubts. But lest the pendulum swing too far toward *this* truth, we had best remember that it, too, is not the whole story. If positive thinking can accomplish *anything*, then if we are unhappily married, poor, or depressed, we have only ourselves to blame. For shame! If only we had tried harder, been more disciplined, less stupid. Failing to appreciate that difficulties sometimes reflect the oppressive power of social situations can tempt us to blame people for their problems and failures, or even to blame ourselves too harshly for our own. Ironically, life's greatest disappointments, as well as its highest achievements, are born of the highest expectations. The bigger we dream, the more we may attain—and the more we risk falling short.

Likewise, researchers Howard Tennen and Glenn Affleck (1987) agree that a positive, hopeful attributional style is generally good medicine—yet remind us that every silver lining has a cloud. Optimists may see themselves as invulnerable and thus fail to take sensible precautions. And when things go wrong in a big way—when the optimist has a Down's syndrome child or encounters a devastating illness—adversity can be shattering. Optimism *is* good for health. But remember: Even optimists have a mortality rate of 100 percent.

The healthiest attitude then is neither blindly positive nor cynically negative. Rather, it mixes ample optimism to provide hope with enough realism to discriminate those things we can control from those we cannot. It was for such wisdom that theologian Reinhold Niebuhr offered his famous "Serenity Prayer": "O God, give us grace to accept with serenity the things that cannot be changed, courage to change the things which should be changed, and the wisdom to distinguish the one from the other."

CONCEPTS TO REMEMBER ·

Self-efficacy   A sense that one is competent and effective. Distinguished from self-esteem, a sense of one's self-worth. A bombardier might feel high self-efficacy and low self-esteem.

Internal locus of control   The perception that one controls one's own fate.

External locus of control   The perception that chance or outside forces beyond one's personal control determine one's fate.

9

Behavior and Belief

————— ❖ —————

W hich comes first, belief or behavior? inner attitude or outer action? character or conduct? What is the relationship between who we *are* (on the inside) and what we *do* (on the outside)?

Opinions on this chicken-and-egg question vary. "The ancestor of every action is a thought," wrote the American essayist Ralph Waldo Emerson in 1841. To the contrary, said British Prime Minister Benjamin Disraeli, "Thought is the child of Action." Most people side with Emerson. Underlying our teaching, preaching, and counseling is the assumption that private beliefs determine public behavior. If we want to alter people's actions, we therefore need to change their hearts and minds.

*D*O ATTITUDES INFLUENCE BEHAVIOR?

Attitudes are beliefs and feelings that may influence our reactions. If we *believe* that someone is threatening, we may *feel* dislike and therefore *act* unfriendly. "Change the way people think," said South African civil rights martyr Steve Biko (echoing Emerson), "and things will never be the same."

Believing this, social psychologists during the 1940s and 1950s studied factors that influence attitudes. Thus they were shocked when dozens of studies during the 1960s revealed that what people say they think and feel often has little to do with how they act (Wicker, 1971). In these studies, students' attitudes toward cheating bore little relation to the likelihood of their actually cheating. People's attitudes toward the church were but modestly linked with church attendance on any given Sunday. Self-described racial attitudes predicted little of the variation in behavior that occurred when people faced an actual interracial situation. People, it seemed, were talking and playing different games.

This realization stimulated more studies during the 1970s and 1980s which revealed that our attitudes *do* influence our actions *when*:

- *External influences on our words and actions are minimal.* Sometimes we adjust our attitude reports to please our listeners. This was vividly demonstrated when the U.S. House of Representatives once overwhelmingly passed a salary increase for itself in an off-the-record vote, and then moments later overwhelmingly defeated the same bill on a roll-call vote. Fear of criticism had distorted the true sentiment on the roll-call vote. Other times social pressure diverts our behavior from the dictates of our attitudes, leading people even to do cruelties toward people they do not dislike. When external pressures do not blur the link between our attitudes and actions, we can see that link more clearly.

- *The attitude is specific to the behavior.* People readily profess honesty while cheating in reporting their taxes, cherish a clean environment while not recycling, or applaud good health while smoking and not exercising. But their more specific attitudes toward jogging better predict whether they jog (Olson & Zanna, 1981). Their attitudes toward recycling do predict whether they recycle (Oskamp, 1991). And their attitudes toward contraception predict their contraceptive use (Morrison, 1989).

- *We are conscious of our attitudes.* Attitudes may lie dormant as we act out of habit or as we flow with the crowd. For our attitudes to guide our action we must pause to consider them. Thus when self-conscious or when reminded how we feel, we act truer to our convictions (Fazio, 1990). Likewise, attitudes formed through a significant experience are more often remembered and acted upon.

So, an attitude will influence our behavior *if* other influences are minimal, *if* the attitude specifically relates to the behavior, and *if* the attitude is potent, perhaps because something brings it to mind. Under these conditions, we *will* stand up for what we believe.

DOES BEHAVIOR INFLUENCE ATTITUDES?

Do we also come to believe in what we've stood up for? Indeed. One of social psychology's big lessons is that we are likely not only to think ourselves into a way of acting but also to act ourselves into a way of thinking. Many streams of evidence confirm that *attitudes follow behavior*.

Role Playing

The word **role** is borrowed from the theater and, as in the theater, refers to prescribed actions—actions expected of those who occupy a particular social position. When stepping into a new social role, we must perform its actions, even if we feel phony. But our sense of phoniness seldom lasts.

Think about a time when you stepped into some new role—perhaps your first days on a job, or at college, or in a sorority or fraternity. That first week on campus, for example, you may have been supersensitive to the new social prescriptions and tried valiantly to meet them and to root out your high school behavior. At such times we feel artificial. We self-consciously observe our new speech and actions, because they aren't natural to us. Then one day an amazing thing happens: We notice that our sorority enthusiasm or our pseudo-intellectual talk no longer feels forced. The role has begun to fit as comfortably as our old jeans and T-shirt.

In one study, researchers observed industrial workers who were promoted to supervisor (a company position) or shop steward (a union position). The new roles demanded new behavior. And, sure enough, the men soon developed new attitudes. The supervisors became more sympathetic to the management's positions, the stewards to the union's (Lieberman, 1956). This hints at the importance of vocational role. The career you choose will affect not only what you do on the job but also your attitudes. Teachers, police officers, soldiers, and managers usually internalize their roles, with significant effects on their attitudes. The U.S. Marines "make a man out of you" not just by indoctrination but by having you act like a tough marine.

In a laboratory study of role playing, college students volunteered to spend time in a simulated prison devised by psychologist Philip Zimbardo (1972). Some he randomly designated as guards; he gave them uniforms, billy clubs, and whistles and instructed them to enforce certain rules. The remainder became prisoners; they were locked in barren cells and forced to wear humiliating outfits. After a day or two of self-consciously "playing" their roles, the simulation became real—too real. The guards devised cruel and degrading routines, and one by one the prisoners either broke down, rebelled, or passively resigned, causing Zimbardo to call the study off after only six days. What began as playacting had become real.

Saying Becomes Believing

In 1785, Thomas Jefferson offered a social psychological observation: "He who permits himself to tell a lie once finds it much easier to do it a second and third time, till at length it becomes habitual; he tells lies without attending to it, and truths without the world's believing him. This falsehood of the tongue leads to that of the heart, and in time depraves all its good dispositions." Experiments have proved Jefferson right. People induced to give spoken or written witness to something about which they have real doubts will often feel bad about their deceit. Nevertheless, they begin to believe what they are saying—provided they weren't bribed or coerced into doing so. When there is no compelling external explanation for one's words, saying becomes believing (Klaas, 1978).

Tory Higgins and his colleagues (Higgins & Rholes, 1978; Higgins & McCann, 1984) illustrate this self-persuasion effect. They had university students read a personality description of someone and then summarize it for someone else who was believed either to like or dislike this person. The students not only wrote a more positive description when the recipient liked the person but also then liked the person more themselves. Asked to recall what they had read, they remembered the description as being more positive than it was. In short, it seems that we are prone to adjust our messages to our listeners and, having done so, to believe the altered message.

The Foot-in-the-Door Phenomenon

Most of us can recall times when, after agreeing to help out with a project or an organization, we ended up more involved than we ever intended, vowing that in the future we would say no to such requests. How does this happen? Experiments suggest that if you want people to do a big favor for you, one technique is to get them to do a small favor first. In the best-known demonstration of this **foot-in-the-door** principle, researchers posing as safety-drive volunteers asked Californians to permit the installation of a huge, poorly lettered "Drive Carefully" sign in their front yards. Only 17 percent consented. Others were first approached with a small request: Would they display a 3-inch "Be a Safe Driver" window sign? Nearly all readily agreed. When approached two weeks later to allow the large, ugly sign in their front yards, 76 percent consented (Freedman & Fraser, 1966).

Other researchers have confirmed the foot-in-the-door effect with altruistic behaviors:

- Patricia Pliner and her collaborators (1974) found 46 percent of Toronto suburbanites willing to give to the Cancer Society when approached directly. Others, asked a day ahead to wear a lapel pin publicizing the drive (which all agreed to do), were nearly twice as likely to donate when the Cancer Society came calling.
- Among the residents of one middle-class Israeli city, 53 percent gave to a collection for the mentally handicapped when approached by canvassers working for Joseph Schwarzwald and his

colleagues (1983). Two weeks earlier, other residents had been approached to sign a petition supporting a recreation center for the handicapped; among these, 92 percent now gave.

- Angela Lipsitz and others (1989) report that ending blood-drive reminder calls with "We'll count on seeing you then, OK? [pause for response]" increased the show-up rate from 62 to 81 percent.

Note that in these experiments the initial compliance—signing a petition, wearing a lapel pin, stating one's intention—was voluntary. We will see again and again that when people commit themselves to public behaviors *and* perceive these acts to be their own doing, they come to believe more strongly in what they have done.

Robert Cialdini and his collaborators (1978) demonstrated a variation on the foot-in-the-door phenomenon by experimenting with the **low-ball technique**, a tactic reportedly used by some car dealers. After the customer agrees to buy a new car because of its great price and begins completing the sales forms, the salesperson removes the price advantage by charging for options the customer thought were included or by checking with a boss who disallows the deal because "We'd be losing money." Folklore has it that more customers stick with their higher-priced purchase than would have agreed to it at the outset. Cialdini and his collaborators found that this technique indeed works. When they invited introductory psychology students to participate in an experiment at 7:00 A.M., only 24 percent showed up. But if the students first agreed to participate without knowing the time and only then were asked to participate at 7:00 A.M., 53 percent came.

Marketing researchers and salespeople have found that the principle works even when we are aware of a profit motive (Cialdini, 1988). A harmless initial commitment—returning a card for more information and a gift, agreeing to listen to an investment possibility—often moves us toward a larger commitment. The day after I wrote this sentence, a life insurance salesperson came to my office and offered a thorough analysis of my family's financial situation. He did not ask whether I wished to buy his life insurance, or even whether I wished to try his free service. His question was instead a small foot-in-the-door, one carefully calculated to elicit agreement: Did I think people should have such information about their financial situation? I could only answer yes, and before I realized what was happening, I had agreed to the analysis. But I'm learning. The other evening a paid fund-raiser came to my door, first soliciting a petition signature supporting environmental cleanup, and then welcoming my contribution to what I'd signed my support of. (I signed but, resisting manipulation, didn't give.)

Salespeople may exploit the power of small commitments when trying to bind people to purchase agreements. Many states now have laws that allow customers of door-to-door salespeople a few days to cancel their purchases. To combat the effect of these laws, many companies use what the sales-training program of one encyclopedia company calls "a very important psychological aid in preventing customers from backing out of their contracts" (Cialdini, 1988, p. 78). They simply have the customer, rather than the salesperson, fill out the agreement. Having written it themselves, people usually live up to their commitment.

The foot-in-the-door phenomenon is well worth being aware of so we won't be naively vulnerable to it. Someone trying to seduce us—financially, politically, or sexually—usually will try to create a momentum of compliance. Before agreeing to the small request, we need to think about what will follow.

Evil Acts and Actors

The action-attitude sequence occurs not just with shading the truth but with more immoral acts as well. Evil sometimes results from gradually escalating commitments. A trifling evil act paves the way for a greater evil. To paraphrase one of La Rochefoucauld's 1665 *Maxims*, it is not as difficult to find a person who has never succumbed to a given temptation as to find a person who has succumbed only once. Consider some examples.

Cruel acts corrode the consciences of those who perform them. Harming an innocent victim—by uttering hurtful comments or delivering electric shocks—typically leads aggressors to disparage their victims, thus helping them justify the behavior (Berscheid & others, 1968; Davis & Jones, 1960; Glass, 1964). In all the studies that have established this, people justify an action especially when coaxed, not coerced, into it. When we agree to the deed, we take more responsibility for it.

In everyday life, oppressors usually disparage their victims. We tend not only to hurt those we dislike but to dislike those we hurt. In times of war, soldiers denigrate their victims: American World War II soldiers called their enemy "the Japs." In the 1960s American soldiers dehumanized the Vietnamese people as "gooks." Action and attitude spiral: The more one commits aggression, the easier it becomes. The same holds for prejudice. A group that enslaves another will likely perceive the slaves as having subhuman traits that justify the oppression. Actions and attitudes feed one another, sometimes to the point of moral numbness. With each little evil, conscience mutates. The human mind is facile in developing justifying beliefs for any behavior, especially for evil.

If evil acts shape the self, so, thankfully, do moral acts. When children resist temptation, they internalize the conscientious act if the deterrent is strong enough to elicit the desired behavior yet mild enough to leave them with a sense of choice. In a dramatic experiment, Jonathan Freedman (1965) introduced elementary schoolchildren to an enticing battery-controlled robot but instructed them not to play with it while he was out of the room. Freedman used a severe threat with half the children and a mild threat with the others. Both were sufficient to deter the children.

Several weeks later a different researcher, with no apparent relation to the earlier events, left each child to play in the same room with the same toys. Of the 18 children who had been given the severe threat, 14 now freely played with the robot; but two-thirds of those who had been given the mild deterrent still resisted playing with it. Having made the conscious choice *not* to play with the toy, the mildly deterred children apparently internalized their decision, and this new attitude controlled their subsequent action. Moral action, especially when chosen rather than coerced, affects moral thinking.

Interracial Behavior and Racial Attitudes

If moral action feeds moral attitudes, will positive interracial behavior reduce racial prejudice? This was part of social scientists' testimony before the Supreme Court's 1954 decision to desegregate schools. Their argument ran like this: If we wait for the heart to change—through preaching and teaching—we will wait a long time for racial justice. But if we legislate moral action, we can, under the right conditions, indirectly affect heartfelt attitudes. Although this idea runs counter to the presumption that "you can't legislate morality," attitude change has, in fact, followed on the heels of desegregation. Consider:

- Since the Supreme Court decision, the percentage of White Americans favoring integrated schools has more than doubled, and now includes nearly everyone.

- In the 10 years after the Civil Rights Act of 1964, the percentage of White Americans who described their neighborhoods, friends, coworkers, or fellow students as all-White declined by about 20 percent for each of these measures. During the same period, the percentage of White Americans who said that Blacks should be allowed to live in any neighborhood increased from 65 percent to 87 percent (ISR Newsletter, 1975).

- More uniform national standards against discrimination were followed by decreasing differences in racial attitudes among people of differing religion, class, and geographic regions. As Americans came to act more alike, they came to think more alike (Greeley & Sheatsley, 1971; Taylor & others, 1978).

Experiments confirm that positive behavior toward someone fosters liking for that person. Doing a favor for an experimenter or another subject, or tutoring a student, usually increases liking of the person helped (Blanchard & Cook, 1976). In 1793, Benjamin Franklin tested the idea that doing a favor engenders liking. As clerk of the Pennsylvania General Assembly, he was disturbed by opposition from another important legislator. So Franklin set out to win him over:

> I did not . . . aim at gaining his favour by paying any servile respect to him but, after some time, took this other method. Having heard that he had in his library a certain very scarce and curious book I wrote a note to him expressing my desire of perusing that book and requesting he would do me the favour of lending it to me for a few days. He sent it immediately and I return'd it in about a week, expressing strongly my sense of the favour. When we next met in the House he spoke to me (which he had never done before), and with great civility; and he ever after manifested a readiness to serve me on all occasions, so that we became great friends and our friendship continued to his death. (Rosenzweig, 1972, p. 769)

B RAINWASHING

Many people assume that the most dramatic influence comes through "brainwashing," a term coined to describe what happened to American prisoners of war (POWs) during the 1950s Korean war. Actually, the Chinese "thought-control" program was not nearly as irresistible as this term suggests. But it was disconcerting that hundreds of prisoners cooperated with their captors, that 21 chose to remain after being granted permission to return to America, and that many of those who did return came home believing that "although communism won't work in America, I think it's a good thing for Asia" (Segal, 1954).

Edgar Schein (1956) interviewed many of the POWs during their journey home and reported that the captors' methods included a gradual escalation of demands. The Chinese, who were experienced at "rehabilitating" people's attitudes, always started with trivial requests and gradually worked up to more significant ones. "Thus after a prisoner had once been 'trained' to speak or write out trivia, statements on more important issues were demanded." Moreover, they always expected active participation, be it just copying something or participating in group discussions, writing self-criticism, or uttering public confessions. Once a prisoner had spoken or written a statement, he felt an inner need to make his beliefs consistent with his acts. This often drove prisoners to persuade themselves of what they had done. The "start-small-and-build" tactic was an effective application of the foot-in-the-door technique, as it continues to be today in the socialization of terrorists and torturers.

In Nazi Germany, too, participation in mass meetings, wearing uniforms, demonstrating, and especially the "German greeting" ("Heil Hitler") established for many a profound inconsistency between behavior and belief. Historian Richard Grunberger (1971, p. 27) reports that for those who had their doubts about Hitler "the 'German greeting' was a powerful conditioning device. Having once decided to intone it as an outward token of conformity, many experienced schizophrenic discomfort at the contradiction between their words and their feelings. Prevented from saying what they believed, they tried to establish their psychic equilibrium by consciously making themselves believe what they said."

From these observations—of the effects of role playing, the foot-in-the-door experience, moral and immoral acts, interracial behavior, and brainwashing—there is a powerful practical lesson: If we want to change ourselves in some important way, it's best not to wait for insight or inspiration. Sometimes we need to act—to begin writing that paper, to make those phone calls, to see that person—even if we don't feel like acting. To strengthen our convictions, it helps to enact them. In this way, faith and love are alike: If we keep them to ourselves, they shrivel. If we enact and express them, they grow.

WHY DOES BEHAVIOR INFLUENCE ATTITUDES?

Social psychologists agree: Our actions influence our attitudes, sometimes turning foes into friends, captives into collaborators, and doubters into believers. Social psychologists debate: Why?

One idea is that, wanting to make a good impression, people may merely express attitudes that *appear* consistent with their attitudes. Let's be honest with ourselves. We do care about appearances—why else all the money we spend on clothes, cosmetics, and calorie counting? To manage the impression we're creating, we may adjust what they say to please rather than offend. To appear consistent we may at times feign attitudes that harmonize with our actions.

But this isn't the whole story. Experiments suggest that some genuine attitude change follows our behavior commitments, for two reasons:

Self-Justifying Our Actions: Cognitive Dissonance Theory

Cognitive dissonance theory, developed by the late Leon Festinger (1957), proposes that we feel motivated to justify our actions. We want to relieve the discomfort—the cognitive dissonance—we feel when aware that our behavior differs from our attitudes (after, say, catching ourselves laughing at a racist or sexist joke). Dissonance, like hunger, motivates its own reduction. Thus if you can get people to choose to act contrary to their usual attitudes, they will feel the discomfort of cognitive dissonance.

They can reduce this discomfort by aligning their attitudes with their actions. "If I chose to do it," they might rationalize, "it must have been worth doing." The more responsible we feel for a troubling act, the more dissonance we feel between our awareness of our behavior and of our attitudes.

Experiments confirm that the more dissonance we feel, the more our attitudes change to justify the act. As part of a survival training program, Philip Zimbardo and others (1965) induced students and Army reservists to eat fried grasshoppers. Zimbardo wondered whether a nasty or a pleasant leader would more effectively induce people to persuade themselves that eating grasshoppers really wasn't so awful. What would you predict? The finding: When the experimenter seemed unpleasant and unfair, the subjects were *more* likely to justify eating grasshoppers than when he seemed pleasant and fair (in which case they could justify their behavior by thinking "I couldn't refuse such a nice guy").

Inferring Our Attitudes: Self-Perception Theory

Cognitive dissonance theory assumes that our need to maintain a consistent and positive self-image motivates us to adopt attitudes that justify our actions. Assuming no such motive, **self-perception theory** says simply that when our attitudes are unclear to us, we observe our behaviors and then infer our attitudes from them. As Anne Frank wrote in her diary, "I can watch myself and my actions just like an outsider." Having done so—having noted how we acted toward that person knocking at our door—we infer how we felt.

In proposing self-perception theory, Daryl Bem (1972) assumed that when we're unsure of our attitudes, we infer them much as we make inferences about others' attitudes. Were we to see someone freely volunteer to write arguments in favor of a drinking ban, we would likely infer that the person favors the ban. Perhaps before writing their pro-ban arguments, many of the Princeton subjects were unsure how they felt, so they inferred their attitudes from what they wrote. And so it goes as we observe our own behavior. What we freely say and do can be self-revealing. To paraphrase an old saying, "How do I know what I think till I hear what I say or see what I do?"

The debate over how to explain the attitudes-follow-behavior effect has inspired hundreds of experiments that reveal the conditions under which dissonance and self-perception processes operate. Dissonance theory best explains what happens when our actions openly contradict our well-defined attitudes. When, say, we hurt someone we like, we feel tension, which we may reduce by viewing the other as a jerk. Self-perception theory best explains what happens when we are unsure of our attitudes: We infer them by observing ourselves. If we lend our new neighbors whom we neither like nor dislike a cup of sugar, our helpful behavior may lead us to infer that we like them.

As often happens in science, each theory provides a partial explanation of a complex reality. If only human nature were simple, one simple theory could describe it. Alas, but thankfully, we are not simple creatures. And that is why there are many miles to go before psychological researchers can sleep.

CONCEPTS TO REMEMBER

Attitude   A favorable or unfavorable evaluative reaction toward something or someone, exhibited in one's beliefs, feelings, or intended behavior.

Role   A set of expectations defining how those in a social position ought to behave.

Foot-in-the-door phenomenon   The tendency for people who have first agreed to a small request to comply later with a larger request.

Low-ball technique   A tactic for getting people to agree to something. People who agree to an initial request will often still comply when the requester ups the ante. People who receive only the costly request are less likely to comply with it.

Cognitive dissonance theory   Cognitive dissonance is tension that arises when one is simultaneously aware of two inconsistent cognitions, as when we realize that we have, with little justification, acted contrary to our attitudes. Cognitive dissonance theory proposes that we act to reduce such tension, as when we adjust our attitudes to correspond with our actions.

Self-perception theory   The theory that when unsure of our attitudes, we infer them much as would someone observing us—by looking at our behavior and the circumstances under which it occurs.

10

Who Is Miserable—and Why?

❖

If you are a typical college student, you may occasionally feel mildly depressed, dissatisfied with your life, discouraged about the future, sad, lacking appetite and energy, unable to concentrate, perhaps even wondering if life is worth it. Maybe you think disappointing grades have jeopardized your career goals. Perhaps the breakup of a relationship has left you in despair. And maybe your self-focused brooding at such times only worsens your feelings. For some 10 percent of men and nearly twice that many women, life's downtimes are not just temporary blue moods but one or more major depressive episodes that last for weeks without any obvious cause.

One of psychology's most intriguing research frontiers concerns the cognitive (thought) processes that accompany such feelings. What are the attributions, expectations, and other thought patterns of troubled people? In the case of depression, the most heavily researched disorder, dozens of new studies are providing some answers.

SOCIAL COGNITION AND DEPRESSION

As we all know from experience, depressed people are negative thinkers. They view life through dark-colored glasses. With seriously depressed people—those who are feeling worthless, lethargic, disinterested in friends and family, and unable to sleep or eat normally—the negative thinking becomes self-defeating. Their intensely pessimistic outlook leads them to magnify bad experiences and minimize good ones. A depressed young woman illustrates: "The real me is worthless and inadequate. I can't move forward with my work because I become frozen with doubt" (Burns, 1980, p. 29).

Distortion or Realism

Are all depressed people unrealistically negative? To find out, Lauren Alloy and Lyn Abramson (1979) studied college students who were either mildly depressed or not depressed. They had the students observe whether their pressing a button was linked with a light coming on. Surprisingly, the depressed students were quite accurate in estimating their degree of control. It was the nondepressives whose judgments were distorted, who exaggerated the extent of their control.

This phenomenon of **depressive realism**, nicknamed the "sadder-but-wiser effect," shows up in many ways (Alloy & others, 1990; Dobson & Franche, 1989). Shelley Taylor (1989, p. 214) explains:

> Normal people exaggerate how competent and well liked they are. Depressed people [unless severely depressed] do not. Normal people remember their past behavior with a rosy glow. Depressed people are more evenhanded in recalling their successes and failures. Normal people describe themselves primarily positively. Depressed people describe both their positive and negative qualities. Normal people take credit for successful outcomes and tend to deny responsibility for failure. Depressed people accept responsibility for both success and failure. Normal people exaggerate the control they have over what goes on around them. Depressed people are less vulnerable to the illusion of control. Normal people believe to an unrealistic degree that the future holds a bounty of good things and few bad things. Depressed people are more realistic in their perceptions of the future. In fact, on virtually every point on which normal people show enhanced self-regard, illusions of control, and unrealistic visions of the future, depressed people fail to show the same biases. "Sadder but wiser" does indeed appear to apply to depression.

Underlying the thinking of depressed people are their attributions of responsibility. Consider: If you fail an exam and blame yourself, you may conclude that you are stupid or lazy, and feel depressed. If you attribute the failure to an unfair exam or to other circumstances beyond your control, you are more likely to feel angry. In over 100 studies involving 15,000 subjects (Sweeney & others, 1985), depressed people have been more likely than nondepressed people to exhibit a negative "attributional style" (Figure 10–1). They are more likely to attribute failure and setbacks to causes that are *stable* ("It's going to last forever"), *global* ("It's going to affect everything I do"), and *internal* ("It's all my fault"). The result of this pessimistic, overgeneralized, self-blaming thinking, say Abramson and her colleagues (1989), is a depressing sense of hopelessness.

Compared to this depressive attributional style, self-serving illusions are adaptive. If this sounds obvious, how much more obvious would

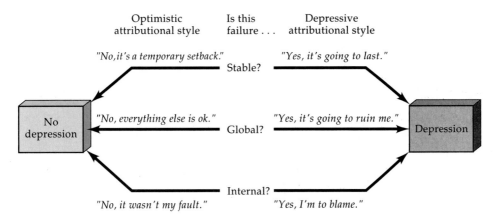

FIGURE 10–1
Depressive attributional style. Depression is linked with a negative, pessimistic way of explaining and interpreting failures.

sound the familiar pronouncement that mental health is based on *accurate* perceptions of ourselves and the world. After amassing the available research, Shelley Taylor and Jonathan Brown (1988) say that mental health derives, rather, from "overly positive self-evaluations, exaggerated perceptions of control or mastery, and unrealistic optimism." Thanks to our positive illusions, we are happier, more productive, and less self-preoccupied than depressed realists.

Positive illusions can also breed the false optimism that ignores real perils and the "I'm-better-than-you" attitude that underlies social conflicts and prejudice. Still, we can understand how La Rochefoucauld could surmise "that Nature, which has so wisely constructed our bodies for our welfare, gave us pride to spare us the painful knowledge of our shortcomings" (*Maxims*, 1665). Even depressed people—though especially those headed toward recovery—compensate for their negative self-concepts with positive views of some of their traits (Pelham, 1991).

Is Negative Thinking a Cause or a Result of Depression?

The cognitive accompaniments of depression raise a chicken-and-egg question: Do depressed moods cause negative thinking, or does negative thinking cause depression?

Depressed Moods Cause Negative Thinking

Without doubt, our moods color our thinking. To West Germans enjoying their team's World Cup soccer victory (Schwarz & others, 1987) and to Australians emerging from a heartwarming movie (Forgas & Moylan, 1987), people seem good-hearted, life seems wonderful. In a happy mood, we find that the world seems friendlier, decisions come more easily, good news more readily comes to mind (Johnson & Tversky, 1983; Isen & Means, 1983; Stone & Glass, 1986). When we *feel* happy, we *think* happy and optimistic thoughts. *Currently* depressed people recall their parents as having been rejecting and punitive. But *formerly* depressed people recall their parents in the same positive terms as never-depressed people (Lewinsohn & Rosenbaum, 1987).

Let our mood turn gloomy, and our thoughts switch onto a different track. Off come the rose-colored glasses; on come the dark glasses. Now the bad mood primes our recollections of negative events (Bower, 1987; Johnson & Magaro, 1987). Our relationships seem to sour, our self-image takes a dive, our hopes for the future dim, people's behavior seems more sinister (Brown & Taylor, 1986; Mayer & Salovey, 1987).

Imagine yourself in an experiment by Joseph Forgas and his colleagues (1984) that used hypnosis to put you in a good or bad mood and then had you watch a videotape (made the day before) of yourself talking with someone. If made to feel happy, you feel pleased with what you see, and you are able to detect many instances of your poise, interest, and social skill. If put in a bad mood, viewing the same tape seems to reveal a quite different you—one who is frequently stiff, nervous, and inarticulate (Figure 10–2). Given how your mood colors your judgments, you feel relieved at how things brighten when the experimenter switches you to a happy mood before leaving the experiment. Curiously, note Michael Ross and Garth Fletcher (1985), we don't attribute our changing perceptions to our mood shifts. Rather, the world really seems different, depending on our mood.

A depressed mood also affects behavior. The person who is withdrawn, glum, and complaining does not elicit joy and warmth in others. So Stephen Strack and James Coyne (1983) found that depressed people were realistic in thinking that others didn't appreciate their behavior. Depressed behavior can trigger hostility, anxiety, and even reciprocal depression in others. College students who have depressed roommates tend to be a little depressed themselves (Burchill & Stiles, 1988; Howes & others, 1985; Sanislow & others, 1989). Depressed people are therefore at risk for being divorced, fired, or shunned, thus magnifying their depression (Coyne & others, 1991; Gotlib & Lee, 1989; Sacco & Dunn, 1990). They may also seek out those whose unfavorable views of them verify, and further magnify, their low self-image (Swann & others, 1991).

Does Negative Thinking Cause Depression?
So being depressed has cognitive and behavioral effects. Does it also have cognitive origins? It's perfectly normal to feel depressed over a *major* loss, such as losing a job, suffering a death in the family, or being rejected or abused. But why are some people so readily depressed by *minor* stresses?

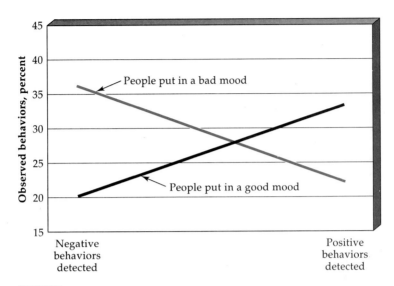

FIGURE 10-2
A temporary good or bad mood strongly influenced people's ratings of
their videotaped behavior. Those in a bad mood detected far fewer
positive behaviors. (Forgas & others, 1984.)

The results have been mixed, because negative thinking tends to rise and
fall with depression (Barnett & Gotlib, 1988; Kuiper & Higgins, 1985). But
new evidence suggests that a negative attributional style contributes to
depressive reactions. Colin Sacks and Daphne Bugental (1987) asked
some young women to get acquainted with a stranger who sometimes
acted cold and unfriendly, creating an awkward social situation. Unlike
optimistic women, those with a pessimistic explanatory style—who characteristically offer stable, global, and internal attributions for bad events—reacted to the social failure by becoming more depressed. Moreover,
they then behaved more antagonistically toward the next person they
met. Their negative thinking had predisposed a negative mood response,
which predisposed negative behavior.

Outside the laboratory, studies of children, teenagers, and adults
confirm that those with the pessimistic explanatory style are more likely
to become depressed when bad things happen (Alloy & Clements, 1991;
Brown & Siegel, 1988; Nolen-Hoeksema & others, 1986). If you think that
negative events (money problems, bad grades, social rejections) are uncontrollable, you are more likely to get depressed.

Researcher Peter Lewinsohn and his colleagues (1985) have assembled these findings into a coherent psychological understanding of depression. In their view, the negative self-image, attributions, and

expectations of a depressed person are an essential link in a vicious cycle that is triggered by negative experience—perhaps academic or vocational failure, or family conflict, or social rejection (Figure 10–3). In those vulnerable to depression, such stresses trigger brooding, self-focused, self-blaming thoughts (Pyszczynski & others, 1991; Wood & others, 1990a,b). Such ruminations create a depressed mood that drastically alters the way a person thinks and acts, which then fuels further negative experiences, self-blame, and depressed mood. Depression is therefore *both* a cause and a consequence of negative cognitions.

Martin Seligman (1988) believes that self-focus and self-blame help explain the near-epidemic levels of depression in America today. Compared with 50 years ago, rates of "unipolar" depression (the type most commonly experienced) have risen tenfold. Seligman believes that the decline of religion and family, plus the growth of the individualist "you can do it" attitude, breeds hopelessness and blame when things don't go well. Failed courses, careers, and marriages produce despair when we stand alone, with nothing and no one to fall back on. If, as a macho *Fortune* ad declared, you can "make it on your own," on "your own drive, your own guts, your own energy, your own ambition," then whose fault is it if you *don't* make it on your own?

These insights into the thinking style linked with depression have prompted social psychologists to study thinking patterns associated with other problems. How do those who are plagued with excessive loneliness, shyness, or substance abuse view themselves? How well do they recall their successes and their failures? To what do they attribute their ups and downs? Is their attention focused on themselves or on others? Here are some of the emerging answers.

FIGURE 10–3
The vicious cycle of depression.

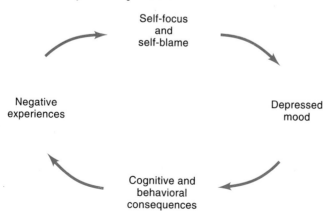

S OCIAL COGNITION AND LONELINESS

If depression is the common cold of psychological disorders, then loneliness is the headache. Loneliness, whether chronic or temporary, is a painful awareness that our social relationships are less numerous or meaningful than we desire. Jenny de Jong-Gierveld (1987) observed in her study of Dutch adults that unmarried and unattached people are more likely to feel lonely. This prompted her to speculate that the modern emphasis on individual fulfillment and the depreciation of marriage and family life may be "loneliness-provoking" (as well as depression-provoking).

But loneliness need not coincide with aloneness. One can feel lonely in the middle of a party. And one can be utterly alone—as I am while writing these words in the solitude of an isolated turret office at a British university 5000 miles from home—without feeling lonely. To feel lonely is to feel excluded from a group, unloved by those around you, unable to share your private concerns, or different and alienated from those in your surroundings (Beck & Young, 1978; Davis & Franzoi, 1986). Adolescents experience such feelings more commonly than adults. When beeped by an electronic pager at various times during a week and asked to record what they were doing and how they felt, adolescents more often than adults reported feeling lonely when alone (Larson & others, 1982). Males and females feel lonely under somewhat different circumstances—males when isolated from group interaction, females when deprived of close one-to-one relationships (Berg & McQuinn, 1988; Stokes & Levin, 1986).

Like depressed people, chronically lonely people seem caught in a vicious cycle of self-defeating social cognitions and social behaviors. They have some of the negative attributional style of the depressed; they blame themselves for their poor social relationships and see most things as beyond their control (Anderson & Riger, 1991; Snodgrass, 1987). Moreover, they perceive others in negative ways. When paired with a stranger of the same sex or with a first-year college roommate, lonely students are more likely to perceive the other person negatively (Jones & others, 1981; Wittenberg & Reis, 1986).

These negative views may both reflect and color the lonely person's experience. Lonely people often do find it hard to introduce themselves, make phone calls, and participate in groups (Rook, 1984; Spitzberg & Hurt, 1987). They tend to be self-conscious and low in self-esteem (Check & Melchior, 1990; Vaux, 1988). When talking with a stranger, they spend more time talking about themselves and take less interest in their conversational partners than nonlonely people (Jones & others, 1982). After such conversations, the new acquaintances often come away with more negative impressions of the lonely people (Jones & others, 1985). Believing in their social unworthiness and feeling pessimistic about others inhibits lonely people from acting to reduce their loneliness.

SOCIAL COGNITION AND SOCIAL ANXIETY

Being interviewed for a much-wanted job, dating someone for the first time, stepping into a roomful of strangers, performing before an important audience, or—that most common of phobias—giving a speech, can make almost anyone feel anxious. Some people, especially those who are shy or easily embarrassed, feel anxious in almost any situation in which they might be evaluated. For these people, anxiety is more a trait than a temporary state.

What causes us to feel anxious in social situations? Why are some people shackled in the prison of their own shyness? Barry Schlenker and Mark Leary (1982, 1985; Leary, 1984, 1986; Maddux & others, 1988) answer these questions by applying self-presentation theory. *Self-presentation theory* assumes that we are eager to present ourselves in ways that make a good impression. The implications for social anxiety are straightforward: *We feel anxious when we are motivated to impress others but doubt our ability to do so.* This simple principle helps explain a variety of research findings, each of which may ring true in your own experience. We feel most anxious when:

- Dealing with powerful, high-status people—people whose impressions matter.
- In an evaluative context, as when making a first impression on the parents of one's fiancé.
- The interaction focuses on something central to our self-image, as when a college professor presents ideas before peers at a professional convention.
- We are in novel situations, such as a first school dance or first formal dinner, where we are unsure of the social rules.
- We are self-conscious (as shy people often are), and our attention is focused on ourselves and how we are coming across.
- In unstructured situations, without clear scripts for how to act. Shy people are noticeably anxious when told merely to "take five minutes to get to know each other," but not when given a set of questions to ask.

The natural tendency in all such situations is to be cautiously self-protective: to talk less; to avoid topics that reveal one's ignorance; to be guarded about oneself; to be unassertive, agreeable, and smiling.

Shyness is a form of social anxiety characterized by self-consciousness and worry about what others think (Anderson & Harvey, 1988; Asendorpf, 1987; Carver & Scheier, 1986). Self-conscious people (whose numbers include many adolescents) see incidental events as somehow relevant to themselves (Fenigstein, 1984). They overpersonalize situations, a tendency that breeds anxious concern and, in extreme cases, paranoia. Shown someone they think is interviewing them live (actually a videotaped interviewer), they perceive the interviewer as less accepting and interested in them (Pozo & others, 1991). They also overestimate the extent to which other people are watching and evaluating them. If their hair won't comb right or they have a facial blemish, they assume everyone else notices and judges them accordingly.

To reduce social anxiety, some people turn to alcohol. Alcohol lowers anxiety as it reduces self-consciousness (Hull & Young, 1983). Thus, chronically self-conscious people are especially likely to drink following a failure. If they become alcoholics, they are more likely than those low in self-consciousness to relapse from treatment when they again experience stress or failure.

Symptoms as diverse as anxiety and alcohol abuse can also serve a self-handicapping function. Labeling oneself as anxious, shy, depressed, or under the influence of alcohol can provide an excuse for failure (Snyder & Smith, 1986). Behind a barricade of symptoms, the person's ego stands secure. "Why don't I date? Because I'm shy, so people don't easily get to know the real me." The symptom is an unconscious strategic ploy to explain away negative outcomes.

What if we were to remove the need for such a ploy by providing people with a handy alternative explanation for their anxiety and there-fore for possible failure? Would a shy person no longer need to be shy? That is precisely what Susan Brodt and Philip Zimbardo (1981) found when they brought shy and not-shy college women to the laboratory and had them converse with a handsome male who posed as another subject. Before the conversation, the women were cooped up in a small chamber and blasted with loud noise. Some of the shy women (but not others) were told that the noise would leave them with a pounding heart, a common symptom of social anxiety. Thus when these women later talked with the man, they could attribute their pounding heart and any conver-sational difficulties to the noise rather than to their shyness or social inadequacy. Compared to the shy women who were not given this handy explanation for their pounding hearts, these women were no longer so shy. They talked fluently once the conversation got going and asked questions of the man. In fact, unlike the other shy women (whom the man could easily spot as shy), these women were to him indistinguishable from the not-shy women. One of these women became so socially attrac-tive that the handsome male confederate later asked her for a date.

SOCIAL-PSYCHOLOGICAL APPROACHES TO TREATMENT

So far we have considered patterns of social thinking that are linked with problems in living, ranging from serious depression to everyday shyness to physical illness. Does the emerging understanding of maladaptive thought patterns suggest any guidelines for treating such difficulties? There is no single social-psychological method of therapy. But therapy is a social encounter, and social psychologists are now suggesting how their principles might be integrated into existing treatment techniques (Leary & Maddux, 1987). Building on what we have already learned, let's consider three examples.

Inducing Internal Change Through External Behavior

In Module 9 on behavior and belief we reviewed a broad range of evidence for a simple but powerful principle: Our actions affect our attitudes. The roles we play, the things we say and do, and the decisions we make help form who we are. When we act, we amplify associated ideas, especially when we feel some responsibility for an action. Our behaviors are self-persuasive.

Consistent with the attitudes-follow-behavior principle, several psychotherapy techniques prescribe action. If we cannot directly control our feelings by sheer will power, we can influence them indirectly through our behavior. Behavior therapists try to shape behavior and, if they care about inner dispositions, assume that these will tag along after the behavior changes. Assertiveness training employs the foot-in-the-door procedure. The individual first role-plays assertiveness in a supportive context, and then gradually becomes assertive in everyday life. Rational-emotive therapy assumes that we generate our own emotions; clients receive "homework" assignments to act in new ways that will generate new emotions. Encounter groups subtly induce participants to behave in new ways in front of the group—to express anger, cry, act with high self-esteem, express positive feelings.

Experiments confirm that what we say about ourselves can affect how we feel. In one experiment, students were induced to write self-laudatory essays (Mirels & McPeek, 1977). These students, more than others who wrote essays about a current social issue, later expressed higher self-esteem when privately rating themselves for a different experimenter. In several more experiments, Edward Jones and his associates (1981; Rhodewalt & Agustsdottir, 1986) influenced students to present themselves to an interviewer in either self-enhancing or self-deprecating ways. Again, the public displays—whether upbeat or downbeat—carried over to later private responses on a test of actual self-esteem. Saying is believing, even when we talk about ourselves. This was especially true when the students were made to feel responsible for how they presented themselves. Uncoerced, effortful behavior commitments can indeed be therapeutic.

Breaking Vicious Cycles

If depression, loneliness, and social anxiety maintain themselves through a vicious cycle of negative experiences, negative thinking, and self-defeating behavior, it should be possible to break the cycle at any of several points—by changing the environment, by training the person to behave more constructively, by reversing negative thinking. And it is. Several different therapy methods can help free people from depression's vicious cycle.

Social Skills Training

Depression, loneliness, and shyness are not just problems in someone's mind. To be around a depressed person for any length of time can be irritating and depressing. As lonely and shy people suspect, they may indeed come across poorly in social situations. In these cases, social skills training may help. By observing and then practicing new behaviors in safe situations, the person may develop the confidence to behave more effectively in other situations.

As the person begins to enjoy the rewards of behaving more skillfully, a more positive self-perception develops. Frances Haemmerlie and Robert Montgomery (1982, 1984, 1986) demonstrated this in several heartwarming studies with shy, anxious college students. They surmised that those who seldom date and are nervous around those of the other sex infer, "I don't date much, so I must be socially inadequate, so I shouldn't try reaching out to anyone." To reverse this negative sequence, Haemmerlie and Montgomery enticed such students into pleasant interactions with people of the other sex.

In one experiment, college men completed social anxiety questionnaires and then came to the laboratory on two different days. Each day they enjoyed 12-minute conversations with each of six young women. The men thought the women were also subjects. Actually, the women had been asked simply to carry on a natural, positive, friendly conversation with each of the men.

The effect of these two and a half hours of conversation was remarkable. As one subject wrote afterward, "I had never met so many girls that I could have a good conversation with. After a few girls, my confidence grew to the point where I didn't notice being nervous like I once did." Such comments were supported by a variety of measures. Unlike men in a control condition, those who experienced the conversations reported considerably less female-related anxiety when retested one week and six months later. Placed alone in a room with an attractive female stranger, they also became much more likely to start a conversation. Outside the laboratory they actually began occasional dating.

Haemmerlie and Montgomery note that not only did all this occur without any counseling but it may very well have occurred *because* there was no counseling. Having behaved successfully on their own, the subjects could now perceive themselves as socially competent. Although seven months later the researchers did debrief the subjects, by that time the men had presumably enjoyed enough social success to maintain their internal attributions for success. "Nothing succeeds like success," concluded Haemmerlie (1987)—"as long as there are no external factors present that the client can use as an excuse for that success!"

Attributional Style Therapy

The vicious cycles that maintain depression, loneliness, and shyness can be broken by social skills training, by positive experiences that alter self-perceptions, *and* by changing negative thought patterns. Some people have social skills, but their experiences with hypercritical friends and family have convinced them they do not. For such people it may be enough to help them reverse their negative beliefs about themselves and their futures. Among the cognitive therapies with this aim is an "attributional style therapy" proposed by social psychologists (Abramson, 1988; Försterling, 1986).

One such program taught depressed college students to change their typical attributions. Mary Anne Layden (1982) first explained the advantages of making attributions more like those of the typical nondepressed person (by accepting credit for successes and seeing how circumstances can make things go wrong). After assigning a variety of tasks, she helped the students see how they typically interpreted success and failure. Then came the treatment phase: Layden instructed each person to keep a diary of daily successes and failures, noting how they contributed to their own successes and noting external reasons for their failures. When they were retested after a month of this attributional retraining and compared with an untreated control group, their self-esteem had risen and their attributional style had become more positive. And the more their attributional style improved, the more their depression lifted. By changing their attributions, they had changed their emotions.

Having emphasized what changed behavior and thought patterns can accomplish, we do well to remind ourselves of their limits. Social skills training and positive thinking cannot transform us into consistent winners who are loved and admired by everyone. Furthermore, temporary depression, loneliness, and shyness are perfectly appropriate responses to profoundly sad events. It is when such feelings exist chronically and without any discernible cause that there is reason for concern and a need to change the self-defeating thoughts and behaviors.

CONCEPTS TO REMEMBER

Depressive realism   The tendency of mildly depressed people to make accurate rather than self-serving judgments, attributions, and predictions.

11

Who Is Happy— and Why?

❖

B ooks, books, and more books have analyzed human misery. During its first century psychology focused far more on negative emotions, such as depression and anxiety, than on positive emotions, such as happiness and satisfaction. Even today, our textbooks say more about suffering than about joy.

That is now changing. A new group of researchers is offering a fresh perspective on an old puzzle: Who is happy—and why? They have, for example, asked people across the industrialized world to reflect on how they feel about life: "Generally speaking, how are things going these days? Would you say you are very happy, pretty happy, or not too happy?" Typically, those who describe themselves as very happy indeed look happy to interviewers (they readily smile and laugh) and seem happy to their friends and family members. Compared to those depressed, they're also less self-focused, more loving, and more helpful. Social psychologists call it the "feel-good, do-good phenomenon." Robert Browning had the idea: "Oh, make us happy and you make us good!"

Psychologists and sociologists have first exploded some myths about what makes for happiness (as I documented in *The Pursuit of Happiness: Who Is Happy—and Why*).

MYTHS OF HAPPINESS

Is Happiness Being Young? Middle-Aged? Retired?

Many people believe there are unhappy times of life—the stress-filled teen years or the crisis midlife years or the declining years of old age. But interviews with representative samples of people of all ages—several hundred thousand people in all—reveal that no time of life is notably happier or unhappier. The ingredients of happiness change with age. And the emotional terrain varies with age (teens, unlike adults, usually come up from gloom or down from elation within an hour's time). Yet tell me how old someone is and you've given me no clue to the person's sense of well-being.

Nor do we find in rates of depression, suicide, or divorce any evidence of increased personal upheaval during the supposed early forties "midlife crisis" years. Many of us do face crisis times, but not at any predictable age. The "empty nest syndrome"—a sense of despondency and lost meaning when children leave the home—also turns out to be extremely rare. For most couples, the empty nest is a happy place—often a place where marital happiness rebounds after the stresses of child rearing.

Does Happiness Have a Favorite Sex?

There are striking gender gaps in misery: Women are twice as vulnerable as men to disabling depression and anxiety, and men are five times as vulnerable as women to alcoholism and antisocial personality disorder. Yet happiness is equally available to either sex. In 1980s surveys of 169,776 carefully sampled people in 16 nations, 80 percent of the men and 80 percent of the women said that they were at least "fairly satisfied" with life (Inglehart, 1990). Slightly less than a quarter of each sex declared themselves "very happy."

Does Happiness Discriminate by Race or Culture?

Knowing someone's race also gives little clue to the person's psychological well-being. African-Americans, for example, experience nearly as much happiness as European-Americans and are actually slightly *less* vulnerable to depression (Robins & Regier, 1991). Blacks and Whites, like women and men, and disabled and nondisabled, also score similarly on tests of self-esteem, report Jennifer Crocker and Brenda Major (1989). (Despite discrimination, people in disadvantaged groups maintain self-esteem by valuing the things at which they excel, by making comparisons within their own groups, and by attributing problems to external sources such as prejudice.) Curiously, though, there are striking national differences in happiness, ranging from Portugal, where 1 in 10 people say they're very happy, to the Netherlands where 4 in 10 people say the same.

Does Money Buy Happiness?

More than ever, the American dream seems to be life, liberty, and the purchase of happiness. In 1991, 74 percent of America's entering collegians declared that a very important life goal was "being very well off financially"—nearly double the 39 percent who said the same in 1970. Most adults share this materialism, believing that 10 to 20 percent more income would make them happier, by relieving the stress of unpaid bills and enabling a few longed-for purchases.

Are they right? Let's make the question more specific: First, are people in rich countries happier than those in poor countries? Are the French happier than Hungarians? A little bit. But the association between national wealth and well-being is surprisingly modest. For example, during the 1980s the Irish had half the incomes and purchasing power of the West Germans. Yet year after year the Irish were a happier people.

Second, within any country, are rich people the happiest? Having food, shelter, and safety is basic to our well-being. But once able to afford life's necessities, increasing levels of affluence matter surprisingly little. Wealth is like health: Although its absence can breed misery, having it is no guarantee of happiness. We need bread, yet happiness does not come by bread alone. In one survey, people on *Forbes'* list of wealthiest Americans reported only slightly greater happiness than other Americans; 37 percent were less happy than the average American (Diener & others, 1985). Even people who have won a state lottery or a British pool gain only a temporary jolt of joy. The emotional effects of some tragedies are likewise temporary: People who become disabled usually recover a near-normal level of well-being. Satisfaction is surprisingly unrelated to one's objective life circumstances. It is much less a matter of getting what you want than wanting what you have.

Third, as cultures become more affluent over time, do their people become happier? In 1957, as economist John Galbraith was about to describe America as *The Affluent Society*, our per person income, expressed in today's dollars, was less than $8000. Today (thanks partly to women's increased employment) it is $16,000, making us *The Doubly Affluent Society*—with double what money buys (not just 10 or 20 percent more). Compared to 1957, we have twice as many cars per person. We have microwave ovens, color TVs, VCRs, air conditioners, answering machines, and $12 billion a year worth of brand-name athletic shoes.

So, are we happier than 35 years ago? We are not. In 1957, 35 percent of Americans told the National Opinion Research Center that they were "very happy." In 1991, with doubled American affluence, 31 percent said the same. If anything, to judge by soaring rates of depression, the quintupling of the violent crime rate since 1960, the doubling of the divorce rate, the slight decline in marital happiness among the marital survivors, and the tripling of the teen suicide rate, we're richer and *un*happier. How can we avoid the shocking conclusion: *Economic growth in affluent countries gives little boost to human morale.*

Dare I suggest a moral to these findings? Realizing our capacity to adapt to changing circumstance—even to becoming rich or to becoming disabled—can be freeing. It can free us from envying the lifestyles of the rich and famous. It can free us from pointless spending on stockpiles of unplayed CDs, on luxury cars, on extravagant vacations—all purchased in a vain quest for an elusive joy. It can free us to share. And it can free us to invest ourselves in developing those attitudes, traits, activities, relationships, and spiritual resources that *do* make for a joyful and joy-spreading spirit.

*H*APPY PEOPLE

So, if happiness is similarly available to those of any age, sex, or race, and to those of most income levels, who is happiest? Through life's ups and downs, some people's capacity for joy persists undiminished. In one National Institute of Aging study of 5000 adults, the happiest of people in 1973 were still relatively happy a decade later, despite changes in their work, their residence, their family status (Costa & others, 1987). Who are these chronically happy people?

The Traits of Happy People

In study after study, four inner traits mark happy people's lives—self-esteem, a sense of personal control, optimism, and extraversion.

First, happy people like themselves. They agree with such statements as "I'm a lot of fun to be with" and "I have good ideas." Contrary to the myth that most Americans are groveling with low self-esteem, most people express moderately high self-esteem by agreeing with such statements. Indeed, as Module 7 explains, most exhibit self-serving bias by believing themselves more ethical, more intelligent, less prejudiced, better able to get along with others, and healthier than average (as illustrated in Freud's joke about the man who said to his wife, "If one of us should die, I think I would go live in Paris"). This generally positive self-esteem helps explain why, contrary to those who would have us believe that happy people are a rare species, 9 in 10 people describe themselves as at least "pretty happy."

Second, happy people typically feel in control. Those who feel empowered rather than helpless typically do better in school, cope better with stress, and live more happily. When deprived of control over one's life—an experience studied in prisoners, nursing home patients, and people living under totalitarian regimes—people suffer lower morale and worse health.

Third, happy people are optimistic. Writing these words in the Norman Vincent Peale Science Center at a college named Hope, it is, I suppose, fitting that I acknowledge the power of positive thinking. Optimists—those who agree, for example, that "when I undertake something new, I expect to succeed"—tend to be more successful, healthier, and happier. If restrained by a realistic awareness of our limits—recognizing that not everyone can be at the top, that half the teams must lose, that the mortality rate remains 100 percent—a hope-filled optimism predisposes venturesome, upbeat living.

Fourth, happy people are outgoing. One could imagine opposite findings—that, for example, pessimists would live with greater gladness as things keep turning out better than expected, or that introverts would be happiest living serenely in their peaceful solitude. But in study after study it's the sociable extraverts who report greater happiness. Outgoing people are temperamentally more high-spirited and less anxious about reaching out to others, which may explain why they marry sooner, get better jobs, and make more friends.

Although genes influence some of these traits of happy people (notably extraversion), people who seek greater happiness can apply one of social psychology's now-familiar principles: We are as likely to act ourselves into a way of thinking as to think ourselves into action. Ergo, to become happier, act as happy people do. In experiments, people who feign high self-esteem actually develop better feelings about themselves. So feign optimism. Simulate outgoingness. Put on a happy face. (Even when manipulated into a smile—"while I attach these wires, please turn up the corners of your mouth"—people feel better; when they scowl the whole world seems to scowl back.) Going through the motions can trigger the emotions.

The Relationships of Happy People

We could easily imagine why close relationships might exacerbate illness and misery. Our closest relationships are fraught with stress. "Hell is others," surmised Sartre. Asked what caused yesterday's greatest emotional strain, people's most frequent answer is "family." But their answer is the same when asked what prompted yesterday's greatest pleasure.

Thankfully, the benefits of close relationships with friends and family outweigh the strains. People who can name several intimate friends with whom they freely share their intimate concerns are healthier, less likely to die prematurely, and happier. In experiments, people relax as they confide painful experiences. In one study, 33 Holocaust survivors spent two hours recalling their experiences, often in intimate detail never before disclosed. Fourteen months later, those who were most self-disclosing had the most improved health (Pennebaker, 1990). Confiding, like confession, is good for the soul.

Some psychologists believe that today's epidemic levels of depression stem from impoverished social connections in our increasingly individualist society. Today, 24 percent of Americans live alone, up from 8 percent a half century ago. Moreover, as Ronald Reagan proclaimed, this is "the age of the individual." In contrast to the interdependence valued in Asian societies, modern western cultures celebrate independence: Be true to yourself. Do your own thing. Be authentically you. And (shudder) don't be codependent (by supporting, loving, and staying tied to a troubled partner). Humanistic psychologist Carl Rogers epitomized today's individualism: "The only question which matters is, 'Am I living in a way which is deeply satisfying to me, and which truly expresses me?'"

For more than 9 in 10 people, the most significant alternative to aloneness is marriage. As with other close social bonds, broken marital relationships are a source of much self-reported unhappiness, while a supportive, intimate relationship is among life's greatest joys. To paraphrase Henry Ward Beecher, "well-married a person is winged; ill-matched, shackled." Happily, 3 out of 4 married people say that their spouse is their best friend, and 4 out of 5 say they would marry the same person again. Such feelings help explain why over the 1970s and 1980s, 24 percent of never-married adults, and 39 percent of married adults, told the National Opinion Research Center that they were "very happy." Without denying that divorce is often a first step toward healing for those physically or emotionally abused, there is a growing consensus that an enduring, equitable, affectionate marriage promotes the well-being of both the partners and their children. Aware of this, American Psychological Association members in a 1990 survey rated "the decline of the nuclear family" as the number one threat to mental health. To live connected and committed to people who know you and care about you is to live at less risk for physical and emotional disorder and with greater happiness.

The "Flow" of Happy People

Turn-of-the-century Russian writer Maksim Gorky anticipated recent studies of work satisfaction: "When work is a pleasure, life is a joy! When work is a duty, life is slavery." Work satisfaction impacts life satisfaction.

Why? And why are out-of-work people so much less likely to feel satisfied with life than those productively engaged? Why is idleness not the bliss we sometimes imagine it to be?

For many people, work provides personal identity: it helps people define who they are. Work also adds to our sense of community: it offers people a network of relationships and a "we feeling." And work can add focus and purpose—a sense that one's life matters.

Work is, however, sometimes unsatisfying, for two reasons. We can be overwhelmed: When challenges exceed our available time and skills, we feel anxious, stressed. Or we can be underwhelmed: When challenges don't engage our time and skills, we feel bored. Between anxiety and boredom lies a middle ground where challenges engage and match our skills. In this zone we enter an optimal state that University of Chicago psychologist Mihaly Csikszentmihalyi (pronounced chick-SENT-me-hi) terms **flow** (Figure 11–1).

To be in flow is to be unself-consciously absorbed. Think of a situation where you get so caught up in an activity that your mind doesn't wander, you become oblivious to your surroundings, and time flies. Csikszentmihalyi formulated the flow concept after studying artists who would spend hour after hour painting or sculpting with enormous concentration. Immersed in a project, they worked as if nothing else mattered, and then promptly forgot about it once they finished. The artists seemed driven less by the external rewards of doing art—money, praise, promotion—than by the intrinsic rewards of creating the work.

FIGURE 11–1

The flow model. When challenges engage our skills, we often become so absorbed in the flow of an activity that we lose consciousness of self and time. (Adapted from Csikszentmihalyi & Csikszentmihalyi, 1988.)

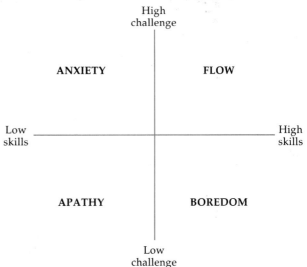

Writer Madeleine L'Engle likens the artist's concentration to a small child at play: "In real play, which is real concentration, the child is not only outside time, he is outside *himself*. He has thrown himself completely into whatever it is that he is doing. A child playing a game, building a sand castle, painting a picture, is completely *in* what he is doing. His *self-consciousness* is gone; his consciousness is wholly focused outside himself."

When beeping people on thousands of occasions with an electronic paging device, triggering them to report on their activities and feelings, Csikszentmihalyi (1988) discovered that happiness comes not from mindless passivity but from engagement in mindful challenge. Whether at work or in leisure, people absorbed in the flow of an activity are enjoying themselves more than when doing nothing meaningful. Csikszentmihalyi concludes that

> We all want to have more free time: But when we get it we don't know what to do with it. Most dimensions of experience deteriorate: People report being more passive, irritable, sad, weak, and so forth. To fill the void in consciousness, people turn on the TV or find some other way of structuring experience vicariously. These passive leisure activities take the worst edge off the threat of chaos, but leave the individual feeling weak and enervated.

Playwright Noel Coward would appreciate Csikszentmihalyi's observation. Involving work, he said, "is more fun than fun."

The Faith of Happy People

In some respects, the links between religion and mental health are impressive (Myers, 1992b). Consider:

Religious people (often defined as those who attend church regularly) are much less likely to become delinquent. To abuse drugs and alcohol. To divorce or be unhappily married. And to commit suicide. Religiously active people even tend to be *physically* healthier and to live longer, due in part to their healthier smoking-eating-drinking habits.

With other mental health indicators the results are mixed. Religious people are somewhat *less* likely to feel in control of their fate. But they also are slightly less vulnerable to two biologically influenced disorders—depression and schizophrenia.

Across North America and Europe, religious people also report higher levels of happiness and satisfaction with life. The most striking finding comes from the Gallup Organization, which compared people low in "spiritual commitment" with highly spiritual people (who consistently agree with statements such as, "My religious faith is the most important influence in my life"). The highly spiritual were *twice* as like to say they were "very happy."

Many studies have focused on the link between religiousness and well-being among the elderly. One statistical research digest revealed that the two best predictors of well-being among older persons are health and religiousness (Okun & Stock, 1987). Elderly people are happier and more satisfied with life if religiously committed and active.

Other studies probe the connection between faith and coping with a crisis. Again, the link is positive. Compared to religiously inactive widows, recently widowed women who worship regularly report more joy in their lives. Compared to irreligious mothers of disabled children, those with a deep religious faith are less vulnerable to depression. Those with a strong faith also retain greater happiness after suffering divorce, unemployment, serious illness, or bereavement.

What explains these positive links between faith and well-being? Although social scientists can neither prove nor refute the ultimate truth of any religious faith, they offer some possibilities. Is it the supportive close relationships often enjoyed by those active in local congregations (of which there are 294,000 in the United States)? Is it the sense of meaning and purpose that many people derive from their faith? Is it the hope that faith affords when people suffer or face what social psychologists Sheldon Solomon, Jeffery Greenberg, and Tom Pyszczynski (1991) call "the terror resulting from our awareness of vulnerability and death." Such are among the proposed explanations.

So, who is happy? Tell me someone's age, sex, race, and income (assuming they have enough to afford life's necessities and basic securities) and you've hardly given me a clue. You will give better clues if you tell me certain traits of the person, whether the person enjoys a supportive network of close relationships (likely including marriage to their best friend), whether the person has work and leisure that suit their skills, and whether the person is actively religious.

CONCEPTS TO REMEMBER

Flow   Unself-conscious absorption in an activity that is well-suited to one's skills, often accompanied by the swift passage of time.

Social Influence

East Meets West: Individualism, Collectivism, and Communitarianism

❖

In many important ways we humans—members of one species, one great family with common ancestors—are all alike. We share not only a common biology but common behavior tendencies. We perceive the world, feel thirst, and develop grammar through identical mechanisms.

Our social behavior, too, is characteristically human: We all know how to read frowns and smiles. We all feel a liking for people whose attitudes and attributes are similar to our own. We join groups, conform, and organize ourselves into status hierarchies. We show favoritism to our own groups and, when confronting other groups, react with negative behaviors ranging from wariness to genocide. Such commonalities define our shared human nature. To a social psychologist, we are more alike than different.

Perhaps the most important of all our similarities is our brain's capacity to learn and adapt. Our shared biology enables our social diversity. It enables those in one culture to value promptness, welcome frankness, and accept premarital sex, while those in other cultures live by different standards. Whether we equate beauty with slimness or shapeliness depends on where and when in the world we live. Whether we define social justice as equality (all receive the same) or as equity (those who produce more receive more) depends on whether Marxism or capitalism shapes our ideology. Whether we tend to be expressive or reserved, casual or formal, hinges partly on whether we have spent our lives in an African, European, or Asian culture.

A CULTURE DIFFERENCE: INDIVIDUALISM VERSUS COLLECTIVISM

One pervasive culture difference arises from social values that stress either individual control and achievement or the bonds of social solidarity. To reflect on your own orientation, consider these questions from the Individualism-Collectivism Scale, developed by University of Hong Kong social psychologist C. Harry Hui (1988): Would you agree that

> I would help if a colleague at work told me that he/she needed money to pay utility bills.
>
> Young people should take into consideration their parents' advice when making education/career plans.
>
> I am often influenced by the moods of my neighbors.

Do your answers suggest that you place a greater value on your individual goals and identity or on your social bonds? Are you more a "me" thinker or a "we" thinker?

Industrialized western cultures typically value **individualism**. They give more priority to self-reliance and personal well-being than to social identity. Western literature, from the *Iliad* and *Odyssey* to *The Adventures of Huckleberry Finn*, often celebrates rugged individuals who, rather than fulfilling others' expectations, seek their own fulfillment. Individualists stand up for their rights, knowing that "the squeaky wheel gets the grease."

Asian and third world cultures place a greater value on **collectivism**. They give more priority to the goals and welfare of their groups—their family, their clan, their company. They are like athletes who place a greater value on their team's performance than their personal achievements. Eastern literature often celebrates those who, despite temptations to self-indulgence, remember who they are and do their social duty. Collectivists avoid confrontation and blunt honesty, knowing that "the nail that stands out gets pounded down."

Without discounting individual differences within cultures, cross-cultural psychologists such as Harry Triandis, Richard Brislin, and C. Harry Hui (1988) have shown how a culture's individualism or collectivism affects people's self-concept, social relations, and child rearing.

Self-Concept

Shorn of their social connections—separated from family, friends, and work group—individualists retain their identity, their sense of "me." Thus individualists feel free to leave jobs, homes, churches, and extended families in search of better opportunities for themselves. As adolescents they struggle to separate from parents and define their own personal sense of self. "Get in touch with yourself, accept yourself, be true to yourself," they hear from their culture's individualistic advice-givers. Don't be "codependent" (by supporting, loving, and staying tied to a troubled partner). Therapist Fritz Perls (1973, p. 70) epitomized the individualism of western popular psychology: "I do my thing, and you do your thing. I am not in this world to live up to your expectations. And you are not in this world to live up to mine." Superstar Frank Sinatra's theme song sums up the aim of individualism: "I gotta be me."

In collectivist cultures, where communal solidarity is prized, such words would not be spoken. For collectivists, social networks provide one's bearings and help define who one is. Extended families are close-knit. One's name may even be written to put first one's family identity (Hui Harry).

Social Relations

Collectivists may have fewer relationships, but they are deeper, more stable, longer-lasting. Compared to North American students, university students in Hong Kong talk during a day with fewer people for longer periods (Wheeler & others, 1989). Employer-employee relations are marked by mutual loyalty. Valuing social solidarity, people in collectivist cultures seek to maintain harmony by showing respect and allowing others to save face. They avoid blunt honesty, stay away from touchy topics, and display a self-effacing humility (Markus & Kitayama, 1991). People do favors for one another and remember who has done favors for them. For collectivists, no one is an island. The self is not independent but *inter*dependent.

Because social identity is so important, collectivists are, however, somewhat quicker to prejudge people by their groups. In their culture, they explain, it *helps* to know people's group identities: "Tell me a person's family, schooling, and employment and you tell me a lot about the person." Individualists warn against stereotyping and prefer not to judge people by their backgrounds and affiliations: "Everyone's an individual, so you shouldn't make assumptions just from knowing a person's sex, race, or background." Individualists do prejudge people, but more often by obvious personal attributes such as physical attractiveness (Dion & others, 1990).

Child Rearing

In individualist cultures, parents and schools teach children to be independent and to think for themselves. Children and adolescents typically decide their own restaurant orders, open their own mail, choose their own boyfriends and girlfriends, and chart their own goals en route to leaving the family nest. Schools teach children to clarify their own values. As young adults, individualists dream their own dreams, chart their own goals, and separate from their parents, who already live separated from the grandparents.

If you live in a western culture, you probably take all this for granted. If you live in Asia, you may wince at such individualism. You were probably strongly bonded with your mother from birth on—sleeping with her, bathing with her, moving about on her back. Rather than leaving children to form their own identity and values, you may instead prefer to teach them communal sensitivity and cooperation, to guide or decide their choices, and to maintain the extended family by providing care for aging parents (Hui, 1990).

Communicating across Cultures

When people from different cultures interact, sensitivity to their differences helps minimize misunderstandings and awkward moments. When visiting collectivist cultures, Triandis, Brislin, and Hui (1988) advise individualists to:

- Avoid confrontation
- Cultivate long-term relationships without expecting instant intimacy
- Present oneself modestly
- Attend to people's positions in their group hierarchies
- Let them know one's own social position

When visiting individualist cultures, collectivists should feel freer than usual to:

- Criticize
- Get right to business
- Disclose one's skills and accomplishments
- Pay more attention to personal attitudes than to group memberships and positions

Each cultural tradition offers benefits, for a price. In competitive, individualist cultures, people enjoy more personal freedom, take greater pride in their own achievements, enjoy more privacy, live with more spontaneity, and feel freer to move about and choose their own lifestyles. But the price is more frequent loneliness, more divorce, more homicide, and more vulnerability to stress-related disease (Triandis & others, 1988). Thus, notes clinical researcher Martin Seligman (1988), "rampant individualism carries with it two seeds of its own destruction. First, a society that exalts the individual to the extent ours now does will be ridden with depression. . . . Second, and perhaps most important, is meaninglessness [which occurs when there is no] attachment to something larger than you are."

A GENDER DIFFERENCE: INDEPENDENCE VERSUS CONNECTEDNESS

The growing appreciation of a culture difference in individualism versus collectivism parallels a growing appreciation of a gender difference in independence versus social connectedness. To be sure, individuals differ within any cultural or gender group. Individual men display outlooks and behavior varying from fierce competitiveness to caring nurturance. So do individual women. Without denying that, psychologists Nancy Chodorow (1978, 1989), Jean Baker Miller (1986), and Carol Gilligan and her colleagues (1982, 1990) contend that women more than men give priority to relationships.

The difference surfaces in childhood. Boys strive for independence; they define their identity in separation from the caregiver, usually their mother. Girls value interdependence; they define their identity through their social connections. Boys' play often involves group activity. But girls' play occurs in smaller groups, with less aggression, more sharing, more imitation of relationships, and more intimate discussion (Lever, 1978). Adult relationships extend this gender difference. In conversation, men more often focus on tasks, women on relationships. In groups, men contribute more task-oriented behaviors, such as giving information; women contribute more positive social-emotional behaviors, such as giving help or showing support (Eagly, 1987). Women spend more time caring for both preschoolers and aging parents (Eagly & Crowley, 1986). They buy most birthday gifts and greeting cards (DeStefano & Colasanto, 1990; Hallmark, 1990). In most of the U.S. caregiving professions—such as social worker, teacher, and nurse—women outnumber men. Among first-year college students, 5 in 10 males and 7 in 10 females say it is *very* important to "help others who are in difficulty" (Astin & others, 1991). Women's greater social concern helps explain why, in survey after survey, American women are more likely than men to support Democratic party candidates and to oppose military initiatives (*American Enterprise*, 1991).

When surveyed, women are far more likely to describe themselves as having **empathy**, as being able to feel what another feels—to rejoice with those who rejoice and weep with those who weep. To a lesser extent, the empathy difference extends to laboratory studies, in which women are more likely to cry or report feeling distressed at another's distress (Eisenberg & Lennon, 1983). Shown slides or told stories, girls, too, react with more empathy (Hunt, 1990). The gender empathy difference helps explain why, compared to friendships with men, both men and women report friendships with women to be more intimate, enjoyable, and nurturing (Rubin, 1985; Sapadin, 1988). When they want empathy and understanding, someone to whom they can disclose their joys and hurts, both men and women usually turn to women.

Women's greater connectedness also gets expressed in their smiling. When Marianne LaFrance (1985) analyzed 9000 college yearbook photos, she found females more often smiling. So did Amy Halberstadt and Martha Saitta (1987) in their analyses of 1100 magazine and newspaper photos and 1300 people in shopping malls, parks, and streets.

One explanation for this male-female empathy difference is that women tend to be better at reading others' emotions. In her analysis of 125 studies of men's and women's sensitivity to nonverbal cues, Hall (1984) discerned that women are generally superior at decoding others' emotional messages. When shown a two-second silent film clip of the face of an upset woman, women guess more accurately whether she is angry or discussing a divorce. Women also are more skilled at expressing emotions nonverbally, reports Hall.

Whether considered feminine or human, traits such as gentleness, sensitivity, and warmth are a boon to close relationships. In a study of 108 married couples in Sydney, Australia, John Antill (1983) found that when either the husband or the wife had these traditionally feminine qualities—or, better, when *both* did—marital satisfaction was higher. Both husbands and wives find marriage rewarding when their spouse is nurturant and emotionally supportive.

COMMUNITARIANISM

Gender research on the valuing of social connections converges with cross-cultural research on collectivist values. Both research strands remind us of alternatives to power-oriented, self-reliant individualism. In view of such findings, social psychologists Hazel Markus and Shinobu Kitayama (1991) propose a new understanding of dependence: "Being dependent does not invariably mean being helpless, powerless, or without control. It often means being *inter*dependent." It means valuing close relationships, being sensitive and responsive to others, giving and receiving support. It means defining oneself not just as a unique self but also as loyally attached to important others.

Hoping to blend the best of individualist and collectivist values, some social scientists are now exploring a **communitarian** synthesis that aims to balance individual rights with the collective right to communal well-being. Communitarians welcome incentives for individual initiative and appreciate why Marxist economies have crumbled. "If I were, let's say, in Albania at this moment," said communitarian sociologist Amitai Etzioni (1991), "I probably would argue that there's too much community and not enough individual rights." They also question the other extreme—in the United States the rugged individualism and self-indulgence of the 1960s ("Do your own thing"), the 1970s (the "me decade"), and the 1980s ("Greed is good"). Unrestrained personal freedom, they say, destroys a culture's social fabric; unrestrained commercial freedom, they add, plunders our shared environment. Echoing the French revolutionists, their motto might well be "liberty, equality, *and* fraternity."

During the last half century, western individualism has intensified. Parents have become more likely to prize independence and self-reliance in their children, and less concerned with obedience (Alwin, 1990; Remley, 1988). Clothing and grooming styles have become more diverse, personal freedoms have increased, and common values have waned (Schlesinger, 1991). Accompanying this growing individualism has been not only increased depression and teen suicide but other indicators of social recession. In the United States since 1960:

- The divorce rate has doubled, and marital happiness among the marital survivors has nevertheless slightly declined (Glenn, 1990, 1991).
- The percent of babies born to unmarried women has quintupled, from 5 percent to 28 percent, in many cases destining both mother and child to educational and economic impoverishment.
- The proportion of children not living with two parents has risen from 1 in 10 to nearly 3 in 10. Although children of caring, hard-working single parents usually develop into mature, productive adults, family status matters: children of single parent homes are at increased risk for school problems, delinquency, and eventual unhappiness. This fact helps explain a new "consensus" among child and family researchers as reported by developmental psychologists Edward Zigler and Elizabeth Gilman (1990): "In the past 30 years of monitoring the indicators of child well-being, never have the indicators looked so negative."
- The known rape rate—the tip of the sexual coercion iceberg—has quadrupled. Judging from surveys of women's rates of reporting crimes, and from the increasing rape reports of younger women, this appears mostly to represent a real increase in women's vul-

nerability to sexual aggression. Moreover, the rape increase parallels the increase in other forms of social violence as reflected in the quintupling of the violent crime rate. (Rape is, however, a worldwide problem.)

Some words of caution. First, such trends have multiple causes. Second, the mere correlation over time between increased individualism and decreased social well-being does not prove cause and effect. Third, communitarians are not advocating a nostalgia trip—a return, for example, to the more restrictive and unequal gender roles of the 1950s. Rather, they propose a middle ground between the individualism of the west and the collectivism of the east, between the macho independence traditionally associated with males and the caregiving connectedness traditionally associated with females, between concerns for individual rights and for communal well-being, between liberty and fraternity, between me-thinking and we-thinking.

A communitarian blend of individualist and collectivist values can already be seen in some western cultures, as in Britain's attempt to strengthen the individual incentives of a free market economy while restricting individual rights of gun ownership, in Canada's openness to cultural diversity while imposing restraints on violent pornography, and in America's effort to foster a "new covenant" of mutual responsibility between the government and the governed, between what society gives individuals (as in funding public colleges) and what individuals give back in voluntary service. In each case, there is an effort to affirm some individual liberties while constraining others that, unhindered, might harm collective well-being.

As with luggage searches at airports, smoking bans on planes, and sobriety checkpoints and speeding limits on highways, societies are accepting some adjustments to individual rights in order to protect the public good. Environmental restraints on individual freedoms (to pollute, to whale, to deforest) similarly exchange certain short-term liberties for long-term communal gain. Some individualists warn that such constraints on individual liberties may plunge us down a slippery slope leading to the loss of more important liberties. If today we let them search our luggage, tomorrow they'll be knocking down the doors of our houses. If today we censor cigarette ads or sexual violence on television, tomorrow they'll be removing books from our libraries. If today we ban handguns, tomorrow they'll take our hunting rifles. In protecting the interests of the majority do we risk suppressing the basic rights of minorities? Communitarians reply that if we don't balance concern for individual rights with concern for our collective well-being, we risk worse civic disorder, which in turn *will* fuel cries for an autocratic crackdown. As the political debate between individual and collective rights heats up, the new cross-cultural and gender scholarship illuminates alternative cultural values and makes visible our own assumed values.

CONCEPTS TO REMEMBER

Individualism "Me" thinking—giving priority to one's own goals over group goals and defining one's identity in terms of personal attributes rather than group identifications.

Collectivism "We" thinking—giving priority to the goals of one's groups (often one's extended family or work group) and defining one's identity accordingly.

Empathy The vicarious experience of another's feelings; putting oneself in another's shoes.

Communitarianism An effort to synthesize aspects of both individualism (respecting basic individual rights) and collectivism (caring for the well-being of families and communities).

MODULE

13

Gender and Genes

———— ❖ ————

There are many obvious dimensions of human diversity—height, weight, hair color, to name just a few. But for people's self-concepts and social relationships, the two dimensions that matter most, and that people first attune to, are race and, especially, sex. Later, we will see how race and sex affect the way others regard and treat us. For now, let's consider **gender**—the behaviors believed characteristic of male and female. What behaviors *are* characteristic and expected of males and of females?

The sexes are not only similar in many physical traits—such as age of sitting, teething, and walking—but also alike in many psychological traits—such as overall vocabulary, intelligence, and happiness. But the occasional differences are what capture attention and make news. Women are twice as vulnerable to anxiety disorders and depression, though only one-fifth as vulnerable to alcoholism and one-third as likely to commit suicide. Women have a slightly better sense of smell. They more easily become rearoused immediately after orgasm. They are much less likely to suffer hyperactivity or speech disorders as children and to display antisocial personalities as adults. And they give greater priority to their human connections.

During the 1970s, many scholars worried that studies of such gender differences might reinforce stereotypes and that gender differences might be construed as women's deficits. Focusing attention on gender differences will provide "battle weapons against women," they warned (Bernard, 1975, p. 13). And it's true that explanations for differences usually focus on the group that's seen as different (Miller & others, 1991). In discussing the "gender gap" in American presidential voting, commentators more often wonder why women so often vote Democratic than why men so often vote Republican. People more often wonder what causes homosexuality than what causes heterosexuality (or what determines sexual orientation). People ask why Asian-Americans so often excel in math and science,

126

not why other groups less often excel. In each case, people define the standard by one group and wonder why the other is "different." From "different" it is but a short leap to "deviant" or "substandard."

Since the 1980s, scholars have felt freer to explore gender diversity (Ashmore, 1990). Some argued that gender difference research has "furthered the cause of gender equality" by reducing overblown stereotypes and that we can accept and value gender diversity (Eagly, 1986). The two sexes, like two sides of a coin, can differ yet be equal. Let's consider, as an example, another dimension of gender diversity, and then ask what forces create such differences.

S OCIAL DOMINANCE

In both modern and traditional societies around the world, from Asia to Europe, people expect men to be, and perceive them as, more dominant and driven than women (Williams & Best, 1990a). And in essentially every society, men *are* socially dominant. They have been 93 percent of the world's legislators (Harper's, 1989). They are half of all jurors but 90 percent of elected jury leaders and most of the leaders of ad hoc laboratory groups (Davis & Gilbert, 1989; Kerr & others, 1982). As is typical of those in higher-status positions, men initiate most of the inviting for dates.

Men's style of communicating undergirds their social power. As leaders in situations where roles aren't rigidly scripted, men tend to be directive, women to be democratic (Eagly & Johnson, 1990). Men tend to excel as task-focused leaders, women as social leaders who build team spirit (Eagly & Karau, 1991; Wood & Rhodes, 1991). In everyday conversation, men are more likely to act as powerful people often do—talking assertively, interrupting, touching with the hand, staring more, smiling less (Ellyson & others, 1991; Carli, 1991; Major & others, 1990). Stating the results from a female perspective, women's influence style (especially in mixed-sex groups) tends to be more indirect—less interruptive, more sensitive, more polite, less cocky.

Aware of such findings, Nancy Henley (1977) has argued that women should stop feigning smiles, averting their eyes, and tolerating interruptions and should instead look people in the eye and speak assertively. Judith Hall (1984), however, values women's less autocratic communication style and therefore objects to the idea

> . . . that women should change their nonverbal style so as to appear more affectively distant and insensitive. . . . What would be sacrificed is the deeper value to self and society of a behavioral style that is adaptive, socially wise, and likely to facilitate positive interaction, understanding, and trust. . . . Whenever it is assumed that women's nonverbal behavior is undesirable, yet another myth is perpetuated: that male behavior is "normal"

and that it is women's behavior that is deviant and in need of explanation. (pp. 152–153)

In acknowledging any gender difference between the *average* woman and the *average* man, let's remember that individual differences within each gender are much greater. It's true that there is a gender difference in life expectancy, but age-of-death differences among individual men (and among women) are far greater. Also, to describe gender differences is neither to justify nor to explain them. So what does explain them?

GENDER ROLES

All the world's a stage,
And all the men and women merely players:
They have their exits and their entrances;
And one man in his time plays many parts.

William Shakespeare

Role theorists assume, as did William Shakespeare, that social life is like acting on a theatrical stage, with all its scenes, masks, and scripts. Like the role of Jaques, who speaks these lines in *As You Like It*, social roles—such as parent, student, and friend—outlast those who play them. And, as Jaques says, these roles allow some freedom of interpretation to those who act them out; great performances are defined by the way the role is played. However, some aspects of any role *must* be performed. A student must at least show up for exams, turn in papers, and maintain some minimum grade point average.

When only a few expectations are associated with a social category (for example, sidewalk pedestrians should keep to the right and not jaywalk), we do not regard the position as a social role. But a whole cluster of expectations defines a **role**. I could readily generate a long list of expectations prescribing my activities as a professor or as a father. Although I may acquire my particular image by violating the least important expectations (I am occasionally a couple minutes late to class), violating my role's most important expectations (failing to meet my classes, abusing my children) could lead to my being fired or divorced.

The shaping power of cultural expectations is conspicuous in our ideas about how men and women should behave. Even in contemporary, dual-career, North American marriages, men do most of the household repairs and women arrange the child care (Biernat & Wortman, 1991). Such behavior expectations for males and females define **gender roles**.

In an experiment with Princeton University undergraduate women, Mark Zanna and Susan Pack (1975) showed the impact of gender role expectations. The women answered a questionnaire on which they described themselves to a tall, unattached, senior man they expected to meet. Those led to believe that his ideal woman was home-oriented and deferential to her husband presented themselves as more traditionally feminine than those women expecting to meet a man who liked strong, ambitious women. Moreover, given a problem-solving test, those expecting to meet the nonsexist man behaved more intelligently: They solved 18 percent more problems than those expecting to meet the man with the traditional views. This adapting of themselves to fit the man's image was much less pronounced if the man was less desirable—a short, already attached freshman.

But does culture construct gender roles? Or do gender roles merely reflect behavior naturally appropriate for men and women? The variety of gender roles across cultures and over time show that culture indeed constructs our gender roles.

Gender Roles Vary with Culture

Should women do the housework? Should they be more concerned with promoting their husband's career than with their own? John Williams, Debra Best, and their collaborators (1990b) asked such questions of university students in 14 cultures. In nearly every one, women students had slightly more egalitarian views than their male peers. But the differences between the countries were far greater. Nigerian and Pakistani students, for example, had much more traditional ideas about distinct roles for men and women than Dutch and German students. Iftikhar Hassan (1980) of Pakistan's National Institute of Psychology describes the traditional status of Pakistani women:

> She knows that parents are not happy at the birth of a girl and she should not complain about parents not sending her to school as she is not expected to take up a job. She is taught to be patient, sacrificing, obedient. . . . If something goes wrong with her marriage she is the one who is to be blamed. If any one of her children do not succeed in life, she is the main cause of their failure. And in the rare circumstance that she seeks a divorce or receives a divorce her chances of second marriage are very slim because Pakistani culture is very harsh on divorced women.

These differing ideas about gender roles are displayed in differing behaviors. In the United States women during the 1980s accounted for 3 percent of the top executives at the 1000 largest corporations, 4 percent of the Marine Corps, 97 percent of all nurses, and 99 percent of secretaries (Castro, 1990; Saltzman, 1991; Williams, 1989). In countries everywhere, girls spend more time helping with housework and child care, while boys spend more time in unsupervised play (Edwards, 1991). In some countries the boy-girl roles differ sharply. In rural central India, for example, girls spend two-thirds of their time doing household work, while their brothers spend two-thirds of their time in leisure (Sarawathi & Dutta, 1988).

Gender Roles Vary over Time

In the last half century—a thin slice of our long history—gender roles have changed dramatically. In 1938, 1 in 5 Americans approved "of a married woman earning money in business or industry if she has a husband capable of supporting her." By the end of the 1980s, 4 in 5 approved (Niemi & others, 1989)—although nearly 2 in 3 still think that for children the "ideal family situation" is "father has a job and mother stays home and cares for the children" (Gallup, 1990). In 1967, 57 percent of first-year American collegians agreed that "the activities of married women are best confined to the home and family." In 1990, 25 percent agreed (Astin & others, 1987a, 1991).

Behavior changes have accompanied this attitude shift. Between 1960 and 1990, the proportion of American women in the work force increased from 1 in 3 to nearly 3 in 5. Between 1965 and 1985, American women were spending progressively less time in household tasks and men more time, raising the proportion of housework done by men from 15 to 33 percent (Robinson, 1988). But cultural variations in the extent to which men are found standing in front of the stove or bending over the laundry remain huge. Japanese husbands devote about 4 hours a week to domestic chores; their Swedish counterparts devote 18 hours a week (Juster & Stafford, 1991).

CULTURE OR BIOLOGY?

So far in this module we have affirmed our biological kinship as members of one human family. We have acknowledged our social diversity. And we have noted how roles vary with culture, and how cultures change over time. Remember that our primary quest in social psychology is not to catalog differences but to identify universal principles of behavior. Our aim is what cross-cultural psychologist Walter Lonner (1989) calls "a universalistic psychology—a psychology that is as valid and meaningful in Omaha and Osaka as it is in Rome and Botswana." Attitudes and behaviors will always vary with culture, but the processes by which attitudes influence behavior vary much less. People in Nigeria and Japan define gender roles differently than those in Europe and North America, but in all cultures role expectations guide social relations. G. K. Chesterton had the idea nearly a century ago: When someone "has discovered why men in Bond Street wear black hats he will at the same moment have discovered why men in Timbuktu wear red feathers."

To see how biology and culture work together, let's consider two more gender differences—in physical aggression and in sexual initiative.

By **aggression**, psychologists mean behavior intended to hurt. Throughout the world, hunting, fighting, and warring are primarily men's activities. In surveys, men admit to more aggression than do women. In laboratory experiments, men indeed exhibit more physical aggression, for example, by administering what they believe are hurtful electric shocks (Eagly & Steffen, 1986; Hyde, 1986). In the United States, men are arrested for violent crimes eight times more often than women— a trend found in every society that has kept crime records (Kenrick, 1987).

There is also a gender gap in sexual attitudes and assertiveness. It's true that in their physiological and subjective responses to sexual stimuli, women and men are "more similar than different" (Griffitt, 1987). Yet Susan Hendrick and her colleagues (1985) report that many studies, including their own, reveal that women are "moderately conservative" about casual sex and men are "moderately permissive." The American Council on Education's recent survey of a quarter million first-year college students is illustrative. "If two people really like each other, it's all right for them to have sex even if they've known each other for only a very short time," agreed 66 percent of the men but only 39 percent of the women (Astin & others, 1991).

The gender difference in sexual attitudes carries over to behavior. "With few exceptions anywhere in the world," report cross-cultural psychologist Marshall Segall and his colleagues (1990, p. 244), "males are more likely than females to initiate sexual activity." Moreover, among people of both sexual orientations (though especially among those with a homosexual orientation) "men without women have sex more often, with more different partners, than women without men" (Baumeister, 1991, p. 151). Like their human counterparts, the males of most animal species, too, are more sexually assertive and less selective about their partners (Hinde, 1984). Not only in sexual relations but also in courtship and touching, males tend to take more initiative (Hendrick, 1988; Kenrick 1987).

As detectives are more intrigued by crime than virtue, so psychological detectives are more intrigued by differences than similarities. In explaining gender roles, and gender differences in aggression and sexual initiative, inquiry has focused on two culprits: biology and culture.

BIOLOGY

"What do you think is the main reason men and women have different personalities, interests, and abilities?" asked the Gallup Organization (1990) in a national survey. "Is it mainly because of the way men and women are raised, or are the differences part of their biological makeup?" Among the 99 percent who answered the question (apparently without questioning its assumptions), nearly equal numbers answered "upbringing" and "biology."

There are, of course, salient biological sex differences. Men have penises; women have vaginas. Men produce sperm, women eggs. Men have the muscle mass to hunt with a spear; women can breast-feed. Are biological sex differences limited to these obvious distinctions in reproduction and physique? Or do men's and women's genes and hormones differ in ways that also contribute to behavior differences? Social scientists have recently been giving increased attention to biological influences on social behavior. Consider the biosocial view of gender differences.

The Evolution of the Sexes: Doing What Comes Naturally

Since Darwin, most biologists have assumed that for millions of years organisms have competed to survive and leave descendants. Genes that increased the odds of leaving descendants became more abundant. In the snowy Arctic environment, for example, polar bear genes programming a thick coat of camouflaging fur have won the genetic competition and now predominate.

Simplified, Darwin assumed that the way organisms evolve is adaptive: otherwise they wouldn't be here. Organisms well adapted to their environment are more likely to leave their genes for descendants. **Evolutionary psychology** studies how this process may predispose not just adaptive physical traits, such as polar bear coats, but also psychological traits and social behaviors (Buss, 1991).

Evolutionary theory offers a ready explanation for why males exert more sexual initiative. The average male produces over 8 trillion sperm in his lifetime, making sperm cheap compared to eggs. Moreover, while a female brings one fetus to term and then nurses it, a male can spread his genes by fertilizing many females. Thus females invest their reproductive opportunities carefully, looking for signs of health and resources. Meanwhile, males compete with other males for chances to send their genes into the future. Moreover, evolutionary psychology suggests, physically dominant males gained more access to females, which over generations enhanced male aggression and dominance.

Mind you, little of this is conscious. No one stops to calculate, "How can I maximize the number of genes I leave to posterity?" Rather, say evolutionary psychologists, our natural yearnings are our genes' way of making more genes. And that, they say, helps explain not only male social dominance and aggression but also the differing sexual attitudes and behaviors of females and males. Although our genes endow us with the adaptive flexibility that permits cultural influence, studies in 37 cultures worldwide reveal that men everywhere feel attracted to women whose youthful features suggest fertility and that women everywhere feel attracted to men whose wealth, power, and ambition promise resources needed to protect and nurture offspring (Buss, 1989).

Without disputing the principle of natural selection—that nature tends to select physical and behavioral traits that enhance gene survival—critics see two problems with evolutionary explanations. First, such an explanation often starts with an effect (such as the male-female difference in sexual initiative) and then works backward to conjecture an explanation for it. This approach is reminiscent of functionalism, a dominant theory in psychology during the 1920s. "Why does that behavior occur? Because it serves such and such a function." The theorist can hardly lose at this game.

The way to prevent the hindsight bias is to imagine things turning out otherwise. Let's try it. If human males were never known to have extra-marital affairs, might we not see the evolutionary wisdom behind their fidelity? After all, there's more to bringing offspring to maturity than merely depositing seed in a fertile woman. Males who are loyal to their mates and offspring are more apt to ensure that their young will survive to perpetuate their genes. (This is, in fact, an evolutionary explanation for why humans, and certain other species whose young require a heavy parental investment, tend to pair off and be monogamous.) Or imagine that women were the stronger, more physically aggressive sex. "But of course!" someone might say. "All the better for protecting their young."

Evolutionary psychologists reply that their field is more and more an empirical science that tests ideas with data from animal behavior, cross-cultural observations, and hormonal and genetic studies. Also, as the evolutionary psychologist would caution us, evolutionary wisdom is *past* wisdom. It tells us what behaviors worked in the past. Whether such tendencies are still adaptive is a different question.

Critics acknowledge that evolution helps explain both our commonalities and our differences (a certain amount of diversity aids survival). But they say our common evolutionary heritage does not, by itself, predict the enormous cultural variation in human marriage patterns (from one spouse to a succession of spouses to multiple wives to multiple husbands to spouse swapping). Nor does it explain cultural changes in behavior patterns over mere decades of time. The most significant trait that nature has endowed us with, it seems, is the capacity to adapt—to learn and to change. Therein lies what all agree is culture's shaping power.

Hormones

The results of architectural blueprints can be seen in physical structures. In humans, the effect of our genetic blueprints can be seen in the sex hormones that differentiate males and females. To what extent do hormonal differences predispose psychological differences?

Infants have built-in abilities to suck, grasp, and cry. Do mothers have a corresponding built-in predisposition to respond? Advocates of the biosocial perspective, such as sociologist Alice Rossi (1978), argue that they do. Behaviors critical to survival, such as the attachment of nursing mothers to their dependent infants, tend to be innate and culturally universal. For example, an infant's crying and nursing stimulate the mother's secretion of oxytocin, the same sex hormone that causes the nipples to become erect during lovemaking. For most of human history, the physical pleasure of breast-feeding probably helped forge the mother-infant bond. Thus Rossi found it not surprising that, while many cultures expect men to be loving fathers, *all* cultures expect women to be closely attached to their young children. She would also not be surprised that in one study of more than 7000 passers-by in a Seattle shopping mall, teenage and young adult women were more than twice as likely as similar-age men to pause to look at a baby (Robinson & others, 1979).

The gender gap in aggression reflects the influence of another hormone, *testosterone*. In various animals, administering testosterone heightens aggressiveness. In humans, violent male criminals have higher than normal testosterone levels, as do National Football League players (Dabbs & Morris, 1990). Moreover, for both humans and monkeys the gender difference in aggression appears early in life (before culture has much effect) and wanes as testosterone levels decline during adulthood. No one of these lines of evidence is conclusive. But taken together, they convince most scholars that sex hormones matter. But so does culture.

BIOLOGY AND CULTURE

As people mature to middle age and beyond, a curious thing happens. Women become more assertive and self-confident, men more empathic and less domineering (Lowenthal & others, 1975; Pratt & others, 1990). Hormone changes are one possible explanation for the shrinking gender differences. Role demands are another. Some speculate that during courtship and early parenthood, social expectations lead both sexes to emphasize traits that enhance their roles. While courting, providing, and protecting, men play up their macho sides and forgo their needs for interdependence and nurturance (Gutmann, 1977). While courting and rearing young children, young women restrain their impulses to assert and be independent. As men and women graduate from these early adult roles, they supposedly express more of their restrained tendencies. Each becomes more *androgynous*—more capable of exhibiting traits associated with both traditional masculinity (such as assertiveness) and femininity (such as nurturance).

But we needn't think of biology and culture as absolute competitors. Cultural expectations subtly but powerfully affect our attitudes and behavior. But they needn't do so independent of biology. What biology initiates, culture may accentuate. If their genes and hormones predispose males to be more physically aggressive than females, culture may amplify this difference by socializing males to be tough and females to be the kinder, gentler sex.

Biology and culture may also **interact**. In humans, biological traits influence how the environment reacts. People respond differently to a Sylvester Stallone than to a Woody Allen. Men, being 8 percent taller and averaging almost double the proportion of muscle mass, may likewise have different experiences than women (Kenrick, 1987). Or consider this: A very strong cultural norm dictates that males should be taller than their female mates. In one study, only 1 in 720 married couples violated this expectation (Gillis & Avis, 1980). With hindsight, we can speculate a psychological explanation: Perhaps being taller (and older) helps men perpetuate their social power over women. But we can also speculate biological wisdom that might underlie the cultural norm: If people preferred partners of the same height, tall men and short women would often be without partners. As it is, biology dictates that men tend to be taller than women, and culture dictates the same for couples. So the height norm might well be biology *and* culture, hand in hand.

In her book *Sex Differences in Social Behavior*, Alice Eagly (1987) theorizes a process by which biology and culture interact (Figure 13–1). She believes that a variety of factors, including biological influences and childhood socialization, predispose a sexual division of labor. In adult life the immediate causes of gender differences in social behavior are the *roles* that reflect this sexual division of labor. Men tend to be found in roles

FIGURE 13–1
A social-role theory of gender differences in social behavior. Various influences, including childhood experiences and biological factors, bend males and females toward differing roles. It is the expectations and the skills and beliefs associated with these differing roles that affect men's and women's behavior.   (Adapted from Eagly, 1987, and Eagly & Wood, 1991.)

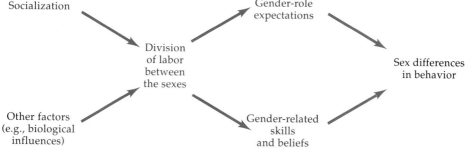

demanding social and physical power, and women in more nurturant roles. Each sex tends to exhibit the behaviors expected of those who fill such roles and to have their skills and beliefs shaped accordingly. The effects of biology and socialization may be important insofar as they influence the social roles that people play, for the roles we play influence who we become.

CONCEPTS TO REMEMBER

Gender   In psychology, the characteristics, whether biologically or socially influenced, by which people define male and female. Because "sex" is a biological category, social psychologists often refer to biologically based gender differences as "sex differences."

Role   A set of expectations (norms) that define how people in a given social position ought to behave.

Gender role   A set of behavior expectations (norms) for males or females.

Aggression   Physical or verbal behavior intended to hurt someone. In laboratory experiments, this might mean delivering electric shocks or saying something likely to hurt another's feelings. By this social psychological definition, one can be socially assertive without being aggressive.

Evolutionary psychology   The study of how natural selection predisposes adaptive traits and behavior tendencies.

Interaction   The effect of one factor (such as biology) depends on another factor (such as environment).

14

How Nice People Get Corrupted

❖

Researchers who study social influence often construct miniature social worlds—laboratory microcultures that simplify and simulate important features of everyday life. Two famous sets of experiments—Solomon Asch's studies of conformity and Stanley Milgram's studies of obedience—illustrate the process. They also offer startling evidence of the powers of social influence.

A SCH'S STUDIES OF CONFORMITY

From his boyhood, Asch recalls a traditional Jewish seder at Passover:

> I asked my uncle, who was sitting next to me, why the door was being opened. He replied, "The prophet Elijah visits this evening every Jewish home and takes a sip of wine from the cup reserved for him."
>
> I was amazed at this news and repeated, "Does he really come? Does he really take a sip?"
>
> My uncle said, "If you watch very closely, when the door is opened you will see—you watch the cup—you will see that the wine will go down a little."
>
> And that's what happened. My eyes were riveted upon the cup of wine. I was determined to see whether there would be a change. And to me it seemed—it was tantalizing, and of course, it was hard to be absolutely sure—that indeed something was happening at the rim of the cup, and the wine did go down a little. (Quoted by Aron & Aron, 1989, p. 27)

Years later, social psychologist Asch re-created his boyhood experience in his laboratory. Imagine yourself as one of Asch's volunteer subjects. You are seated sixth in a row of seven people. After explaining that you will be taking part in a study of perceptual judgments, the experimenter asks you to say which of the three lines in Figure 14–1 matches the standard line. You can easily see that it's line 2. So it's no surprise when the five people responding before you all say "line 2."

The next comparison proves as easy, and you settle in to endure a boring experiment. But the third trial startles you. Although the correct answer seems just as clear-cut, the first person gives a seemingly wrong answer. When the second person gives the same answer, you sit up in your chair and stare at the cards. The third person agrees with the first two. Your jaw drops; you start to perspire. "What is this?" you ask yourself. "Are they blind? Or am I?" The fourth and fifth people agree with the others. Then the experimenter looks at you. Now you are experiencing an "epistemological nightmare": "How am I to know what is true? Is it what my peers tell me or what my eyes tell me?"

Dozens of college students experienced this conflict during Asch's experiments. Those in a control condition who answered alone were correct more than 99 percent of the time. Asch wondered: If several others ("confederates" coached by the experimenter) gave identical wrong answers, would people declare what they would otherwise have denied? Although some people never conformed, three-fourths did so at least once. All told, 37 percent of the responses were conforming. Of course, that means 63 percent of the time people did not conform. Despite the independence shown by many of his subjects, Asch's (1955) feelings

FIGURE 14–1
Sample comparison from Solomon Asch's conformity procedure. The participants judged which of three comparison lines matched the standard.

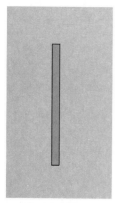

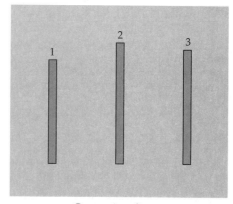

Standard line   Comparison lines

In one of Asch's conformity experiments, the subject, number 6, experienced uneasiness and conflict after hearing incorrect responses from the five persons who answered a question before him.

about the conformity were as clear as the correct answers to his questions: "That reasonably intelligent and well-meaning young people are willing to call white black is a matter of concern. It raises questions about our ways of education and about the values that guide our conduct."

Asch's results are startling because his experiments created no obvious pressure to conform: there were no rewards for "team play," no punishments for individuality. One wonders: If people are this compliant in response to such minimal pressure, how much more compliant will they be if they are directly coerced? Could someone force the average North American to perform cruel acts like those of the Nazis in Germany? I would have guessed not: North Americans' democratic and individualistic values would make them resist such pressure. Besides, the easy verbal pronouncements of these experiments are a giant step away from actually harming someone; you and I would never yield to coercion to hurt another. Or would we? Stanley Milgram wondered.

*M*ILGRAM'S OBEDIENCE EXPERIMENTS

Milgram's (1965, 1974) experiments on what happens when the demands of authority clash with the demands of conscience have become the most famous and controversial experiments in all social psychology. "Perhaps more than any other empirical contributions in the history of social science," notes Lee Ross (1988), "they have become part of our society's shared intellectual legacy—that small body of historical incidents, biblical parables, and classic literature that serious thinkers feel free to draw on when they debate about human nature or contemplate human history."

Here is the scene: Two men come to Yale University's psychology laboratory to participate in a study of learning and memory. A stern experimenter in a gray technician's coat explains that this is a pioneering study of the effect of punishment on learning. The experiment requires one of them to teach a list of word pairs to the other and to punish errors by delivering shocks of increasing intensity. To designate the roles, they draw slips out of a hat. One of the men, a mild-mannered 47-year-old accountant who is the experimenter's confederate, pretends that his slip says "learner" and is ushered into an adjacent room. The "teacher" (who has come in response to a newspaper ad) takes a mild sample shock and then looks on as the experimenter straps the learner into a chair and attaches an electrode to his wrist.

Teacher and experimenter then return to the main room where the teacher takes his place before a "shock generator" with switches ranging from 15 to 450 volts in 15-volt increments. The switches are labeled "Slight Shock," "Very Strong Shock," "Danger: Severe Shock," and so forth. Under the 435 and 450 volt switches appears "XXX." The experimenter tells the teacher to "move one level higher on the shock generator" each time the learner gives a wrong answer. With each flick of a switch, lights flash, relay switches click, and an electric buzz sounds.

If the subject complies with the experimenter's requests, he hears the learner grunt at 75, 90, and 105 volts. At 120 volts the learner shouts that the shocks are painful. And at 150 volts he cries out, "Experimenter, get me out of here! I won't be in the experiment anymore! I refuse to go on!" By 270 volts his protests have become screams of agony, and he continues to insist to be let out. At 300 and 315 volts he screams his refusal to answer. After 330 volts he falls silent. In answer to the teacher's inquiries and pleas to end the experiment, the experimenter states that the non-responses should be treated as wrong answers. To keep the subject going, he uses four verbal prods:

Prod 1: Please continue (*or* Please go on).
Prod 2: The experiment requires that you continue.

Prod 3: It is absolutely essential that you continue.

Prod 4: You have no other choice; you *must* go on.

How far would you go? Milgram described the experiment to 110 psychiatrists, college students, and middle-class adults. People in all three groups guessed that they would disobey by about 135 volts; none expected to go beyond 300 volts. Recognizing that self-estimates may reflect self-serving bias, Milgram asked them how far they thought *other* people would go. Virtually no one expected anyone to proceed to XXX on the shock panel. (The psychiatrists guessed about 1 in 1000.)

But when Milgram conducted the experiment with 40 men—a vocational mix of 20- to 50-year-olds—25 of them (63 percent) went clear to 450 volts. In fact, all who reached 450 volts complied with a command to *continue* the procedure until, after two further trials, the experimenter called a halt.

Given this disturbing result, Milgram next made the learner's protests even more compelling. As the learner was strapped into the chair, the teacher heard him mention his "slight heart condition" and heard the experimenter's reassurance that "although the shocks may be painful, they cause no permanent tissue damage." The learner's anguished protests were to little avail; of 40 new men in this experiment, 26 (65 percent) fully complied with the experimenter's demands (Figure 14–2).

The obedience of his subjects disturbed Milgram. The procedures he used disturbed many social psychologists (Miller, 1986). The "learner" in these experiments actually received no shock (he disengaged himself from the electric chair and turned on a tape recorder that delivered the protests). Nevertheless, some critics said that Milgram did to his subjects what they did to their victims: He stressed them against their will. Indeed, many of the "teachers" did experience agony. They sweated, trembled, stuttered, bit their lips, groaned, or even broke into uncontrollable nervous laughter. A *New York Times* reviewer complained that the cruelty inflicted by the experiments "upon their unwitting subjects is surpassed only by the cruelty that they elicit from them" (Marcus, 1974). Critics also argued that the participants' self-concepts may have been altered. One participant's wife told him, "You can call yourself Eichmann" (referring to Nazi death camp administrator Adolf Eichmann).

In his own defense, Milgram pointed first to the lessons his nearly two dozen experiments with some 1000 people taught us, and second to the support he received from the participants after the deception was revealed and the experiment explained. When surveyed afterward, 84 percent said they were glad to have participated; only 1 percent regretted volunteering. A year later, a psychiatrist interviewed 40 of those

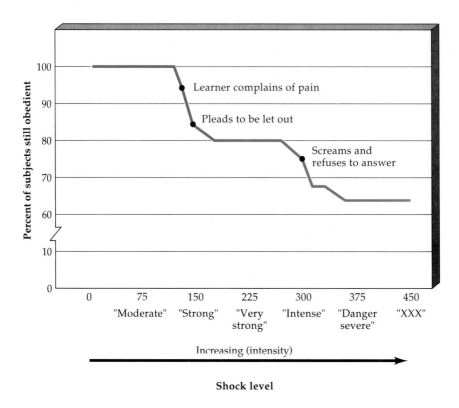

FIGURE 14–2
The Milgram obedience experiment. Percentage of subjects complying despite the learner's cries of protest and failure to respond.   (From Milgram, 1965.)

who had suffered most and concluded that, despite the temporary stress, none was harmed.

What Breeds Obedience?

Milgram did more than reveal the extent to which people will obey an authority; he also examined the conditions that breed obedience. Milgram wondered: Under what conditions can someone seduce good people into doing evil? In further experiments, he varied the social conditions and got compliance ranging from 0 to 93 percent fully obedient. The determining factors were these four: the victim's emotional distance, the authority's closeness and legitimacy, whether or not the authority is institutionalized, and the liberating effects of a disobedient fellow subject.

The Victim's Emotional Distance

Milgram's subjects acted with least compassion when the "learners" could not be seen (and could not see them). When the victim was remote and the teachers heard no complaints, nearly all obeyed calmly to the end. When the learner was in the same room, "only" 40 percent obeyed to 450 volts. Full compliance dropped to 30 percent when teachers were required to force the learner's hand into contact with a shock plate.

In everyday life, too, it is easiest to abuse someone who is distant or depersonalized. People will be unresponsive even to great tragedies. Executioners depersonalize those being executed by placing hoods over their heads. The ethics of war allow one to bomb a helpless village from 40,000 feet but not to shoot an equally helpless villager. In combat with an enemy they can see, many soldiers either do not fire or do not aim. Such disobedience is rare among those given orders to kill with the more distant artillery or aircraft weapons (Padgett, 1989).

On the positive side, people act most compassionately toward those who are personalized. This is why appeals for the unborn or the hungry are nearly always personalized with a compelling photograph or description. In his 1790 *Theory of Moral Sentiments*, Scottish economist Adam Smith imagined that "the great empire of China, with all its myriads of inhabitants, was suddenly swallowed up by an earthquake." Your average European, he guessed, would on hearing the news "express very strongly his sorrow for the misfortune of that unhappy people, would make many melancholy reflections upon the precariousness of human life . . . and when all this fine philosophy was over [would resume] his business or his pleasure . . . as if no such accident had happened."

Closeness and Legitimacy of the Authority

The physical presence of the experimenter also affected obedience. When Milgram gave the commands by telephone, full obedience dropped to 21 percent (although many lied and said they were obeying). Other studies confirm that when the one making the request is physically close, compliance increases. Given a light touch on the arm, people are more likely to lend a dime, sign a petition, or sample a new pizza (Kleinke, 1977; Smith & others, 1982; Willis & Hamm, 1980).

However, the authority must be perceived as legitimate. In another twist on the basic experiment, the experimenter received a rigged telephone call that required him to leave the laboratory. He said that since the equipment recorded data automatically, the teacher should just go ahead. After the experimenter left, another subject who had been assigned a clerical role (actually a second confederate) assumed command. The clerk "decided" that the shock should be increased one level for each wrong answer and instructed the teacher accordingly. Now 80 percent of the teachers refused to comply fully. The confederate, feigning disgust at this defiance, then came and sat down in front of the shock generator and tried to take over the teacher's role. At this point most of the defiant participants protested. Some tried to unplug the generator. One large man lifted the zealous shocker from his chair and threw him across the room. This rebellion against an illegitimate authority contrasted sharply with the deferential politeness usually shown the experimenter.

It also contrasts with the behavior of hospital nurses who in one study were called by an unknown physician and ordered to administer an obvious overdose of a drug (Hofling & others, 1966). The researchers told one group of nurses and nursing students about the experiment and asked how they would react. Nearly all said they would not have given the medication as ordered. One explained that she would have replied, "I'm sorry, sir, but I am not authorized to give any medication without a written order, especially one so large over the usual dose and one that I'm unfamiliar with. If it were possible, I would be glad to do it, but this is against hospital policy and my own ethical standards." Nevertheless, when 22 other nurses were actually given the phoned-in overdose order, all but one obeyed without delay (until being intercepted on their way to the patient). Although not all nurses are so compliant (Rank & Jacobson, 1977), these nurses were following a familiar script: Doctor (a legitimate authority) orders; nurse obeys.

Compliance with legitimate authority was also apparent in the strange case of the "rectal earache" (Cohen & Davis, 1981, cited by Cialdini, 1988). A doctor ordered ear drops given to a patient suffering infection in the right ear. On the prescription, the doctor abbreviated "place in right ear" as "place in R ear." Reading the order, the compliant nurse put the required drops in the compliant patient's rectum.

Institutional Authority

If the prestige of the authority is this important, then perhaps the institutional prestige of Yale University legitimized the commands. In postexperimental interviews, many participants volunteered that had it not been for Yale's reputation, they would not have obeyed. To see whether this was true, Milgram moved the experiment to Bridgeport, Connecticut. He set himself up in a modest commercial building as the "Research Associates of Bridgeport." When the usual "heart disturbance" experiment was run with the same personnel, what percentage of the men do you suppose fully obeyed? Though reduced, the rate remained remarkably high—48 percent.

The Liberating Effects of Group Influence

These classic experiments give us a negative view of conformity. Can conformity be constructive? Perhaps you can recall a time you felt justifiably angry at an unfair teacher, or with someone's offensive behavior, but you hesitated to object. Then one or two others objected, and you followed their example. Milgram captured this liberating effect of conformity by placing the teacher with two confederates who were to help conduct the procedure. During the experiment, both defied the experimenter, who then ordered the real subject to continue alone. Did he? No. Ninety percent liberated themselves by conforming to the defiant confederates.

REFLECTIONS ON THE CLASSIC STUDIES

The common response to Milgram's results is to note their counterparts in recent history: the "I was only following orders" defenses of Adolf Eichmann; of Lieutenant William Calley, who directed the unprovoked slaughter of hundreds of Vietnamese villagers in My Lai; and of the participants in various government scandals. Soldiers are trained to obey superiors. In the United States, the military acknowledges that even Marines should disobey *inappropriate* orders, but the military does not train soldiers to recognize an illegal or immoral order (Staub, 1989). Thus one participant in the My Lai massacre recalled:

> [Lieutenant Calley] told me to start shooting. So I started shooting, I poured about four clips into the group. . . . They were begging and saying, "No, no." And the mothers were hugging their children and. . . . Well, we kept right on firing. They was waving their arms and begging. (Wallace, 1969)

The obedience experiments differ from the other conformity experiments in the strength of the social pressure: Compliance is explicitly commanded. Without the coercion, people did not act cruelly. Yet both the Asch and Milgram experiments share certain commonalities. They show how compliance can take precedence over moral sense. They succeeded in pressuring people to go against their own conscience. They did more than teach us an academic lesson; they sensitize us to moral conflicts in our own lives. And they illustrate and affirm some familiar social psychological principles. Let us recall some of these.

Behavior and Attitudes

In Module 9 on behavior and belief we noted that attitudes fail to determine behavior when external influences override inner convictions. These experiments are a vivid illustration. When responding alone, Asch's subjects nearly always gave the correct answer. It was another matter when they stood alone against a group. In the obedience experiments, a powerful social pressure (the experimenter's commands) overcame a weaker one (the remote victim's pleas). Torn between the pleas of the victim and the orders of the experimenter, between the desire to avoid doing harm and the desire to be a good subject, a surprising number chose to obey. As Milgram explained:

> Some subjects were totally convinced of the wrongness of what they were doing [yet] felt that—within themselves, at least—they had been on the side of the angels. What they failed to realize is that subjective feelings are largely irrelevant to the moral issue at hand so long as they are not transformed into action. Political control is effected through action. . . . Tyrannies are perpetuated by difficult men who do not possess the courage to act out their beliefs. Time and again in the experiment people disvalued what they were doing but could not muster the inner resources to translate their values into action. (Milgram, 1974, p. 10)

Why were the participants unable to disengage themselves? How had they become trapped? Imagine yourself as the teacher in yet another version of Milgram's experiment, one he never conducted. Assume that when the learner gives the first wrong answer, the experimenter asks you to zap him with 330 volts. After flicking the switch, you hear the learner scream, complain of a heart disturbance, and plead for mercy. Do you continue?

I think not. Recall the step-by-step entrapment of the foot-in-the-door phenomenon (from Module 9) as we compare this hypothetical experiment to what Milgram's subjects experienced. Their first commitment was mild (15 volts), and it elicited no protest. You, too, would agree to do that much. By the time they delivered 75 volts and heard the learner's first groan, they already had complied five times. On the next trial the experimenter asked them to commit an act only slightly more extreme than what they had already repeatedly committed. By the time they delivered 330 volts, after 22 acts of compliance, the subjects had reduced some of their dissonance. They were therefore in a different psychological state from that of someone beginning the experiment at that point. External behavior and internal disposition can feed one another, sometimes in an escalating spiral. Thus, reported Milgram (1974, p. 10):

> Many subjects harshly devalue the victim *as a consequence* of acting against him. Such comments as "He was so stupid and stubborn he deserved to get shocked," were common. Once having acted against the victim, these subjects found it necessary to view him as an unworthy individual, whose punishment was made inevitable by his own deficiencies of intellect and character.

During the early 1970s, the military junta then in power in Greece used this "blame-the-victim" process to train torturers (Haritos-Fatouros, 1988; Staub, 1989). In Greece, as in the training of SS officers in Nazi Germany, the military selected future torturers based on their respect for and submission to authority. But such tendencies alone do not a torturer make. Thus they would first assign the trainee to guard prisoners, then to participate in arrest squads, then to hit prisoners, then to observe torture, and only then to practice it. Step by step, an obedient but otherwise decent person evolved into an agent of cruelty. Compliance bred acceptance.

From his study of human genocide across the world, Ervin Staub (1989) shows where this process can lead. Too often, criticism produces contempt, which licenses cruelty, which, when justified, leads to brutality, then killing, then systematic killing. Evolving attitudes both follow and justify actions. Staub's disturbing conclusion: "Human beings have the capacity to come to experience killing other people as nothing extraordinary" (p. 13).

The Power of the Situation

The most important lesson of the modules on individualism and gender—that culture is a powerful shaper of lives—and this module's most important lesson—that immediate situational forces are similarly powerful—reveal the strength of the social context. To feel this for yourself, imagine violating some minor norms: standing up in the middle of a class, singing out loud in a restaurant, greeting some distinguished senior professors by their first names, wearing shorts to church, playing golf in a suit, munching Cracker Jacks at a piano recital. In trying to break with social constraints, we suddenly realize how strong they are.

Some of Milgram's own students learned this lesson when he and John Sabini (1983) asked their help in studying the effects of violating a simple social norm: asking riders on the New York City subway system for their seats. To their surprise, 56 percent gave up their seats, even when no justification was given. The students' own reactions to making the request were as interesting: Most found it extremely difficult. Often, the words got stuck in their throat, and they had to withdraw. Once having made a request and gotten a seat, they sometimes justified their norm violation by pretending to be sick. Such is the power of the unspoken rules governing our public behavior.

There is also a lesson here about evil. Evil sometimes results from a few bad apples. That's the image of evil symbolized by depraved killers in suspense novels and horror movies. In real life we think of Hitler's extermination of Jews, of Saddam Hussein's extermination of Kurds, of Pol Pot's extermination of Cambodians. But evil also results from social forces—from the heat, humidity, and disease that help make a whole barrel of apples go bad. As these experiments show, situations can induce ordinary people to agree to falsehoods or capitulate to cruelty. Like the seductive power of the ring in J. R. R. Tolkien's *Lord of the Rings*, evil situations have enormous corrupting power.

This is especially true when, as happens often in complex societies, the most terrible evil evolves from a sequence of small evils. German civil servants surprised Nazi leaders with their willingness to handle the paperwork of the Holocaust. They were not killing Jews, of course; they were merely pushing paper (Silver & Geller, 1978). When fragmented, evil becomes easier. Milgram studied this compartmentalization of evil by involving yet another 40 men more indirectly. Rather than trigger the shock, they had only to administer the learning test. Now, 37 of the 40 fully complied.

So it is in our everyday lives: The drift toward evil usually comes in small increments, without any conscious intent to do evil. Procrastination involves a similar unintended drift, toward self-harm (Sabini & Silver, 1982). A student knows the deadline for a term paper weeks ahead. Each diversion from work on the paper—a video game here, a TV program there—seems harmless enough. Yet gradually the student veers toward not doing the paper without ever consciously deciding not to do it.

The Fundamental Attribution Error

Why do the results of these classic experiments so often startle people? Isn't it because we expect people to act in accord with their dispositions? It doesn't surprise us when a surly person is nasty, but we expect those with pleasant dispositions to be kind. Bad people do bad things; good people do good things.

When you read about Milgram's experiments, what impressions did you form of the subjects? Most people attribute negative qualities to them. When told about one or two of the obedient subjects, people judge them to be aggressive, cold, and unappealing—even after learning that their behavior was typical (A. G. Miller & others, 1973). Cruelty, we presume, is inflicted by the cruel at heart.

Günter Bierbrauer (1979) tried to eliminate this underestimation of social forces (the fundamental attribution error). He had university students observe a vivid reenactment of the experiment or play the role of obedient teacher themselves. Regardless, they still predicted that their friends would, in a repeat of Milgram's experiment, be only minimally compliant. Bierbrauer concluded that although social scientists accumulate evidence that our behavior is a product of our social history and current environment, most people continue to believe that people's inner qualities reveal themselves—that only good people do good and that only evil people do evil.

It is tempting to assume that Eichmann and the Auschwitz camp commanders were uncivilized monsters. But after a hard day's work, the Auschwitz commanders would relax by listening to Beethoven and Schubert. Eichmann himself was outwardly indistinguishable from common people with ordinary jobs (Arendt, 1963). Milgram's conclusion makes it harder to attribute the Holocaust to unique character traits in the German people: "The most fundamental lesson of our study," he noted, is that "ordinary people, simply doing their jobs, and without any particular hostility on their part, can become agents in a terrible destructive process" (Milgram, 1973, p. 6). As Mister Rogers often reminds his preschool television audience, "Good people sometimes do bad things." Perhaps then, we should be more wary of political leaders whose genial and charming dispositions lull us into supposing that they would never do evil. Under the sway of corrosive social forces, even nice people sometimes get corrupted.

15

Two Routes to Persuasion

————— ❖ —————

O ur opinions come from somewhere. Persuasion—whether we call it education (when we agree) or propaganda (when we don't)—is therefore inevitable. Indeed, persuasion is everywhere—at the heart of politics, marketing, courtship, parenting, negotiation, evangelism, and courtroom decision making. Social psychologists therefore seek to understand what makes a message effective: What factors influence us to change? And how, as persuaders, can we most effectively "educate" others?

Imagine that you are a marketing or advertising executive, one of those responsible for the $100 + billion spent annually just in the United States on ads promoting products and services (Wachtel, 1989). Or imagine that you are a preacher, trying to increase love and charity among your parishioners. Or imagine that you want to promote energy conservation, to encourage breast-feeding, or to campaign for a political candidate. What could you do to make yourself, and your message, persuasive? Or, if you are wary of being manipulated by such appeals, what tactics should you be alert to?

THE TWO ROUTES

In choosing tactics, you must first decide: Should you focus mostly on building strong, *central arguments*? Or should you make your message appealing by associating it with favorable *peripheral cues*? Persuasion researchers Richard Petty and John Cacioppo (1986) and Alice Eagly and Shelly Chaiken (1992) report that people who are able and motivated to think through an issue are best persuaded through a **central route** to persuasion—one that marshals systematic arguments to stimulate favorable thinking. Computer ads, for example, seldom feature Hollywood stars or great athletes; instead they offer their analytical customers competitive features and prices.

Some people are analytical, note Petty and Cacioppo. They like to think about issues and mentally elaborate them. Such people rely not just on the cogency of an appeal but on their own cognitive responses to it. It's not so much the arguments that are persuasive, as what they get people thinking. And when people think deeply rather than superficially, any changed attitude will likely persist (Verplanken, 1991).

On issues that don't and won't engage people's thinking, a **peripheral route**—one that provides cues that trigger acceptance without much thinking—works better. Instead of providing product information, cigarette ads merely associate the product with images of beauty and pleasure. Even analytical people sometimes form tentative opinions using simple heuristics (Chaiken, 1987). Residents of my community recently voted on a complicated issue involving the legal ownership of our local hospital. I didn't have the time or interest to study this question myself (I had this book to write). But I noted that referendum supporters were all people I either liked or regarded as experts. So I used a simple heuristic—friends and experts can be trusted—and voted accordingly. We all make snap judgments using other rule-of-thumb heuristics: If a speaker is articulate and appealing, has apparently good motives, and has several arguments (or better, if the different arguments come from different sources), we take the easy peripheral route and accept the message without much thought (Figure 15–1).

FIGURE 15–1
The central and peripheral routes to persuasion. Computer ads typically take the central route, by assuming that their audience wants to systematically compare features and prices. Soft-drink ads usually take the peripheral route, by merely associating their product with glamour, pleasure, and good moods.

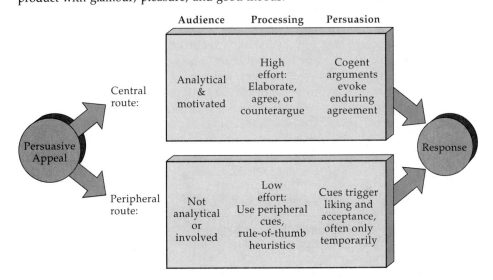

*T*HREE FACTORS IN PERSUASION

Among the ingredients of persuasion explored by social psychologists are these three: the communicator, the message, and the audience. In other words, *who* says *what* to *whom*? Let's see how each of these factors takes the central or peripheral route to persuasion.

Who Says? The Effect of the Communicator

Imagine the following scene: I. M. Wright, a middle-aged American, is watching the evening news. In the first segment, a small group of radicals is shown burning an American flag. As they do, one shouts through a bullhorn that whenever any government becomes oppressive, "it is the right of the people to alter or to abolish it. . . . It is their right, it is their duty, to throw off such government!" Angered, Mr. Wright mutters to his wife, "It's sickening to hear them spouting that Communist line." In the next segment, a presidential candidate speaking before an antitax rally declares, "Thrift should be the guiding principle in our government expenditure. It should be made clear to all government workers that corruption and waste are very great crimes." An obviously pleased Mr. Wright relaxes and smiles: "Now that's the kind of good sense we need. That's my kinda guy."

Now switch the scene. Imagine Mr. Wright hearing the same revolutionary line at a July 4 oration of the Declaration of Independence (from which the line comes) and hearing a Communist speaker read the thrift quote from *Quotations from Chairman Mao Tse-tung* (from which they come). Would he now react differently?

Social psychologists have found that who is saying something makes a big difference. In one experiment, when the Socialist and Liberal leaders in the Dutch parliament argued identical positions using the same words, each was most effective with members of his own party (Wiegman, 1985). Obviously, it's not just the central message that matters, but a *peripheral cue*—who says it. But what makes one communicator more persuasive than another?

Credibility

All of us, I suspect, would find a statement about the benefits of exercise more believable if it came from the National Academy of Sciences rather than the *National Enquirer*. Credible communicators seem both *expert* (confidently knowledgeable) and *trustworthy*. They speak unhesitatingly and without any selfish motive. Some television ads are obviously constructed to make the communicator appear both expert and trustworthy. Drug companies peddle pain relievers using a white-coated speaker, who declares confidently that most doctors recommend their ingredient (the ingredient, of course, is aspirin). Given such peripheral cues, people who don't care enough to analyze the evidence may reflexively infer the product's value. Other ads seem not to use the credibility principle. Is Bill Cosby really a trustworthy expert on Jell-O desserts? And are you and I more likely to drink Gatorade because Michael Jordan recommends it?

The effects of source **credibility** diminish after a month or so. If a message is persuasive but its source is forgotten or dissociated from the message, the impact of a high-credibility communicator decreases. The impact of a low-credibility communicator may correspondingly *increase* over time (if people remember the message better than the reason for discounting it) (Cook & Flay, 1978; Gruder & others, 1978; Pratkanis & others, 1988). This delayed persuasion, after people forget the source or its connection with the message, is called the **sleeper effect**.

Attractiveness

Most people deny that endorsements by star athletes and entertainers affect them. Everyone knows that stars are seldom knowledgeable about the products. Besides, we know the intent is to persuade us; we don't just accidentally eavesdrop on Cosby lapping Jell-O. Such ads are based on another characteristic of an effective communicator: attractiveness. We may think we are not influenced by how attractive or likeable the person is, but researchers have found otherwise. Our liking of them may open us to their arguments (central route persuasion) or may serve simply to trigger positive associations when we later see the product (peripheral route persuasion).

Attractiveness varies in several ways. *Physical appeal* is one. Arguments, especially emotional ones, are often more influential when they come from beautiful people (Chaiken, 1979; Dion & Stein, 1978; Pallak & others, 1983). *Similarity* is another. As Module 28 will emphasize, we tend to like people who are like us. We also are influenced by them. For example, Theodore Dembroski, Thomas Lasater, and Albert Ramirez (1978) gave African-American junior high students a taped appeal for proper dental care. When a dentist assessed the cleanliness of their teeth the next day, those who heard the appeal from an African-American dentist had cleaner teeth than those who heard the same appeal from a Caucasian dentist. As a general rule, people are better able to hear and respond to a message that comes from someone in their group (Mackie & others 1990; Wilder, 1990).

*W*HAT IS SAID? THE CONTENT OF THE MESSAGE

It matters not only who says a thing (a peripheral cue) but *what* that person says. If you were to help organize an appeal to get people to vote for school taxes, or to stop smoking, or to give money to world hunger relief, you might wonder how to concoct a recipe for central route persuasion. Common sense can be made to argue on either side of these questions:

- How discrepant (different) should the message be from the audience's existing opinions: Will you get more opinion change by advocating a position only slightly discrepant from the listeners' existing opinions? Or by advocating an extreme point of view? (That depends on the communicator's credibility. Highly credible people elicit the greatest opinion changes when they argue an extreme position; less credible people are more successful when they advocate positions closer to those of the audience.)
- Should the message express your side only, or should it acknowledge and attempt to refute opposing views? (This depends on the listeners. When the audience already agrees with the message, is unaware of opposing arguments, and is unlikely later to consider the opposition, then a one-sided appeal is most effective. With more sophisticated audiences or with those not already agreeing, two-sided messages are most successful.)
- If people present both sides, say in successive talks at a community meeting, is there an advantage to going first or last? (Information presented early is often the most potent, especially when it affects one's interpretation of later information. However, if a time gap separates the two sides, the effect of the early information diminishes; if a decision is also made right after hearing the second side, which is still fresh in mind, the advantage will likely go to the second presentation.)

Let's look closer at a fourth question: Is a carefully reasoned message more persuasive, or one that arouses emotion?

Reason versus Emotion

Suppose you were campaigning in support of world hunger relief. Would it be best to itemize your arguments and cite an array of impressive statistics? Or would you be more effective with an emotional approach, say by presenting the compelling story of one starving child? Of course, an argument need not be unreasonable to arouse emotion. Still, which is more influential—reason or emotion? Was Shakespeare's Lysander right when he said, "The will of man is by his reason sway'd"? Or was Lord Chesterfield's advice wiser: "Address yourself generally to the senses, to the heart, and to the weaknesses of mankind, but rarely to their reason"?

The answer: It depends on the audience. Well-educated or analytical people are more responsive to rational appeals than less educated or less analytical people (Cacioppo & others, 1983; Hovland & others, 1949). Involved audiences travel the central route; they are more responsive to reasoned arguments. Audiences that care little travel the peripheral route; they are more affected by how much they like the communicator (Chaiken, 1980; Petty & others, 1981). To judge from interviews before the 1980 U.S. presidential election, many voters were uninvolved. Their voting preferences were more predictable from emotional reactions to the candidates (for example, whether Ronald Reagan ever made them feel happy) than from their beliefs about the candidates' traits and likely behaviors (Abelson & others, 1982). In 1988, too, many people who agreed more with Michael Dukakis nevertheless *liked* George Bush more and therefore voted for Bush.

The Effect of Good Feelings

Messages also become more persuasive through association with good feelings. Irving Janis and his colleagues (1965; Dabbs & Janis, 1965) found that Yale students were more convinced by persuasive messages if they were allowed to enjoy peanuts and Pepsi while reading them (Figure 15–2). Similarly, Mark Galizio and Clyde Hendrick (1972) found Kent State University students more persuaded by folk-song lyrics accompanied by pleasant guitar music than by unaccompanied lyrics. Those who like conducting business over sumptuous lunches with soft background music can celebrate these results.

Good feelings enhance persuasion partly by enhancing positive thinking (Petty & others, 1991). In a good mood, people view the world through rose-colored glasses. They also make faster, more impulsive decisions; they rely less on systematic thinking, more on peripheral cues (Schwarz & others, 1991). Because unhappy people ruminate more before reacting, they are less easily swayed by weak arguments. Thus, if you can't make a strong case, it's a smart idea to put your audience in a good mood and hope they'll feel good about your message without thinking too much about it.

The Effect of Arousing Fear

Messages also can be effective by evoking negative emotions. In trying to convince people to cut down on smoking, brush their teeth more often, get a tetanus shot, or drive carefully, a fear-arousing message can be potent (Muller & Johnson, 1990). Showing cigarette smokers the horrible things that sometimes happen to people who smoke too much adds to persuasiveness. But how much fear should you arouse? Should

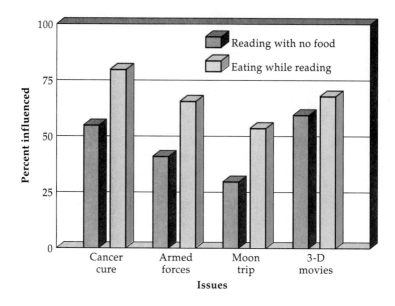

FIGURE 15–2
People who snacked as they read were more persuaded than those who read without snacking.   (Data from Janis, Kaye, & Kirschner, 1965.)

you evoke just a little fear, lest people become so frightened that they tune out your painful message? Or should you try to scare the daylights out of them? Experiments by Howard Leventhal (1970) and his collaborators at the University of Wisconsin and by Ronald Rogers and his collaborators at the University of Alabama (Robberson & Rogers, 1988) show that, often, the more frightened people are, the more they respond.

The effectiveness of fear-arousing communications is being applied in ads discouraging smoking, drinking and driving, and risky sexual behaviors. Dawn Wilson and her colleagues (1987, 1988) had doctors send a letter to their patients who smoked. Of those who received a positively framed message (explaining that by quitting they would live longer), 8 percent tried to quit smoking. Of those who received a fear-framed message (explaining that by continuing to smoke they would likely die sooner), 30 percent tried to quit. Similarly, researcher Claude Levy-Leboyer (1988) found that attitudes toward alcohol and drinking habits among French youth were more effectively changed by fear-arousing pictures, leading the French government to incorporate fear-arousing information into its TV spots.

But playing on fear won't always make a message more potent. If you don't tell people how to avoid the danger, frightening messages can be too much to cope with (Leventhal, 1970; Rogers & Mewborn, 1976). Such messages are more effective if you lead people not only to fear the severity and likelihood of a threatened event (say, a lung cancer death due to cigarette smoking) but also to believe there is an effective protective strategy they can follow (Maddux & Rogers, 1983). Many ads aimed at reducing sexual risks attempt both to arouse fear—"AIDS kills"—and to offer a protective strategy: abstain or wear a condom. During the 1980s, fear of AIDS indeed persuaded many men to alter their behavior. One study of 5000 gay men found that between 1984 and 1986 the number saying they were celibate or monogamous rose from 14 to 39 percent (Fineberg, 1988).

TO WHOM IS IT SAID? THE AUDIENCE

It also matters who receives a message. Consider, for example, the *age* and the *thoughtfulness* of the audience.

How Old Are They?

People today tend to have different social and political attitudes depending on their age. There are two explanations for the difference. One is a *life-cycle explanation*: Attitudes change (for example, become more conservative) as people grow older. The other is a *generational explanation*: The attitudes older people adopted when they were young persist largely unchanged; because these attitudes are different from those now being adopted by young people today, a generation gap develops.

The evidence supports the generational explanation. In surveying and resurveying groups of younger and older people over several years, it is almost always found that the attitudes of older people change less than those of young people. As David Sears (1979, 1986) puts it, researchers have "almost invariably found generational rather than life cycle effects."

The point is not that older adults are inflexible; most people in their fifties and sixties have more liberal sexual and racial attitudes than they had in their thirties and forties (Glenn, 1980, 1981). The point is that the teens and early twenties are important formative years (Krosnick & Alwin, 1989), and the attitudes formed then tend to be stable thereafter. If you are an 18- to 25-year-old, you may want to choose carefully your own social influences—the groups you join, the books you read, the roles you adopt.

Experiences during adolescence and early adulthood are formative partly because they make deep and lasting impressions. When Howard Schuman and Jacqueline Scott (1989) asked people to name the one or two most important national or world events over the last half century, most recalled events from their teens or early twenties. For those who experi-

enced the Great Depression or World War II as 16- to 24-year-olds, those
events overshadowed the Civil Rights movement and the Kennedy assas-
sination of the early sixties, the Vietnam war and moon landing of the late
sixties, and the women's movement of the seventies, each of which
imprinted themselves on the minds of those who experienced them as 16-
to 24-year-olds. For today's young adults, we may expect that memories
of the Persian Gulf war, or of the fall of the Berlin Wall and the democra-
tization of eastern Europe and the Soviet Union will be indelible turning
points in world history.

What Are They Thinking?

In central route persuasion, what's crucial is not the message itself but
what responses it evokes in a person's mind. Our minds are not sponges
that soak up whatever messages pour over them. If the message sum-
mons favorable thoughts, it persuades us. If it provokes us to think of
contrary arguments, we remain unpersuaded.

Forewarned Is Forearmed—If You Care Enough to Counterargue
What circumstances breed counterarguing? One is a low-credibility communicator with a disagreeable message (Perloff & Brock, 1980). Another
is a *forewarning* that someone is going to try to persuade you. If you had to
tell your parents that you wanted to drop out of school, you would
anticipate their trying to persuade you to stay. So, you might develop a
list of arguments to counter every conceivable argument they might
make. Jonathan Freedman and David Sears (1965) demonstrated the
difficulty of trying to persuade someone under such circumstances. They
forewarned one of two large groups of California high school seniors that
they were going to hear a talk: "Why Teenagers Should Not Be Allowed to
Drive." Those forewarned did not budge; those not forewarned did.
    Sneak attacks on attitudes are especially useful with involved people.
Given several minutes' forewarning, such people will prepare defenses
(Petty & Cacioppo, 1977, 1979a). But when people regard an issue as
trivial, even blatant propaganda can be effective. Would you bother to
construct counterarguments for two brands of toothpaste? Similarly,
when someone slips a premise into a casual conversation—"Why was
Sue hostile to Mark?"—people often accept the premise (that Sue was, in
fact, hostile) (Swann, Giuliano, & Wegner, 1982).

Distraction Disarms Counterarguing
Verbal persuasion also increases by distracting people with something
that attracts their attention just enough to inhibit counterarguing (Festinger & Maccoby, 1964; Keating & Brock, 1974; Osterhouse & Brock, 1970).
Political ads often use this technique. The words promote the candidate,

and the visual images keep us occupied so we don't analyze the words. Distraction is especially effective when the message is simple (Harkins & Petty, 1981; Regan & Cheng, 1973). This research on how persuasion becomes more effective as counterarguing decreases makes me wonder: Does television shape important attitudes more through its subtle or hidden messages (for example, concerning gender roles) than through its explicit persuasive appeals? After all, if we don't notice a message, we won't examine and counterargue it.

Uninvolved Audiences Use Peripheral Cues

Recall again the two routes to persuasion—the central route of systematic thinking and the peripheral route of heuristic cues. Like the road through town, the central route has starts and stops as the mind analyzes arguments and formulates responses. Like the freeway around town, the peripheral route zips people to their destination. Analytical people—those with a high "need for cognition"—prefer central routes. Image-conscious people who care less about whether they're right or wrong than what sort of impression they are making are quicker to respond to such peripheral cues as the communicator's attractiveness and the pleasantness of the surroundings (Snyder, 1991). But the issue matters too. All of us struggle actively with issues that involve us while making snap judgments about things that matter little (Johnson & Eagly, 1990). As we mentally elaborate upon an important issue, the strength of the arguments and the tenor of our own thoughts determine our attitudes.

This basically simple theory—that what you think in response to a message is crucial *if* you are motivated and able to think about it—helps us understand several findings. For example, we more readily believe expert communicators, because when we trust the source we think favorable thoughts and are less likely to counterargue. When we mistrust the source, we are more likely mentally to defend our preconceptions by refuting the disagreeable message.

The theory has also generated many predictions, most of which have been confirmed by Petty, Cacioppo, and others (Axsom & others, 1987; Harkins & Petty, 1987; Leippe & Elkin, 1987). Many experiments have explored ways to stimulate people's thinking—by using *rhetorical questions*, by presenting *multiple speakers* (for example, having three speakers each give one argument instead of one speaker giving three), by making people *feel responsible* for evaluating or passing along the message, by using *relaxed* rather than standing postures, by *repeating* the message, and by getting people's *undistracted attention*. Their consistent finding: Each of these techniques for stimulating thinking makes strong messages more persuasive and (because of counterarguing) weak messages less persuasive.

The theory also has practical implications. Effective communicators care not only about their images and their messages but also about how their audience is likely to react. How they will react depends not only on their interest in the issue but also on their dispositions—their analytical inclinations, their tolerance for uncertainty, their need to be true to themselves (Cacioppo & others, 1986; Snyder & DeBono, 1987; Sorrentino & others, 1988).

So, are people likely to think and remember thoughts that favor the persuader's point of view? If the answer is yes, quality arguments will be persuasive. During the closing days of the closely contested 1980 presidential campaign, Ronald Reagan effectively used rhetorical questions to stimulate desired thoughts in voters' minds. His summary statement in the presidential debate began with two potent rhetorical questions that he repeated often during the campaign's remaining week: "Are you better off than you were four years ago? Is it easier for you to go and buy things in the stores than it was four years ago?" Most people answered no, and Reagan, thanks partly to this bit of central route persuasion, won by a bigger-than-expected margin.

THE TWO ROUTES TO PERSUASION IN THERAPY

One constructive use of persuasion powers is in counseling and psychotherapy, which social-counseling psychologist Stanley Strong views "as a branch of applied social psychology" (1978, p. 101). By the 1990s, psychologists more and more accepted the idea that social influence—one person affecting another—is at the heart of therapy.

Early analyses of social influence in psychotherapy focused on how therapists establish credible expertise and trustworthiness and how their credibility enhances their influence (Strong, 1968). More recent analyses have focused less on the therapist than on how the interaction affects the client's thinking (Cacioppo & others, 1991; McNeill & Stoltenberg, 1988; Neimeyer & others, 1991). Peripheral cues, such as therapist credibility, may open the door for ideas which the therapist can now get the client to think about. But the central route to persuasion provides the most enduring attitude and behavior change. Therapists should therefore aim not to elicit a client's superficial agreement with their expert judgment but to change the client's own thinking.

Fortunately, most clients entering therapy are motivated to take the central route, thinking deeply about their problems under the therapist's guidance. The therapist's task is to offer arguments and raise questions calculated to elicit favorable thoughts. The cogency of the therapist's insights matters less than the thoughts they evoke in the client. The therapist needs to put things in ways that a client can hear and understand, that will prompt agreement rather than counterargument, and that allow time and space for the client to reflect. Questions, such as, "How do you respond to what I just said?" can stimulate the client's thinking.

Martin Heesacker (1989) illustrates with the case of Dave, a 35-year-old male graduate student. Having seen what Dave denied—an underlying substance abuse problem—the counselor drew on his knowledge of Dave, an intellectual person who liked hard evidence, in persuading him to accept the diagnosis and join a treatment-support group. The counselor said, "OK, if my diagnosis is wrong, I'll be glad to change it. But let's go through a list of the characteristics of a substance abuser to check out my accuracy." The counselor then went through each criterion slowly, giving Dave time to think about each point. As he finished, Dave sat back and exclaimed, "I don't believe it: I'm a damned alcoholic."

In an experiment, John Ernst and Heesacker (1991) showed the effectiveness of escorting participants in an assertion training workshop through the central route to persuasion. Some participants experienced the typical assertiveness workshop by learning and rehearsing concepts of assertiveness. Others learned the same concepts but also volunteered a time when they hurt themselves by being unassertive. Then they heard arguments that, from pretesting, Ernst and Heesacker knew were likely to trigger favorable thoughts (for example, "By failing to assert yourself, you train others to mistreat you"). At the workshop's end, Ernst and Heesacker asked the people to stop and reflect on how they now felt about all they had learned. Compared to those in the first group, those who went through the thought-evoking workshop left the experience with more favorable attitudes and intentions regarding assertiveness. Moreover, their roommates noticed greater assertiveness during the ensuing two weeks.

In his 1620 *Penseés*, the philosopher Pascal foresaw this principle: "People are usually more convinced by reasons they discover themselves than by those found by others." It's a principle worth remembering in our own lives.

CONCEPTS TO REMEMBER

Central route persuasion   Persuasion that occurs when interested people focus on the arguments and respond with favorable thoughts.

Peripheral route persuasion   Persuasion that occurs when people are influenced by incidental cues, such as a speaker's attractiveness.

Credibility   Believability. A credible communicator is perceived as both expert and trustworthy.

Sleeper effect   A delayed impact of a message; occurs when we remember the message but forget a reason for discounting it.

Attractiveness   Having qualities which appeal to an audience. An appealing communicator (often someone similar to the audience) is most persuasive on matters of subjective preference.

16

Indoctrination and Inoculation

❖

Persuasion principles are being applied, consciously or not, in ways that reveal their power. Consider Joseph Goebbels, Nazi Germany's minister of "popular enlightenment" and propaganda. Given control of publications, radio programs, motion pictures, and the arts, he undertook to persuade Germans to accept Nazi ideology. Julius Streicher, another member of the Nazi group, published *Der Stürmer*, a weekly anti-Semitic (anti-Jewish) newspaper with a circulation of 500,000 and the only paper read cover to cover by his intimate friend, Adolf Hitler. Streicher also published anti-Semitic children's books and along with Goebbels spoke at the mass rallies that became a part of the Nazi propaganda machine. How effective were Goebbels, Streicher, and other Nazi propagandists? Did they, as the Allies alleged at Streicher's Nuremberg trial, "inject poison into the minds of millions and millions" (Bytwerk, 1976)? Most Germans were not persuaded to feel raging hatred for the Jews. But some were. Others became sympathetic to anti-Semitic measures. And most of the rest became either sufficiently uncertain or sufficiently intimidated to allow the Holocaust to happen.

Or consider the social influences that have caused hundreds of thousands of people to join religious cults.

*C*ULT INDOCTRINATION

What persuades people to adopt radically new beliefs as when joining a **cult**—a group marked by (1) the distinctive ritual of its devotion to a god or a person, (2) isolation from the surrounding "evil" culture, and (3) a charismatic leader? Do their experiences illustrate the dynamics of human persuasion? Bear two things in mind: First, this is hindsight analysis. It uses persuasion principles as categories for explaining, after the fact, a fascinating social phenomenon.

Second, explaining *why* people believe something says nothing about the *truth* of their beliefs. That is a logically separate issue. A psychology of religion that could tell us *why* a theist believes in God and an atheist disbelieves would not tell us who is right. Explaining either belief does not explain it away. So if someone tries to discount your beliefs by saying, "You just believe that because . . . ," you might recall the reply of Archbishop William Temple. After giving an address at Oxford, a questioner opened the discussion with a challenge: "Well, of course, Archbishop, the point is that you believe what you believe because of the way you were brought up." To which the Archbishop replied: "That is as it may be. But the fact remains that you believe I believe what I believe because of the way I was brought up, because of the way you were brought up."

In recent decades, two religious cults have gained much publicity: Sun Myung Moon's Unification Church and Jim Jones' People's Temple. The Reverend Moon's mixture of Christianity, anticommunism, and glorification of Moon himself as a new messiah attracted a worldwide following. In response to Moon's declaration, "What I wish must be your wish," many committed themselves and their incomes to the Unification Church. How were they persuaded to do so?

In 1978 in Guyana, 911 followers of the Reverend Jones, who had followed him there from San Francisco, shocked the world when they died by following his order to down a strawberry drink laced with tranquilizers, painkillers, and a lethal dose of cyanide. How could such a thing happen? And what about the 85 followers of David Koresh who perished when their Waco, Texas cult torched their compound? How did Koresh persuade them to give him their possessions and submit to his sexual exploitation?

Attitudes Follow Behavior

Compliance Breeds Acceptance

As the module on behavior and belief showed, people usually internalize commitments made voluntarily, publicly, and repeatedly. Cult leaders seem to know this. New converts soon learn that membership is no trivial matter. They are quickly made active members of the team, not mere spectators. Rituals within the cult community, and public canvassing and fund-raising, strengthen the initiates' identities as members. As those in social-psychological experiments come to believe in what they bear witness to (Aronson & Mills, 1959; Gerard & Mathewson, 1966), so cult initiates become committed advocates. And the greater the personal commitment, the more the need to justify it.

The Foot-in-the-Door Phenomenon

How are we induced to make commitments? Seldom by an abrupt, conscious decision. One does not just decide, "I'm through with mainstream religion. I'm gonna find a cult." Nor do cult recruiters approach people on the street with, "Hi. I'm a Moonie. Care to join us?"

Rather, the recruitment strategy exploits the foot-in-the-door principle. Unification Church recruiters would invite people to a dinner and then to a weekend of warm fellowship and discussions of philosophies of life. At the weekend retreat, they encouraged the attenders to join in songs, activities, and discussion. Once the recruiters identified potential converts, they urged them to sign up for longer training retreats. Eventually the activities become more arduous—soliciting contributions and attempting to convert others. Persuading others to join the cause intensifies their own commitment.

Jim Jones used this foot-in-the-door technique with his People's Temple members. At first, monetary offerings were voluntary. He next inaugurated a required 10-percent-of-income contribution, which soon increased to 25 percent. Finally, he ordered members to turn over to him everything they owned. Work loads also became progressively more demanding. Grace Stoen recalls:

> Nothing was ever done drastically. That's how Jim Jones got away with so much. You slowly gave up things and slowly had to put up with more, but it was always done very gradually. It was amazing, because you would sit up sometimes and say, wow, I really have given up a lot. I really am putting up with a lot. But he did it so slowly that you figured, I've made it this far, what the hell is the difference? (Conway & Siegelman, 1979, p. 236).

Persuasive Elements

We can also analyze cult persuasion in terms of the factors described in the persuasion module: *Who* (the communicator) said *what* (the message) to *whom* (the audience)?

The Communicator

Successful cults have a charismatic leader—someone who attracts and directs the members. As in experiments on persuasion, a credible communicator is someone the audience perceives as expert and trustworthy, for example, as "Father" Moon.

Jim Jones reportedly used "psychic readings" to establish his credibility. Newcomers were asked to identify themselves as they entered the church before services. Then one of his aides would call the person's home and say, "Hi. We're doing a survey, and we'd like to ask you some questions." During the service, recalls one ex-member, Jones would call out the person's name and say:

> Have you ever seen me before? Well, you live in such and such a place, your phone number is such and such, and in your living room you've got this, that, and the other, and on your sofa you've got such and such a pillow. . . . Now do you remember me ever being in your house? (Conway & Siegelman, 1979, p. 234)

Trust is another aspect of credibility. Cult researcher Margaret Singer (1979b) noted that middle-class Caucasian youths are more vulnerable because they are more trusting. They lack the "street smarts" of lower-class youths (who know how to resist a hustle) and the wariness of upper-class youths (who have been warned of kidnappers since childhood). Many cult members have been recruited by friends or relatives, people they trust (Stark & Bainbridge, 1980).

The Message

To lonely or depressed people, the vivid, emotional messages and the warmth and acceptance with which the group showers them can be strikingly appealing: Trust the master, join the family; we have the answer, the "one way." The message echoes through channels as varied as lectures, small-group discussions, and direct social pressure. And it is delivered intensively for long periods, with support from previous converts.

The Audience

Recruits are often young—people under 25 and still at that comparatively open age before attitudes and values stabilize. Some, such as the followers of Jim Jones, are less educated people who like the simplicity of the message and find it difficult to counterargue. More are well-educated and middle-class people who, taken by the ideals, overlook the contradictions in those who profess selflessness and practice greed, who pretend concern and behave indifferently.

Potential converts often are at a turning point in their lives or facing a personal crisis. They have needs; the cult offers them an answer (Lofland & Stark, 1965; Singer, 1979a). Times of social and economic upheaval are therefore especially conducive to an ayatollah or a "father" who can make apparent simple sense out of the confusion (O'Dea, 1968; Sales, 1972).

Group Effects

Cults illustrate a theme of several modules to come: the power of a group to shape members' views and behavior. Members are usually separated from their previous social support systems and isolated with other cultists. There may then occur what Rodney Stark and William Bainbridge (1980) call a "social implosion": External ties weaken until the group socially collapses inward, each person engaging only with other group members. Cut off from families and former friends, they lose access to counterarguments. The group now defines reality. Because the cult frowns on or punishes disagreements, the apparent consensus helps eliminate any lingering doubts.

Contrary to the idea that cults turn hapless people into mindless robots, these techniques—binding behavioral commitments, persuasion, and group isolation—do not have unlimited power. The Unification Church successfully recruits fewer than 1 in 10 people who attend its workshops (Ennis & Verrilli, 1989). As Jim Jones made his demands more extreme, he increasingly had to control people with intimidation. He used threats of harm to those who fled the community, beatings for noncompliance, and drugs to neutralize disagreeable members. By the end, he was as much an arm twister as a mind bender.

Moreover, cult influence techniques are in some ways similar to techniques used by groups more familiar to us. Fraternity and sorority members, for example, have reported that the initial "love bombing" of potential cult recruits is not unlike their own "rush" period, during which members lavish prospective pledges with attention and make them feel special. During the pledge period, new members are somewhat isolated, cut off from old friends who did not pledge. They spend time studying the history and rules of their new group. They suffer and commit time on its behalf. And they are expected to comply with all its demands. Not surprisingly, the result is usually a committed new member.

Much the same is true of some therapeutic communities for recovering drug and alcohol abusers. Like religious cults, zealous self-help groups form a cohesive "social cocoon," have intense beliefs, and exert a profound influence on members' behavior (Galanter, 1989, 1990). Terrorist organizations exploit some of these principles in recruiting and indoctrinating members (McCauley & Segal, 1987).

I chose the examples of fraternities, sororities, and self-help groups not to disparage them but to illustrate two concluding observations. First, if we attribute cult indoctrination to the leader's mystical force or to the followers' peculiar weaknesses, we may delude ourselves into thinking we are immune to social control techniques. In truth, as the fraternity and sorority example suggests, our own groups—and countless salespeople, political leaders, and other persuaders—successfully use many of these tactics on us. Second, that Jim Jones abused the power of persuasion does not mean that the power is itself intrinsically bad. Nuclear power enables us to light up homes or wipe out cities. Sexual power enables us to express and celebrate committed love or exploit people for selfish gratification. Persuasive power enables us to enlighten or deceive. That these powers can be harnessed for evil purposes should alert us to guard against their immoral use. But the powers themselves are neither inherently evil nor inherently good; how we use them determines whether their effect is destructive or constructive.

RESISTING PERSUASION: ATTITUDE INOCULATION

This consideration of persuasive influences has perhaps made you wonder if it is possible to *resist* unwanted persuasion. Of course it is. If, because of an aura of credibility, the repairperson's uniform and doctor's title have intimidated us into unquestioning agreement, we can rethink our habitual responses to authority. We can seek more information before committing time or money. We can question what we don't understand.

Strengthening Personal Commitment

There is a way to resist: Before encountering others' judgments, make a public commitment to your position. Having stood up for your convictions, you will become less susceptible (or should we say less "open"?) to what others have to say.

Challenging Beliefs

How might we stimulate people to commit themselves? From his experiments, Charles Kiesler (1971) offers one possible way: Mildly attack their position. Kiesler found that when committed people were attacked strongly enough to cause them to react, but not so strongly as to overwhelm them, they became even more committed. Kiesler explains:

> When you attack a committed person and your attack is of inadequate strength, you drive him to even more extreme behaviors in defense of his previous commitment. His commitment escalates, in a sense, because the number of acts consistent with his belief increases. (p. 88)

Perhaps you can recall a time when this happened in an argument, as those involved escalated their rhetoric, committing themselves to increasingly extreme positions.

Developing Counterarguments

There is a second reason a mild attack might build resistance. Like inoculations against disease, weak arguments prompt counterarguments, which are then available for a stronger attack. Social psychologist William McGuire (1964) documented this in a series of experiments. McGuire wondered: Could we inoculate people against persuasion much as we inoculate them against a virus? Is there such a thing as **attitude inoculation**? Could we take people raised in a "germ-free ideological environment"—people who hold some unquestioned belief—and stimulate their mental defenses? And would subjecting them to a small "dose" of belief-threatening material inoculate them against later persuasion?

That is what McGuire did. First, he found some cultural truisms, such as, "It's a good idea to brush your teeth after every meal if at all possible." He then showed that people were vulnerable to a massive, credible assault upon these truisms (for example, prestigious authorities were said to have discovered that too much toothbrushing can damage one's gums). If, however, before having their belief attacked, they were "immunized" by first receiving a small challenge to their belief, *and* if they read or wrote an essay in refutation of this mild attack, then they were better able to resist the powerful attack.

Large-Scale Inoculation Programs

Inoculating Children against Peer Pressure to Smoke

In a clear demonstration of how laboratory research findings can lead to practical application, a research team led by Alfred McAlister (1980) had high school students "inoculate" seventh graders against peer pressures to smoke. The seventh graders were taught to respond to advertisements implying that liberated women smoke by saying, "She's not really liberated if she is hooked on tobacco." They also acted in role plays in which, after being called "chicken" for not taking a cigarette, they answered with statements like, "I'd be a real chicken if I smoked just to impress you." After several such sessions during the seventh and eighth grades, the inoculated students were half as likely to begin smoking as uninoculated students at another junior high school that had an identical parental smoking rate (Figure 16-1).

Other research teams have confirmed that education-inoculation procedures can indeed greatly reduce the teenage smoking rate (Evans & others, 1984; Flay & others, 1985). Most newer efforts emphasize strategies for resisting social pressure. One study exposed sixth to eighth graders to antismoking films or to information about smoking, together with role plays of student-generated ways of refusing a cigarette (Hirschman & Leventhal, 1989). A year and a half later 31 percent of those who watched the antismoking films had taken up smoking, but only 19 percent had done so among those who role-played refusing. Another study involved the entire seventh grade class in a diverse sample of 30 junior high schools. It warned students about pressures to smoke and use drugs and offered them strategies for resisting (Ellickson & Bell, 1990). Among nonusers of marijuana, the training curbed initiation by a third; among users, it reduced usage by half.

Antismoking and drug education programs apply other persuasion principles too. They use attractive peers to communicate information.

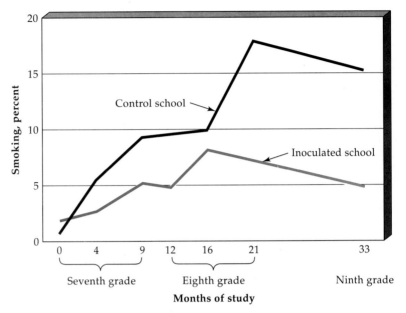

FIGURE 16–1

The percentage of cigarette smokers at an "inoculated" junior high school was much less than at a matched control school using a more typical smoking education program.   (Data from McAlister & others, 1980; Telch & others, 1981.)

They trigger the students' own cognitive processing ("Here's something you might want to think about"). They get the students to make a public commitment (by making a rational decision about smoking and then announcing it, along with their reasoning, to their classmates). Some of these smoking-prevention programs require only 2 to 6 one-hour class sessions, using prepared printed materials or videotapes. Today any school district or teacher wishing to use the social-psychological approach to smoking prevention can do so easily, inexpensively, and with the hope of significant reductions in future smoking rates and associated health costs.

Inoculating Children against the Influence of Advertising

Researchers have also now studied how to immunize young children so they can more effectively analyze and evaluate television commercials. This research is prompted partly by studies showing that children, especially those under eight years, (1) have trouble distinguishing commercials from programs and fail to grasp their persuasive intent, (2) trust television advertising rather indiscriminately, and (3) desire and badger their parents for advertised products (Adler & others, 1980; S. Feshbach,

1980; Palmer & Dorr, 1980). Children, it seems, are an advertiser's dream: gullible, vulnerable, an easy sell. Moreover, half the 20,000 ads the typical child sees in a year are for low-nutrition, often sugary foods.

Armed with such data, citizens' groups have given the advertisers of such products a chewing out (Moody, 1980): "When a sophisticated advertiser spends millions to sell unsophisticated, trusting children an unhealthy product, this can only be called exploitation. No wonder the consumption of dairy products has declined since the start of television, while soft-drink consumption has almost doubled." On the other side are the commercial interests, who claim that such ads allow parents to teach their children consumer skills and, more important, finance children's television programs. In the United States, the Federal Trade Commission has been in the middle, pushed by research findings and political pressures while trying to decide whether to place new constraints on TV ads aimed at young children.

Meanwhile, researchers have wondered whether children can be taught to resist deceptive ads. In one such effort, a team of investigators led by Norma Feshbach (1980; S. Cohen, 1980) gave small groups of Los Angeles–area elementary schoolchildren three half-hour lessons in analyzing commercials. The children were inoculated by viewing ads and discussing them. For example, after viewing a toy ad, they were immediately given the toy and challenged to make it do what they had just seen in the commercial. Such experiences helped breed a more realistic understanding of commercials.

Implications

This inoculation research also has some provocative implications. The best way to build resistance to brainwashing may not be, as some senators thought after the Korean war, to introduce more courses on patriotism and Americanism. William McGuire advised that teachers use inoculation techniques: Challenge the concepts and principles of democracy and explain alternatives such as communism and constitutional monarchy, and so help students to develop defenses.

For the same reason, religious educators should be wary of creating a "germ-free ideological environment" in their churches and schools. An attack, if refuted, is more likely to solidify one's position than to undermine it, particularly if the threatening material can be examined with like-minded others. Cults apply this principle by forewarning members of how families and friends will attack the cult's beliefs. When the expected challenge comes, the member is armed with counterarguments.

Another implication is that, for the persuader, an ineffective appeal can be worse than none. Can you see why? Those who reject one appeal are inoculated against further appeals. Consider an experiment in which

Susan Darley and Joel Cooper (1972) invited students to write essays advocating a strict dress code. Because this was against the students' own positions and the essays were to be published, all chose *not* to write the essay—even those offered money to do so. After turning down the money, they became even more extreme and confident in their anti-dress-code opinions. Having made an overt decision against the dress code, they became even more resistant to it. Those who have rejected initial appeals to quit smoking may likewise become immune to further appeals. Thus, ineffective persuasion, by stimulating the listener's defenses, may be counterproductive. Rebuffed appeals "harden the heart" against later appeals.

Inoculation research has a personal implication too. Do you want to build your resistance to persuasion without becoming closed to valid messages? Be an active listener and a critical thinker. Force yourself to counterargue. After hearing a political speech, discuss it with others. In other words, don't just listen; react. If the message cannot withstand careful analysis, so much the worse for it. If it can, its effect on you will be the more enduring for your having done the analytical work.

C ONCEPTS TO REMEMBER

Cult   A group typically characterized by (1) the distinctive ritual of its devotion to a god or a person, (2) isolation from the surrounding "evil" culture, and (3) a living, charismatic leader.

Attitude inoculation   Exposing people to weak attacks upon their attitudes so that when stronger attacks come, they will have refutations available.

The Mere Presence of Others

❖

Our world contains not only 5.4 billion individuals but also 200 nation-states, 4 million local communities, 20 million economic organizations, and hundreds of millions of other formal and informal groups—couples on dates, families, churches, housemates in bull sessions. How do these groups influence individuals?

Let's begin with social psychology's most elementary question: Are we affected by the mere presence of another person? "Mere presence" means people are not competing, do not reward or punish, and in fact do nothing except be present as a passive audience or as **coactors**. Would the mere presence of others affect a person's jogging, eating, typing, or exam performance? The search for the answer makes a scientific mystery story.

THE PRESENCE OF OTHERS

A century ago, Norman Triplett (1898), a psychologist interested in bicycle racing, noticed that cyclists' times were faster when racing together than when racing alone against the clock. Before he peddled his hunch (that the presence of others boosts performance), Triplett conducted one of social psychology's early laboratory experiments. Children told to wind string on a fishing reel as rapidly as possible wound faster when they worked with coactors than when they worked alone.

Subsequent experiments in the early decades of this century found that the presence of others also improves the speed with which people do simple multiplication problems and cross out designated letters. It also improves the accuracy with which people perform simple motor tasks, such as keeping a metal stick in contact with a dime-sized disk on a moving turntable (F. H. Allport, 1920; Dashiell, 1930; Travis, 1925). This **social-facilitation** effect, as it came to be called, also occurs with animals. In the presence of others of their species, ants excavate more sand and chickens eat more grain (Bayer, 1929; Chen, 1937).

Other studies conducted about the same time revealed that on other tasks the presence of others hinders performance. In the presence of others, cockroaches, parakeets, and green finches learn mazes more slowly (Allee & Masure, 1936; Gates & Allee, 1933; Klopfer, 1958). This disruptive effect also occurs with people. The presence of others diminishes efficiency at learning nonsense syllables, completing a maze, and performing complex multiplication problems (Dashiell, 1930; Pessin, 1933; Pessin & Husband, 1933).

Saying that the presence of others sometimes facilitates performance and sometimes hinders it is about as satisfying as a weather forecast predicting that it might be sunny but then again it might rain. By 1940, research activity in this area had ground to a halt. It lay dormant for 25 years until awakened by the touch of a new idea.

Social psychologist Robert Zajonc (pronounced *Zy-ence*, rhymes with *science*) wondered whether these seemingly contradictory findings could be reconciled. As often happens at creative moments in science, Zajonc (1965) used one field of research to illuminate another. In this case the illumination came from a well-established principle in experimental psychology: Arousal enhances whatever response tendency is dominant. Increased arousal enhances performance on easy tasks for which the most likely—"dominant"—response is the correct one. People solve easy anagrams, such as *akec*, fastest when they are anxious. On complex tasks, for which the correct answer is not dominant, increased arousal promotes *incorrect* responding. On harder anagrams people do worse when anxious.

Could this principle solve the mystery of social facilitation? It seemed reasonable to assume that others' presence will arouse or energize people. (Most of us can recall feeling more tense or excited when before an audience.) If social arousal facilitates dominant responses, it should boost performance on easy tasks and hurt performance on difficult tasks. Now the confusing results made sense. Winding fishing reels, doing simple multiplication problems, and eating were all easy tasks for which the responses were well learned or naturally dominant. And sure enough, having others around boosted performance. On the other hand, learning new material, doing a maze, or solving complex math problems were more difficult tasks for which the correct responses were initially less probable. And sure enough, the presence of others increased the number of *incorrect* responses on these tasks. The same general rule—*arousal facilitates dominant responses*—worked in both cases. Suddenly, what had looked like contradictory results no longer seemed contradictory.

Zajonc's solution, so simple and elegant, left other social psychologists thinking what Thomas H. Huxley thought after first reading Darwin's *Origin of Species*: "How extremely stupid not to have thought of that!" It seemed obvious—once Zajonc had pointed it out. Perhaps, however, the pieces appeared to merge so neatly only because we viewed them through the spectacles of hindsight. Would the solution survive direct experimental tests?

After almost 300 studies conducted with the help of more than 25,000 volunteer subjects, it has survived (Bond & Titus, 1983; Guerin, 1986). Several experiments in which Zajonc and his associates manufactured an arbitrary dominant response confirmed that an audience enhanced this response. In one, Zajonc and Stephen Sales (1966) asked people to pronounce various nonsense words between 1 and 16 times. Then they told the people that the same words would appear on a screen, one at a time. Each time, they were to guess which had appeared. When the people were actually shown only random black lines for a hundredth of a second, they "saw" mostly the words they had pronounced most frequently. These words had become the dominant responses. People who took the same test in the presence of two others were even more likely to guess the dominant words (Figure 17–1).

FIGURE 17–1
Social facilitation of dominant responses. People responded with dominant words (practiced 16 times) more frequently, and subordinate words (practiced only once) less frequently, when observers were present.   (Data from Zajonc & Sales, 1966.)

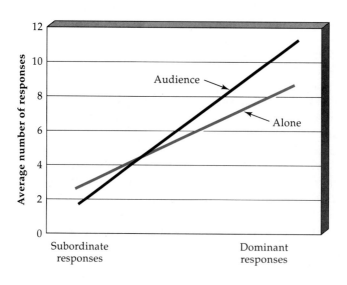

In various ways, later experiments confirmed that social arousal facilitates dominant responses, whether right or wrong. Peter Hunt and Joseph Hillery (1973) found that in the presence of others, University of Akron students took less time to learn a simple maze and more time to learn a complex one (just as the cockroaches do). And James Michaels and his collaborators (1982) found that good pool players in the Virginia Polytechnic Institute student union (who had made 71 percent of their shots while being unobtrusively observed) did even better (80 percent) when four observers came up to watch them play. Poor shooters (who had previously averaged 36 percent) did even worse (25 percent) when closely observed.

CROWDING: THE PRESENCE OF MANY OTHERS

So, people do respond to the presence of others. But does the presence of observers really arouse people? In times of stress, a comrade can be comforting. Nevertheless, researchers have found that with others present, people perspire more, breathe faster, tense their muscles more, and have higher blood pressure and a faster heart rate (Geen & Gange, 1983; Moore & Baron, 1983).

The effect of other people increases with their number (Jackson & Latané, 1981; Knowles, 1983). Sometimes the arousal and self-conscious attention created by a large audience interfere with well-learned, automatic behaviors, such as speaking. Stutterers tend to stutter more in front of larger audiences than when speaking to just one or two people (Mullen, 1986b). College basketball players become slightly *less* accurate in their free throw shooting when highly aroused by a packed fieldhouse (Sokoll & Mynatt, 1984). In baseball's World Series, home teams have won 60 percent of the first two games but only 40 percent of the final games (Baumeister & Steinhilber, 1984; Heaton & Sigall, 1989, 1991). The arousal created by playing before the home fans helps to a point: home teams win two-thirds of their college basketball games (Hirt & Kimble, 1981). But under the pressure of a World Series final game, the home team players sometimes choke, producing twice as many fielding errors in final games as in games 1 and 2.

Being *in* a crowd also intensifies positive or negative reactions. When they sit close by, friendly people are liked even more, and *un*friendly people are *dis*liked even more (Schiffenbauer & Schiavo, 1976; Storms & Thomas, 1977). In experiments with Columbia University students and with Ontario Science Center visitors, Jonathan Freedman and his co-workers (1979; 1980) had an accomplice listen to a humorous tape or watch a movie with other subjects. When all sat close together, the accomplice could more readily induce them to laugh and clap. As theater directors and sports fans know, and as researchers have confirmed

(Aiello & others, 1983; Worchel & Brown, 1984), a "good house" is a full house.

Perhaps you've noticed that a class of 35 students feels more warm and lively in a room that seats just 35 than when spread around a room that seats 100. This occurs partly because we are more likely when others are close by to notice and join in their laughter or clapping. But crowding also enhances arousal, as Gary Evans (1979) found. He tested 10-person groups of University of Massachusetts students, either in a room 20 by 30 feet or in one 8 by 12 feet. Compared to those in the large room, those densely packed had higher pulse rates and blood pressure (indicating arousal). Though their performance on simple tasks did not suffer, on difficult tasks they made more errors. In their study of university students in India, Dinesh Nagar and Janak Pandey (1987) also found that crowding hampered performance only on complex tasks, such as solving difficult anagrams.

WHY ARE WE AROUSED IN THE PRESENCE OF OTHERS?

To this point we have seen that what you do well, you will be energized to do best in front of others (unless you become hyperaroused and self-conscious). What you find difficult may seem impossible in the same circumstances. What is it about other people that causes arousal? Is it their mere presence? There is evidence to support three possible factors.

Evaluation Apprehension

Nickolas Cottrell surmised that observers make us apprehensive because we wonder how they are evaluating us. To test whether **evaluation apprehension** exists, Cottrell and his associates (1968) repeated Zajonc and Sales' nonsense-syllable study at Kent State University and added a third condition. In this "mere presence" condition they blindfolded observers, supposedly in preparation for a perception experiment. In contrast to the effect of the watching audience, the mere presence of these blindfolded people did *not* boost well-practiced responses. Other experiments confirmed Cottrell's conclusion: The enhancement of dominant responses is strongest when people think they are being evaluated. In one experiment, joggers on a University of California at Santa Barbara jogging path sped up as they came upon a woman seated on the grass—*if* she was facing them rather than sitting with her back turned (Worringham & Messick, 1983).

Evaluation apprehension also helps explain:

- Why people perform best when their coactor is slightly superior (Seta, 1982)
- Why arousal may lessen when a high-status group is diluted by the addition of people whose opinions we don't much care about (Seta & Seta, 1992)
- Why people who worry most about others' evaluations are the ones most affected by their presence (Gastorf & others, 1980; Geen & Gange, 1983)
- Why social-facilitation effects are greatest when the others are unfamiliar and hard to keep an eye on (Guerin & Innes, 1982)

The self-consciousness we feel when being evaluated can also interfere with behaviors that we perform best automatically—without thinking about how we're doing them (Mullen & Baumeister, 1987). If self-conscious basketball players analyze their body movements while shooting critical free throws, they are more likely to miss.

Driven by Distraction

Glenn Sanders, Robert Baron, and Danny Moore (1978; Baron, 1986) carry evaluation apprehension a step farther. They theorize that when people wonder how coactors are doing or how an audience is reacting, they get distracted. This *conflict* between paying attention to others and paying attention to the task overloads the cognitive system, causing arousal. Evidence that people are indeed "driven by distraction" comes from experiments that produce social facilitation not just by the presence of another person but even by a nonhuman distraction, such as bursts of light (Sanders, 1981a, 1981b).

Mere Presence

Zajonc, however, believes that the mere presence of others produces some arousal even without evaluation apprehension or distraction. For example, people's color preferences are stronger when they make judgments with others present (Goldman, 1967). On such a task, there is no "good" or "right" answer for others to evaluate and thus no reason to be concerned with their reactions.

That response facilitation effects also occur with animals, which probably are not consciously worrying about how other animals are evaluating them, hints at an innate social arousal mechanism common to much of the zoological world. At the human level, most joggers feel energized when jogging with someone else, even one who neither competes nor evaluates.

This is a good time to consider the purpose of a theory. A good theory is a scientific shorthand: It simplifies and summarizes a variety of observations. Social-facilitation theory does this well. It is a simple summary of many research findings. A good theory also offers clear predictions that (1) help confirm or modify the theory, (2) guide new exploration, and (3) suggest practical application. Social-facilitation theory has definitely generated the first two types of prediction: (1) The basics of the theory (that the presence of others is arousing and that this social arousal enhances dominant responses) have been confirmed, and (2) the theory has brought new life to a long dormant field of research. Does it also suggest (3) some practical applications?

Application is properly the last research phase. In their study of social facilitation, researchers have yet to work much on this. That gives us the opportunity to speculate on what some applications might be. For example, as Figure 17-2 shows, many new office buildings are replacing private offices with large open areas divided by low partitions. Might the

FIGURE 17-2
In the "open-office plan" people work in the presence of others. How might this affect worker efficiency?   (Photo courtesy of Herman Miller Inc.)

resulting awareness of others' presence help energize the performance of well-learned tasks but disrupt creative thinking on complex tasks? Can you think of other possible applications?

CONCEPTS TO REMEMBER

Coactors A group of people working simultaneously and individually on a noncompetitive task.

Social facilitation (1) Original meaning: the tendency of people to perform simple or well-learned tasks better when others are present. (2) Current meaning: the strengthening of dominant (prevalent, likely) responses due to the presence of others.

Evaluation apprehension Concern for how others are evaluating us.

18

Many Hands Make Diminished Responsibility

❖

Imagine a team tug-of-war, a popular sport in the summer highland games around Scotland. Will eight people on a side exert as much force as the sum of their best efforts? More effort, thanks to social facilitation (the strengthening of well-learned responses in others' presence)? Less effort, due to the diffusion of responsibility?

Social facilitation usually occurs when people work toward individual goals and when their efforts, whether winding fishing reels or solving math problems, can be individually evaluated. These situations parallel some everyday work situations, but not those where people cooperatively pool their efforts toward a *common* goal and where individuals are *not* accountable for their efforts. A team tug-of-war provides one such example. Organizational fund-raising—pooling candy sale proceeds to pay for the class trip—provides another. People on a work crew or a class group project where all get the same grade are another. On such "additive tasks"—tasks where the group's achievement depends on the sum of the individual efforts—will team spirit boost productivity? Will bricklayers lay bricks faster when working as a team than when working alone? One way to attack such questions is with laboratory simulations.

MANY HANDS MAKE LIGHT WORK

Nearly a century ago, French engineer Max Ringelmann (reported by Kravitz & Martin, 1986) found that the collective effort of tug-of-war teams was but half the sum of the individual efforts. Contrary to the common notion that "in unity there

In this tug-of-war at the Garnock Highland Games in Scotland, are group members likely pulling as hard as they might in an individual tug-of-war? Harder? Less hard?

is strength," this suggests that group members may actually be *less* motivated when performing additive tasks. Maybe, though, the group's poor performance stemmed from poor coordination—people pulling in slightly different directions at slightly different times. A group of Massachusetts researchers led by Alan Ingham (1974) cleverly eliminated this problem by making individuals think that others were pulling with them, when in fact they were pulling alone. Blindfolded participants assigned the first position in the apparatus shown in Figure 18–1 and told to "pull as hard as you can" pulled 18 percent harder when they knew they were pulling alone than when they believed that behind them two to five people were also pulling.

At Ohio State University, researchers Bibb Latané, Kipling Williams, and Stephen Harkins (1979; Harkins & others, 1980) kept their ears open for other ways to investigate this phenomenon, which they labeled **social loafing**. They observed that the noise produced by six people shouting or clapping "as loud as you can" was less than three times that produced by one person alone. However, like the tug-of-war task, noisemaking is vulnerable to group inefficiency. So Latané and his associates followed Ingham's example by leading participants to believe that others were shouting or clapping with them, when in fact they were doing so alone.

Their method was to blindfold six people, seat them in a semicircle, and have them put on headphones, over which they were blasted with

FIGURE 18–1
The rope-pulling apparatus. People in the first position pulled less hard when
they thought that people behind them were also pulling.   (Data from Ingham,
Levinger, Graves, & Peckham, 1974. Photo by Alan G. Ingham.)

the sound of people shouting or clapping. People could not hear their
own shouting or clapping, much less that of others. On various trials they
were instructed to shout or clap either alone or along with the group.
People who were told about this experiment guessed that the subjects
would shout louder when with others, because they would be less embarrassed (Harkins, 1981). The actual result? Once again, social loafing:
When the participants believed that five others were also either shouting
or clapping, they produced one-third less noise than when they thought
themselves alone. (Curiously, those who clapped both alone and in
groups did not view themselves as loafing; they perceived themselves
clapping equally in both situations. This parallels what happens when
students work on group projects yielding a shared grade. Williams reports that all agree that loafing occurs—by others. No one admits to doing
the loafing.) Social loafing occurred even when the subjects are high
school cheerleaders who believe themselves to be cheering together or
alone (Hardy & Latané, 1986).

John Sweeney (1973), a political scientist interested in the policy
implications of social loafing, obtained similar results in an experiment at
the University of Texas. He found that students pumped exercise bicycles
more energetically (as measured by electrical output) when they knew
they were being individually monitored than when they thought their

output was being pooled with that of other riders. In the group condition, people were tempted to **free-ride** on the group effort.

In this and some four dozen other studies (Figure 18–2), we see a twist on one of the psychological forces that makes for social facilitation: evaluation apprehension. In the social-loafing experiments, individuals believe they are evaluated only when they act alone. The group situation (rope pulling, shouting, and so forth) *decreases* evaluation apprehension; when people are not accountable and cannot evaluate their own efforts, responsibility is diffused across all group members (Harkins & Jackson, 1985; Kerr & Bruun, 1981). By contrast, the social-facilitation experiments *increased* people's exposure to evaluation. When made the center of attention, people self-consciously monitor their behavior (Mullen & Baumeister, 1987). So the principle is the same: When being observed *increases* evaluation concerns, social facilitation occurs; when being lost in a crowd *decreases* evaluation concerns, social loafing occurs.

To motivate group members, one strategy is to make performance individually identifiable. Some football coaches do this by individually filming and evaluating each player. The Ohio State researchers had group members wear individual microphones while engaged in group shouting

FIGURE 18–2
A statistical digest of 49 studies, involving more than 4000 participants, revealed that effort decreases (loafing increases) as the size of the group increases. Each dot represents the aggregate data from one of these studies.   (From Jackson & Williams, 1988.)

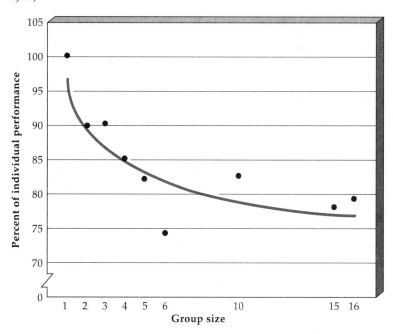

(Williams & others, 1981). Whether in a group or not, people exert more effort when their outputs are individually identifiable: University swim team members swim faster in intrasquad relay races when someone monitors and announces their individual times (Williams & others, 1989).

SOCIAL LOAFING IN EVERYDAY LIVING

How widespread is social loafing? In the laboratory, the phenomenon occurs not only among people who are pulling ropes, cycling, shouting, and clapping but also among those who are pumping water or air, evaluating poems or editorials, producing ideas, typing, and detecting signals. Do these results generalize to everyday worker productivity?

On their collective farms under communism, Russian peasants worked one field one day, another field the next, with little direct responsibility for any given plot. For their own use, they were given small private plots. In one analysis, the private plots occupied 1 percent of the agricultural land yet produced 27 percent of the Soviet farm output (H. Smith, 1979). In Hungary, private plots accounted for only 13 percent of the farmland but produced one-third of the output (Spivak, 1979). In China, where farmers are now allowed to sell food grown in excess of that owed to the state, food production increased 8 percent each year after 1978—$2^{1}/_{2}$ times the rate in the preceding 26 years (Church, 1986). In the early 1990s, long lines of frustrated people outside sparsely stocked state-run Russian food stores helped persuade government leaders to begin moving toward private ownership with profit incentives.

In North America, workers who do not pay dues or volunteer time to their union or professional association nevertheless are usually happy to accept its benefits. So, too, are public television viewers who don't respond to their station's fund drives. This hints at another possible explanation of social loafing. When rewards are divided equally, regardless of how much one contributes to the group, any individual gets more reward per unit of effort by free-riding on the group. So people may be motivated to slack off when their efforts are not individually monitored and rewarded.

In a pickle factory, for example, the key job is picking the right-size dill-pickle halves off the conveyor belt and stuffing them in jars. Unfortunately, workers are tempted to stuff any size pickle in, because their output is not identifiable (the jars go into a common hopper before reaching the quality control section). Williams, Harkins, and Latané (1981) note that research on social loafing suggests "making individual production identifiable, and raises the question: 'How many pickles could a pickle packer pack if pickle packers were only paid for properly packed pickles?'"

But surely collective effort does not always lead to slacking off. Sometimes the goal is so compelling and maximum output from everyone is so essential that team spirit maintains or intensifies effort. In an Olympic crew race, will the individual rowers in an eight-person crew pull their oars with less effort than those in a one- or two-person crew?

My hunch is that they will not. Experiments show that people in groups loaf less when the task is *challenging, appealing,* or *involving* (Brickner & others, 1986; Jackson & Williams, 1985). On challenging tasks, people may perceive their efforts as indispensable (Harkins & Petty, 1982; Kerr, 1983; Kerr & Bruun, 1983). When people see others in their group as unreliable or as unable to contribute much, they work harder (Vancouver & others, 1991; Williams & Karau, 1991). Adding incentives or challenging a group to strive for certain standards also promotes collective effort (Harkins & Szymanski, 1989; Shepperd & Wright, 1989).

Latané notes that Israel's communal kibbutz farms have actually outproduced Israel's noncollective farms (Leon, 1969), and Williams (1981) and Loren Davis and his associates (1984) report that groups of friends loaf much less than groups of strangers. Perhaps cohesiveness somehow intensifies effort. If so, will social loafing not occur in group-centered cultures? To find out, Latané and his coresearchers (Gabrenya & others, 1985) headed for Asia where they repeated their sound production experiments in Japan, Thailand, Taiwan, India, and Malaysia. Their findings? Social loafing was evident in all these countries too. In collectivist China, however, social loafing was notably absent (Early, 1989). And as we noted in a previous module, loyalty to family and work groups runs strong in collectivist cultures. In Japanese corporate culture, and within families of Asian immigrants, if less so in momentary laboratory groups, team spirit fuels achievement.

Some of these findings parallel those from studies of everyday work groups. When groups are given challenging objectives, when they are rewarded for group success, and when there is a spirit of commitment to the "team," group members work hard (Hackman, 1986). So, while social loafing is a common occurrence when group members work collectively and without individual accountability, many hands need not always make light work.

CONCEPTS TO REMEMBER

Social loafing   The tendency for people to exert less effort when they pool their efforts toward a common goal than when they are individually accountable.

Free riders   People who benefit from the group but give little in return.

Doing Together What We Would Never Do Alone

❖

I n 1991 an eyewitness videotaped four Los Angeles police officers hitting unarmed Rodney King more than 50 times—fracturing his skull in nine places with their nightsticks and leaving him brain damaged and missing teeth—while 23 other officers watched passively. Replays of the tape shocked the nation into a prolonged discussion of police brutality and group violence. People wondered: Where was the officers' humanity? What had happened to standards of professional conduct? What evil force could unleash such behavior?

DEINDIVIDUATION

Social-facilitation experiments show that groups can arouse people. Social-loafing experiments show that groups can diffuse responsibility. When arousal and diffused responsibility combine, normal inhibitions may diminish. The result may be acts ranging from a mild lessening of restraint (throwing food in the dining hall, snarling at a referee, screaming during a rock concert) to impulsive self-gratification (group vandalism, orgies, thefts) to destructive social explosions (police brutality, riots, lynchings). In a 1967 incident, 200 University of Oklahoma students gathered to watch a disturbed fellow student threatening to jump from a tower. They began to chant "Jump. Jump. . . ." The student jumped to his death (UPI, 1967).

These unrestrained behaviors have something in common: They are somehow provoked by the power of a group. Groups can provoke a sense of excitement, of being caught up in something bigger than the self. It is harder to imagine

From George Holliday 3 1991

The beating of defenseless Rodney King makes us wonder: How do group situations release people from normal restraints?

a single rock fan screaming deliriously at a private rock concert, a single Oklahoma student trying to coax someone to suicide, or even a single police officer beating a defenseless motorist. In certain kinds of group situations people are more likely to abandon normal restraints, to lose their sense of individual responsibility, to become what Leon Festinger, Albert Pepitone, and Theodore Newcomb (1952) labeled **deindividuated**. What circumstances elicit this psychological state?

Group Size

A group has the power not only to arouse its members but also to render them unidentifiable. The snarling crowd hides the snarling basketball fan. A lynch mob enables its members to believe they will not be prosecuted; they perceive the action as the *group's*. Rioters, made faceless by the mob, are freed to loot. In an analysis of 21 instances in which crowds were present as someone threatened to jump from a building or bridge, Leon Mann (1981) found that when the crowd was small and exposed by daylight, people usually did not try to bait the person. But when a large crowd or the cover of night gave people anonymity, the crowd usually baited and jeered. Brian Mullen (1986a) reports a similar effect of lynch mobs: The bigger the mob, the more its members lose self-awareness and become willing to commit atrocities, such as burning, lacerating, or dismembering the victim. In each of these examples, from sports crowds to lynch mobs, evaluation apprehension plummets. And because "everyone is doing it," all can attribute their behavior to the situation rather than to their own choices.

Philip Zimbardo (1970) speculated that the mere immensity of crowded cities produces anonymity and thus norms that permit vandalism. He purchased two 10-year-old cars and left them with the hoods up and license plates removed, one on a street near the old Bronx campus of New York University and one near the Stanford University campus in Palo Alto, a much smaller city. In New York the first auto strippers arrived within 10 minutes, taking the battery and radiator. After three days and 23 incidents of theft and vandalism (by neatly dressed White people), the car was reduced to a battered, useless hulk of metal. By contrast, the only person observed to touch the Palo Alto car in over a week was a passer-by who lowered the hood when it began to rain.

Physical Anonymity

How can we be sure that the crucial factor, among all the differences between the Bronx and Palo Alto, is greater anonymity in the Bronx? We can't. But we can experiment with anonymity to see if it actually lessens inhibitions. In one creative experiment, Zimbardo (1970) dressed New York University women in identical white coats and hoods, rather like Ku Klux Klan members (Figure 19–1). Asked to deliver electric shocks to a woman, they pressed the shock button twice as long as women who were visible and wearing large name tags.

A research team led by Ed Diener (1976) cleverly demonstrated the effect both of being in a group *and* of being physically anonymous. At Halloween, they observed 1352 Seattle children trick-or-treating. As the children, either alone or in groups, approached 1 of 27 homes scattered throughout the city, an experimenter greeted them warmly, invited them to "take *one* of the candies," and then left the room. Hidden observers noted that, compared to solo children, those in groups were more than twice as likely to take extra candy. Also, compared to children who had been asked their names and where they lived, those left anonymous were also more than twice as likely to transgress. The transgression rate thus varied dramatically with the situation. As Figure 19–2 shows, when group immersion was combined with anonymity, the deindividuated children usually stole extra candy.

These experiments make me wonder about the effect of wearing uniforms. Robert Watson (1973) scrutinized anthropological files and discovered that the cultures with depersonalized warriors (wearing masks or face paints) were also the cultures that tortured, killed, or

FIGURE 19–1
Anonymous, although obviously poised, women delivered more shock to help-less victims than did identifiable women.

FIGURE 19–2
Children were more likely to transgress by taking extra Halloween candy when trick-or-treating in a group, when anonymous, and, especially, when deindividuated by the combination of group immersion and anonymity.   (Data from Diener & others, 1976.)

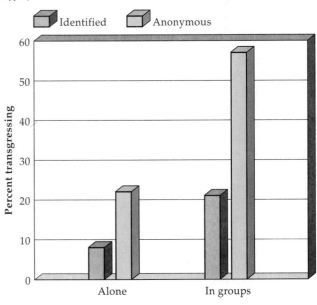

mutilated their enemies. The uniformed Los Angeles police officers who beat Rodney King were aroused by their apprehension of him, enjoying one another's camaraderie, and unaware that outsiders would view their actions. Thus, forgetting their normal standards, they were swept away by their worst impulses.

In William Golding's (1962) *Lord of the Flies*, a group of marooned boys gradually descend into savagery. One decent boy who could not kill a pig for food does so gleefully, and later kills a scorned peer, after painting his face and body. (Zimbardo tells me that reading this literary episode inspired his New York University deindividuation experiment.)

Does becoming physically anonymous *always* evoke our worst impulses? Fortunately, no. For one thing, the situations in which some of these experiments took place had clear antisocial cues. Robert Johnson and Leslie Downing (1979) point out that the Klan-like outfits worn by Zimbardo's subjects may have encouraged hostility. In an experiment at the University of Georgia, they had women put on nurses' uniforms before deciding how much shock someone should receive. When those wearing the nurses' uniforms were made anonymous, they became *less* aggressive in administering shock than when their names and personal identities were stressed. Evidently being anonymous makes one less self-conscious and more responsive to cues present in the situation, whether negative (Klan uniforms) or positive (nurses' uniforms). Given altruistic cues, deindividuated people even give more money (Spivey & Prentice-Dunn, 1990).

This helps explain why wearing black uniforms—which are traditionally associated with evil and death, as worn by medieval executioners, Darth Vader, and Ninja warriors—has an effect opposite to that of wearing a nurse's uniform. Mark Frank and Thomas Gilovich (1988) report that, led by the Los Angeles Raiders and the Philadelphia Flyers, black-uniformed teams consistently ranked near the top of the National Football and Hockey Leagues in penalties assessed between 1970 and 1986. Follow-up laboratory research suggests that just putting on a black jersey can trigger wearers to behave more aggressively.

Even if anonymity does unleash our impulses, as well as make us more responsive to social cues, we must remember that not all our impulses are sinister. Consider the heartwarming outcome of an experiment conducted by Swarthmore College researchers Kenneth Gergen, Mary Gergen, and William Barton (1973). Imagine that, as a subject in this experiment, you are ushered into a totally darkened chamber, where you spend the next hour (unless you choose to leave) with seven strangers of both sexes. You are told, "There are no rules as to what you should do together. At the end of the time period you will be escorted from the room alone, and will subsequently depart from the experimental site alone. There will be no opportunity to [formally] meet the other participants."

Control participants, who spent the hour in a lighted room with more conventional expectations, chose simply to sit and talk. By contrast, the

experience of being anonymous in the dark room with unclear expectations "unleashed" intimacy and affection. People in the dark talked less,
but they talked more about "important" things. Ninety percent purposefully touched someone; 50 percent hugged another. Few disliked the
anonymity; most deeply enjoyed it and volunteered to return without
pay. Anonymity had "freed up" intimacy and playfulness.

Arousing and Distracting Activities

Aggressive outbursts by large groups are often preceded by minor actions
that arouse and divert people's attention. Group shouting, chanting,
clapping, or dancing serve both to hype people up and to reduce self-
consciousness. One Moonie observer recalls how the "choo-choo" chant
helped deindividuate:

> All the brothers and sisters joined hands and chanted with increasing inten-
> sity, choo-choo-choo, Choo-choo-choo, CHOO-CHOO-CHOO! YEA! YEA!
> POWW!!! The act made us a group, as though in some strange way we had all
> experienced something important together. The power of the choo-choo
> frightened me, but it made me feel more comfortable and there was some-
> thing very relaxing about building up the energy and releasing it. (Zimbardo
> & others, 1977, p. 186)

In Golding's *Lord of the Flies*, the boys sometimes preceded savage acts
with group activities, such as dancing in a circle and chanting, *"Kill the
beast! Cut his throat! Spill his blood!"* In so doing, the group became "a single
organism" (p. 182).

Ed Diener's experiments (1976, 1979) have shown that such activities
as throwing rocks and group singing can set the stage for more disin-
hibited behavior. There is a self-reinforcing pleasure in doing an impulsive act while observing others doing it also. When we see others act as we
are acting, we think they feel as we do, and so feel reinforced in our own
feelings (Orive, 1984). Moreover, impulsive group action absorbs our
attention. When we yell at the referee, we are not thinking about our
values; we are reacting to the immediate situation. Later, when we stop to
think about what we have done or said, we sometimes feel chagrined.
Sometimes. At other times we seek deindividuating group experiences—
dances, worship experiences, group encounters—where we can enjoy
intense positive feelings and a sense of closeness with others.

DIMINISHED SELF-AWARENESS

Group experiences that diminish self-consciousness tend to disconnect
behavior from attitudes. Experiments by Ed Diener (1980) and Steven
Prentice-Dunn and Ronald Rogers (1980, 1989) reveal that unself-con-

scious, deindividuated people are less restrained, less self-regulated, more likely to act without thinking about their own values, more responsive to the situation. These findings complement and reinforce the experiments on *self-awareness*. Self-awareness is the other side of the coin from deindividuation. Those made self-aware, say by acting in front of a mirror or TV camera, exhibit *increased* self-control, and their actions more clearly reflect their attitudes. People made self-aware are less likely to cheat (Beaman & others, 1979; Diener & Wallbom, 1976). So are those who generally have a strong sense of themselves as distinct and independent (Nadler & others, 1982). People who are self-conscious, or who are made so, exhibit greater consistency between their words outside a situation and their deeds in it.

Circumstances that diminish self-awareness (as alcohol consumption does—Hull & others, 1983) therefore increase deindividuation. And deindividuation decreases in circumstances that increase self-awareness: mirrors and cameras, small towns, bright lights, large name tags, undistracted quiet, individual clothes and houses (Ickes & others, 1978). When a teenager leaves for a party, a parent's parting advice could well be: "Have fun, and remember who you are." In other words, enjoy the group, but be self-aware; don't become deindividuated.

CONCEPTS TO REMEMBER

Deindividuation   Loss of self-awareness and evaluation apprehension; occurs in group situations that foster anonymity and draw attention away from the individual.

20

How Groups Intensify Decisions

❖

W hich effects—good or bad—does group interaction more often have? Police brutality and mob violence demonstrate its destructive potential. Yet support-group leaders, management consultants, and educational theorists proclaim its benefits. And social and religious movements urge their members to strengthen their identities by fellowship with like-minded others.

Research helps clarify our understanding of such effects. From studies of people in small groups, a principle emerges that helps explain both destructive and constructive outcomes: Group discussion often strengthens members' initial inclinations, good or bad. The unfolding of this research on "group polarization" and "groupthink" illustrates the process of inquiry—how an interesting discovery often leads researchers to hasty and erroneous conclusions, which ultimately get replaced with more accurate conclusions. This is one scientific mystery I can discuss firsthand, having been one of the detectives.

*T*HE CASE OF THE RISKY SHIFT

A research literature of more than 300 studies began with a surprising finding by James Stoner (1961), then an MIT graduate student. For his master's thesis in industrial management, Stoner compared risk taking by individuals and groups. To test the commonly held belief that groups are more cautious than individuals, Stoner posed decision dilemmas faced by fictional characters. The participant's task was to advise the character about how much risk to take. Put yourself in the participant's shoes: What advice would you give the character in this situation?

> Helen is a writer who is said to have considerable creative talent but who so far has been earning a comfortable living by writing cheap westerns. Recently she has come up with an idea for a potentially significant novel. If it could be written and accepted, it might have considerable literary impact and be a big boost to her career. On the other hand, if she cannot work out her idea or if the novel is a flop, she will have expended considerable time and energy without remuneration.
>
> Imagine that you are advising Helen. Please check the *lowest* probability that you would consider acceptable for Helen to attempt to write the novel.
>
> Helen should attempt to write the novel if the chances that the novel will be a success are at least:
>
> _____ 1 in 10
> _____ 2 in 10
> _____ 3 in 10
> _____ 4 in 10
> _____ 5 in 10
> _____ 6 in 10
> _____ 7 in 10
> _____ 8 in 10
> _____ 9 in 10
> _____ 10 in 10 (Place a check here if you think Helen should attempt the novel only if it is certain that the novel will be a success.)

After making your decision, guess what this book's average reader would advise.

Having marked their advice on a dozen such items, five or so individuals would then discuss and reach agreement on each item. How do you think their group decisions compared to the average decision before the discussions? Would the groups be likely to take greater risks? become more cautious? stay the same?

To everyone's amazement, the group decisions were usually *riskier*. Dubbed the risky shift phenomenon, this finding set off a wave of investigation into group risk taking. The studies revealed that this effect occurs not only when a group decides by consensus; after a brief discussion, individuals, too, will alter their decisions. What is more, researchers successfully repeated Stoner's finding with people of varying ages and occupations in a dozen different nations.

Opinions did converge during discussion. Curiously, however, the point toward which they converged was usually a lower (riskier) number than their initial average. Here was a delightful puzzle. The small risky shift effect was reliable, unexpected, and without any immediately obvious explanation. What group influences produce such an effect? And

how widespread is the effect? Do discussions in juries, business committees, and military organizations also promote risk taking?

After several years of study and speculation about group risk taking,
we became aware that the risky shift was not universal. We could write
decision dilemmas on which people became more *cautious* after discussion. One of these featured "Roger," a young married man with two
school-age children and a secure but low-paying job. Roger can afford
life's necessities but few of its luxuries. He hears that the stock of a
relatively unknown company may soon triple in value if its new product
is favorably received or decline considerably if it does not sell. Roger has
no savings; so in order to invest in the company, he is considering selling
his life insurance policy.

Is there a general principle that will predict people's giving riskier
advice after discussing Helen's situation and more cautious advice after
discussing Roger's? Yes. If you are like most people, you would likely
advise Helen to take greater risk than Roger, even before talking with
others. It turns out that there is a strong tendency for discussion to
accentuate these initial leanings.

We therefore began to realize that this group phenomenon was not,
as originally assumed, a consistent shift to risk, but rather a tendency for
group discussion to *enhance* the individuals' initial leanings. This idea led
investigators to propose what Serge Moscovici and Marisa Zavalloni
(1969) termed a **group polarization** phenomenon: Discussion typically
strengthens the average inclination of group members.

DO GROUPS INTENSIFY OPINIONS?

Experiments on Group Polarization

This new view of the changes induced by group discussion prompted
experimenters to have people discuss statements that most of them
favored or most of them opposed. Would talking in groups enhance their
initial inclinations as it did with the decision dilemmas? That's what the
group polarization hypothesis predicts (Figure 20–1).

Dozens of studies confirm group polarization. Moscovici and
Zavalloni observed that discussion enhanced French students' initially
positive attitude toward their premier and negative attitude toward
Americans. Mititoshi Isozaki (1984) found that Japanese university students gave more pronounced judgments of "guilty" after discussing a
traffic case. And Glen Whyte (1992) reports that group decision making
exacerbates the "too much invested to quit" phenomenon that has cost
many businesses huge sums of money. Canadian business students
imagined themselves having to decide whether to invest more money in
the hope of preventing losses in various failing projects (for example,

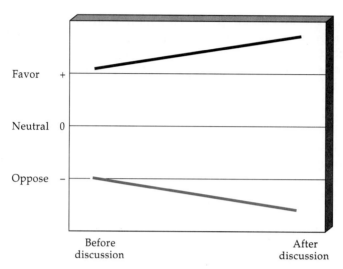

FIGURE 20–1

The group-polarization hypothesis predicts that discussion will strengthen an attitude shared by group members. If people initially tend to favor something (say, risk taking) they tend to favor it even more after discussion. If they tend to oppose risk, they tend to oppose it even more after discussion.

whether to make a high-risk loan to protect an earlier investment). They exhibited the typical effect: 72 percent reinvested money they would seldom have invested if they were considering the new investment on its own merits. When making the same decision as groups, 94 percent opted for reinvestment.

Another research strategy has been to pick issues on which opinions are divided and then isolate people who hold the same view. Does discussion with like-minded people strengthen shared views? Does it magnify the attitude gap that separates the two sides?

George Bishop and I wondered. So we set up groups of relatively prejudiced and unprejudiced high school students and asked them to respond—before and after discussion—to issues involving racial attitudes, such as property rights versus open housing (Myers & Bishop, 1970). We found that the discussions among like-minded students did indeed increase the initial gap between the two groups (Figure 20–2).

Naturally Occurring Group Polarization

In everyday life people associate mostly with others whose attitudes are similar to their own. (Look at your own circle of friends.) So, does

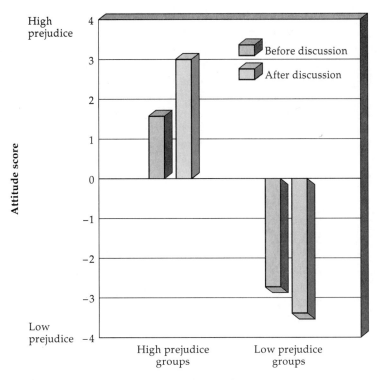

FIGURE 20–2
Group polarization. Talking over racial issues increased prejudice in groups of high-prejudice high school students, and decreased prejudice in low-prejudice groups.
(Data from Myers & Bishop, 1970.)

everyday group interaction with like-minded friends intensify shared attitudes? In natural situations it's hard to disentangle cause and effect. But the laboratory phenomenon does have real-life parallels.

One such parallel is what education researchers have called the "accentuation phenomenon": Over time, initial differences among college student groups become accentuated. If the students at college X are initially more intellectual than the students at college Y, that gap is likely to grow during college. Likewise, compared to fraternity and sorority members, independents tend to have more liberal political attitudes, a difference that grows with time in college (Pascarella & Terenzini, 1991). Researchers believe this results partly from group members reinforcing shared inclinations (Chickering & McCormick, 1973; Feldman & Newcomb 1969; Wilson & others, 1975).

Polarization also occurs in communities. During community conflicts, like-minded people increasingly associate with one another. This amplifies their shared tendencies. Gang delinquency emerges from a process of mutual reinforcement within neighborhood gangs whose members have a common socioeconomic and ethnic background (Cartwright, 1975). From their analysis of terrorist organizations around the world, Clark McCauley and Mary Segal (1987) note that terrorism does not erupt suddenly. Rather, it arises among people whose shared grievances bring them together. As they interact in isolation from moderating influences, they become progressively more extreme. The result is violent acts which the individuals, apart from the group, might never have contemplated.

EXPLAINING GROUP POLARIZATION

Why do groups adopt stances more exaggerated than the average opinions of their individual members? Researchers hoped that solving the mystery of group polarization might provide insights into social influence. Solving small puzzles sometimes provides clues for solving larger ones.

Among several proposed theories of group polarization, two survived scientific scrutiny. One deals with the arguments presented during a discussion; the other, with how members of a group view themselves vis-a-vis the other members. The first idea is an example of what Morton Deutsch and Harold Gerard (1955) called **informational influence** (influence that results from accepting evidence about reality). The second is an example of **normative influence** (influence based on a person's desire to be accepted or admired by others).

Informational Influence

According to the best-supported explanation, group discussion elicits a pooling of ideas, most of which favor the dominant viewpoint. These ideas may include persuasive arguments that some group members had not previously considered (Stasser, 1991). When discussing Helen the writer, someone may say, "Helen should go for it because she has little to lose: if her novel flops, she can always go back to writing cheap westerns." Such statements often entangle information about the person's *arguments* with cues concerning the person's *position* on the issue. But when people hear relevant arguments without learning the specific stands other people assume, they still shift their positions (Burnstein & Vinokur, 1977; Hinsz & Davis, 1984). *Arguments*, in and of themselves, matter.

Normative Influence

A second explanation of polarization involves comparison with others. As Leon Festinger (1954) argued in his influential theory of **social comparison**, it is human nature to want to evaluate our opinions and abilities, something we can do by comparing our views with others'. We are most persuaded by people in groups we identify with (Abrams & others, 1990; Hogg & others, 1990). Moreover, wanting people to like us, we may express stronger opinions after discovering that others share our views.

Perhaps you can recall a time when you and others were guarded and reserved in a group, until someone broke the ice and said, "Well, to be perfectly honest, I think . . ." Soon you were all surprised to discover strong support for your views. When people are asked (as you were earlier) to predict how others would respond to items, such as the "Helen" dilemma, they typically exhibit social ignorance: They don't realize how much others support the socially preferred tendency (in this case, writing the novel). A typical person will advise writing the novel even if its chance of success is only 4 in 10 but estimate that most other people would require 5 or 6 in 10. When the discussion begins, most people discover they are not outshining the others as they had supposed. In fact, some of the others are ahead of them, having taken an even stronger position for writing the novel. No longer restrained by a misperceived group norm, they are liberated to voice their preferences more strongly.

This social comparison theory prompted experiments that exposed people to others' positions without exposing them to others' arguments. This is roughly the experience we have when reading the results of an opinion poll. When people learn others' positions—without discussion —will they adjust their responses to maintain a socially favorable position? When people have not already made a prior commitment to a particular response, seeing others' responses does indeed stimulate a small polarization (Goethals & Zanna, 1979; Sanders & Baron, 1977). Polarization from mere social comparison is usually less than that produced by a lively discussion. Still, it's surprising that, instead of simply conforming to the group average, people often go it one better.

Group polarization research illustrates the complexity of social-psychological inquiry. Much as we like our explanations to be simple, one explanation of a phenomenon seldom accounts for all the data. Because people are complex, more than one factor frequently influences a phenomenon. In group discussions, persuasive arguments predominate on issues that have a factual element ("Is she guilty of the crime?"). Social comparison sways responses on value-laden judgments ("How long a sentence should she serve?") (Kaplan, 1989). On the many issues that have both factual and value-laden aspects, the two factors work together. Discovering that others share one's feelings (social comparison) unleashes arguments (informational influence) supporting what everyone secretly favors.

*G*ROUPTHINK

Do the social-psychological phenomena we have been considering in this book occur in sophisticated groups like corporate boards or the President's Cabinet? Is there likely to be self-justification? Self-serving bias? A cohesive "we feeling" provoking conformity and rejection of dissent? Public commitment producing resistance to change? Group polarization? Social psychologist Irving Janis (1971, 1982) wondered whether such phenomena might help explain good and bad group decisions made by recent American presidents and their advisers. To find out, he analyzed the decision-making procedures that led to several major fiascoes:

- *Pearl Harbor:* In the weeks preceding the December 1941 Pearl Harbor attack that put the United States into World War II, military commanders in Hawaii received a steady stream of information about Japan's preparations for attack on the United States— somewhere in the Pacific. Then military intelligence lost radio contact with Japanese aircraft carriers, which had begun moving straight for Hawaii. Air reconnaissance could have spotted the carriers or at least provided a few minutes' warning. But complacent commanders decided against such precautions. The result: No alert was sounded until the attack on virtually defenseless ships and airfields was under way.

- *The Bay of Pigs invasion:* In 1961 President John Kennedy and his advisers tried to overthrow Fidel Castro by invading Cuba with 1400 CIA-trained Cuban exiles. Nearly all the invaders were soon killed or captured, the United States was humiliated, and Cuba allied itself even closer to the U.S.S.R. "How could we have been so stupid?" Kennedy asked after learning the outcome.

- *The Vietnamese war:* From 1964 to 1967 President Lyndon Johnson and his "Tuesday lunch group" of policy advisers escalated the war in Vietnam on the assumption that U.S. aerial bombardment, defoliation, and search and destroy missions would bring North Vietnam to the peace table with the appreciative support of the South Vietnamese populace. They continued the escalation despite warnings from government intelligence experts and nearly all U.S. allies. The resulting disaster cost 46,500 American and more than 1 million Vietnamese lives, drove the President from office, and created huge budget deficits that helped fuel inflation in the 1970s.

Janis believes these blunders were bred by the tendency of decision-making groups to suppress dissent in the interests of group harmony, a phenomenon he calls **groupthink**. In work groups, a cohesive camaraderie boosts productivity (Evans & Dion, 1991). But when making decisions, close-knit groups may pay a price. The soil from which groupthink sprouts includes an amiable, *cohesive* group; relative *isolation* of the group from dissenting viewpoints; and a *directive leader* who signals what decision he or she favors. When planning the ill-fated Bay of Pigs invasion, the newly elected President Kennedy and his advisers enjoyed a strong esprit de corps. Arguments critical of the plan were suppressed or excluded, and the President himself soon endorsed the invasion.

Symptoms of Groupthink

From historical records and the memoirs of participants and observers, Janis identified eight groupthink symptoms. These symptoms are a collective form of dissonance reduction that surfaces as group members try to maintain their positive group feeling in the face of a threat (Turner & others, 1992). The first two symptoms lead group members to *overestimate their group's might and right*.

- *An illusion of invulnerability:* The groups Janis studied all developed an excessive optimism that blinded them to warnings of danger. Told that his forces had lost radio contact with the Japanese carriers, Admiral Kimmel, the chief naval officer at Pearl Harbor, joked that maybe they were about to round Honolulu's Diamond Head. Kimmel's laughing at the idea dismissed the very possibility of its being true.
- *Unquestioned belief in the group's morality:* Group members assume the inherent morality of their group and ignore ethical and moral issues. The Kennedy group knew that adviser Arthur Schlesinger, Jr., and Senator J. William Fullbright had moral reservations about invading a small neighboring country. But the group never entertained or discussed these moral qualms.

Group members also become *close-minded*:

- *Rationalization:* The groups discounted challenges by collectively justifying their decisions. President Johnson's Tuesday lunch group spent far more time rationalizing (explaining and justifying) than reflecting upon and rethinking prior decisions to escalate. Each initiative became an action to defend and justify.
- *Stereotyped view of opponent:* Participants in these groupthink tanks consider their enemies too evil to negotiate with or too weak and

unintelligent to defend themselves against the planned initiative. The Kennedy group convinced itself that Castro's military was so weak and his popular support so shallow that a single brigade could easily overturn his regime.

Finally, the group suffers from *pressures toward uniformity*:

- *Conformity pressure:* Group members rebuffed those who raised doubts about the group's assumption and plans, at times not by argument but by personal sarcasm. Once, when President Johnson's assistant Bill Moyers arrived at a meeting, the President derided him with, "Well, here comes Mr. Stop-the-Bombing." To avoid disapproval, most people fall into line when faced with such ridicule.

- *Self-censorship:* Since disagreements were often discomforting and the groups seemed in consensus, members withheld or discounted their misgivings. In the months following the Bay of Pigs invasion, Arthur Schlesinger (1965, p. 255) reproached himself "for having kept so silent during those crucial discussions in the Cabinet Room, though my feelings of guilt were tempered by the knowledge that a course of objection would have accomplished little save to gain me a name as a nuisance."

- *Illusion of unanimity:* Self-censorship and pressure not to puncture the consensus create an illusion of unanimity. What is more, the apparent consensus confirms the group's decision. This appearance of consensus was evident in the three fiascoes and in other fiascoes before and since. Albert Speer (1971), an adviser to Adolf Hitler, describes the atmosphere around Hitler as one where pressure to conform suppressed all deviation. The absence of dissent created an illusion of unanimity:

   In normal circumstances people who turn their backs on reality are soon set straight by the mockery and criticism of those around them, which makes them aware they have lost credibility. In the Third Reich there were no such correctives, especially for those who belonged to the upper stratum. On the contrary, every self-deception was multiplied as in a hall of distorting mirrors, becoming a repeatedly confirmed picture of a fantastical dream world which no longer bore any relationship to the grim outside world. In those mirrors I could see nothing but my own face reproduced many times over. No external factors disturbed the uniformity of hundreds of unchanging faces, all mine. (p. 379)

- *Mindguards:* Some members protect the group from information that would dispute the effectiveness or morality of its decisions. Before the Bay of Pigs invasion, Robert Kennedy took Schlesinger aside and told him, "Don't push it any further." Secretary of State Dean Rusk withheld diplomatic and intelligence experts' warnings against the invasion. They thus served as the President's "mind-guards," protecting him from disagreeable facts rather than physical harm.

Groupthink in Action

Groupthink symptoms cause several problems in making decisions, which involve a failure to seek and discuss contrary information and alternative possibilities (Figure 20-3). When a leader promotes an idea and when a group insulates itself from dissenting views, beware of groupthink (McCauley, 1989).

Groupthink was tragically evident in the decision process by which NASA decided to launch the space shuttle *Challenger* on its fateful mission in January 1986 (Esser & Lindoerfer, 1989). Engineers at Morton Thiokol, which makes the shuttle's rocket boosters, and at Rockwell International, which manufactures the orbiter, opposed the launch because of dangers posed to equipment by the subfreezing temperatures. The Thiokol engineers feared the cold would make the rubber seals between the rocket's four segments too brittle to contain the superhot gases. Several months before the doomed mission, the company's top expert had warned in a memo that it was a "jump ball" whether the seal would hold and that if it failed, "the result would be a catastrophe of the highest order" (Magnuson, 1986).

In a telephone discussion the night before the launch, the engineers argued their case with their uncertain managers and with NASA officials, who were eager to proceed with the already delayed launch. One Thiokol official later testified: "We got ourselves into the thought process that we

FIGURE 20-3
Theoretical analysis of groupthink.   (From Janis & Mann, 1977, p. 132.)

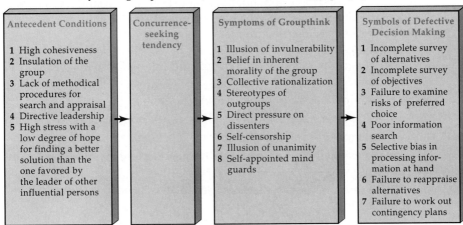

Antecedent Conditions	Concurrence-seeking tendency	Symptoms of Groupthink	Symbols of Defective Decision Making
1 High cohesiveness 2 Insulation of the group 3 Lack of methodical procedures for search and appraisal 4 Directive leadership 5 High stress with a low degree of hope for finding a better solution than the one favored by the leader of other influential persons		1 Illusion of invulnerability 2 Belief in inherent morality of the group 3 Collective rationalization 4 Stereotypes of outgroups 5 Direct pressure on dissenters 6 Self-censorship 7 Illusion of unanimity 8 Self-appointed mind guards	1 Incomplete survey of alternatives 2 Incomplete survey of objectives 3 Failure to examine risks of preferred choice 4 Poor information search 5 Selective bias in processing information at hand 6 Failure to reappraise alternatives 7 Failure to work out contingency plans

were trying to find some way to prove to them [the booster] wouldn't work. We couldn't prove absolutely that it wouldn't work." The result was an *illusion of invulnerability*.

Conformity pressures also operated. One NASA official complained, "My God, Thiokol, when do you want me to launch, next April?" The top Thiokol executive declared, "We have to make a management decision," and then asked his engineering vice president to "take off his engineering hat and put on his management hat."

To create an *illusion of unanimity*, this executive then proceeded to poll only the management officials and ignore the engineers. The go-ahead decision now made, one of the engineers belatedly pleaded with a NASA official to reconsider: "If anything happened to this launch," he said prophetically, "I sure wouldn't want to be the person that had to stand in front of a board of inquiry to explain why I launched."

Thanks, finally, to *mindguarding*, the top NASA executive who made the final decision never learned about the engineers' concerns, nor about the reservations of the Rockwell officials. Protected from disagreeable information, he confidently gave the go-ahead to launch the *Challenger* on its tragic flight.

Preventing Groupthink

Does this bleak analysis imply that group decision making is inherently defective? To pose the question with contradictory proverbs, do too many cooks always spoil the broth? Or are two or more heads sometimes better than one?

Janis also analyzed two highly successful group decisions: the Truman administration's formulation of the Marshall Plan for getting Europe back on its feet after World War II and the Kennedy administration's handling of the U.S.S.R.'s attempts to install missile bases in Cuba in 1962. Janis's (1982) recommendations for preventing groupthink incorporate many of the effective group procedures used by both the Marshall Plan and the missile-crisis groups:

- Tell group members about groupthink—its causes and consequences.
- Be impartial; do not endorse any position.
- Ask everyone to critically evaluate; encourage doubts.
- Assign someone the role of "devil's advocate."
- Occasionally form subgroups to meet separately and then air differences.
- After a preliminary decision, invite dissent at a "second-chance" meeting.

- Invite outside experts to evaluate the group's decision.
- Encourage members to share group deliberations and seek feedback from trusted others.

When such steps are taken, group decisions may take longer yet ultimately prove less defective and more effective.

CONCEPTS TO REMEMBER

Group polarization Group-produced enhancement of members' preexisting tendencies; a strengthening of the members' *average* tendency, not a split within the group.

Informational influence Influence that results from accepting evidence about reality provided by other people.

Normative influence Conformity based on a person's desire to fulfill others' expectations or to gain acceptance.

Social comparison Evaluating one's opinions and abilities by comparing oneself to others.

Groupthink "The mode of thinking that persons engage in when concurrence-seeking becomes so dominant in a cohesive ingroup that it tends to override realistic appraisal of alternative courses of action" (Janis, 1971).

21

Power to the Person

❖

"There are trivial truths and great truths," declared the physicist Niels Bohr. "The opposite of a trivial truth is plainly false. The opposite of a great truth is also true." The modules in this unit on social influence teach a great truth: the power of the social situation. This great truth about the power of external pressures would sufficiently explain our behavior if we were passive, like tumbleweed. But unlike tumbleweed, we are not just blown here and there by the environment. We act; we react. We respond, and we get responses. We can resist the social situation and sometimes even change it. Let us therefore conclude by affirming the power of the person.

Perhaps these modules on the power of social influences have at times made you uncomfortable. Most of us resent any suggestion that external forces determine our behavior; we see ourselves as free beings, as the originators of our actions (well, at least of our good actions). We sense that believing in social determinism might lead to what philosopher Jean-Paul Sartre called "bad faith"— evading responsibility by blaming something or someone for one's fate.

Actually, social control (the power of the situation) and personal control (the power of the person) no more compete with one another than do biological and cultural explanations. Social and personal explanations of our social behavior are both valid, for at any moment we are both the creatures and the creators of our social worlds. We may well be the products of our genes and environment. But it is also true that the future is coming, and it is our job to decide where it is going. Our choices today determine our environment tomorrow.

INTERACTING PERSONS AND SITUATIONS

Social situations do profoundly influence individuals. But individuals also influence the social situation. The two *interact*. Asking whether external situations or inner dispositions determine behavior is like asking whether length or width determines the area of a field.

The interaction occurs in at least three ways (Snyder & Ickes, 1985). First, a given social situation often affects different people differently. Because our minds do not see reality identically, we each respond to a situation as we construe it. And some people are more sensitive and responsive to social situations than others (M. Snyder, 1983). The Japanese, for example, are more responsive to social expectations than the British (Argyle & others, 1978).

Second, interaction between persons and situations also occurs because people can choose to be part of a particular situation (Ickes & others, 1990). Given a choice, sociable people elect situations that evoke social interaction. When you chose your college, you were also choosing to expose yourself to a specific set of social influences. Liberal political activists are unlikely to settle in Orange County, California, join the Chamber of Commerce, or read *U.S. News and World Report*. They are more likely to live in San Francisco, join a civil rights organization, and read the *New Republic*—in other words, to choose a social world that reinforces their inclinations.

Third, people often create their situations. Recall again that our preconceptions can be self-fulfilling: If we expect someone to be extraverted, hostile, feminine, or sexy, our actions toward the person may induce the very behavior we expect. Moreover, what composes a social situation but the people in it? A liberal political environment is one created by political liberals. What takes place at the Elks Club bar is created by the patrons. The social environment is not like the weather—something that just happens to us. It is more like our homes—something we make for ourselves.

This reciprocal causation between situations and persons allows us to see people as either *reacting to* or *acting upon* their environment. Each perspective is correct, for we are both the products and the architects of our social worlds. Is one perspective wiser? In one sense, it is wise to see ourselves as the products of our environments (lest we become too proud of our achievements and blame ourselves too much for our problems), and to see others as free actors (lest we become paternalistic and manipulative).

However, perhaps we would do well more often to assume the reverse—to view ourselves as free agents and to view others as influenced by their environments. We would then assume self-efficacy as we view ourselves and seek understanding and social reform as we relate to others. (If we view others as influenced by their situations, we are more likely to understand and empathize and less likely to judge negative behavior as freely chosen by "immoral," "sadistic," or "lazy" persons.) Most religions encourage us to take responsibility for ourselves but to refrain from judging others. Does religion teach this because our natural inclination is to excuse our own failures while blaming others for theirs?

RESISTING SOCIAL PRESSURE

Social psychology offers other reminders of the power of the person. We are not just billiard balls. Knowing that someone is trying to coerce us may actually prompt us to react in the *opposite* direction.

Reactance

Individuals value their sense of freedom and self-efficacy (Baer & others, 1980). So when social pressure becomes so blatant that it threatens their sense of freedom, they often rebel. Think of Romeo and Juliet, whose love was intensified by their families' opposition. Or think of children asserting their freedom and independence by doing the opposite of what their parents ask. Savvy parents therefore offer their children choices instead of commands: "It's time to clean up: Do you want a bath or a shower?"

Experiments reveal psychological **reactance**—people's acting to protect their sense of freedom—by showing that attempts to restrict a person's freedom often produce a "boomerang effect" (Brehm & Brehm, 1981). Suppose someone stops you on the street and asks you to sign a petition that advocates something you mildly support. While considering the petition, you are told that someone else believes "people absolutely should not be allowed to distribute or sign such petitions." Reactance theory predicts that such blatant attempts to limit freedom will actually increase the likelihood of your signing. When Madeline Heilman (1976) staged this experiment on the streets of New York City, that is precisely what she found. Clinical psychologists sometimes use the reactance principle by ordering resistant clients to enact the to-be-eliminated behavior (Brehm & Smith, 1986; Seltzer, 1983). By resisting the therapist, the clients get better.

Reactance may also contribute to underage drinking. In the United States, where alcohol sales are illegal to persons under age 21, a survey of 3375 students on a cross section of 56 campuses revealed a 25 percent rate of abstinence among students of legal drinking age, but only a 19 percent abstinence rate among students under 21. The researchers, Ruth Engs and David Hanson (1989), also found that 15 percent of the legal-age students and 24 percent of the underage students were heavy drinkers. They suspect this reflects a reactance against the restriction. It probably also reflects peer influence. With alcohol use, as with drugs, peers influence attitudes, provide the substance, and provide a context for its use. This helps explain why college students, living in a peer culture that often supports alcohol use, drink more alcohol than their noncollege peers (Atwell, 1986).

Reactance can escalate into social rebellion. Like obedience, rebellion can be produced and observed in experiments. William Gamson, Bruce Fireman, and Steven Rytina (1982) posed as members of a commercial research firm. They recruited people from towns near the University of Michigan to come to a hotel conference room for "a group discussion of community standards." Once there, the people learned that the discussions were to be videotaped on behalf of a large oil company seeking to win a legal case against a local station manager who had spoken out against high gas prices. In the first discussion, virtually everyone sided with the station manager. Hoping to convince the court that people in the local community were on its side, the "company representative" then began to tell more and more group members to defend the company. In the end, he told everyone to attack the station manager and asked them to sign an affidavit giving the company permission to edit the tapes and use them in court. By leaving the room from time to time, the experimenter gave the group members repeated opportunities to interpret and react to the injustice.

Most rebelled, objecting to and resisting the demand that they misrepresent their opinions to help the oil company. Some groups even mobilized themselves to stop the whole effort. They made plans to go to a newspaper, the Better Business Bureau, a lawyer, or the court.

By brewing small social rebellions, the researchers saw how a revolt is born. They found that successful resistance often begins very quickly. The more a group complies with unjust demands, the more trouble it later has breaking free. And someone must be willing to seed the process by expressing the reservations the others are feeling.

These demonstrations of reactance reassure us that people are not puppets. Sociologist Peter Berger (1963) expressed the point vividly:

> We see the puppets dancing in their miniature stage, moving up and down as the strings pull them around, following the prescribed course of their various little parts. We learn to understand the logic of this theater and we find ourselves in its motions. We locate ourselves in society and thus recognize our own position as we hang from its subtle strings. For a moment we see ourselves as puppets indeed. But then we grasp a decisive difference between the puppet theater and our own drama. Unlike the puppets, we have the possibility of stopping in our movements, looking up and perceiving the machinery by which we have been moved. In this act lies the first step towards freedom. (p. 176)

Asserting Uniqueness

Imagine a world of complete conformity where there were no differences among people. Would such a world be a happy place? If nonconformity can create discomfort, can sameness create comfort?

People feel uncomfortable when they appear too different from others. But, at least in western cultures, they also feel uncomfortable when they appear exactly like everyone else. As experiments by C. R. Snyder and Howard Fromkin (1980; see also Duval, 1976) have shown, people feel better when they see themselves as unique. Moreover, they act in ways that will assert their individuality. In one experiment, Snyder (1980) led Purdue University students to believe that their "10 most important attitudes" were either distinct from or nearly identical with the attitudes of 10,000 other students. When they then participated in a conformity experiment, those deprived of their feeling of uniqueness were most likely to assert their individuality by nonconformity. In another experiment, people who heard others express attitudes identical with their own altered their positions to maintain their sense of uniqueness.

Seeing oneself as unique also appears in people's "spontaneous self-concepts." William McGuire and his Yale University colleagues (McGuire & Padawer-Singer, 1978; McGuire & others, 1979) report that when children are invited to "tell us about yourself," they are most likely to mention their distinctive attributes. Foreign-born children are more likely than others to mention their birthplace. Redheads are more likely than black- and brown-haired children to volunteer their hair color. Light and heavy children are the most likely to refer to their body weight. Minority children are the most likely to mention their race. Likewise we become more keenly aware of our gender when we are with people of the other sex (Cota & Dion, 1986).

The principle, says McGuire, is that "one is conscious of oneself insofar as, and in the ways that, one is different." Thus, "If I am a Black woman in a group of White women, I tend to think of myself as a Black; if I move to a group of Black men, my blackness loses salience and I become more conscious of being a woman" (McGuire & others, 1978). This insight helps us understand why any minority group tends to be conscious of its distinctiveness and how the surrounding culture relates to it. The majority group, being less conscious of race, may see the minority group as "hypersensitive."

So it seems that while we do not like being greatly deviant, we are, ironically, all alike in wanting to feel distinctive and noticing how we are distinctive. But as research on self-serving bias makes clear, it is not just any kind of distinctiveness we seek, but distinctiveness in the right direction. Our quest is not merely to be different from the average, but *better* than average.

MINORITY INFLUENCE

We have seen that while cultural situations mold us, we also help create and choose these situations; that while pressures to conform sometimes overwhelm our better judgment, blatant pressure can motivate us to assert our individuality and freedom; and that while persuasive forces are indeed powerful, we can resist persuasion by making public commitments and by anticipating persuasive appeals. Consider, finally, how individuals can influence their groups.

At the beginning of most social movements, a small minority will sometimes sway, and then even become, the majority. "All history," wrote Ralph Waldo Emerson, "is a record of the power of minorities, and of minorities of one." Think of Copernicus and Galileo, of Martin Luther, of the suffragettes. Technological history is also made by innovative minorities. As Robert Fulton developed his steamboat—"Fulton's Folly"—he endured constant derision: "Never did a single encouraging remark, a bright hope, a warm wish, cross my path" (Cantril & Bumstead, 1960).

What makes a minority persuasive? Experiments initiated by Serge Moscovici in Paris have identified several determinants of minority influence: consistency, self-confidence, defection.

Consistency

More influential than a minority that wavers is a minority that unswervingly sticks to its position. Moscovici and his associates (1969, 1985) have found that if a minority consistently judges blue slides as green, members of the majority will occasionally agree. But if the minority wavers, saying "blue" to one-third of the blue slides and "green" to the rest, virtually no one in the majority will ever agree with "green."

Still debated is the nature of this influence (Clark & Maass, 1990; Levine & Russo, 1987). Moscovici believes that a minority's following the majority usually reflects mere public compliance, but a majority's following a minority usually reflects genuine acceptance—really recalling the blue slide as greenish. A minority influences us by making us think more deeply; a majority can also influence by intimidating us or by giving us a rule of thumb for deciding truth ("All those smart cookies can't be wrong") (Burnstein & Kitayama, 1989; Mackie, 1987). Minority influence is therefore more likely to take the thought-filled central route to persuasion.

Experiments show—and experience confirms—that nonconformity, especially persistent nonconformity, is often painful (Levine, 1989). If you set out to be Emerson's minority of one, prepare yourself for ridicule—especially when you argue an issue that's personally relevant to the majority and when the group is wanting to settle an issue (Kruglanski & Webster, 1991; Trost & others, 1992). People may attribute your dissent to psychological peculiarities, such as your presumed dogmatism (Papastamou & Mugny, 1990). When Charlan Nemeth (1979) planted a minority of two within a simulated jury and had them oppose the majority's opinions, the duo was inevitably disliked. Nevertheless, the majority acknowledged that the persistence of the two did more than anything else to make them rethink their positions. In so doing, a minority may stimulate creative thinking on problem-solving tasks (Mucchi-Faina & others, 1991; Nemeth, 1992). With dissent from within one's own group, people take in more information, think about it in new ways, and often make better decisions. Believing that one need not win friends to influence people, Nemeth quotes Oscar Wilde: "We dislike arguments of any kind; they are always vulgar, and often convincing."

A persistent minority is influential, even if not popular, partly because it soon becomes the focus of debate (Schachter, 1951). Being the center of conversation allows one to contribute a disproportionate number of arguments. And Nemeth reports that in experiments on minority influence, as in the studies dealing with group polarization, the position supported by the most arguments usually wins. Talkative group members are usually influential (Mullen & others, 1989).

Self-Confidence

Consistency and persistence convey self-confidence. Furthermore, Nemeth and Joel Wachtler (1974) reported that any behavior by a minority that conveys self-confidence—for example, taking the head seat at the table—tends to raise self-doubts among the majority. By being firm and forceful, the minority's apparent self-assurance may prompt the majority to reconsider its position.

Defections from the Majority

A persistent minority punctures any illusion of unanimity. When a minority consistently doubts the majority wisdom, members of the majority who might otherwise have self-censored their own doubts feel freer to express them and may even switch to the minority position. In research with University of Pittsburgh students, John Levine (1980) found that a minority person who had defected from the majority was more persuasive than a consistent minority voice. In her jury-simulation experiments, Nemeth found that once defections begin, others often soon follow, initiating a snowball effect. As President Carter slipped in the polls in the months preceding the 1980 election, some of his former supporters began to yearn for another alternative and called for an "open" Democratic National Convention. Speculating from the experiments, we might surmise that observing these defections aroused doubts among the President's remaining supporters.

Are these factors that strengthen minority influence unique to minorities? Sharon Wolf and Bibb Latané (1985; Wolf, 1987) believe not. They argue that the same social forces work for both majorities and minorities. If consistency, self-confidence, and defections from the other side strengthen the minority, such variables strengthen a majority also. The social impact of any position—whether held by a majority or a minority—depends on the strength, immediacy, and number of those who support it. Minorities have less influence than majorities simply because they are smaller.

However, Anne Maass and Russell Clark (1984, 1986) agree with Moscovici that minorities are more likely to convert people to *accepting* their views. Nemeth (1986) also believes that the stress of being in the minority differs from the more relaxed reflection of the majority. And from their analyses of how groups evolve over time, John Levine and Richard Moreland (1985) conclude that new recruits to a group exert a different type of minority influence than longtime members. Newcomers exert influence through the attention they receive and the group awareness they trigger in the old-timers. Established members feel freer to dissent and to exert leadership.

There is a delightful irony in this new emphasis on how individuals can influence the group. Until recently, the idea that the minority could sway the majority was itself a minority view in social psychology. Nevertheless, by arguing consistently and forcefully, Moscovici, Nemeth, and others have convinced the majority of group influence researchers that minority influence is a phenomenon worthy of study.

*I*S LEADERSHIP MINORITY INFLUENCE?

One example of the power of the person is **leadership**, the process by which certain individuals mobilize and guide groups. Some leaders are formally appointed or elected; others emerge informally as the group interacts. What makes for good leadership often depends on the situation—the best person to lead the engineering team may not make the best leader of the sales force. Some people excel at *task leadership*—at organizing work, setting standards, and focusing on goal attainment. Others excel at *social leadership*—at building teamwork, mediating conflicts, and being supportive.

Task leaders often have a directive style—one that can work well if the leader is bright enough to give good orders (Fiedler, 1987). Being goal-oriented, such leaders also keep the group's attention and effort focused on its mission. Experiments show that the combination of specific, challenging goals and periodic progress reports helps motivate high achievement (Locke & Latham, 1990).

Social leaders often have a democratic style—one that delegates authority and welcomes input from team members. Many experiments reveal that such leadership is good for morale. Group members usually feel more satisfied when they participate in making decisions (Spector, 1986; Vanderslice & others, 1987). Given control over their tasks, workers also become more motivated to achieve (Burger, 1987). People who value good group feeling and take pride in achievement therefore thrive under democratic leadership.

Democratic leadership can be seen in the move by many businesses toward "participative management," a management style common in Sweden and Japan (Naylor, 1990; Sundstrom & others, 1990). Ironically, a major influence on this "Japanese-style" management was MIT social psychologist Kurt Lewin. In laboratory and factory experiments, Lewin and his students demonstrated the benefits of inviting workers to participate in decision making. Shortly before World War II, Lewin visited Japan and explained his findings to industrial and academic leaders (Nisbett & Ross, 1991). Japan's collectivist culture provided a receptive audience for Lewin's group-centered ideas about teamwork. Eventually, his influence circled back to North America.

The once-popular "great person" theory of leadership—that all great leaders share certain traits—has fallen into disrepute. Effective leadership styles, we now know, vary with the situations. Recently, however, social psychologists have again wondered if there might be qualities that mark a good leader in many situations (Mumford, 1986). British social psychologists Peter Smith and Monir Tayeb (1989) report that studies done in India, Taiwan, and Iran have found that the most effective supervisors in coal mines, banks, and government offices score high on tests of *both* task and social leadership. They are sensitive to the needs of their subordinates *and* actively concerned for how work is progressing.

Studies also reveal that many effective leaders of laboratory groups, work teams, and large corporations exhibit the behaviors known to enable minority influence. They engender trust by consistently sticking to their goals. And they often exude a self-confident charisma that kindles the allegiance of their followers (Bennis, 1984; House & Singh, 1987). Charismatic leaders typically have a compelling *vision* of some desired state of affairs, an ability to *communicate* this to others in clear and simple language, and enough optimism and faith in their group to *inspire* others to follow.

To be sure, groups also influence their leaders. Sometimes those at the front of the herd have simply sensed where it is already heading. Political candidates know how to read the opinion polls. A leader who deviates too radically from the group's standards may be rejected. Smart leaders usually remain with the majority and spend their influence prudently. Nevertheless, effective individual leaders exhibit minority influence by energizing and guiding their group's majority.

CONCEPTS TO REMEMBER

Reactance   A motive to protect or restore one's sense of freedom. Reactance arises when someone threatens our freedom of action.

Leadership   The process by which certain group members motivate and guide the group. Task leaders organize work, set standards, and focus on goals. Social leaders build teamwork, mediate conflicts, and offer support.

Social Relations

The Dislike of Diversity

❖

P rejudice comes in many forms—prejudices against "northeastern liberals" or "southern rednecks," against Arab "terrorists" or Christian "fundamentalists," against people who are short, or fat, or homely. Consider a few actual occurrences:

> In 1961 Charlayne Hunter, now PBS newscaster Charlayne Hunter-Gault, needed a federal judge to compel the University of Georgia to admit her (as an African-American). A week after she enrolled, state officials asked the court whether they also were compelled to allow her to eat on campus (Menand, 1991).

> A group of homosexual students at the University of Illinois announced that the motto for one spring day would be: "If you are gay, wear blue jeans today." When the day dawned, many students who usually wore jeans woke up with an urge to dress up in a skirt or slacks. The gay group had made its point—that attitudes toward homosexuals are such that many would rather give up their usual clothes lest anyone suspect (RCAgenda, 1979).

> Prejudice against girls and women is sometimes subtle, sometimes devastating. Nowhere in the modern world are female infants left on a hillside to die of exposure, as was the occasional practice in ancient Greece. Yet in many developing countries, girls' death rates exceed boys'. During the 1976–1977 Bangladesh famine, preschool girls were more malnourished than boys (Bairagi, 1987). In South Korea, where would-be parents often test to learn the sex of their fetus, male births exceed female births by 14 percent. Under China's one-child policy, unmarried males now greatly exceed the number of unmarried females (Time, 1990).

Yoshio, one of a group of Japanese university students visiting my college, matter-of-factly reveals to his Japanese peers that he is a Burakumin, one of Japan's "ghetto people" whose ancestors had an occupation regarded as polluting. Their response: Hands come to the mouth and brows furrow, revealing their shock and astonishment. Though physically indistinguishable from other Japanese, the Burakumin have for generations been segregated in Japan's slums, considered eligible only for the most menial occupations and unfit for intermarriage with other Japanese. So, how could this obviously bright, attractive, ambitious student be a Burakumin?

WHAT IS PREJUDICE?

Prejudice, stereotyping, discrimination, racism, sexism—the terms often overlap. Before seeking to understand prejudice, let's clarify the terms. Each of the situations just described involved a negative evaluation of some group. And that is the essence of **prejudice**: an unjustifiable negative attitude toward a group and its individual members. Prejudice is *prejudgment*; it biases us against a person based solely on our identifying the person with a particular group.

Prejudice is an attitude. An attitude is a distinct combination of feelings, inclinations to act, and beliefs. This combination is the ABC of attitudes: *a*ffect (feelings), *b*ehavior tendency (inclination to act), and *c*ognition (beliefs). A prejudiced person might *dislike* the Burakumin and *behave* in a discriminatory manner, *believing* them ignorant and dangerous.

The negative evaluations that mark prejudice can stem from emotional associations, from the need to justify behavior, or from negative beliefs, called **stereotypes** (Stroebe & Insko, 1989; Zanna & others, 1990). To stereotype is to generalize. To simplify the world, we generalize all the time: The British are reserved; Americans are outgoing. Professors are absentminded. Women who assume the title of "Ms." are more assertive and ambitious than those who call themselves "Miss" or "Mrs." (Dion, 1987; Dion & Cota, 1991; Dion & Schuller, 1991). Such generalizations can have a germ of truth. People do in fact differ.

The problem with stereotypes arises when they are *overgeneralized* or just plain wrong. Pretend you told me I was about to meet Mike, an avid organic gardener. I might form an image of someone in bib overalls sporting a neatly trimmed beard and driving a van displaying a "Ban Handguns" bumper sticker. Certainly I would not expect someone to pull up in a Cadillac and emerge wearing a three-piece blue suit with a National Rifle Association lapel button. My stereotype of organic gardeners may contain a kernel of truth, just as people's beliefs about the employment rates, crime rates, and single-parent birthrates of different racial groups sometimes mirror actual census statistics (McCauley & Stitt, 1978). Yet my stereotype is likely an overgeneralization. There may be some conservatively dressed, Cadillac-driving organic gardeners. But were I to meet one, I might shrug it off by telling myself, "Every rule has its exceptions."

Prejudice is a negative *attitude*; **discrimination** is negative *behavior.* Discriminatory behavior often, but not always, has its source in prejudicial attitudes. As an earlier module emphasized, attitudes and behavior are often loosely linked, partly because our behavior reflects more than our inner convictions. Prejudiced attitudes need not breed hostile acts, nor does all oppression spring from prejudice. **Racism** and **sexism** are institutional practices that discriminate, even when there is no prejudicial intent.

Imagine a state police force that set a height requirement of 5 feet, 10 inches for all its officers. If this requirement were irrelevant to on-the-job effectiveness and tended to exclude Hispanics, Asians, and women, someone might label the requirement racist and sexist. Note that we could make this allegation even if no one intended discrimination. Similarly, if word-of-mouth hiring practices in an all-White business have the effect of excluding non-White employees, the practice could be called racist—even if the open-minded employer intended no discrimination. Racist and sexist policies need not involve prejudiced attitudes.

HOW PERVASIVE IS PREJUDICE?

Is prejudice inevitable? Can we eradicate it? As a case example, let's look at racial and gender prejudice in a heavily studied country, the United States.

Racial Prejudice

In the context of the world, every race is a minority. Non-Hispanic Whites, for example, are but one-fifth of the world's people and will be but one-eighth within another half century. Thanks to mobility and migration during the past two centuries, the world's races now intermingle, with relations that are sometimes hostile, sometimes amiable.

Is Racial Prejudice Becoming Extinct?

To judge from what Americans tell survey takers, racial prejudice toward African-Americans has plummeted since the early 1940s. In 1942, most Americans agreed, "There should be separate sections for Negroes on streetcars and buses" (Hyman & Sheatsley, 1956); today, the question would seem bizarre. In 1942, fewer than a third of all Whites (only 1 in 50 in the south) supported school integration; by 1980, support for it was 90 percent. Considering what a thin slice of history is covered by the years since 1942, or even since slavery was practiced, the changes are dramatic.

African-Americans' attitudes also have changed since the 1940s, when Kenneth Clark and Mamie Clark (1947) demonstrated that many held anti-Black prejudices. In making its historic 1954 decision declaring segregated schools unconstitutional, the Supreme Court found it noteworthy that when the Clarks gave African-American children a choice between Black dolls and White dolls, most chose the White. In studies from the 1950s through the 1970s, Black children were increasingly likely to prefer Black dolls. And adult Blacks came to view Blacks and Whites as similar in traits such as intelligence, laziness, and dependability (Jackman & Senter, 1981; Smedley & Bayton, 1978).

So, shall we conclude that racial prejudice is extinct in the United States? No. Although no longer fashionable, racial prejudice still exists, surfacing when a person thinks it is safe to express it.

Prejudice appears in the residue of White Americans who, as Figure 22–1 shows, openly dislike African-Americans. During the late 1980s and into the 1990s, "hate crimes"—slurs, vandalism, physical violence—victimized a growing number of African-Americans and gay men and lesbians (Goleman, 1990; Herek, 1990; Levine, 1990). In other cultures, open ethnic hostilities are common, as Israel's Palestinians and Jews, Northern Ireland's Protestants and Catholics, and Serbs and Croatians in the former Yugoslavia know well.

Questions concerning intimate interracial contacts still detect prejudice. "I would probably feel uncomfortable dancing with a Black person in a public place," detects more racial feeling than, "I would probably feel uncomfortable riding a bus with a Black person." In one survey, only 3 percent of the Whites said they wouldn't want their child to attend an integrated school, but 57 percent acknowledged they would be unhappy if their child *married* a Black person (*Life*, 1988). This phenomenon of *greatest prejudice in the most intimate social realms* seems universal. In India, people who accept the prejudices of the caste system typically allow someone from a lower caste into their home but would not consider marrying such a person (Sharma, 1981).

Subtle Forms of Prejudice

Much prejudice remains hidden, until evoked by circumstance. When White students indicate racial attitudes, they typically deny prejudice—unless hooked up to a supposed lie detector (Jones & Sigall, 1971). Other researchers have invited people to evaluate someone's behavior, that someone being either White or Black. Birt Duncan (1976) had White students at the University of California, Irvine, observe a videotape of one man lightly shoving another during a brief argument. When a White

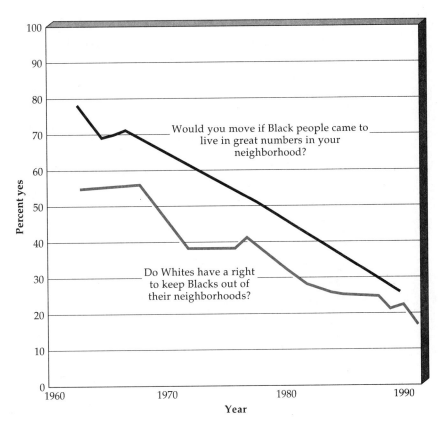

FIGURE 22-1
Expressed racial attitudes of White Americans from 1963 to 1990.   (Data from
Gallup & Hugick, 1990; Niemi & others, 1989; Smith, 1990.)

shoved a Black man, only 13 percent of the observers rated the act as
"violent behavior." Rather, they interpreted the shove as "playing
around" or "dramatizing." Not so when a Black shoved a White man:
Then, 73 percent said the act was "violent."

Many experiments have assessed people's *behavior* toward Blacks and
Whites (Gaertner & Dovidio, 1977, 1986). Whites are equally helpful to
any person in need—except when the needy person is remote (say, a
wrong-number caller with a Black accent who needs a message relayed).
Likewise, when asked to use electric shocks to "teach" a task, White
people give no more (if anything less) shock to a Black than a White
person—except when they are angered or when the recipient can't retaliate or know who did it (Crosby & others, 1980; Rogers & Prentice-Dunn,
1981) (Figure 22-2). Thus, discriminatory behavior surfaces not when a
behavior would *look* prejudicial but when it can hide behind the screen of
some other motive.

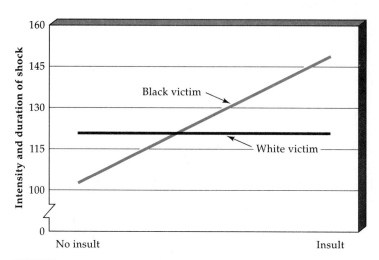

FIGURE 22-2

Does anger trigger latent prejudice? When White students administered electric shock, supposedly as part of a "behavior-modification experiment," they behaved less aggressively toward an agreeable Black victim than toward a White victim. But when the victim insulted the subjects, they responded with more aggression if the victim was Black.   (Data from Rogers & Prentice-Dunn, 1981.)

As blatant prejudice subsides, automatic, emotional reactions linger. Patricia Devine and her colleagues (1989, 1991) report that those low and high in prejudice often have similar automatic reactions. They differ because the low-prejudice person consciously suppresses prejudicial thoughts and feelings. It's like consciously breaking a bad habit, says Devine. Thomas Pettigrew (1987, p. 20) illustrates: "Many [people] have confessed to me . . . that even though in their minds they no longer feel prejudice toward Blacks, they still feel squeamish when they shake hands with a Black. These feelings are left over from what they learned in their families as children." Thus prejudice operates partly as an unconscious emotional response (Greenwald, 1990). As in the experiments with the shoves, shocks, and wrong phone numbers, unconscious prejudice appears mostly when people react to someone for the first time, with their conscious attention focused on something other than the person's race.

To summarize, there is good news: During the past four decades, open prejudice against Black Americans has nearly vanished. White racial attitudes are far more egalitarian than a generation ago. The bad news pertains to all people of color, including Native Americans and Hispanics (Ramirez, 1988; Trimble, 1988): Though now camouflaged by a more pleasant exterior, resentments and partiality still lurk beneath the surface. And what is true in the United States is true everywhere: In a world still torn by ethnic tensions, old hatreds die slowly.

Prejudice against Women

How pervasive is prejudice against women? In an earlier module, we examined gender-role norms—people's ideas about how women and men *ought* to behave. Here we first consider gender *stereotypes*—people's beliefs about how women and men *do* behave.

Gender Stereotypes

From research on stereotypes, two conclusions are indisputable: Strong gender stereotypes exist, and, as often happens, members of the stereotyped group accept the stereotypes. Men and women agree that you *can* judge the book by its sexual cover. Analyzing responses from a University of Michigan survey, Mary Jackman and Mary Senter (1981) found that gender stereotypes were much stronger than racial stereotypes. For example, only 22 percent of the men thought the two sexes equally "emotional." Of the remaining 78 percent, those who believed females were more emotional outnumbered those who thought males were by 15 to 1. And what did the women believe? To within 1 percentage point, their responses were identical.

Consider, too, a study by Natalie Porter, Florence Geis, and Joyce Jennings Walstedt (1983). They showed students pictures of "a group of graduate students working as a team on a research project" (Figure 22–3). Then they gave them a test of "first impressions," asking them to guess who contributed the most to the group. When the group was either all-male or all-female, the students overwhelmingly chose the person at the head of the table. When the group was a mix of males and females, a man occupying the head position was again overwhelmingly chosen. But a woman occupying that position was usually ignored. Each of the men in Figure 22–3 received more of the leadership choices than all three women combined! This stereotype of men as leaders was true not only of women as well as men but also of feminists as well as nonfeminists. How pervasive are gender stereotypes? Quite pervasive.

Remember that stereotypes are generalizations about a group of people and may be true, false, or overgeneralized from a kernel of truth. As previous modules explained, the average man and woman do differ somewhat in social connectedness, aggressiveness, and sexual initiative. Do we then conclude that gender stereotypes are accurate?

They are often overgeneralizations. Carol Lynn Martin (1987) surmised as much after querying visitors to the University of British Columbia. She asked them to check which of several traits described themselves and to estimate what percentage of North American males and females had each trait. Males were *slightly* more likely than females to describe themselves as assertive and dominant and were *slightly* less likely to describe themselves as tender and compassionate. But stereotypes of these differences were greatly exaggerated: The people perceived North American males as almost twice as likely as females to be assertive and

FIGURE 22-3
Which one of these people would you guess is the group's strongest contributor? Shown this picture, college students usually guessed one of the two men, although those shown photos of same-sex groups most commonly guessed the person at the head of the table.

dominant and roughly half as likely to be tender and compassionate. The conclusion: Although actual differences between the sexes are small, stereotypes are strong.

Stereotypes (beliefs) are not prejudices (attitudes). Stereotypes may support prejudice. But then again one might believe, without prejudice, that men and women are "different yet equal." Let us therefore see how researchers probe for gender prejudice.

Gender Attitudes

Judging from what people tell survey researchers, attitudes toward women have changed as rapidly as racial attitudes. In 1937, one-third of Americans said they would vote for a qualified woman whom their party nominated for President; in 1988, 9 in 10 said they would. In 1967, 56 percent of first-year American college students agreed that "the activities of married women are best confined to the home and family"; by 1990, only 25 percent agreed (Astin & others, 1987a, 1991). In 1970, Americans were split 50-50 on whether they favored or opposed "efforts to strengthen women's status." By the end of the decade, this tenet of the women's movement was favored by better than 2 to 1 (Figure 22-4). And should there be "equal pay for women and men when they are doing the

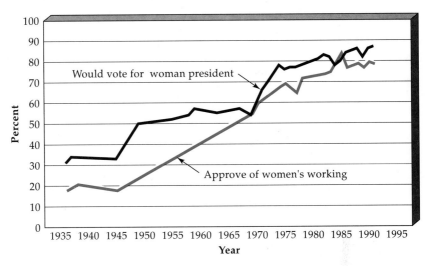

FIGURE 22–4
Prejudice against women: an idea whose time has passed? The percentage of
Americans who say that they approve of a married woman's working for money
if she has a capable husband and that they would vote for a qualified women
candidate for President has steadily increased since the mid-1930s.   (Data from
Niemi & others, 1989; Tom Smith, 1990, personal correspondence.)

same job"? (NBC, 1977). Yes, say both men and women—by a 16 to 1
margin, as close to absolute consensus as Americans ever get.

Alice Eagly and her associates (1991) also report that people don't
respond to women with gut-level negative emotions as they do to certain
other groups. If anything, their emotional evaluations of women exceed
those of men, thanks largely to the common perception that women are
more kind, understanding, and helpful.

There is still more good news for those who are upset by sex bias. One
heavily publicized finding of prejudice against women no longer holds
true. In one study, Philip Goldberg (1968) gave women students at
Connecticut College several short articles, asking them to judge the value
of each. Sometimes a given article was attributed to a male author (for
example, John T. McKay), other times to a female author (for example,
Joan T. McKay). In general, the articles received lower ratings when
attributed to a female. The historic mark of oppression—self-depreca-
tion—surfaced again. Women were prejudiced against women.

Eager to demonstrate the subtle reality of gender prejudice, I obtained Goldberg's materials and repeated the experiment for my own
students' benefit. They showed no such tendency to deprecate women's
work. So, Janet Swim, Eugene Borgida, Geoffrey Maruyama, and I (1989)
searched the literature and corresponded with investigators to learn all

we could about studies of gender bias in the evaluation of men's and women's work. To our surprise, the biases that occasionally surfaced were as often against men as women. But the most common result across 104 studies involving almost 20,000 people was *no difference*. On most comparisons, judgments of someone's work were unaffected by whether the work was attributed to a female or a male.

The attention given highly publicized studies of prejudice against women's work illustrates a familiar point: Social scientists' values often penetrate their conclusions. The researchers who conducted the publicized studies did as they should in reporting their findings. However, my colleagues and I more readily accepted and reported findings supporting our preconceived biases than those opposing them.

So, is gender bias fast becoming extinct in the United States? Has the women's movement nearly completed its work? No. As with race prejudice, blatant gender prejudice is dying, but subtle bias lives. Men who believe an experimenter can read their true attitudes with a sensitive lie detector express less sympathy toward women's rights. Even on paper-and-pencil questionnaires, Janet Swim and her coresearchers (1991) found a subtle sexism that parallels subtle racism. Both appear in denials of discrimination and in antagonism toward efforts to promote equality.

We can also detect bias in behavior. That's what a research team led by Ian Ayres (1991) did while visiting 90 Chicago-area car dealers and using a uniform strategy to negotiate the lowest price on a new car that cost the dealer about $11,000. White males were given a final price that averaged $11,362; White females were given an average price of $11,504; Black males were given an average price of $11,783; and Black females were given an average price of $12,237.

Most women know that gender bias exists. They believe that sex discrimination affects most working women, as shown by the lower salaries for women and for jobs such as child care worker that are filled mostly by women. Curiously, however, Faye Crosby and her colleagues (1989) have repeatedly found that most women deny feeling personally discriminated against. Discrimination, they believe, is something *other* women face. Their employer is not villainous. They are doing better than the average woman. Hearing no complaints, managers—even in discriminatory organizations—can persuade themselves that justice prevails. Similar denials of personal disadvantage, while perceiving discrimination against one's group, occur among unemployed people, out-of-the-closet lesbians, African-Americans, and Canadian minorities (Taylor & others, 1990).

To conclude, overt prejudice against people of color and against women is far less common today than it was four decades ago. Although stereotypes remain, blatant racial and gender prejudices have largely disappeared. Nevertheless, techniques that are sensitive to subtle prejudice still detect widespread bias.

CONCEPTS TO REMEMBER

Prejudice An unjustifiable negative attitude toward a group and its individual members.

Stereotype A belief about the personal attributes of a group of people. Stereotypes can be overgeneralized, inaccurate, and resistant to new information.

Discrimination Unjustifiable negative behavior toward a group or its members.

Racism (1) Individual's prejudicial attitudes and discriminatory behavior toward people of a given race, or (2) institutional practices (even if not motivated by prejudice) that subordinate people of a given race.

Sexism (1) Individual's prejudicial attitudes and discriminatory behavior toward people of a given sex, or (2) institutional practices (even if not motivated by prejudice) that subordinate people of a given sex.

23

The Roots of Prejudice

--- ❖ ---

I n Northern Ireland, hostilities between British-heritage Protestants and Irish-heritage Catholics have claimed 3000 lives since 1969. (A similar proportion of Americans would number 400,0000 and of Canadians 40,000.) Elsewhere, whole countries—Yugoslavia, the Soviet Union, Iraq, among them—have been ripped apart by seething ethnic tensions. Thanks to modern travel and migration, most other modern nations are more and more a mix of cultures, as Albanians mix with Italians, Pakistanis with English, Turks with Germans, and as European-, African-, Asian-, and Hispanic-heritage people mix in Canada and the United States. In such environments, what produces prejudice?

Prejudice springs from several sources, because it serves several functions (Herek, 1986, 1987). Prejudice may express our sense of who we are and gain us social acceptance. It may defend our sense of self against anxiety that arises from insecurity or inner conflict. And it may promote our self-interest by supporting what brings us pleasure and opposing what doesn't. Let's consider the social, emotional, and cognitive roots of prejudice, beginning with how people use prejudice to defend their social position.

SOCIAL SOURCES OF PREJUDICE

Inequality and Prejudice

A principle to remember: *Unequal status breeds prejudice.* Masters view slaves as lazy, irresponsible, lacking ambition—as having just those traits that justify the slavery. Historians debate the forces that create unequal status. But once inequalities exist, prejudice helps justify the economic and social superiority of those who have wealth and power. Thus, prejudice and discrimination support each other: Discrimination breeds prejudice, and prejudice legitimizes discrimination.

In times of conflict, attitudes easily adjust to behavior. People often view enemies as subhuman and depersonalize them with a label. During World War II, the Japanese people became "the Japs." After the war was over, they became "the intelligent, hardworking Japanese" whom Americans admire today. Attitudes are amazingly adaptable.

Gender stereotypes, too, help rationalize differing gender roles. After studying gender stereotypes worldwide, John Williams and Deborah Best (1990a) noted that if women provide most of the care to young children, it is reassuring to think women are naturally nurturant. And if males run the businesses, hunt, and fight wars, it is comforting to suppose that men are aggressive, independent, and adventurous. In experiments, people perceive members of unknown groups as having traits that suit their roles (Hoffman & Hurst, 1990).

Discrimination's Impact: The Self-Fulfilling Prophecy

Attitudes may coincide with the social order not only as a rationalization for it but also because discrimination affects its victims. "One's reputation," wrote Gordon Allport, "cannot be hammered, hammered, hammered into one's head without doing something to one's character" (1958, p. 139). In his classic book, *The Nature of Prejudice*, Allport cataloged 15 possible effects of victimization. Allport believed these reactions were reducible to two basic types—those that involve blaming oneself (withdrawal, self-hate, aggression against one's own group) and those that involve blaming external causes (fighting back, suspiciousness, increased group pride). If the net results are negative—say, higher rates of crime—people can use them to justify the discrimination that helps maintain them: "If we let those people in our nice neighborhood, property values will plummet."

Does discrimination affect its victims as this analysis supposes? We must be careful not to overstate the point, lest we feed the idea that the "victims" of prejudice are of necessity socially deficient. The soul and style of Black culture are for many a proud heritage, not just a response to victimization (Jones, 1983). Cultural differences need not imply social deficits.

Nevertheless, social beliefs *can* be self-confirming, as demonstrated in a clever pair of experiments by Carl Word, Mark Zanna, and Joel Cooper (1974). In the first experiment, Princeton University White men interviewed White and Black job applicants. When the applicant was Black, the interviewers sat farther away, ended the interview 25 percent sooner, and made 50 percent more speech errors than when the applicant was White. Imagine being interviewed by someone who sat at a distance, stammered, and ended the interview rather quickly. Would it affect your performance or your feelings about the interviewer?

To find out, the researchers conducted a second experiment in which trained interviewers treated students as the interviewers in the first experiment had treated either the White or Black applicants. When videotapes of the interviews were later rated, those who were treated like the Blacks in the first experiment seemed more nervous and less effective. Moreover, the interviewees could themselves sense a difference; those treated as were the Blacks judged their interviewers as less adequate and less friendly. The experimenters concluded "that the 'problem' of Black performance resides not entirely within the Blacks, but rather within the interaction setting itself."

Ingroup and Outgroup

The social definition of who you are—your race, religion, sex, academic major—implies a definition of who you are not. The circle that includes "us" (the **ingroup**) excludes "them" (the **outgroup**). Thus, the mere experience of people's being formed into groups may promote **ingroup bias**. Ask children, "Which are better, the children in your school or the children at [another school nearby]?" Virtually all will say that their own school has the better children.

In a series of experiments, British social psychologists Henri Tajfel and Michael Billig (1974; Tajfel, 1970, 1981, 1982) discovered how little it takes to provoke favoritism toward *us* and unfairness toward *them*. They found that even when the us-them distinction is trivial, people still favor their own group. In one study Tajfel and Billig had British teenagers evaluate modern abstract paintings and then told them that they and some others had favored the art of Paul Klee over that of Wassily Kandinsky. Finally, without ever meeting the other members of their group, the teens divided some money among members of both groups. In experiment after experiment, defining groups even in this trivial way produced favoritism. David Wilder (1981) summarizes the typical result: "When given the opportunity to divide 15 points [worth money], subjects generally award 9 or 10 points to their own group and 5 or 6 points to the other group." This bias occurs with both sexes and with people of all ages and nationalities, though especially with people from individualist cultures (Gudykunst, 1989). (People in communal cultures identify more with all their peers and so treat everyone more the same.)

We also are more prone to ingroup bias when our group is small, relative to the outgroup (Mullen, 1991). When we're part of a small group surrounded by a larger group, we are also more conscious of our group membership; when our ingroup is the majority, we think less about it. To be a foreign student, or to be a Black student on a mostly White campus or a White student on a mostly Black campus, is to feel one's social identity more keenly and to react accordingly.

Even forming conspicuous groups on *no* logical basis—say, merely by composing groups X and Y with the flip of a coin—will produce some ingroup bias (Billig & Tajfel, 1973; Brewer & Silver, 1978; Locksley & others, 1980). In Kurt Vonnegut's novel *Slapstick*, computers gave everyone a new middle name; all "Daffodil-11's" then felt unity with one another and distance from "Raspberry-13's." The self-serving bias rides again, enabling people to achieve a more positive social identity: "We" are better than "they," even when "we" and "they" are alike.

Because we evaluate ourselves partly by our group memberships, seeing our own groups as superior helps us feel good about ourselves. What is more, our whole self-concept—our sense of who we are—contains not just our personal identity (our sense of our personal attributes and attitudes) but our *social identity* (Hogg & Abrams, 1988). Having a sense of "we-ness" strengthens our self-concept. It *feels* good. So much so, report Charles Perdue and his associates (1990), that just pairing a nonsense syllable such as *yof* with words like "we" and "us" makes the syllable seem more pleasant than if it is associated with "they" or "them."

Conformity

Once established, prejudice is maintained largely by inertia. If prejudice is a social norm, many people will follow the path of least resistance and conform to the fashion. They will act not so much out of a need to hate as from a need to be liked and accepted.

Studies by Thomas Pettigrew (1958) of Whites in South Africa and the American south revealed that during the 1950s those who conformed most to other social norms were also most prejudiced; those who were less conforming mirrored less of the surrounding prejudice. The price of nonconformity was painfully clear to the ministers of Little Rock, Arkansas, where the Supreme Court's 1954 school desegregation decision was implemented. Most ministers favored integration but usually only privately; they feared that advocating it vigorously would lose them members and contributions (Campbell & Pettigrew, 1959). Or consider the Indiana steelworkers and West Virginia coal miners of the same era. In the mills and the mines, the workers accepted integration. In the neighborhood, the norm was rigid segregation (Minard, 1952; Reitzes, 1953). Prejudice was clearly *not* a manifestation of "sick" personalities but simply of the norms that operated in a given situation.

Conformity also maintains gender prejudice. "If we have come to think that the nursery and the kitchen are the natural sphere of a woman," wrote George Bernard Shaw in an 1891 essay, "we have done so exactly as English children come to think that a cage is the natural sphere of a parrot—because they have never seen one anywhere else." Children who *have* seen women elsewhere—children of employed women—have less stereotyped views of men and women (Hoffman, 1977).

Popular prejudices often gain support from political leaders, schools, and the media. When Arkansas Governor Orval Faubus barred the doors of Little Rock's Central High School, he was not only representing his constituents, but also legitimating their views. When advertisers, photographers, and artists picture men's faces and women's bodies, this "face-ism" makes men seem more intelligent and ambitious (Archer & others, 1983; Schwarz & Kurz, 1989).

In all this, there is a message of hope. If prejudice is not deeply ingrained in personality, then as fashions change and new norms evolve, prejudice can diminish. And so it has.

EMOTIONAL SOURCES OF PREJUDICE

Although prejudice is bred by social situations, emotional factors often add fuel to the fire: Frustration and aggression can feed prejudice, as can personality factors like status needs and authoritarian tendencies. Let's see how.

Frustration and Aggression: The Scapegoat Theory

Pain and frustration (the blocking of a goal) often evoke hostility. When the cause of our frustration is intimidating or vague, we often redirect our hostility. This phenomenon of "displaced aggression" may have contributed to the lynchings of African-Americans in the south after the Civil War. Between 1882 and 1930, there were more lynchings in years when cotton prices were low and economic frustration was therefore presumably high (Hepworth & West, 1988; Hovland & Sears, 1940).

Targets for this displaced aggression vary. Following their defeat in World War I and their country's subsequent economic chaos, many Germans saw Jews as villains. Long before Hitler came to power, one German leader explained: "The Jew is just convenient. . . . If there were no Jews, the anti-Semites would have to invent them" (quoted by G. W. Allport, 1958, p. 325). In earlier centuries people vented their fear and hostility on witches, whom they sometimes burned or drowned in public. Today's economic frustrations are often attributed to targets such as "lazy welfare bums" or "greedy corporations."

A famous experiment by Neal Miller and Richard Bugelski (1948) confirmed the scapegoat theory. They asked college-age men working at a summer camp to state their attitudes toward Japanese and Mexicans.

Some did so before, and then after, being forced to stay in camp to take tests rather than attend a long-awaited free evening at a local theater. Compared to a control group that did not undergo this frustration, the deprived group afterward displayed increased prejudice. Passions provoked prejudice.

One source of frustration is competition. When two groups compete for jobs, housing, or social prestige, one group's goal fulfillment can become the other group's frustration. Thus the **realistic group conflict theory** suggests that prejudice arises when groups compete for scarce resources. A corresponding ecological principle, Gauss' law, states that maximum competition will exist between species with identical needs. In western Europe, for example, some people agree that "over the last five years people like yourself have been economically worse off than most [name of country's minority group]." These frustrated people express relatively high levels of blatant prejudice (Pettigrew & Meertens, 1991). Researchers have consistently detected the strongest anti-Black prejudice among Whites who are closest to Blacks on the socioeconomic ladder (Greeley & Sheatsley, 1971; Pettigrew, 1978; Tumin, 1958). When interests clash, prejudice pays, for some people.

Personality Dynamics

But any two people, with equal reason to feel frustrated or threatened, will often not be equally prejudiced. This suggests that prejudice serves other functions besides advancing our competitive self-interest. Sometimes, suggested Sigmund Freud, people hold to beliefs and attitudes that satisfy unconscious needs.

Need for Status
Status is relative: To perceive ourselves as having status, we need people below us. Thus one psychological benefit of prejudice, or of any status system, is the feeling of superiority it offers. Most of us can recall a time when we took secret satisfaction in another's failure—perhaps we saw a brother or sister punished or heard of a classmate's failing a test. Our own esteem derives a boost from such comparisons. So prejudice is often greater among those low or slipping on the socioeconomic ladder and among those whose positive self-image is being threatened (Lemyre & Smith, 1985; Thompson & Crocker, 1985). In one study at Northwestern University, members of lower-status sororities were more disparaging of other sororities than members of higher-status sororities (Crocker & others, 1987). Perhaps people whose status is secure have less need to feel superior.

But other factors associated with low status could also account for prejudice. Imagine yourself as one of the Arizona State University students who took part in an experiment by Robert Cialdini and Kenneth Richardson (1980). You are walking alone across campus. Someone approaches you and asks for your help with a five-minute survey. You agree. After the researcher gives you a brief "creativity test," he deflates you with the news that "you have scored relatively low on the test." The researcher then completes the survey by asking you some evaluative questions about either your school or its traditional rival, the University of Arizona. Would your feelings of failure affect your ratings of either school? Compared with those in a control group whose self-esteem was not threatened, the students who experienced failure gave higher ratings to their own school and lower ratings to their rival. Apparently, boasting of one's own group and denigrating outgroups can boost one's ego.

James Meindl and Melvin Lerner (1984) found that a humiliating experience—accidentally knocking over a stack of someone's important computer cards—provoked English-speaking Canadian students to express increased hostility toward French-speaking Canadians. And Teresa Amabile and Ann Glazebrook (1982) found that Dartmouth College men who were made to feel insecure judged others' work more harshly. Thinking about your own mortality—by writing a short essay on dying and the emotions aroused by thinking about death—also provokes enough insecurity to intensify ingroup favoritism and outgroup prejudice (Greenberg & others, 1990).

The Authoritarian Personality

The emotional needs that contribute to prejudice are said to predominate in the "authoritarian personality." In the 1940s, a group of University of California, Berkeley, researchers—two of whom had fled Nazi Germany—set out on an urgent research mission. They wanted to uncover the psychological roots of an anti-Semitism so poisonous that it caused the slaughter of millions of Jews and turned many millions of Europeans into indifferent spectators. In studies of American adults, Adorno and his colleagues (1950) discovered that hostility toward Jews often coexisted with hostility toward other minorities. Moreover, these **ethnocentric** people shared authoritarian tendencies—an intolerance for weakness, a punitive attitude, and a submissive respect for their ingroup's authorities, as reflected in their agreement with such statements as, "Obedience and respect for authority are the most important virtues children should learn."

As children, authoritarian people often were harshly disciplined. This apparently led them to repress their hostilities and impulses and to "project" them onto outgroups. The insecurity of authoritarian children seemed to predispose them toward an excessive concern with power and status and an inflexible right-wrong way of thinking that made ambiguity difficult to tolerate. Such people therefore tended to be submissive to those with power over them and aggressive or punitive toward those beneath them.

Although scholars criticized the research for its focus on right-wing authoritarianism, overlooking dogmatic authoritarianism of the left, its main conclusion has survived: Authoritarian tendencies, sometimes reflected in ethnic tensions, surge during threatening times of economic recession and social upheaval (Doty & others, 1991; Sales, 1973). Moreover, contemporary studies of right-wing authoritarians by University of Manitoba psychologist Bob Altemeyer (1988, 1992) confirm that there *are* individuals whose fears and self-righteous hostilities surface as prejudice. Feelings of moral superiority may go hand in hand with brutality toward perceived inferiors. Although the prejudices that maintained *apartheid* in South Africa arose from social inequalities, socialization, and conformity (Louw-Potgieter, 1988), those who most strongly favored separation usually had authoritarian attitudes (van Staden, 1987). In repressive regimes across the world, people who become torturers typically have an authoritarian liking for hierarchical chains of command and a contempt for those who are weak or resistant (Staub, 1989). Moreover, different forms of prejudice—toward Blacks, gays and lesbians, women, old people—*do* tend to coexist in the same individuals (Bierly, 1985; Snyder & Ickes, 1985). As Altemeyer concludes, right-wing authoritarians tend to be "equal opportunity bigots."

COGNITIVE SOURCES OF PREJUDICE

Much of the explanation of prejudice so far could have been written in the 1960s—but not what follows. This new look at prejudice reflects the new research on social thinking. The basic point is this: Stereotyped beliefs and prejudiced attitudes exist not only because of social conditioning, or because they enable people to displace and project their hostilities, but also as by-products of normal thinking processes. Many stereotypes spring less from malice than from the way we all simplify our complex worlds. They are like perceptual illusions, a by-product of our knack for simplifying.

Categorization

One way we simplify our environment is to "categorize"—to organize the world by clustering objects into groups. A biologist organizes the world by classifying plants and animals. Once we organize people into categories, we can think about them more easily. If persons in a group are similar, it helps to know their group. Customs inspectors and airplane antihijack personnel are therefore taught "profiles" of suspicious individuals (Kraut & Poe, 1980). Such categorization provides useful information with a minimum amount of effort. When pressed for time (Kaplan & others, 1992), when preoccupied (Gilbert & Hixon, 1991), when tired (Bodenhausen, 1990), or when too young to appreciate diversity (Biernat, 1991), it's easy and efficient to rely on stereotypes.

Ethnicity and sex are, in our current world, powerful ways of categorizing people. Imagine Tom, a 40-year-old African-American real estate agent in New Orleans. I suspect that your image of "Black male" predominates over the categories "middle-aged," "businessperson," and "southerner." Experiments expose our spontaneous categorization of people by race. When subjects view different people making statements, they often forget who said what, yet remember the race of the person who made each statement (Hewstone & others, 1991; Stroessner & others, 1990; Taylor & others, 1978). By itself, such categorization is not prejudice, but it does provide a foundation for prejudice.

Perceived Similarities and Differences

Picture the following objects: apples, chairs, pencils.

There is a strong tendency to see objects within a group as being more uniform than they really are. Were your apples all red? your chairs all straight-backed? your pencils all yellow? It's the same with people. Once we assign people to groups—athletes, drama majors, math professors—we are likely to exaggerate the similarities within the groups and the differences between them (S. E. Taylor, 1981; Wilder, 1978). Mere division into groups can create an **outgroup homogeneity effect**—a sense that *they* are "all alike" and different from "us" and "our" group (Allen & Wilder, 1979). Because we generally like people we think are similar to us and dislike those we perceive as different, the natural result is ingroup bias (Byrne & Wong, 1962; Rokeach & Mezei, 1966; Stein & others, 1965).

When the group is our own, we are more likely to see the diversity among its members. White Americans readily identify "Black leaders" who supposedly can speak for Black Americans, and White reporters sometimes find it newsworthy that the "Black community is divided" on such an issue as the Persian Gulf war. Whites apparently presume that their own racial group is more diverse: They do not assume there are "White leaders" who can speak for White America, nor is it newsworthy that not all Whites agree on an issue. (No newspapers headlined, "White leaders divided over Persian Gulf war.") In general, the greater our familiarity with a social group, the more we see its diversity (Linville & others, 1989). The less our familiarity, the more we stereotype.

Perhaps you have noticed: *They*—the members of any racial group other than your own—even *look* alike. Many of us can recall embarrassing ourselves by confusing two people of another racial group, prompting the person we've misnamed to say, "You think we all look alike." Experiments by John Brigham, June Chance, Alvin Goldstein, and Roy Malpass in the United States and by Hayden Ellis in Scotland reveal that people of other races do in fact appear to look more alike than people of one's own race (Brigham & Williamson, 1979; Chance & Goldstein, 1981; Ellis, 1981). When White students are shown faces of a few White and a few Black individuals and then asked to pick these individuals out of a photographic lineup, they more accurately recognize the White faces than the Black.

I am White. When I first read this research I thought, "Of course! White people *are* more physically diverse than Blacks." But my reaction was apparently just an illustration of the phenomenon. For if my reaction were correct, Black people, too, would better recognize a White face among a lineup of Whites than a Black face in a lineup of Blacks. But in fact the opposite appears true: Blacks more easily recognize another Black than they do a White (Bothwell & others, 1989). And Hispanics more readily recognize another Hispanic than an Anglo whom they saw a couple of hours earlier (Platz & Hosch, 1988).

This intriguing "own-race bias" appears to be an automatic cognitive phenomenon, for it is usually unrelated to the perceiver's racial attitudes (Brigham & Malpass, 1985). But experience may play a role. June Chance (1985) reports that White students have difficulty recognizing individual Japanese faces (although Japanese facial features are actually as varied as those of White faces). But White students become markedly better at recognizing Japanese faces if, over several training sessions, they view pairs of Japanese faces, which they must learn to differentiate. Chance's hunch is that experience enables people to become attuned to the types of faces they frequently encounter. This helps explain why Black people in White cultures are slightly better than Whites at recognizing faces from another race (Anthony & others, 1992). It also explains why to me all Cabbage Patch dolls looked alike, though they hardly looked alike to my nine-year-old daughter and her friends.

Distinctive Stimuli

Distinctive People Draw Attention

Other ways we perceive our worlds also breed stereotypes. Distinctive people and vivid or extreme occurrences often capture attention and distort judgments.

Have you ever found yourself in a situation where you were the only person present of your sex, race, or nationality? If so, your difference from the others probably made you more noticeable and the object of more attention. A Black in an otherwise White group, a man in an otherwise female group, or a woman in an otherwise male group seems more prominent and influential and appears to have exaggerated good and bad qualities (Crocker & McGraw, 1984; S. E. Taylor & others, 1979). This occurs because when someone in a group is made salient (conspicuous), we tend to see that person as causing whatever happens (Taylor & Fiske, 1978). If we are positioned to look at Joe, an average group member, Joe will seem to have a greater than average influence upon the group. People who capture our attention seem more responsible for what happens.

Ellen Langer and Lois Imber (1980) asked Harvard students to watch a videotape of a man reading. They discovered that the students paid closer attention when they were led to think he was out of the ordinary— a cancer patient, a homosexual, or a millionaire. They detected characteristics of the man that other viewers ignored, and their evaluation of him was more extreme. Those who thought the man a cancer patient noticed his distinctive facial characteristics and bodily movements and thus perceived him as much more "different from most people" than did the other viewers. The extra attention we pay to distinctive people creates an illusion that they differ more from others than they really do. If people thought you had the IQ of a genius, they would probably notice things about you that otherwise would pass unnoticed.

However, sometimes we perceive others as reacting to our distinctiveness when actually they aren't. At Dartmouth College, researchers Robert Kleck and Angelo Strenta (1980) discovered this when they led college women to feel disfigured. The women thought the purpose of the experiment was to assess how someone would react to a facial scar created with theatrical makeup on the right cheek, running from the ear to the mouth. Actually, the purpose was to see how the women themselves, when made to feel deviant, would perceive others' behavior toward them. After applying the makeup, the experimenter gave each subject a small hand mirror so she could see the authentic-looking scar. When she put the mirror down, he then applied some "moisturizer" to "keep the makeup from cracking." What the "moisturizer" really did was remove the scar.

The scene that followed was poignant. A young woman, feeling terribly self-conscious about her supposedly disfigured face, is talking with another woman who sees no such disfigurement and knows nothing of what has gone before. If you have ever felt similarly self-conscious— perhaps about a physical handicap, acne, or even just "awful-looking hair"—then perhaps you can sympathize with the self-conscious woman. Compared to women led to believe their conversational partner merely thought they had an allergy, the "disfigured" women became acutely sensitive to how their partners were looking at them. They rated their partners as more tense, distant, and patronizing. But in fact, observers who later analyzed videotapes of how the partners treated "disfigured" persons could find no such differences in treatment. Self-conscious about being different, the "disfigured" women misinterpreted mannerisms and comments they would otherwise not notice.

Vivid, Distinctive Cases

Our minds also use distinctive cases as a shortcut to judging groups. Are Blacks good athletes? "Well, there's Carl Lewis and Florence Griffith Joyner and Michael Jordan. Yeah, I'd say so." Note the thought processes at work here: We recall instances of a particular category and, based on those recalled, generalize. The problem is that vivid instances, though persuasive because of their greater availability in memory, are seldom representative of the larger group. Exceptional athletes, though distinctive and memorable, are not the best basis for judging the distribution of athletic talent among an entire ethnic group.

Myron Rothbart and his colleagues (1978) showed how distinctive people fuel stereotypes. They had University of Oregon students view 50 slides, each of which stated the man's height. For one group of students, 10 of the men were slightly over 6 feet (up to 6 feet, 4 inches). For other students, these 10 men were well over 6 feet (up to 6 feet, 11 inches). When asked later how many of the men were over 6 feet, those given the moderately tall examples recalled 5 percent too many. In a follow-up experiment, students read descriptions of the actions of 50 men, 10 of whom had committed either nonviolent crimes, such as forgery, or violent crimes, such as rape. Of those shown the list with the violent crimes, most overestimated the number of criminal acts.

Because they are distinctive, we most easily remember extreme cases: and because they alone are newsworthy, they dominate our images of various groups. The attention-getting power of distinctive, extreme cases helps explain why middle-class people so greatly exaggerate the dissimilarities between themselves and the underclass. Contrary to stereotypes of "welfare queens" driving Cadillacs, people living in poverty generally share the aspirations of the middle class and would rather provide for themselves than accept public assistance (Cook & Curtin, 1987). Moreover, the less we know about a group, the more we are influenced by a vivid case or two (Quattrone & Jones, 1980). To see is to believe.

Attribution: Is It a Just World?

In explaining others' actions, we frequently commit the fundamental attribution error. We attribute their behavior so much to their inner dispositions that we discount important situational forces. The error occurs partly because our attention focuses on the persons themselves, not on their situations. A person's race or sex is vivid and attention-getting; the situational forces working upon that person are less visible. Slavery was often overlooked as an explanation for slave behavior; the behavior was instead attributed to the slaves' own nature. Until recently, the same was true of how we explained the perceived differences between women and men. Because gender-role constraints were hard to see, we attributed men's and women's behavior solely to their innate dispositions.

In a series of experiments conducted at the Universities of Waterloo and Kentucky, Melvin Lerner and his colleagues (Lerner & Miller, 1978; Lerner, 1980) discovered that merely *observing* another person being innocently victimized is enough to make the victim seem less worthy. Imagine that you along with some others are participating in a study on the perception of emotional cues (Lerner & Simmons, 1966). One of the participants, a confederate, is selected by lottery to perform a memory task. This person receives painful shocks whenever she gives a wrong answer. You and the others note her emotional responses. After watching the victim receive these apparently painful shocks, the experimenter asks you to evaluate her. How would you respond? With compassionate sympathy? We might legitimately expect such. As Ralph Waldo Emerson wrote, "The martyr cannot be dishonored." On the contrary, the experiments revealed that when observers were powerless to alter the victim's fate, they often rejected and devalued the victim. Juvenal, the Roman satirist, anticipated these results: "The Roman mob follows after Fortune . . . and hates those who have been condemned."

Linda Carli and her colleagues (1989, 1990) report that this **just-world phenomenon** colors our impressions of rape victims. Carli had people read detailed descriptions of interactions between a man and a woman. Some read a scenario that has a happy ending: "Then he led me to the couch. He held my hand and asked me to marry him." In hindsight, people find the ending unsurprising and admire the man's and woman's character traits. Others read the same scenario with a different ending: "But then he became very rough and pushed me onto the couch. He held me down on the couch and raped me." Given this ending, people see it as more inevitable and blame the woman for behavior that seems faultless when it has a happier outcome.

Likewise, people may reason, if Blacks or Jews have been abused, they must somehow have brought it on themselves. When the British marched a group of German civilians around the Bergen-Belsen concentration camp at the close of World War II, one German responded: "What terrible criminals these prisoners must have been to receive such treatment."

Lerner (1980) believes that such disparaging of hapless victims results from our need to believe, "I am a just person living in a just world, a world where people get what they deserve." From early childhood, he argues, we are taught that good is rewarded and evil punished. Hard work and virtue pay dividends; laziness and immorality do not. From this it is but a short leap to assuming that those who flourish must be good and those who suffer must deserve their fate. The classic illustration is the Old Testament story of Job, a good person who suffers terrible misfortune. Job's friends surmise that, this being a just world, Job must have done something wicked to elicit such terrible suffering.

All this suggests that people are indifferent to social injustice not because they have no concern for justice but because they *see* no injustice. What is more, believing in a just world—believing, as many people do, that rape victims must have behaved seductively (Borgida & Brekke, 1985), that battered spouses must have provoked their beatings (Summers & Feldman, 1984), that poor people don't deserve better (Furnham & Gunter, 1984), that sick people are responsible for their illness (Gruman & Sloan, 1983)—enables successful people to reassure themselves that they deserve what they have. The wealthy and healthy can see their own good fortune and others' misfortune as justly deserved. Linking good fortune with virtue and misfortune with moral failure enables the fortunate to feel pride in their achievements and to avoid responsibility for the unfortunate.

Social psychologists have been more successful in explaining prejudice than in alleviating it. Because prejudice results from many interrelated factors, there is no simple remedy. Nevertheless, we can now anticipate techniques for reducing prejudice. If unequal status breeds prejudice, then we can seek to create cooperative, equal-status relationships. If prejudice often rationalizes discriminatory behavior, then we can mandate nondiscrimination. If outgroups seem more unlike one's own group than they really are, then we can make efforts to personalize their members. These are some of the antidotes for the poison of prejudice.

Since the end of World War II in 1945, a number of these antidotes have been applied, and racial and gender prejudices have indeed diminished. It now remains to be seen whether, during the remaining years of this century, progress will continue or whether, as could easily happen in a time of increasing population and diminishing resources, antagonisms will again erupt into open hostility.

CONCEPTS TO REMEMBER

Ingroup "Us"—group of people who share a sense of belonging, a feeling of common identity.

Outgroup "Them"—group that people perceive as distinctively different from or apart from their ingroup.

Ingroup bias The tendency to favor one's own group.

Realistic group conflict theory The theory that prejudice arises from competition between groups for scarce resources.

Ethnocentrism A belief in the superiority of one's own ethnic and cultural group, and a corresponding disdain for all other groups.

Outgroup homogeneity effect Perception of outgroup members as more similar to one another than ingroup members. Thus "they are alike; we are diverse."

Just-world phenomenon The tendency of people to believe the world is just and that people therefore get what they deserve and deserve what they get.

24

The Nature and Nurture of Aggression

❖

O ur behavior toward one another is at times strangely destructive. Although Woody Allen's one-time prediction that "by 1990 kidnapping will be the dominant mode of social interaction" has not been fulfilled, the odds of someone's being hit by violent crime have quintupled since 1960. In the United States, reported assaults now exceed 1 million annually. Worldwide, spending for arms and armies approaches $3 billion per day—$3 billion that could feed, educate, and protect the environment of impoverished hundreds of millions.

To a social psychologist, **aggression** is any behavior intended to hurt or destroy. This definition excludes accidents, dental treatments, and assertive go-getting behavior. But it includes slaps, insults, and gossipy digs, whether done coolly (as a calculated means to some end) or in an emotional outburst. When Iraqis killed Kuwaitis while capturing their country, and when Allied forces killed 100,000 Iraqis while taking it back, their motives were instrumental: killing people was simply a way to seize territory. But their behavior was nevertheless aggressive.

Aggression, like other human behaviors, emerges from the mix of nature and nurture. For a gun to fire, or for a person to explode, a trigger must be pulled. With some people, as with hair-trigger guns, the trigger pulls easily. Let's consider biological factors that influence how easily our trigger pulls, and psychological factors that pull it.

BIOLOGICAL INFLUENCES ON AGGRESSION

Is Aggression an Instinct?

Philosophers have long debated whether our human nature is that of a benign "noble savage" or that of an explosive brute. The first view, espoused by eighteenth-century philosopher Jean-Jacques Rousseau, blames social evils on society, not human nature. The second, espoused by philosopher Thomas Hobbes (1588–1679), sees society's restrictions as necessary to restrain and control the human brute. In this century, the brutish view—that aggressive drive is inborn and thus inevitable—was argued by Sigmund Freud in Vienna and by animal behavior theorist Konrad Lorenz in Germany.

Freud theorized that our positive survival instincts coexist with a self-destructive "death instinct." He believed that we usually release the energy of this primitive death urge in socially approved activities such as sports or displace the energy toward others as aggression. Lorenz similarly argued that aggressive energy swells until released. Although gestures of submission inhibit aggression, he feared the consequences of our arming our "fighting instinct" without comparably arming our inhibitions.

The idea that aggression is an instinct collapsed as the list of supposed human instincts grew to include nearly every conceivable human behavior and as scientists became aware how much behavior varies from person to person and culture to culture. Yet biology clearly does influence behavior. Nurture works upon nature. Our experiences interact with the nervous system engineered by our genes.

Neural Influences

Because aggression is a complex behavior, no one spot in the brain controls it. But in both animals and humans, researchers have found neural systems that facilitate aggression. When they activate these areas in the inner brain, hostility increases; when they deactivate them, hostility decreases. Docile animals can thus be provoked into rage, and raging animals into submission.

In one experiment, researchers placed an electrode in an aggression-inhibiting area of a domineering monkey's brain. Given a button that activated the electrode, one small monkey learned to push it every time the tyrant monkey got intimidating. Comparable effects have been observed with human patients. After receiving painless electrical stimulation in her amygdala (a part of the brain core), one woman became enraged and smashed her guitar against the wall, barely missing her psychiatrist's head (Moyer, 1976).

Genetic Influences

Individuals of any species vary in their neural system's sensitivity to aggressive cues. One source of the difference is heredity. It has long been known that animals of many species can be bred for aggressiveness. Sometimes this is done for practical purposes (the breeding of fighting cocks). Sometimes, breeding is done for research. Kirsti Lagerspetz (1979), a Finnish psychologist, took normal albino mice and bred the most aggressive ones together and the least aggressive ones. After repeating the procedure for 26 generations, she had one set of fierce mice and one set of placid mice.

Aggressiveness similarly varies among primates and humans (Asher, 1987; Olweus, 1979). Our temperament—how intense and reactive we are—is partly something we bring with us into the world, influenced by our sympathetic nervous system's reactivity (Kagan, 1989). A person's temperament, observed in infancy, therefore endures (Larsen & Diener, 1987; Wilson & Matheny, 1986). Identical twins, when asked separately, are more likely than fraternal twins to agree on whether they have "a violent temper" (Rushton & others, 1986).

Blood Chemistry

Blood chemistry is another influence on neural sensitivity to aggressive stimulation. Both laboratory experiments and police data indicate that when people are provoked, alcohol diminishes their restraints on aggression (Bushman & Cooper, 1990; Taylor & Leonard, 1983). The U.S. Department of Justice estimates that nearly a third of the nation's 523,000 state prisoners drank heavily before committing rapes, burglaries, and assaults (Desmond, 1987). Alcohol enhances aggressiveness by reducing people's self-awareness and their ability to consider the results of their actions (Hull & Bond, 1986; Steele & Southwick, 1985). Alcohol therefore deindividuates and disinhibits.

There are other biochemical influences. Low blood sugar can boost aggressiveness. In males, aggressiveness is also influenced by the male sex hormone, testosterone (Moyer, 1983). Although hormonal influences appear much stronger in lower animals than in humans, drugs that diminish testosterone levels in violent human males will subdue their aggressive tendencies. After age 25 testosterone and rates of violent crime both decrease. Among both male and female prisoners convicted of unprovoked violent crimes, testosterone levels tend to be higher than among those imprisoned for nonviolent crimes (Dabbs & others, 1988). And among the normal range of teen boys and adult men, those with high testosterone levels are more prone to delinquency, hard drug use, and aggressive responses to provocation (Archer, 1991; Dabbs & Morris, 1990; Olweus & others, 1988).

So, there exist important neural, genetic, and biochemical influences on aggression. But is aggression so much a part of human nature that it makes peace unattainable? To counter such pessimism, the Council of Representatives of the American Psychological Association and the directors of the International Council of Psychologists have joined other organizations in unanimously endorsing a "statement on violence" developed by scientists from a dozen nations (Adams, 1991). "It is scientifically incorrect," declares the statement, to say that "war or any other violent behavior is genetically programmed into our human nature," or that "war is caused by 'instinct' or any single motivation." Thus there are, as we will see, ways to reduce human aggression.

PSYCHOLOGICAL INFLUENCES ON AGGRESSION

Frustration and Aggression

It is a warm evening. Tired and thirsty after two hours of studying, you borrow some change from a friend and head for the nearest soft-drink machine. As the machine devours the change, you can almost taste the cold, refreshing cola. But when you push the button, nothing happens. You push it again. Then you flip the coin return button. Still nothing. Your throat is now feeling parched. Again, you hit the buttons. You slam them. And finally you shake and whack the machine. You stomp back to your studies, empty-handed and short-changed. Should your roommate beware? Are you now more likely to say or do something hurtful?

One of the first psychological theories of aggression, the popular frustration-aggression theory, answers yes. **Frustration**, said Dollard and his colleagues (1939), is anything (such as the malfunctioning vending machine) that blocks our attaining a goal. Frustration grows when our motivation to achieve a goal is very strong, when we expected gratification, and when the blocking is complete.

As Figure 24–1 suggests, the aggressive energy need not explode directly against its source. We learn to inhibit direct retaliation, especially when others might disapprove or punish; instead we *displace* our hostilities to safer targets. **Displacement** occurs in the old anecdote about a man who, humiliated by his boss, berates his wife, who yells at their son, who kicks the dog, which bites the mail carrier.

Laboratory tests of the frustration-aggression theory produce mixed results: Sometimes frustration increases aggressiveness, sometimes not.

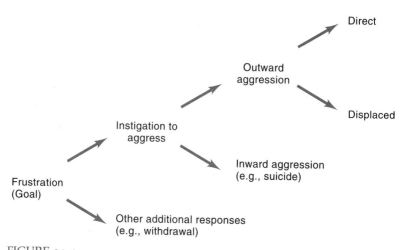

FIGURE 24-1
The classic frustration-aggression theory. Frustration creates a
motive to aggress. Fear of punishment or disapproval for aggressing against the source of frustration may cause the aggressive
drive to be displaced against some other target or even redirected
against oneself.   (Based on Dollard & others, 1939; and Miller, 1941.)

For example, if the frustration is understandable—if, as in one experiment by Eugene Burnstein and Philip Worchel (1962), a confederate
disrupts a group's problem solving because his hearing aid malfunctions
(rather than just because he paid no attention)—then frustration leads to
irritation but not aggression.

Knowing that the original theory overstated the frustration-aggression connection, Leonard Berkowitz (1978, 1989) revised it. Berkowitz
theorized that frustration produces anger, an emotional readiness to
aggress. Anger arises when someone who frustrates us could have chosen to act otherwise (Averill, 1983; Weiner, 1981). A frustrated person is
especially likely to lash out when aggressive cues pull the cork, releasing
bottled-up anger. Sometimes the cork will blow without such cues. But
cues associated with aggression amplify aggression (Carlson & others,
1990).

Berkowitz (1968, 1981) and others have found that the sight of a
weapon is one such cue. In one experiment, children who had just played
with toy guns became more willing to knock down another child's blocks.
In another, angered University of Wisconsin men gave more electric
shocks to their tormentor when a rifle and a revolver were nearby (supposedly left over from a previous experiment) than when badminton
rackets had been left behind (Berkowitz & LePage, 1967). Thus Berkowitz
is not surprised that half of all U.S. murders are committed with handguns and that handguns in homes are far more likely to kill household
members than intruders. "Guns not only permit violence," he reported,

"they can stimulate it as well. The finger pulls the trigger, but the trigger may also be pulling the finger."

Nor would Berkowitz be surprised that countries which ban handguns have lower murder rates. Britain, for example, has one-fourth as many people as the United States and one-sixteenth as many murders. The United States has 10,000 handgun homicides a year; Britain has about 10. Vancouver, British Columbia, and Seattle, Washington, have similar populations, climates, economies, and rates of criminal activity and assault—except that Vancouver, which carefully restricts handgun ownership, has one-fifth as many handgun murders as Seattle and thus a 40 percent lower overall murder rate (Sloan & others, 1988). When Washington, D.C., adopted a law restricting handgun possession, the numbers of gun-related murders and suicides each abruptly dropped about 25 percent. No changes occurred in other methods of murder and suicide, nor did adjacent areas outside the reach of the law experience any such declines (Loftin & others, 1991).

Guns not only serve as aggression cues but also put psychological distance between aggressor and victim. As Milgram's obedience studies taught us, remoteness from the victim facilitates cruelty. A knife attack can kill someone but is more difficult and less likely than pulling a trigger from a distance.

The Learning of Aggression

The theories of aggression based on instinct and frustration assume that hostile urges erupt from inner emotions, which naturally "push" aggression from within. Social psychologists contend that learning also "pulls" aggression out of us.

The Rewards of Aggression

By experience and by observing others, we learn that *aggression often pays.* Through a series of successful bouts, experiments have transformed animals from docile creatures into ferocious fighters. Severe defeats, on the other hand, create submissiveness (Ginsburg & Allee, 1942; Kahn, 1951; Scott & Marston, 1953).

People, too, can learn the rewards of aggression. A child whose aggressive acts successfully intimidate other children will likely become increasingly aggressive (Patterson & others, 1967). Aggressive hockey players—the ones sent most often to the penalty box for rough play— score more goals than nonaggressive players (McCarthy & Kelly, 1978a, 1978b). Canadian teenage hockey players whose fathers applaud physically aggressive play show the most aggressive attitudes and style of play (Ennis & Zanna, 1991). In these cases, aggression is instrumental in achieving certain rewards.

Collective violence can also pay. After the 1980 riot in Miami's Liberty City neighborhood, President Carter came to the neighborhood to assure residents personally of his concern and of forthcoming federal aid. After the 1967 Detroit riot, the Ford Motor Company accelerated its efforts to hire minority workers, prompting comedian Dick Gregory to joke, "Last summer the fire got too close to the Ford plant. Don't scorch the Mustangs, baby." After the 1985 riots in South Africa became severe, the government repealed laws forbidding mixed marriages, offered to restore Black "citizenship rights" (not including the right to vote), and eliminated the hated pass laws controlling the movement of Blacks. The point is not that people consciously plan riots for their instrumental value but that aggression sometimes has payoffs. If nothing more, it gets attention.

The same is true of terrorist acts, which enable powerless people to garner widespread attention. "Kill one, frighten ten thousand," asserts an ancient Chinese proverb. In this age of global communications, killing only a few can frighten tens of millions—as happened when the terrorist-caused deaths of 25 Americans in several incidents during 1985 struck more fear into the hearts of travelers than the car-accident deaths of 46,000. Deprived of what Margaret Thatcher called "the oxygen of publicity," terrorism would surely diminish, concludes Jeffrey Rubin (1986). It's like the 1970s incidents of naked spectators "streaking" onto football fields for a few seconds of television exposure, which ended once the networks decided to ignore the incidents.

Observational Learning

Albert Bandura, the leading proponent of the **social learning theory** of aggression, believes that we learn aggression not only by experiencing its payoffs but also by observing others. Like many social behaviors, we acquire aggression by watching others act and noting the consequences.

Bandura (1979) believes that in everyday life aggressive models appear in (1) the family, (2) the subculture, and (3) the mass media. Children of physically punitive parents tend to use similar aggression when relating to others. The parents of violent teenage boys and of abused children often themselves had parents who were physically punitive (Bandura & Walters, 1959; Strauss & Gelles, 1980). Although most abused children do not become criminals or abusive parents, 30 percent do later abuse their own children—four times the national rate (Kaufman & Zigler, 1987; Widom, 1989). Within families, violence often leads to violence.

The social environment outside the home also provides models. In communities where "macho" images are admired, aggression is readily transmitted to new generations (Cartwright, 1975; Short, 1969). The violent subculture of teenage gangs, for instance, provides its junior members with numerous aggressive models. At sporting events such as soccer games, player violence precedes most incidents of fan violence (Goldstein, 1982).

Although family or subculture may model aggression, television offers a much wider range of violent models. As the next module explains, viewing televised violence tends to (1) increase aggressiveness, (2) desensitize viewers to violence, and (3) shape their assumptions about social reality.

So, people learn aggressive responses both by experience and by observing aggressive models. But when will aggressive responses actually occur? Bandura (1979) contends that aggressive acts are motivated by a variety of aversive experiences—frustration, pain, insults (Figure 24-2). Such experiences arouse us emotionally. But whether we act aggressively depends upon the consequences we anticipate. Aggression is most likely when we are aroused *and* it seems safe and rewarding to aggress.

Environmental Influences

Social learning theory offers a perspective from which we can examine specific influences on aggression. Under what conditions are we most likely to aggress? What environmental influences pull our trigger?

Painful Incidents
Researcher Nathan Azrin wanted to know if switching off foot shocks would reinforce two rats' positive interactions with each other. Azrin planned to turn on the shock and then, once the rats approached each other, cut off the pain. To his great surprise, the experiment proved impossible. As soon as the rats felt pain, they attacked each other, before the experimenter could switch off the shock.

FIGURE 24-2
The social learning view of aggression. The emotional arousal stemming from an aversive experience motivates aggression. Whether aggression or some other response actually occurs depends on what consequences we have learned to expect.   (Based on Bandura, 1979.)

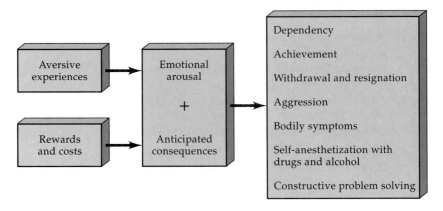

Is this true of rats alone? The researchers found that with a wide variety of species, the cruelty the animals imposed upon each other matched zap for zap the cruelty imposed upon them. (Under today's ethical guidelines, animals' welfare is better protected.) As Azrin (1967) explained, the pain-attack response occurred

> . . . in many different strains of rats. Then we found that shock produced attack when pairs of the following species were caged together: some kinds of mice, hamsters, opossums, raccoons, marmosets, foxes, nutria, cats, snapping turtles, squirrel monkeys, ferrets, red squirrels, bantam roosters, alligators, crayfish, amphiuma (an amphibian), and several species of snakes including the boa constrictor, rattlesnake, brown rat-snake, cottonmouth, copperhead, and black snake. The shock-attack reaction was clearly present in many very different kinds of creatures. In all the species in which shock produced attack it was fast and consistent, in the same "push-button" manner as with the rats.

The animals were not choosy about their targets. They would attack animals of their own species and also those of a different species, or stuffed dolls, or even tennis balls.

Azrin and his colleagues also varied the source of pain. They found that not just shocks induce attack; intense heat and "psychological pain"—for example, suddenly not rewarding hungry pigeons that have been trained to expect a grain reward after pecking at a disk—brought the same reaction. Such "psychological pain" is, of course, what we call frustration.

Pain heightens aggressiveness in humans, also. Many of us can recall such a reaction after stubbing a toe or suffering a headache. Leonard Berkowitz and his associates demonstrated this by having University of Wisconsin students hold one hand in lukewarm water or painfully cold water. Those whose hands were submerged in the cold water reported feeling more irritable and more annoyed, and they were more willing to blast another person with unpleasant noise. In view of such results, Berkowitz (1983, 1989) now believes that aversive stimulation rather than frustration is the basic trigger of hostile aggression. Frustration is certainly one important type of unpleasantness. But any aversive event—whether a dashed expectation, a personal insult, or physical pain—can incite an emotional outburst. Even the torment of a depressed state increases the likelihood of hostile aggressive behavior.

Heat

An uncomfortable environment also heightens aggressive tendencies. Offensive odors, cigarette smoke, and air pollution have all been linked with aggressive behavior (Rotton & Frey, 1985). But the most-studied environmental irritant is heat. William Griffitt (1970; Griffitt & Veitch, 1971) found that compared to students who answered questionnaires in a room with a normal temperature, those who did so in an uncomfortably hot room (over 90°F) reported feeling more tired and aggressive and expressed more hostility toward a stranger. Follow-up experiments revealed that heat also triggers retaliative actions (Bell, 1980; Rule & others, 1987).

Does uncomfortable heat increase aggression in the real world as well as in the laboratory? Consider:

- The riots occurring in 79 U.S. cities between 1967 and 1971 were more likely on hot than on cool days.
- When the weather is hot in Houston, Texas, violent crimes are more likely. The same is true in Des Moines, Iowa (Cotton, 1981); Dayton, Ohio (Rotton & Frey, 1985); Indianapolis, Indiana (Cotton, 1986); and Dallas, Texas (Harries & Stadler, 1988).
- Not only do hotter days have more violent crimes, so do hotter seasons of the year and hotter summers (Anderson, 1989).
- In heat-stricken Phoenix, Arizona, drivers without air conditioning are more likely to honk at a stalled car (Kenrick & MacFarlane, 1986).
- During the 1986 to 1988 major league baseball seasons, the number of batters hit by a pitch was two-thirds greater for games played in 90° temperatures than for games played below 80° (Reifman & others, 1991). Pitchers weren't wilder on hot days: they had no more walks and wild pitches. They just clobbered more batters.

Attacks

Being attacked by another is especially conducive to aggression. Experiments at Kent State University by Stuart Taylor (Taylor & Pisano, 1971), at Washington State University by Harold Dengerink (Dengerink & Myers, 1977), and at Osaka University by Kennichi Ohbuchi and Toshihiro Kambara (1985) confirm that intentional attacks breed retaliatory attacks. In most of these experiments one person competes with another in a reaction-time contest. After each test trial, the winner chooses how much shock to give the loser. Actually, each subject is playing a programmed opponent, who steadily escalates the amount of shock. Do the real subjects respond charitably, "turning the other cheek"? Hardly. Extracting "an eye for an eye" is the more likely response. When attacked, subjects usually retaliate in kind.

Crowding

To feel **crowded**, to feel one doesn't have enough space, is to feel stressed. Crammed in the back of a bus, trapped in slow-moving freeway traffic, or living three to a small room in a college dorm diminishes one's sense of control (Baron & others, 1976; McNeel, 1980). Might such experiences also heighten aggression?

The stress experienced by animals allowed to overpopulate a confined environment does heighten aggressiveness (Calhoun, 1962; Christian & others, 1960). But it is a rather large leap from rats in an enclosure or deer on an island to human beings in a city. Nevertheless, it's true that dense urban areas do experience higher rates of crime and emotional distress (Fleming & others, 1987; Kirmeyer, 1978). Even when they don't suffer higher crime rates, residents of crowded cities may *feel* more fearful. Toronto's crime rate is four times higher than Hong Kong's. Yet people from Hong Kong, which is four times more densely populated than Toronto, report feeling more fearful on their city's streets than people from Toronto (Gifford & Peacock, 1979).

REDUCING AGGRESSION

We have examined instinct, frustration-aggression, and social learning theories of aggression, and we have scrutinized influences on aggression. How, then, can we reduce aggression? Do theory and research suggest ways to control aggression?

Catharsis

"Youngsters should be taught to vent their anger." So advised Ann Landers (1973). If a person "bottles up his rage, we have to find an outlet. We have to give him an opportunity of letting off steam." So asserted the prominent psychiatrist Fritz Perls (1973). Both statements assume the "hydraulic model"—that, like dammed-up water, accumulated aggressive energy, whether derived from instinctual impulses or from frustrations, needs a release.

The concept of **catharsis**—emotional release through action or fantasy—is usually credited to Aristotle. Although Aristotle actually said nothing about aggression, he did argue that we can purge emotions by experiencing them and that viewing the classic tragedies therefore enabled a catharsis ("purgation") of pity and fear. To have an emotion excited, he believed, is to have that emotion released (Butcher, 1951). The catharsis hypothesis has been extended to include the emotional release supposedly obtained not only by observing drama but also through recalling and reliving past events, through expressing emotions, and through various actions. In such ways, we supposedly "blow off a little steam."

Catharsis sometimes occurs. Confiding, as we noted in an earlier module, is good for both soul and body. Even expressing anger can temporarily calm us *if* it doesn't leave us feeling guilty or anxious about retaliation (Geen & Quanty, 1977; Hokanson & Edelman, 1966). But in the long run expressing anger is more likely to breed anger. Robert Arms and his associates report that Canadian and American spectators of football, wrestling, and hockey exhibit *more* hostility after viewing the event than before (Arms & others, 1979; Goldstein & Arms, 1971; Russell, 1983). Not even war seems to purge aggressive feelings. After a war, a nation's murder rate tends to jump (Archer & Gartner, 1976).

In experiments, too, aggressing has led to heightened aggression. Ebbe Ebbesen and his coresearchers (1975) interviewed 100 engineers and technicians shortly after they were angered by layoff notices. Some were asked questions that gave them an opportunity to express hostility against their employer or supervisor—for example, "What instances can you think of where the company has not been fair with you?" Afterward, they answered a questionnaire assessing attitudes toward the company and the supervisor. Did the previous opportunity to "vent" or "drain off" their hostility reduce it? To the contrary, their hostility increased. Expressing hostility bred more hostility.

Sound familiar? Recall from Module 9 on behavior and belief that cruel acts beget cruel attitudes. Furthermore, as we noted in analyzing Stanley Milgram's obedience experiments, little aggressive acts can breed their own justification. People derogate their victims, rationalizing further aggression. Even if retaliation sometimes (in the short run) reduces tension, in the long run it reduces inhibitions. We can speculate that this will be true especially when, as often happens, the force of the aggressive outburst is an overreaction to the provocation.

Should we therefore bottle up anger and aggressive urges? Silent sulking is hardly more effective, because it allows us to continue reciting our grievances as we conduct conversations in our head. Fortunately, there are other nonaggressive ways to express our feelings and to inform others how their behavior affects us. Stating "I'm angry" or "When you talk like that I feel irritated" communicates our feelings in a way that leads the other person to make amends rather than further escalate the aggression. It is possible to be assertive without being aggressive.

A Social Learning Approach

If aggressive behavior is learned rather than instinctive, then there is hope for its control. Let us briefly review factors that influence aggression and speculate how to counteract them.

Aversive experiences such as frustrated expectations create a readiness to aggress. So it is wise to refrain from planting false, unreachable expectations in people's minds. Anticipated rewards and costs control instrumental aggression. This suggests that we should reward cooperative, nonaggressive behavior. In experiments, children become less aggressive when their aggressive behavior is ignored (rather than rewarded with attention) and when their nonaggressive behavior is reinforced (Hamblin & others, 1969).

Observing aggressive models can lower inhibitions and elicit imitation. This suggests new ways to reduce brutal, dehumanizing portrayals in films and on television, steps comparable to those already taken to reduce racist and sexist portrayals. It also suggests inoculating children against the effects of media violence. Despairing that the TV networks would ever "face the facts and change their programming," Eron and Huesmann (1984) taught 170 Oak Park, Illinois, children that television portrays the world unrealistically, that aggression is less common and effective than TV suggests, and that aggressive behavior is undesirable. (Drawing upon attitude research, Eron and Huesmann encouraged children to draw these inferences themselves and to attribute their expressed criticisms of television to their own convictions.) When restudied two years later, these children were less influenced by TV violence than were untrained children.

Aggression is also triggered by aggressive stimuli. This suggests reducing the availability of weapons such as handguns. Jamaica in 1974 implemented a sweeping anticrime program that included strict gun control and censorship of gun scenes from television and movies (Diener & Crandall, 1979). In the following year, robberies dropped 25 percent, nonfatal shootings 37 percent. In Sweden, the toy industry has discontinued the sale of war toys. The Swedish Information Service (1980) states the national attitude: "Playing at war means learning to settle disputes by violent means."

Suggestions such as these can help us minimize aggression. But given the complexity of aggression's causes and the difficulty of controlling them, who can feel the optimism expressed by Andrew Carnegie's forecast that in the twentieth century "to kill a man will be considered as disgusting as we in this day consider it disgusting to eat one." Since Carnegie uttered those words in 1900, some 200 million human beings have been killed. It is a sad irony that although today we understand human aggression better than ever before, humanity's inhumanity is hardly diminished.

CONCEPTS TO REMEMBER

Aggression   Physical or verbal behavior intended to hurt someone.

Frustration   The blocking of goal-directed behavior.

Displacement   The redirection of aggression to a target other than the source of the frustration. Generally, the new target is a safer or more socially acceptable target.

Social learning theory   The theory that we learn social behavior by observing and imitating and by being rewarded and punished.

Crowding   A subjective feeling of not enough space per person.

Catharsis   Emotional release through action or fantasy. The catharsis view of aggression is that aggressive drive is reduced when one "releases" aggressive energy, either by acting aggressively or by fantasizing aggression.

MODULE

25

Do the Media Influence Social Behavior?

❖

The quintupled American violent crime rate and the quadrupled rape rate since 1960 prompt our wondering: Why the change? What social forces have caused the mushrooming violence?

Alcohol contributes to aggression; but alcohol use has actually *declined* slightly since 1960 (Gallup & Newport, 1990). Might the surging violence instead be fueled by the growth in individualism and materialism? by the growing gap between the empowered rich and the powerless poor? by the media's increasing modeling of violence and unrestrained sexuality? The latter question arises because increased rates of violence and sexual coercion and harassment have coincided with increases in media mayhem and sexual suggestion. Is the historical correlation a mere coincidence? What are the effects of modeling violence in movies and on television? And what are the social consequences of pornography (which *Webster's* defines as erotic depictions intended to excite sexual arousal)?

TELEVISION

Picture this scene from one of Albert Bandura's experiments (Bandura & others, 1961). A Stanford nursery school child is put to work on an interesting art activity. An adult is in another part of the room, where there are Tinker Toys, a mallet, and a big inflated doll. After a minute of working with the Tinker Toys, the adult gets up and for almost 10 minutes attacks the inflated doll. She pounds it with the

257

mallet, kicks it, and throws it, all the while yelling, "Sock him in the nose. . . . Knock him down. . . . Kick him."

After observing this outburst, the child goes to a different room with many very attractive toys. But after two minutes the experimenter interrupts, saying these are her best toys and she must "save them for the other children." The frustrated child now goes into another room with various toys for aggressive and nonaggressive play, two of which are a Bobo doll and a mallet.

Seldom did children not exposed to the aggressive adult model display any aggressive play or talk. Although frustrated, they nevertheless played calmly. Those who had observed the aggressive adult were many times more likely to pick up the mallet and lash out at the doll. Watching the adult's aggressive behavior lowered their inhibitions. Moreover, the children often reproduced the model's acts and said her words. Observing aggressive behavior had both lowered their inhibitions and taught them ways to aggress.

If watching an aggressive model can unleash children's aggressive urges and teach them new ways to aggress, would watching aggressive models on television similarly affect children? Consider these few facts about watching television. In 1945, the Gallup poll asked Americans, "Do you know what television is?" (Gallup, 1972, p. 551). Today, in America, as in much of the industrialized world, 98 percent of all households have a TV set, more than have bathtubs or telephones. In the average home, the set is on seven hours a day, with a household member watching it four hours.

During all those hours, what social behaviors are modeled? Since 1967, George Gerbner and other TV watchers (1990) at the University of Pennsylvania have been sampling U.S. network prime-time and Saturday morning entertainment programs. Their findings? Seven out of ten programs contain violence ("physically compelling action that threatens to hurt or kill, or actual hurting or killing"). Prime-time programs average five violent acts per hour; Saturday morning children's programs, twenty-five per hour. Since 1967 the yearly rates of televised cruelty have never varied by more than 30 percent from the average for the whole period. Reflecting on his 22 years of cruelty counting, Gerbner (in press) lamented, "Humankind has had more bloodthirsty eras but none as filled with *images* of violence as the present. We are awash in a tide of violent representations the world has never seen . . . drenching every home with graphic scenes of expertly choreographed brutality."

These two facts—(1) more than 1000 hours a year of television watching per person and (2) a heavy dose of aggression in the typical television diet—arouse concern about the cumulative effects of viewing. Does prime-time crime stimulate the behavior it depicts? Or, as viewers vicariously participate in aggressive acts, do the shows drain off aggressive energy?

The latter idea, a variation on the catharsis hypothesis, maintains that watching violent drama enables people to release their pent-up hostilities. Defenders of the media cite this theory frequently and remind us that violence predates television. In an imaginary debate with one of television's critics, the medium's defender might argue, "Television played no role in the genocides of Jews and Native Americans. Television just reflects and caters to our tastes." "Agreed," responds the critic, "but it's also true that during America's TV age violent crime has increased several times faster than the population rate. Surely you don't mean that the popular arts are mere passive reflections, without any power to influence public consciousness." The defender replies: "The violence epidemic results from many factors. TV may even reduce aggression by keeping people off the streets and by offering them a harmless opportunity to vent their aggression."

Television's Effects on Behavior

Do viewers imitate violent models? Examples abound of people reenacting television crimes. In one informal survey of 208 prison convicts, 9 out of 10 admitted that by watching crime programs they learned new criminal tricks. And 4 out of 10 said they had attempted specific crimes seen on television (*TV Guide*, 1977).

Correlation of TV Viewing and Behavior
Crime stories are not scientific evidence. Nor do they tell us how television affects those who have never committed violent crimes. Researchers therefore use correlational and experimental studies to examine the effects of viewing violence. One technique, commonly used with schoolchildren, asks whether their TV watching predicts their aggressiveness. To some extent it does. The more violent the content of the child's TV viewing, the more aggressive the child (Eron, 1987; Turner & others, 1986). The relationship is modest but consistently found in the United States, Europe, and Australia.

So can we conclude that a violent TV diet fuels aggression? Perhaps you are already thinking that because this is a correlational study, the cause-effect relation could also work in the opposite direction. Maybe aggressive children prefer aggressive programs. Or maybe some underlying third factor, such as lower intelligence, predisposes some children both to prefer aggressive programs and to act aggressively.

Researchers have developed two ways to test these alternative explanations. They test the "hidden third factor" explanation by statistically pulling out the influence of some of these possible factors. For example, British researcher William Belson (1978; Muson, 1978) studied 1565 London boys. Compared to those who watched little violence, those who watched a great deal (especially realistic rather than cartoon violence) admitted to 50 percent more violent acts during the preceding six months (for example, "I busted the telephone in a telephone box"). Belson also examined 22 likely third factors, such as family size. The heavy and light viewers still differed after equating them with respect to potential third factors. So Belson surmised that the heavy viewers were indeed more violent *because* of their TV exposure.

Similarly, Leonard Eron and Rowell Huesmann (1980, 1985) found that violence viewing among 875 eight-year-olds correlated with aggressiveness even after statistically pulling out several obvious possible third factors. Moreover, when they restudied these individuals as 19-year-olds, they discovered that violence viewing at age 8 modestly predicted aggressiveness at age 19, but that aggressiveness at age 8 did *not* predict the violence viewing at age 19. Thus aggression followed viewing, not the reverse. They confirmed these findings in follow-up studies of 758 Chicago-area and 220 Finnish youngsters (Huesmann & others, 1984). What is more, when Eron and Huesmann (1984) examined the later criminal conviction records of their initial sample of 8-year-olds, they found that at age 30, those men who as children had watched a great deal of violent television were more likely to have been convicted of a serious crime (Figure 25–1).

FIGURE 25–1
Children's television viewing and later criminal activity. Violence viewing at age 8 was a predictor of a serious criminal offense by age 30.   (Data from Eron & Huesmann, 1984.)

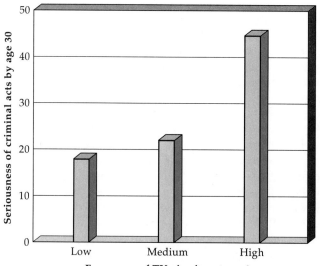

Even murder rates increase when and where television comes. In Canada and the United States, the homicide rate doubled between 1957 and 1974 as violent television spread. In census regions where television came later, the homicide rate jumped later too. In White South Africa, where television was not introduced until 1975, a similar near doubling of the homicide rate did not begin until after 1975 (Centerwall, 1989). And in a closely studied rural Canadian town where television came late, playground aggression doubled soon after (Williams, 1986).

Notice that these studies illustrate how researchers are now using correlational findings to *suggest* cause and effect. Yet, an infinite number of possible third factors could be creating a merely coincidental relation between viewing violence and aggression. Fortunately, however, the experimental method can control these extraneous factors. If we randomly assign some children to watch a violent film and others a nonviolent film, any later aggression difference between the two groups will be due to the only factor that distinguishes them: what they watched.

TV Viewing Experiments

The pioneering experiments by Albert Bandura and Richard Walters (1963) sometimes had young children view the adult pounding the inflated doll on film instead of observing it live—with much the same effect. Then Leonard Berkowitz and Russell Geen (1966) found that angered college students who viewed a violent film acted more aggressively than similarly angered students who viewed nonaggressive films. These laboratory experiments, coupled with growing public concern, were sufficient to prompt the U.S. Surgeon General to commission 50 new research studies during the early 1970s. By and large, these studies confirmed that viewing violence amplifies aggression.

In a later series of experiments, research teams led by Ross Parke (1977) in the United States and Jacques Leyens (1975) in Belgium showed institutionalized American and Belgian delinquent boys a series of either aggressive or nonaggressive commercial films. Their consistent finding: "Exposure to movie violence . . . led to an increase in viewer aggression." Compared to the week preceding the film series, physical attacks increased sharply in cottages where boys were viewing violent films.

The Convergence of Evidence

Television research has involved a variety of methods and participants. One ambitious researcher, Susan Hearold (1986), assembled results from 230 correlational and experimental studies involving more than 100,000 people. Her conclusion: Viewing antisocial portrayals is indeed associated with antisocial behavior. The effect is not overwhelming and is, in fact, at times so modest that some critics doubt it exists (Freedman, 1988; McGuire, 1986). Moreover, the aggression provoked in these experiments is not assault and battery; it's more on the scale of a shove in the lunch line, a cruel comment, a threatening gesture.

Nevertheless, the convergence of evidence is striking. Experimental studies point most clearly to cause and effect, but they are sometimes remote from real life (for example, pushing a hurt button). Moreover, the experiments can but hint at the cumulative effects of witnessing more than 100,000 violent episodes and some 20,000 murders, as the average American child does before becoming the average American teenager (Murray & Lonnborg, 1989). Uncontrolled influences complicate the correlational studies, but such studies do tap the cumulative effects of real-life viewing.

Why Does TV Viewing Affect Behavior?

We know from experiments that prolonged violence viewing has two effects on thinking. It desensitizes people to cruelty. (Emotionally numbed, they say, "It doesn't bother me at all.") And it distorts their perceptions of reality. (They exaggerate the frequency of violence and become more fearful.) But why does violence viewing also affect *behavior*. The conclusion drawn by the Surgeon General and by these researchers is *not* that television is the primary cause of social violence, any more than cyclamates are a primary cause of cancer. Rather, they say, television is *a* cause. Even if it is just one ingredient in a complex recipe for violence, it is one that, like cyclamates, is potentially controllable. Given the convergence of correlational and experimental evidence, researchers have explored *why* viewing violence has this effect.

Consider three possibilities (Geen & Thomas, 1986). One is that it's not the violent content per se that causes social violence but the *arousal* produced by the exciting action (Mueller & others, 1983; Zillmann, 1989). Experiments show that arousal can feed one emotion or another, depending on how we interpret and label it (Schachter & Singer, 1962). Pumped up—whether by physical exercise, sexual stimulation, or anger—our arousal may spill over into another emotion. Thus love is never so passionate as after a fight or a fright. Likewise, if aroused, people respond to provocation with heightened anger and aggression. One type of arousal energizes other behaviors.

Other research shows that viewing violence *disinhibits*. Viewing others performing an antisocial act can loosen our own restraints. In Bandura's experiment, the adult's punching the Bobo doll seemed to legitimate such outbursts and to lower the children's own inhibitions. Viewing violence primes the viewer for aggressive behavior by activating violence-related thoughts (Berkowitz, 1984; Bushman & Geen, 1990; Josephson, 1987).

Media portrayals also evoke *imitation*. The children in Bandura's experiments reenacted the specific behaviors they had witnessed. Even publicized suicides, whether fictional or real, have triggered a noticeable increase in copycat suicides (Jonas, 1991; Phillips & others, 1985, 1989). The commercial television industry is hard-pressed to dispute that television leads viewers to imitate what they have seen. Its advertisers model consumption. Television's critics agree—and are troubled that on TV programs acts of assault outnumber affectionate acts 4 to 1 and that, in other ways as well, television models an unreal world. TV cops fire their guns in almost every episode; actual Chicago police officers fire their guns an average of once every 27 years (Radecki, 1989). Nearly half of all beverages consumed on TV are alcoholic. In real life, no more than one-sixth of beverages are alcoholic (NCTV, 1988).

If the ways of relating and problem solving modeled on television do trigger imitation, especially among young viewers, then modeling **prosocial behavior** (positive, helpful behavior) should be socially beneficial. Happily, it is: Television's subtle influence can indeed teach children positive lessons in behavior. Susan Hearold (1986) statistically combined 108 comparisons of prosocial programs with neutral programs or no program. She found that, on average, "if the viewer watched prosocial programs instead of neutral programs, he would [at least temporarily] be elevated from the 50th to the 74th percentile in prosocial behavior—typically altruism."

In one such study, researchers Lynette Friedrich and Aletha Stein (1973; Stein & Friedrich, 1972) showed preschool children *Mister Rogers' Neighborhood* episodes each day for four weeks as part of their nursery school program. (*Mister Rogers* is an educational program designed to enhance young children's social and emotional development.) During this viewing period, children from less educated homes became more cooperative, helpful, and likely to state their feelings. In a follow-up study, kindergartners who viewed four *Mister Rogers* programs were able to state its prosocial content, both on a test and in puppet play (Friedrich & Stein, 1975; also Coates & others, 1976).

PORNOGRAPHY AND SEXUAL VIOLENCE

Repeated exposure to fictional eroticism has several effects. It can decrease attraction for one's less exciting real-life partner (Kenrick & others, 1989). It may also increase acceptance of extramarital sex and of women's sexual submission to men (Zillmann, 1989). Rock video images of macho men and sexually acquiescent women similarly color viewers' perceptions of men and women (Hansen, 1989; Hansen & Hansen 1988, 1990; St. Lawrence & Joyner, 1991). But social-psychological research has focused mostly on depictions of sexual violence.

A typical sexually violent episode finds a man forcing himself upon a woman. She at first resists and tries to fight off her attacker. Gradually she becomes sexually aroused, and as she does, her resistance melts. By the end she is in ecstasy, pleading for more. We have all viewed or read nonpornographic versions of this sequence: She resists; he persists. Dashing man grabs and forcibly kisses protesting woman. Within moments, the arms that were pushing him away are clutching him tight, her resistance overwhelmed by her unleashed passion. In *Gone with the Wind*, Scarlett O'Hara is carried to bed protesting and kicking, and wakes up singing.

Social psychologists report that viewing such fictional scenes of a man overpowering and arousing a woman can (1) distort one's perceptions of how women actually respond to sexual coercion and (2) increase men's aggression against women, at least in laboratory settings.

Distorted Perceptions of Sexual Reality

Does viewing sexual violence reinforce the myth that some women would welcome sexual assault—that "'no' doesn't really mean no"? To find out, Neil Malamuth and James Check (1981) showed University of Manitoba men either two nonsexual movies or two movies depicting a man sexually overcoming a woman. A week later, when surveyed by a different experimenter, those who saw the films with mild sexual violence were more accepting of violence against women. Viewing slasher movies has much the same effect. Men shown films such as the *Texas Chainsaw Massacre* become desensitized to brutality and more likely to view rape victims unsympathetically (Linz & others, 1988, 1989). On the basis of such findings, 21 social science researchers attending a Surgeon General's workshop (Koop, 1987) reached a consensus: "Pornography that portrays sexual aggression as pleasurable for the victim increases the acceptance of the use of coercion in sexual relations." In fact, say researchers Edward Donnerstein, Daniel Linz, and Steven Penrod (1987), what better way for an evil character to enable people to react calmly to the torture and mutilation of women than to show a gradually escalating series of such films.

Aggression against Women

Evidence also accumulates that pornography may contribute to men's actual aggression toward women. Correlational studies suggest that possibility. John Court (1984) notes that across the world, as pornography became more widely available during the 1960s and 1970s, the rate of reported rapes sharply increased—except in countries and areas where pornography has been controlled. (The examples that counter this trend—such as Japan, where violent pornography is available but the rape rate is low—remind us that other factors are also important.) In

Hawaii, the number of reported rapes rose ninefold between 1960 and 1974, then dropped when restraints on pornography were temporarily imposed, and then rose again when the restraints were lifted.

In another correlational study, Larry Baron and Murray Straus (1984) discovered that the sales of "soft-core" sexually explicit magazines (such as *Hustler* and *Playboy*) in each of the 50 states correlate with state rape rates. After controlling for other factors, such as the percentage of young males in each state, a positive relationship remained. Alaska ranked first in sex magazine sales and first in rape. Nevada was second on both measures.

When interviewed, Canadian and American sexual offenders commonly acknowledge pornography use. For example, William Marshall (1989) reports that Ontario rapists and child molesters use pornography much more than men who are not sexual offenders. An FBI study also reports considerable exposure to pornography among serial killers (Ressler & others, 1988). Of course, this *correlation* cannot prove that pornography is a contributing *cause* of rape. Maybe the offenders' use of pornography is merely a symptom and not a cause of their basic deviance.

Although limited to the sorts of short-term behaviors that can be studied in the laboratory, controlled experiments reveal that—to quote another of the consensus statements—"exposure to violent pornography increases punitive behavior toward women" (Koop, 1987). One of these social scientists, Edward Donnerstein (1980), had shown 120 University of Wisconsin men either a neutral, an erotic, or an aggressive-erotic (rape) film. Then, the men, supposedly as part of another experiment, "taught" a male or female confederate some nonsense syllables by choosing how much shock to administer for incorrect answers. The men who had watched the rape film administered markedly stronger shocks—but only to female victims (Figure 25–2).

If the ethics of conducting experiments such as these trouble you, rest assured that these researchers appreciate the controversial and powerful experience they are giving participants, and they are careful to warn participants what they might be shown. Only after giving their knowing consent do people participate. Moreover, after the experiment researchers debunk any myths the film communicated. One hopes that such debriefing sufficiently offsets the vivid image of a supposedly euphoric rape victim. Judging from studies with University of Manitoba and Winnipeg students by James Check and Neil Malamuth (1984; Malamuth & Check, 1984), it does. Those who read erotic rape stories and were then debriefed became *less* accepting of the "women-enjoy-rape" myth than students who had not seen the film. Similarly, Donnerstein and Berkowitz (1981) found that Wisconsin students who viewed pornography *and* were then thoroughly debriefed were later less likely than other students to agree that "being roughed up is sexually stimulating to many women."

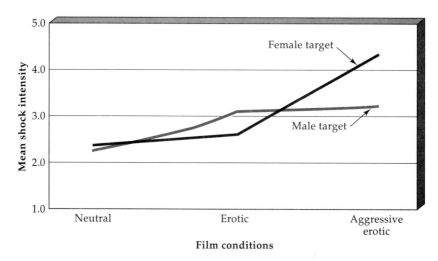

FIGURE 25–2
After viewing an aggressive-erotic film, college men delivered stronger shocks than before, especially to a woman. (Data from Donnerstein, 1980.)

Justification for this experimentation is not only scientific but also humanitarian. In 1990, some 103,000 U.S. women—one every five minutes—were known to have suffered the horror of forcible rape, four times the rate of 30 years earlier (FBI *Uniform Crime Reports*, 1971 to 1990). Does this increase merely reflect an increasing willingness to *report* rapes? Consider: In the government's annual National Crime Survey, the percentage of acknowledged rapes reported to police has *not* been increasing (Koss, 1992). Moreover, today's women under 45—who are more vulnerable to rape—are two to three times more likely than those over 65 to report *ever* having been raped (Sorenson & others, 1987). (Those over 65 were young women in an earlier era when—if you believe their reports—rape was much less common.) Finally, the quadrupled rape rate parallels the quintupled violent crime rate since 1960. Ergo, it seems that sexual violence has indeed increased.

In surveys of 6200 college students nationwide and 2200 Ohio working women, Mary Koss and her colleagues (1988, 1989, 1990) found that 28 percent of the women reported an experience that meets the legal definition of rape or attempted rape (although most, having been overcome on a date or by an acquaintance, didn't label it as such). Three in four stranger rapes and nearly all acquaintance rapes went unreported to police. Thus the known rape rate *greatly* underestimates the actual rape rate. Moreover, many more women—half in one recent survey of college women (Sandberg & others, 1985)—report having suffered some form of sexual assault while on a date, and even more have experienced verbal sexual coercion or harassment (Craig, 1990; Pryor, 1987).

Malamuth, Donnerstein, and Zillmann are among those alarmed by women's increasing risk of being sexually harassed or raped. They caution against oversimplifying the complex causes of rape—which is no more attributable to any one cause than cancer. Yet they conclude that viewing violence, especially sexual violence, can have antisocial effects. Just as most Germans quietly tolerated the degrading anti-Semitic images that fed the Holocaust, so most people today tolerate media images of women that feed what some call the growing "female holocaust" of sexual harassment, abuse, and rape.

Is the answer censorship? Most people support censorship in instances where one person's rights are trampled by another's free expression (as in cases involving child pornography, slander, and false advertising). In 1992 the Supreme Court of Canada extended such protection to women when it unanimously upheld an antipornography law that suppresses materials deemed harmful to the equal rights of women. "If true equality between male and female persons is to be achieved, we cannot ignore the threat to equality resulting from exposure to audiences of certain types of violent and degrading material," the court declared.

In the contest of individual versus collective rights, most western nations, however, side with individual rights. Thus, as an alternative to censorship, many psychologists favor "media awareness training." Recall that pornography researchers have successfully resensitized and educated participants to women's actual responses to sexual violence. Could educators similarly promote critical viewing skills? By sensitizing people to the view of women that predominates in pornography and to issues of sexual harassment and violence, it should be possible to counter the myth that women enjoy being coerced. "Our utopian and perhaps naive hope," say Edward Donnerstein, Daniel Linz, and Steven Penrod (1987, p. 196), "is that in the end the truth revealed through good science will prevail and the public will be convinced that these images not only demean those portrayed but also those who view them."

Is the hope naive? Consider: Without prohibition, growing health consciousness and alcohol awareness has increased the number of nondrinkers in the United States from 29 percent in 1978 to 43 percent in 1990 (Gallup & Newport, 1990). Without banning cigarettes (though with a ban on TV cigarette ads), the number of smokers has dropped from 43 percent in 1972 to 27 percent in 1989 (Gallup Organization, 1989). Without censoring racism, once-common media images of African-Americans as childlike, superstitious buffoons have nearly disappeared. As public consciousness changed, script writers, producers, and media executives decided that exploitative images of minorities were not good. More recently they have decided that drugs are not glamorous, as many films and songs from the 1960s and 1970s implied, but dangerous—and high school seniors' marijuana use during the previous month has plunged from 37 percent in 1979 to 14 percent in 1991 (Johnston & others, 1992). Will we one day look back with embarrassment on the time when movies entertained people with scenes of exploitation, mutilation, and sexual coercion?

CONCEPTS TO REMEMBER

Prosocial behavior   Positive, constructive, helpful social behavior; the opposite of antisocial behavior.

26

Causes of Conflict

❖

There is a speech that has been spoken in many languages by the leaders of many countries. It goes like this: "The intentions of our country are entirely peaceful. Yet, we are also aware of the world's unrest, and that other nations, with their new weapons, threaten us. Thus we must defend ourselves against attack. By so doing, we shall protect our way of life and preserve the peace" (L. F. Richardson, 1969). Almost every nation claims concern only for peace but, mistrusting other nations, arms itself in self-defense. The result: a world in which developing countries have eight soldiers for every doctor, a world with 51,000 nuclear weapons stockpiled (Sivard, 1991).

The elements of such **conflict** (a perceived incompatibility of actions or goals) are similar at all levels, from nations in an arms race to labor-management disputes to marital spats. Let's consider these conflict elements.

SOCIAL DILEMMAS

Several of the problems that most threaten our human future—nuclear arms, the greenhouse effect, pollution, overpopulation, natural resource depletion—arise as various parties pursue their self-interest but do so, ironically, to their collective detriment. Anyone can think: "It would cost me lots to buy expensive pollution controls. Besides, by itself my pollution is trivial." Many others reason similarly, and the result is befouled air and water. Thus, choices that are individually rewarding become collectively punishing when others choose the same. We therefore have an urgent dilemma: How can we reconcile the well-being of individual parties—their right to pursue freely their personal interests—with the well-being of the community?

To isolate and illustrate this dilemma, social psychologists have used laboratory games that expose the heart of many real social conflicts. By showing us how well-meaning people become trapped in mutually destructive behavior, they illuminate some fascinating, yet troubling, paradoxes of human existence. Consider two examples: the Prisoner's Dilemma and the Tragedy of the Commons.

The Prisoner's Dilemma

One dilemma derives from an anecdote concerning two suspects questioned separately by the district attorney (Rapoport, 1960). They are jointly guilty; however, the DA has only enough evidence to convict them of a lesser offense. So the DA creates an incentive for each to confess privately: If one confesses and the other doesn't, the DA will grant the confessor immunity (and will use the confession to convict the other of a maximum offense). If both confess, each will receive a moderate sentence. If neither confesses, each will receive a light sentence. Faced with such a dilemma, would you confess?

To minimize their own sentence, many would, despite the fact that mutual confession elicits more severe joint sentences than mutual nonconfession. In some 2000 studies (Dawes, 1991), university students have faced variations of the Prisoner's Dilemma with the outcomes being not prison terms but chips, money, or course points. As Figure 26–1 illustrates, on any given decision, a person is better off defecting (because such behavior exploits the other's cooperation or protects against the other's exploitation). However—and here's the rub—by not cooperating, both parties end up far worse off than if they trusted each other and gained a joint profit. This dilemma often traps each one in a maddening predicament in which both realize they *could* mutually profit but, mistrusting one another, become "locked in" to not cooperating.

The Tragedy of the Commons

Unlike conflicts between two nations, many other pressing social dilemmas involve many parties. The predicted greenhouse effect will stem mostly from widespread deforestation and from the carbon dioxide emissions of countless cars, oil burners, and coal-fired power plants. Similarly, each person who pollutes and exploits limited natural resources contributes infinitesimally to the world's pollution, and the harm each does is diffused over many people. To model such social predicaments, researchers have developed laboratory dilemmas that involve multiple people.

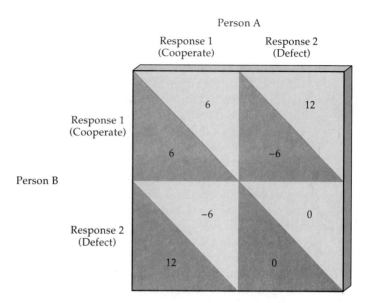

FIGURE 26-1
Laboratory version of the Prisoner's Dilemma. The numbers represent some reward, such as money. In each box, the number above the diagonal lines is the outcome for person A.

A metaphor for the insidious nature of social dilemmas is what ecologist Garrett Hardin (1968) called the "tragedy of the commons." He derived the name from the centrally located pasture in old English towns. However, the "commons" can be air, water, whales, cookies, or any shared and limited resource. If all use the resource in moderation, it may replenish itself as rapidly as it's harvested. The grass will grow, the whales will reproduce, and the cookie jar gets restocked.

Imagine 100 farmers surrounding a commons capable of sustaining 100 cows. When each grazes one cow, the common feeding ground is optimally used. But then someone reasons: "If I put a second cow in the pasture, I'll double my output, minus the mere 1 percent overgrazing." So this farmer adds a second cow. Then so does each of the other farmers. The inevitable result? The tragedy of the commons—a grassless mud field.

Many real predicaments parallel this story. Environmental pollution is the sum of many minor pollutions, each of which benefits the individual polluters much more than they could benefit themselves (and the environment) if they stopped their small pollution. We litter public places—dorm lounges, parks, zoos—but keep our personal spaces clean. And we deplete our natural resources, because the immediate personal benefits of, say, taking a long, hot shower outweigh the seemingly inconsequential costs. Whalers knew others would exploit the whales if they didn't and that taking a few whales would hardly diminish the species. Therein lay the tragedy. Everybody's business (conservation) became nobody's business.

The elements of the Commons Dilemma have been isolated in laboratory games. Put yourself in the place of Arizona State University students playing Julian Edney's Nuts Game (1979). You and several others sit around a shallow bowl that initially has ten metal nuts. The experimenter explains that your goal is to accumulate as many nuts as possible. Each of you at any time may take as many as you want, and every 10 seconds the number of nuts remaining in the bowl will be doubled. Would you leave the nuts in the bowl to regenerate, thus producing a greater harvest for all?

Likely not. Unless they were given time to devise and agree upon a conservation strategy, 65 percent of Edney's groups never reached the first 10-second replenishment. Often the people knocked the bowl on the floor grabbing for their share.

Edney's nut bowl reminds me of the cookie jar in our home. What we *should* do is conserve cookies during the interval between weekly restockings, so that each day we can each munch two or three. Lacking regulation and fearing that other family members will soon deplete the resource, what we actually do is maximize our individual cookie consumption by downing one after the other. The result: Within 24 hours the cookie glut ends, the jar sits empty, and we again await its replenishment.

The Prisoner's Dilemma and Commons Dilemma games have several similar features. First, both tempt people to explain their own behavior situationally ("I had to protect myself against exploitation by my opponent") and to explain their partners' behavior dispositionally ("She was greedy," "He was untrustworthy"). Most never realize that their counterparts are viewing them with the same fundamental attribution error.

Second, motives often change. At first, people are eager to make some easy money, then to minimize their losses, and finally to save face and avoid defeat (Brockner & others, 1982; Teger, 1980). These shifting motives are strikingly similar to President Johnson's apparently shifting motives during the buildup of the Vietnam war. At first, his speeches described America's concern for democracy, freedom, and justice. As the conflict escalated, his expressed concern became protecting America's honor and avoiding the national humiliation of losing a war.

Third, most real-life conflicts, like the Prisoner's Dilemma and Commons Dilemma, are **non-zero-sum games**. The two sides' profits and losses need not add up to zero. Both can win; both can lose. Each game pits the immediate interests of individuals against the well-being of the group. Each is a social trap that shows how, even when individuals behave "rationally," harm can result. No malicious person planned for

Los Angeles to be smothered in smog, or for the horrendous destruction of the Vietnam conflict, or for the earth's atmosphere to be warmed by a blanket of carbon dioxide.

Not all self-serving behavior leads to collective doom. In a plentiful commons—as in the world of the eighteenth-century capitalist economist Adam Smith—individuals who seek to maximize their own profit may also give the community what it needs: "It is not from the benevolence of the butcher, the brewer, or the baker, that we expect our dinner, but from their regard to their own interest" (Smith, 1976, p. 18).

But in those situations that are indeed social traps, how can we induce people to cooperate for their mutual betterment?

Resolving Social Dilemmas

Research with the laboratory dilemmas has revealed several methods for promoting cooperation.

Regulation

If taxes were entirely voluntary, how many would pay their full share? Surely, many would not, which is why modern societies do not depend on voluntary charity to meet their needs for social and military security. We also develop laws and regulations for our common good. An International Whaling Commission sets an agreed-upon "harvest" that enables whales to regenerate.

Small Is Beautiful

In laboratory dilemma games, people who interact with only a few others cooperate more than those in larger groups (Dawes, 1980). In small commons, each person feels more responsible, effective, and identified with the group's success (Kerr, 1989). Although group identification occurs more readily in small groups, anything that gives people a "we feeling"—even just a few minutes of discussion or just believing that one shares similarities with others in the group—will increase cooperation (Brewer, 1987; Orbell & others, 1988). On the Puget Sound island where I grew up, our small neighborhood shared a communal water supply. On hot summer days when the reservoir ran low, a light came on, signaling our 15 families to conserve. Recognizing our responsibility to one another, and feeling like our conservation really mattered, each of us conserved. Never did the reservoir run dry. In a much larger commons—say, a city—voluntary conservation is less successful.

Communication

To escape a social trap, people must communicate. Without communication, those who expect others not to cooperate usually refuse to cooperate themselves (Messé & Sivacek, 1979; Pruitt & Kimmel, 1977). One who mistrusts almost has to be uncooperative (to protect against exploitation). Noncooperation, in turn, feeds further mistrust ("What else could I do? It's a dog-eat-dog world"). In experiments, communication reduces mistrust, enabling people to reach agreements that lead to their common betterment.

Changing the Payoffs

Cooperation rises when experimenters change the payoff matrix to make cooperation more rewarding and exploitation less rewarding (Komorita & Barth, 1985; Pruitt & Rubin, 1986). Changing payoffs also helps resolve actual dilemmas. In some cities, freeways clog and skies smog because people prefer the convenience of driving themselves directly to work. To alter the personal cost-benefit calculations, many of these cities now give carpoolers incentives, such as freeway lanes designated for their use.

Appeals to Altruistic Norms

When cooperation obviously serves the public good, one can usefully appeal to what a previous module called the social-responsibility norm. Basketball players will pass up a good shot to offer a teammate a better shot. Struggling for civil rights, many marchers willingly agreed, for the sake of their larger group, to suffer harassment, beatings, and jail. In wartime, people make great personal sacrifices for the good of their group. As Winston Churchill said of the Battle of Britain, the actions of the Royal Air Force pilots were genuinely altruistic: A great many people owed a great deal to those who flew into battle knowing the high probability they would not return.

To summarize, we can minimize destructive entrapment in social dilemmas by establishing rules that regulate self-serving behavior, by keeping groups small, by enabling people to communicate, by changing payoffs to make cooperation more rewarding, and by invoking altruistic norms.

COMPETITION

In the module on prejudice we noted that racial hostilities often arise when groups compete for jobs and housing. When interests clash, conflict erupts.

But does competition by itself provoke hostile conflict? Real-life situations are so complex that it is hard to be sure. If competition is indeed responsible, then it should be possible to provoke conflict in an experiment. We could randomly divide people into two groups, have the groups compete for a scarce resource, and note what happens. This is precisely what Muzafer Sherif (1966) and his colleagues did in a dramatic series of experiments with typical 11- and 12-year-old boys. The inspira-

tion for these experiments dated back to Sherif's witnessing, as a teenager, Greek troops invading his Turkish province in 1919.

> They started killing people right and left. [That] made a great impression on
> me. There and then I became interested in understanding why these things
> were happening among human beings. . . . I wanted to learn whatever
> science or specialization was needed to understand this intergroup savagery.
> (Quoted by Aron & Aron, 1989, p. 131)

After studying the social roots of savagery, Sherif introduced these
apparent essentials into several three-week summer camping experiences. In one such study, he divided 22 unacquainted Oklahoma City
boys into two groups, took them to a Boy Scout camp in separate buses,
and settled them in bunkhouses about a half mile apart. For most of the
first week, they were unaware of the other group's existence. By cooperating in various activities—preparing meals, camping out, fixing up a
swimming hole, building a rope bridge—each group soon became close-
knit. They gave themselves names: "Rattlers" and "Eagles." Typifying
the good feeling, a sign appeared in one cabin: "Home Sweet Home."

Group identity thus established, the stage was set for the conflict.
Toward the end of the first week, the Rattlers "discovered the Eagles on
'our' baseball field." When the camp staff then proposed a tournament of
competitive activities between the two groups (baseball games, tugs-of-
war, cabin inspections, treasure hunts, and so forth), both groups responded enthusiastically. This was win-lose competition. The spoils
(medals, knives) would all go to the tournament victor.

The result? The camp gradually degenerated into open warfare. It
was like a scene from William Golding's novel *Lord of the Flies*, which
depicts the social disintegration of boys marooned on an island. In
Sherif's study, the conflict began with each side calling the other deroga-
tory names during the competitive activities. Soon it escalated to dining
hall "garbage wars," flag burnings, cabin ransackings, even fistfights.
Asked to describe the other group, the boys said "they" were "sneaky,"
"smart alecks," "stinkers," while referring to their own group as
"brave," "tough," "friendly."

The win-lose competition had produced intense conflict, negative
images of the out-group, and strong in-group cohesiveness and pride
(making this, by today's standards, an ethically questionable study). All
this occurred without any cultural, physical, or economic differences
between the two groups and with boys who were their communities'
"cream of the crop." Sherif noted that had we visited the camp at this
point, we would have concluded that these "were wicked, disturbed, and
vicious bunches of youngsters" (1966, p. 85). Actually, their evil behavior
was triggered by an evil situation. Fortunately, as we will see in Module 27, Sherif not only made strangers into enemies but subsequently
made the enemies into friends.

P ERCEIVED INJUSTICE

"That's unfair!" "What a rip-off!" "We deserve better!" Such comments typify conflicts bred by perceived injustice. But what is "justice"? According to some social-psychological theorists, people perceive justice as equity—the distribution of rewards in proportion to individuals' contributions (Walster & others, 1987). If you and I have a relationship (employer-employee, teacher-student, husband-wife, colleague-colleague), it is equitable if:

$$\frac{\text{My outcomes}}{\text{My inputs}} = \frac{\text{your outcomes}}{\text{your inputs}}$$

If you contribute more and benefit less than I do, you will feel exploited and irritated; I may feel exploitative and guilty. Chances are, though, that you more than I will be sensitive to the inequity (Greenberg, 1986; Messick & Sentis, 1979).

We may agree with the equity principle's definition of justice yet disagree on whether our relationship is equitable. If two people are colleagues, what will each consider a relevant input? The one who is older may favor basing pay on seniority; the other, on current productivity. Given such a disagreement, whose definition is likely to prevail? More often than not, those with social power convince themselves and others that they deserve what they're getting (Mikula, 1984). Karl Marx anticipated this finding: "The class, which is the ruling material force of society, is at the same time its ruling intellectual force" (Walster & others, 1978, p. 220). This has been called a "golden" rule: Whoever has the gold makes the rules.

As this suggests, the exploiter can relieve guilt by valuing inputs to justify the existing outcomes. Some men may perceive the lower pay of women as equitable, given women's "less important" inputs. As we noted earlier, those who inflict harm may even blame the victim and thus maintain their belief in a just world.

And those who are exploited? How do they react? Elaine Hatfield, William Walster, and Ellen Berscheid (1978) detect three possibilities. They can accept and justify their inferior position ("We're poor; it's what we deserve, but we're happy"). They can demand compensation, perhaps by harassing, embarrassing, even cheating their exploiter. If all else fails, they may try to restore equity by retaliating.

An interesting implication of equity theory—an implication that has been confirmed experimentally—is that the more competent and worthy people feel (the more they value their inputs), the more they will feel that a given outcome is insufficient and thus retaliate (Ross & others, 1971). Intense social protests generally come from those who believe themselves worthy of more than they are receiving. Since 1970, professional oppor-

TABLE 26–1   GALLUP POLLS REVEAL
INCREASED PERCEPTIONS OF GENDER
INEQUALITY

*All things considered, who has a better life in this
country—men or women?*

	1975	1989
Men	32%	49%
Women	28	22
Same	31	21
No opinion	9	8

SOURCE: DeStefano & Colasanto, 1990.

tunities for women have significantly increased. Ironically, though understandably to an equity theorist, so have people's feelings that
women's status is *in*equitable (Table 26–1).

So long as women compared their opportunities and earnings with
those of other women, they felt generally satisfied (Jackson, 1989; Major,
1989). Now that women are more likely to see themselves as men's
equals, their sense of relative deprivation has grown. If secretarial work
and truck driving have "comparable worth" (for the skills required), then
they deserve comparable pay; that's equity, say advocates of gender
equality (Lowe & Wittig, 1989).

M ISPERCEPTION

Recall that conflict is a *perceived* incompatibility of actions or goals. Many
conflicts contain only a small core of truly incompatible goals; the bigger
problem is the misperceptions of the other's motives and goals. The
Eagles and the Rattlers did indeed have some genuinely incompatible
aims. But their perceptions subjectively magnified their differences (Figure 26–2).

In earlier modules we considered several seeds of such misperception. The *self-serving bias* leads individuals and groups to accept credit for
their good deeds and shuck responsibility for bad deeds, without according others the same benefit of the doubt. A tendency to *self-justify* further
inclines people to deny the wrong of evil acts that cannot be shucked off.
Thanks to the *fundamental attribution error*, each side sees the other's
hostility as reflecting an evil disposition. One then filters the information
and interprets it to fit one's *preconceptions*. Groups frequently *polarize*
these self-serving, self-justifying, biasing tendencies. One symptom of
groupthink is the tendency to perceive one's own group as moral and
strong, the opposition as evil and weak. Terrorist acts that are despicable

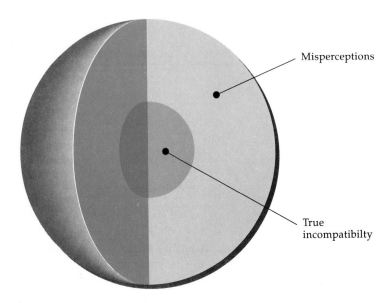

Misperceptions

True
incompatibilty

FIGURE 26–2
Most conflicts contain a core of truly incompatible goals
surrounded by a larger exterior of misperceptions.

brutality to most people are "holy war" to others. Indeed, the mere fact of
being in a group triggers an *ingroup bias*. And negative *stereotypes*, once
formed, are often resistant to contradictory evidence.

Given these seeds of social misperception, it should not surprise us,
though it should sober us, to discover that people in conflict form distorted images of one another. Even the types of misperception are in-
triguingly predictable.

Mirror-Image Perceptions

To a striking degree, the misperceptions of those in conflict are mutual.
People in conflict attribute similar virtues to themselves and vices to the
other. When American psychologist Urie Bronfenbrenner (1961) visited
the Soviet Union in 1960 and conversed with many ordinary citizens in
Russian, he was astonished to hear them saying the same things about
America that Americans were saying about the U.S.S.R. The Soviets said
that the U.S. government was militarily aggressive, that it exploited and
deluded the American people, that in diplomacy it was not to be trusted.
"Slowly and painfully, it forced itself upon one that the Russians' distorted picture of us was curiously similar to our view of them—a mirror
image."

When two sides have clashing perceptions, at least one of the two is
misperceiving the other. And when such misperceptions exist, noted

Bronfenbrenner, "it is a psychological phenomenon without parallel in the gravity of its consequences . . . for *it is characteristic of such images that they are self-confirming.*" If A expects B to be hostile, A may treat B in such a way that B fulfills A's expectations, thus beginning a vicious circle. Morton Deutsch (1986) explains:

> You hear the false rumor that a friend is saying nasty things about you; you snub him; he then badmouths you, confirming your expectation. Similarly, if the policymakers of East and West believe that war is likely and either attempts to increase its military security vis-a-vis the other, the other's response will justify the initial move.

Some observers of the Arab-Israeli conflict have concluded that negative **mirror-image perceptions** are a chief obstacle to peace. Both sides insist that "we" are motivated by our need to protect our security and our territory, while "they" want to obliterate us and gobble up our land (Heradstveit, 1979; White, 1977). Both sides have difficulty appreciating how their own actions sustain the other's fear and anger. Given such intense mistrust, negotiation is difficult.

Northern Ireland, too, suffers from mirror-image perceptions. At the University of Ulster, J. A. Hunter and his colleagues (1991) showed Catholic and Protestant students videos of a Protestant attack at a Catholic funeral and a Catholic attack at a Protestant funeral. Most students attributed the other side's attack to "bloodthirsty" motives but attributed its own side's attack to retaliation or self-defense. Muslims and Hindus in Bangladesh exhibit the same ingroup-favoring perceptions (Islam & Hewstone, 1991).

Destructive mirror-image perceptions also operate in conflicts between small groups and between individuals. As we saw in the dilemma games, both parties may say, "We want to cooperate. But their refusal to cooperate forces us to react defensively." In a study of executives, Kenneth Thomas and Louis Pondy (1977) uncovered similar self-serving attributions. Asked to describe a significant recent conflict, only 12 percent felt that the other party was cooperative; 74 percent perceived themselves as cooperative. The executives explained that they had "suggested," "informed," and "recommended," while their antagonist had "demanded," "disagreed with everything I said," and "refused."

International conflicts are fueled and prolonged by an illusion that the enemy's top leaders are evil and coercive, while their people, though controlled and manipulated, are pro-us. This evil leader–good people perception characterized Americans' and Soviets' views of each other during the cold war.

Another type of mirror-image perception is each side's exaggeration of the other's position. People with opposing views on issues such as abortion and capital punishment often differ less than they suppose. Each side overestimates the extremity of the other side's views and presumes that *our* beliefs *follow* from the facts while *their* beliefs *dictate* their interpretation of facts (Robinson & others, 1991).

Shifting Perceptions

If misperceptions accompany conflict, then they should appear and disappear as conflicts wax and wane. And they do, with startling ease. The same processes that create the enemy's image can reverse that image when the enemy becomes an ally. Thus the "bloodthirsty, cruel, treacherous, buck-toothed little Japs" of World War II became, soon after—in American minds (Gallup, 1972) and in the American media—our "intelligent, hardworking, self-disciplined, resourceful allies." Our World War II allies, the Soviets, then became the "warlike, treacherous" ones. The Germans—whom Americans after two world wars hated, then admired, and then again hated—were once again admired, apparently no longer plagued by what earlier was presumed to be cruelty in their national character. So long as Iraq was attacking Iran, even while using chemical weapons and massacring its own Kurds, many nations supported it. Our enemy's enemy is our friend. When Iraq ended its war with Iran and invaded oil-rich Kuwait, Iraq's behavior suddenly became "barbaric." Clearly, our images of our enemies not only justify our actions but also adjust with amazing ease.

The extent of misperceptions during conflict provides a chilling reminder that people need not be insane or abnormally evil to form distorted, diabolic images of their antagonists. When in conflict with another nation, another group, or simply a roommate or parent, we readily develop misperceptions that allow us to perceive our own motives and actions as wholly good and the other's as totally evil. Our antagonists usually form a mirror-image perception of us. So, trapped in a social dilemma, competing for scarce resources, or perceiving injustice, the conflict continues until something enables us both to peel away our misperceptions and work at reconciling our actual differences.

CONCEPTS TO REMEMBER

Conflict   A perceived incompatibility of actions or goals.

Non-zero-sum games   Games in which outcomes need not sum to zero. With cooperation, both can win; with competition, both can lose. (Also called *mixed-motive situations*.)

Mirror-image perceptions   Reciprocal views of one another often held by parties in conflict; for example, each may view itself as moral and peace-loving and the other as evil and aggressive.

MODULE

27

Blessed Are the Peacemakers

❖

W e have seen how conflicts are ignited: by social traps, competition, perceived injustices, and misperceptions. The picture appears grim— but not hopeless. Sometimes closed fists become open arms as hostilities evolve into friendships. Social psychologists have focused on four strategies for helping enemies become comrades. We can remember these as the four C's of peacemaking: contact, cooperation, communication, conciliation.

CONTACT

Might putting two conflicting individuals or groups into close contact enable them better to know and like each other? We have seen why it might. We have seen that proximity—and the accompanying interaction, anticipation of interaction, and mere exposure—boosts liking. We have noted that the recent downturn in blatant racial prejudice in the United States followed closely on the heels of desegregation, showing that "attitudes follow behavior."

During the last 30 years in the United States, segregation and prejudice have diminished together. But was interracial contact the *cause* of these improved attitudes? Were those who actually experienced desegregation affected by it?

Does Desegregation Improve Racial Attitudes?

School desegregation has produced measurable benefits, such as leading more Blacks to attend and succeed in college (Stephan, 1988). Does desegregation of schools, neighborhoods, and workplaces also produce favorable *social* results? The evidence is mixed.

On the one hand, many studies conducted during and shortly after the desegregation following World War II found Whites' attitudes toward Blacks improving markedly. Whether the people were department store clerks and customers, merchant marines, government workers, police officers, neighbors, or students, racial contact led to diminished prejudice (Amir, 1969; T. F. Pettigrew, 1969). For example, near the end of World War II, the Army partially desegregated some of its rifle companies (Stouffer & others, 1949). When asked their opinions of such desegregation, 11 percent of the White soldiers in segregated companies approved. Of those in desegregated companies, 60 percent approved.

These encouraging findings influenced the Supreme Court's 1954 decision to desegregate U.S. schools and helped fuel the civil rights movement of the 1960s (Pettigrew, 1986). Yet studies of the effects of school desegregation have been less encouraging. Social psychologist Walter Stephan (1986) reviewed all such studies and concluded that racial attitudes have been little affected by desegregation. (For Blacks the more noticeable consequence of desegregated schooling is their increased likelihood of later attending integrated colleges, living in integrated neighborhoods, and working in integrated settings.)

So, sometimes desegregation improves racial attitudes; sometimes it doesn't. Such disagreements excite the scientist's detective spirit. What explains the difference? So far, we've been lumping all desegregation together. Actual desegregation occurs in many ways and under vastly different conditions.

When Does Desegregation Improve Racial Attitudes?

Might the amount of interracial *contact* be a factor? Indeed it seems to be. Researchers have gone into dozens of desegregated schools and observed with whom children of a given race eat, loiter, and talk. Race influences contact. Whites disproportionately associate with Whites, Blacks with Blacks (Schofield, 1982, 1986). Academic tracking programs often amplify resegregation by separating academically advantaged White students into predominantly White classes.

In contrast, the more encouraging older studies of store clerks, soldiers, and housing project neighbors involved considerable interracial contact. Other studies involving prolonged, personal contact—between Black and White prison inmates and between Black and White girls in an interracial summer camp—show similar benefits (Clore & others, 1978; Foley, 1976).

The social psychologists who advocated desegregation never claimed that contact of *any* sort would improve attitudes. They expected less-than-favorable results when contacts were competitive, unsupported by authorities, and unequal (Pettigrew, 1988; Stephan, 1987). Before 1954, many prejudiced Whites had ample contact with Blacks—with the latter in subordinate roles as shoeshine boys and domestic workers. Contacts on such an unequal basis breed attitudes that merely justify the continuation of such relations. So it's important that people in contact have **equal status**. The contacts between the store clerks, the soldiers, the neighbors, the prisoners, the summer campers were of this kind.

COOPERATION

Although equal-status contact can help, it is sometimes not enough. It didn't help when Muzafer Sherif stopped the Eagles versus Rattlers competition and brought the groups together for noncompetitive activities, such as watching movies, shooting off fireworks, and eating. By this time, their hostility was so strong that mere contact provided the opportunity for taunts and attacks. When an Eagle was bumped by a Rattler, his fellow Eagles urged him to "brush off the dirt." Obviously, desegregating the two groups had hardly promoted their social integration.

Given such entrenched hostilities, what can a peacemaker do? Think back to the successful and unsuccessful desegregation efforts. The Army's racial mixing of rifle companies not only brought Blacks and Whites into equal-status contact but also made them interdependent. Together, they were fighting against a common enemy, striving toward a shared goal.

Contrast this interdependence with the competitive situation in the typical classroom, desegregated or not. Students compete for good grades, teacher approval, and various honors and privileges. Is the following scene familiar (Aronson, 1988)? The teacher asks a question. Several students' hands shoot up; other students sit, eyes downcast, trying to look invisible. When the teacher calls on one of the eager faces, the others hope for a wrong answer, giving them a chance to display their knowledge. The losers in this academic sport often resent those who succeed and may disparage them as "nerds" or "geeks." The situation abounds with both competition and painfully obvious status inequalities; we could hardly design it better to create divisions among the children.

Does this suggest a second factor that predicts whether the effect of desegregation will be favorable? Does competitive contact divide and *cooperative* contact unite? Consider what happens to people who together face a common predicament or work together toward a shared goal.

Common External Threats

Together with others, have you ever been victimized by the weather; harassed as part of your initiation into a group; punished by a teacher; or persecuted and ridiculed because of your social, racial, or religious identity? If so, you may recall feeling close to those with whom you shared the predicament. Perhaps previous social barriers were dropped as you helped one another dig out of the snow or struggled to cope with your common enemy.

Such friendliness is common among those who experience a shared threat. John Lanzetta (1955) observed this when he put four-man groups of Naval ROTC cadets to work on problem-solving tasks and then began informing them over a loudspeaker that their answers were wrong, their productivity inexcusably low, their thinking stupid. Other groups did not receive this harassment. Lanzetta observed that the group members under duress became friendlier to one another, more cooperative, less argumentative, less competitive. They were in it together. And the result was a cohesive spirit.

Having a common enemy also unified the groups of competing boys in Sherif's camping experiments and in many subsequent experiments (Dion, 1979). Americans' feeling of patriotism and unity was aroused by conflicts with Germany and Japan during World War II, with the Soviet Union during the cold war, with Iran during 1980, and with Iraq during 1991. Soldiers who together face combat often maintain lifelong ties with their comrades (Elder & Clipp, 1988). Few things so unite a people as having a common hatred.

Times of interracial strife may therefore be times of heightened group pride. For Chinese university students in Toronto, facing discrimination heightens a sense of kinship with other Chinese (Pak & others, 1991). Just being reminded of an outgroup (say, a rival school) heightens people's responsiveness to their own group (Wilder & Shapiro, 1984). When keenly conscious of who "they" are, we also know who "we" are.

Superordinate Goals

Closely related to the unifying power of an external threat is the unifying power of **superordinate goals**, goals compelling for all in a group and requiring cooperative effort. To promote harmony among his warring campers, Sherif introduced such goals. He created a problem with the camp water supply, necessitating their cooperation to restore the water. Given an opportunity to rent a movie, one expensive enough to require the joint resources of both groups, they again cooperated. When a truck "broke down" on a camping trip, a staff member casually left the tug-of-war rope nearby, prompting one boy to suggest that they all pull the truck to get it started. When it started, a backslapping celebration ensued over their victorious "tug-of-war against the truck."

After working together to achieve such superordinate goals, the boys began eating together and enjoyed themselves around a camp fire.

Friendships sprouted across group lines. Hostilities plummeted. On the last day, the boys decided to travel home together on one bus. During the trip they no longer sat by groups. As the bus approached Oklahoma City and home, they, as one, spontaneously sang "Oklahoma" and then bade their friends farewell. With isolation and competition, Sherif made strangers into bitter enemies. With superordinate goals, he made enemies into friends.

Are Sherif's experiments mere child's play? Or can pulling together to achieve superordinate goals be similarly beneficial with adults in conflict? Robert Blake and Jane Mouton (1979) wondered. So in a series of two-week experiments involving more than 1000 executives in 150 different groups, they re-created the essential features of the situation experienced by the Rattlers and Eagles. Each group first engaged in activities by itself, then competed with another group, and then cooperated with the other group in working toward jointly chosen superordinate goals. Their results provided, in the words of the researchers, "unequivocal evidence that adult reactions parallel those of Sherif's younger subjects."

Extending these findings, Samuel Gaertner, John Dovidio, and their collaborators (1989, 1990, 1991) report that working cooperatively has especially favorable effects under conditions that lead people to define a new, inclusive group that dissolves their former subgroups. If, for example, the members of two groups sit alternately around a table (rather than on opposite sides), give their new group a single name, and then work together, their old feelings of bias against the former outsiders will diminish. "Us" and "them" become "we."

Cooperative Learning

So far we have noted the apparently meager social benefits of typical school desegregation and the apparently dramatic social benefits of successful, cooperative contacts between members of rival groups. Could putting these two findings together suggest a constructive alternative to traditional desegregation practices? Several independent research teams speculated yes. Each wondered whether, without restraining academic achievement, we could promote interracial friendships by replacing competitive learning situations with cooperative ones. Given the diversity of their methods—all involving students on integrated study teams, sometimes in competition with other teams—the consistently positive results are striking and very heartening.

One research team, led by Elliot Aronson and Alex Gonzalez (1988), elicited similar group cooperation with a "jigsaw" technique. In experiments in Texas and California elementary schools, they assigned children to racially and academically diverse six-member groups. The subject was then divided into six parts, with each student becoming the expert on his or her part. In a unit on Chile, one student might be the expert on Chile's history, another on its geography, another on its culture, and so on. First, the various "historians," "geographers," and so forth got together to master their material. Then each returned to the home group to teach it to their classmates. Each group member held, so to speak, a piece of the jigsaw. The self-confident students therefore had to listen to and learn from the reticent students, who in turn soon realized they had something important to offer their peers.

With cooperative learning, students learn not only the material but other lessons as well. Cross-racial friendships begin to blossom. The exam scores of minority students improve (perhaps because academic achievement is now peer-supported). Many teachers continue using cooperative learning after the experiments are over (D. W. Johnson & others, 1981; Slavin, 1990). "It is clear," wrote race-relations expert John McConahay (1981), that cooperative learning "is the most effective practice for improving race relations in desegregated schools that we know of to date."

So, cooperative, equal-status contacts exert a positive influence on boy campers, industrial executives, college students, and schoolchildren. Can we assume that the principle extends to all levels of human relations? Are families unified by pulling together to farm the land, restore an old house, or sail a sloop? Are communal identities forged by barn raisings, group singing, or cheering on the football team? Is international understanding bred by international collaboration in science and space, by joint efforts to feed the world and conserve resources, by friendly personal contacts between people of different nations? Indications are that the answer to all these questions is yes (Brewer & Miller, 1988; Desforges & others, 1991; Deutsch, 1985). Thus an important challenge facing our divided world is to identify and agree on our superordinate goals and to structure cooperative efforts to achieve them.

COMMUNICATION

Conflicting parties have other ways to resolve their differences. When husband and wife, or labor and management, or nation X and nation Y disagree, they can **bargain** with one another directly. They can ask a third party to *mediate* by making suggestions and facilitating their negotiations. Or they can **arbitrate** by submitting their disagreement to someone who will study the issues and impose a settlement.

Bargaining

If you or I want to buy or sell a new car, are we better off adopting a tough bargaining stance—opening with an extreme offer so that splitting the difference will yield a favorable result? Or are we better off beginning with a sincere "good-faith" offer?

Experiments suggest no simple answer. On the one hand, those who demand more will often get more. Tough bargaining may lower the other party's expectations, making the other side willing to settle for less (Yukl, 1974).

But toughness can sometimes backfire. Many a conflict is not over a pie of fixed size but over a pie that shrinks if the conflict continues. When a strike is prolonged, both labor and management lose. Being tough can also diminish the chances of actually reaching an agreement. If the other party responds with an equally extreme stance, both may be locked into positions from which neither can back down without losing face. In the weeks before the Persian Gulf war, President Bush threatened, in the full glare of publicity, to "kick Saddam's ass." Saddam Hussein communicated in kind, threatening to make "infidel" Americans "swim in their own blood." After such belligerent statements, it was difficult for each side to evade war and save face.

Mediation

A third-party mediator may offer suggestions that enable conflicting parties to make concessions and still save face (Pruitt, 1981). If my concession can be attributed to a mediator, who is gaining an equal concession from my antagonist, then neither of us will be viewed as caving in to the other's demands.

Turning Win-Lose into Win-Win

Mediators also help resolve conflicts by facilitating constructive communication. By prodding them to set aside their conflicting demands and to think instead about each other's underlying needs, interests, and goals, the mediator aims to replace a competitive "win-lose" orientation with a cooperative "win-win" orientation that aims at a mutually beneficial resolution. In experiments, Leigh Thompson (1990a,b) found that, with experience, negotiators become better able to make mutually beneficial trade-offs and thus to achieve win-win resolutions.

A classic story of such a resolution concerns the two sisters who quarreled over an orange (Follett, 1940). Finally they compromise and split the orange in half, whereupon one sister squeezed her half for juice while the other used the peel to make a cake. In experiments at the State University of New York at Buffalo, Dean Pruitt and his associates induced bargainers to search for **integrative agreements**. If the sisters had agreed to split the orange, giving one sister all the juice and the other all the peel, they would have hit on such an agreement, one that integrates both parties' interests (Kimmel & others, 1980; Pruitt & Lewis, 1975, 1977). Compared to compromises, in which each party sacrifices something important, integrative agreements are more enduring. Because they are mutually rewarding, they also lead to better ongoing relationships (Pruitt, 1986).

Unraveling Misperceptions with Controlled Communications
Communication often helps reduce self-fulfilling misperceptions. Perhaps you can recall experiences similar to that of the following college student:

> Often, after a prolonged period of little communication, I perceive Martha's silence as a sign of her dislike for me. She, in turn, thinks that my quietness is a result of my being mad at her. My silence induces her silence, which makes me even more silent . . . until this snowballing effect is broken by some occurrence that makes it necessary for us to interact. And the communication then unravels all the misinterpretations we had made about one another.

The outcome of such conflicts often depends on *how* people communicate their feelings to one another. Roger Knudson and his colleagues (1980) invited married couples to come to the University of Illinois psychology laboratory and relive, through role playing, one of their past conflicts. Before, during, and after their conversation (which often generated as much emotion as their actual previous conflict), the couples were closely observed and questioned. Couples who evaded the issue—by failing to make their positions clear or failing to acknowledge their spouse's position—left with the illusion that they were more in harmony and agreement than they really were. Often, they came to believe that they now agreed more when actually they agreed less. In contrast, those who engaged the issue—by making their positions clear and by taking one another's views into account—achieved more actual agreement and gained more accurate information about one another's perceptions. That helps explain why happily married couples communicate their concerns directly and openly (Grush & Glidden, 1987).

Conflict researchers believe that a key factor is *trust*. If you believe that the other person is well-intentioned, not out to exploit you, you are then more likely to divulge your needs and concerns. Lacking such trust, you probably will be cautious, fearing that being open will give the other party information that might be used against you.

When the two parties mistrust each other and communicate unproductively, a third-party mediator—a marriage counselor, a labor mediator, a diplomat—sometimes helps. After coaxing the conflicting parties to rethink their perceived win-lose conflict, the mediator often has each party identify and rank its goals. When there is little actual incompatibility of goals, the goal-ranking procedure makes it easier for each to concede on less important goals so that both achieve their chief goals (Erickson & others, 1974; Schulz & Pruitt, 1978). Once labor and management both believe that management's goal of higher productivity and profit is compatible with labor's goal of better wages and working conditions, they can begin to work for an integrative win-win solution.

When the parties then convene to communicate directly, they are usually *not* set loose in the hope that, eyeball to eyeball, the conflict will resolve itself. In the midst of a threatening, stressful conflict, emotions often disrupt the ability to understand the other party's point of view. Communication may become most difficult just when it is most needed (Tetlock, 1985). The mediator will therefore often structure the encounter to help each party understand and feel understood by the other. The mediator may ask the conflicting parties to restrict their arguments to statements of fact, including statements of how they feel and how they respond when the other acts in a given way: "I enjoy having music on. But when you play it loud, I find it hard to concentrate. That makes me crabby." Also, the mediator may ask people to reverse roles and argue the other's position, or to restate one another's positions before replying with their own: "My turning up the stereo bugs you."

Neutral third parties may also suggest mutually agreeable proposals that would be dismissed—"reactively devalued"—if offered by either side. Constance Stillinger and her colleagues (1991) found that a nuclear disarmament proposal which Americans dismissed when attributed to the Soviet Union seemed more acceptable when attributed to a neutral third party. Likewise, people will often reactively devalue a concession offered by an adversary ("They must not value it"); the same concession may seem less like a token gesture when suggested by a third party.

These peacemaking principles, based partly on laboratory experiments and partly on practical experience, have helped mediate both international and industrial conflicts (Blake & Mouton, 1962, 1979; Burton, 1969; Wehr, 1979). One small team of Arab and Jewish Americans, led by social psychologists Herbert Kelman and Stephen Cohen (1986), have conducted workshops bringing together influential Arabs and Israelis, and Pakistanis and Indians. Using methods such as those we've considered, Kelman and Cohen counter misperceptions and have participants creatively seek solutions for their common good. Isolated, the participants are free to speak directly to their adversaries without fearing their constituents' second-guessing what they are saying. The result? Those from both sides typically come to understand the other's perspective and how the other side responds to their own group's actions.

In 1976, Kelman drove an Egyptian social scientist, Boutros Ghali (who in 1991 became the UN Secretary General), to the Boston airport. En route, they formulated plans for an Egyptian conference on misperceptions in Arab-Israeli relations. The conference later took place, and Kelman conveyed its promising results to influential Israelis. A year later, Ghali became Egypt's acting foreign minister, and Egyptian President Anwar Sadat made his historic trip to Israel, opening a road to peace.

Afterward, Ghali said happily to Kelman, "You see the process that we started at the Boston airport last year" (Armstrong, 1981).

A year later, mediator Jimmy Carter secluded Sadat and Israeli Prime Minister Menachem Begin at Camp David. Rather than begin by having each side state their demands, Carter had them identify their underlying interests and goals—security for Israel, authority over its historic territory for Egypt. Thirteen days later, the trio emerged with "A Framework for Peace in the Middle East," granting each what they desired—security in exchange for territory (Rubin, 1989). Six months later, after further mediation by President Carter during visits to both countries, Begin and Sadat signed a treaty ending a state of war that had existed since 1948.

Arbitration

Some conflicts are so intractable, the underlying interests so divergent, that a mutually satisfactory resolution is unattainable. Israelis and Palestinians cannot both have jurisdiction over the same homelands. In a divorce dispute over custody of a child, both parents cannot enjoy full custody. In these and many other cases (involving disputes over tenants' repair bills, athletes' wages, and national territories), a third-party mediator may—or may not—help resolve the conflict.

If not, the parties may turn to *arbitration* by having the mediator or another third party *impose* a settlement. Disputants usually prefer to settle their differences without arbitration, so they retain control over the outcome. Neil McGillicuddy and others (1987) observed this preference in an experiment involving disputants coming to the Dispute Settlement Center in Buffalo, New York. When people knew they would face an arbitrated settlement if mediation failed, they tried harder to resolve the problem, exhibited less hostility, and thus were more likely to reach agreement.

However, in cases where differences seem large and irreconcilable, the prospect of arbitration may have an opposite effect (Pruitt, 1986). The disputants may freeze their positions, hoping to gain an advantage when the arbitrator chooses a compromise. To combat this tendency, some disputes, such as those involving salaries of major league baseball players, are settled with "final-offer arbitration" in which the third party chooses one of the two final offers. Final-offer arbitration motivates each party to make a reasonable proposal.

Typically, however, the final offer is not so reasonable as it would be if each party, free of self-serving bias, saw its own proposal through the other's eyes. Negotiation researchers report that most disputants are made stubborn by overconfidence. Successful mediation is hindered when, as often happens, both parties believe they have a two-thirds chance of winning a final-offer arbitration (Bazerman, 1986).

CONCILIATION

Sometimes tension and suspicion run so high that communication, much less resolution, becomes all but impossible. Each party may threaten, coerce, or retaliate against the other. Unfortunately, such acts tend to be reciprocated, thus escalating the conflict. So, would an opposite strategy—appeasing the other party by being unconditionally cooperative—produce a satisfying result? Often not. In laboratory games, those who are 100 percent cooperative often get exploited. Politically, a one-sided pacifism is out of the question anyway.

GRIT

Is there a third alternative—one that is conciliatory, rather than retaliatory, yet strong enough to discourage exploitation? Social psychologist Charles Osgood (1962, 1980) advocated one such alternative. Osgood calls it "graduated and reciprocated initiatives in tension reduction," nicknamed **GRIT**, a label that suggests the determination it requires. GRIT aims to reverse the conflict spiral by triggering reciprocal deescalation.

GRIT requires one side to initiate a few small deescalatory actions, undertaken after *announcing a conciliatory intent*. The initiator states its desire to reduce tension, declares each conciliatory act prior to making it, and invites the adversary to reciprocate. Such announcements create a framework that helps the adversary interpret correctly what otherwise might be seen as weak or tricky actions. They also elicit public pressure on the adversary to follow the reciprocity norm.

Next, the initiator establishes credibility and genuineness by carrying out, exactly as announced, several verifiable *conciliatory acts*. This intensifies the pressure to reciprocate. Making conciliatory acts diverse—perhaps offering medical information, closing a military base, and lifting a trade ban—keeps the initiator from making a significant sacrifice in any one area and leaves the adversary freer to choose its own means of reciprocation. If the adversary reciprocates voluntarily, its own conciliatory behavior may soften its attitudes.

GRIT *is* conciliatory. But it is not "surrender on the installment plan." The remaining aspects of the plan protect each side's self-interest by *maintaining retaliatory capability*. The initial conciliatory steps entail some small risk but do not jeopardize either one's security; rather, they are calculated to begin edging both sides down the tension ladder. If one side takes an aggressive action, the other side reciprocates in kind, making it clear it will not tolerate exploitation. Yet, the reciprocal act is not an overresponse that would likely reescalate the conflict. If the adversary offers its own conciliatory acts, these, too, are matched or even slightly exceeded. Conflict expert Morton Deutsch (1991) captures the spirit of GRIT in advising negotiators to be "firm, fair, and friendly: *firm* in resisting intimidation, exploitation, and dirty tricks; *fair* in holding to one's moral principles and not reciprocating the other's immoral behavior despite provocation; and *friendly* in the sense that one is willing to initiate and reciprocate cooperation."

Does GRIT really work? In laboratory dilemma games the most successful strategy has proved to be simple "tit-for-tat," which begins with a cooperative opening play and thereafter matches the other party's last response (Axelrod & Dion, 1988; Smith, 1987). Tit-for-tat tries to cooperate and is forgiving, yet does not tolerate exploitation. In a lengthy series of experiments at Ohio University, Svenn Lindskold and his associates (1976 to 1988) have tested other aspects of the GRIT strategy. Lindskold (1978) reports that his own and others' studies provide "strong support for the various steps in the GRIT proposal." In laboratory games, announcing cooperative intent *does* boost cooperation. Repeated conciliatory acts *do* breed greater trust (although self-serving biases often make one's own acts seem more conciliatory and less hostile than those of the adversary). Maintaining an equality of power *does* protect against exploitation.

GRIT-like strategies have occasionally been tried outside the laboratory, with promising results. To many, the most significant attempt at GRIT was the so-called Kennedy experiment (Etzioni, 1967). On June 10, 1963, President Kennedy gave a major speech, "A Strategy for Peace." In it he noted, "Our problems are man-made . . . and can be solved by man," and then announced his first conciliatory act: The United States was stopping all atmospheric nuclear tests and would not resume them unless another country did. In the Soviet Union, Kennedy's speech was published in full. Five days later Premier Khrushchev reciprocated, announcing he had halted production of strategic bombers. There soon followed further reciprocal gestures: The United States agreed to sell wheat to Russia, the Soviets agreed to a "hot line" between the two countries, and the two countries soon achieved a test-ban treaty. For a time, these conciliatory initiatives warmed relations between the two countries.

As they warmed again, within all our memories, President Bush in 1991 ordered the elimination of all land-based U.S. tactical nuclear warheads and took strategic bombers off high alert, putting their bombs in storage. Although leaving intact his least vulnerable and most extensive nuclear arsenal—submarine-based missiles—he invited Mikhail Gorbachev to reciprocate his conciliatory gesture. Eight days later Gorbachev did, taking his bombers off alert, storing their bombs, and announcing the removal of nuclear weapons from short-range rockets, ships, and submarines.

Might conciliatory efforts also help reduce tension between individuals? There is every reason to expect so. When a relationship is strained and communication nonexistent, it sometimes takes only a conciliatory gesture—a soft answer, a warm smile, a gentle touch—for both parties to begin easing down the tension ladder to a rung where contact, cooperation, and communication again become possible.

CONCEPTS TO REMEMBER

Equal-status contact   Contact made on an equal basis. Just as a relationship between people of unequal status breeds attitudes consistent with their relationship, so do relationships between those of equal status. Thus, to reduce prejudice, interracial contact should be between persons equal in status.

Superordinate goal   A shared goal that necessitates cooperative effort; a goal that overrides people's differences from one another.

Bargaining   Seeking an agreement through direct negotiation between parties to a conflict.

Mediation   An attempt by a neutral third party to resolve a conflict by facilitating communication and offering suggestions.

Arbitration   Resolution of a conflict by a neutral third party who studies both sides and imposes a settlement.

Integrative agreements   Win-win agreements that reconcile both parties' interests to their mutual benefit.

GRIT   Acronym for "graduated and reciprocated initiatives in tension reduction"—a strategy designed to deescalate international tensions.

28

Who Likes Whom?

❖

I n the beginning there was attraction—the attraction between a particular man and a particular woman to which we each owe our existence. Our lifelong dependence on one another puts relationships at the core of our existence. Asked "What is it that makes your life meaningful?" or "What is necessary for your happiness?" most people mention—before anything else—satisfying close relationships with friends, family, or romantic partners (Berscheid, 1985; Berscheid & Peplau, 1983).

What predisposes one person to like, or to love, another? So much has been written about liking and loving that almost every conceivable explanation—and its opposite—has been already proposed. Does absence make the heart grow fonder? Or is someone who is out of sight also out of mind? Is it likes that attract? Or opposites?

Consider a simple but powerful **reward theory of attraction**: We like those whose behavior is rewarding to us, or whom we associate with rewarding events. Friends reward each other. Without keeping score, they do favors for one another. Likewise, we develop a liking for those whom we associate with pleasant happenings and surroundings. Thus, surmised researchers Elaine Hatfield and William Walster (1978), "romantic dinners, trips to the theatre, evenings at home together, and vacations never stop being important. . . . If your relationship is to survive, it's important that you *both* continue to associate your relationship with good things."

But as with most sweeping generalizations, the reward theory of attraction leaves many questions unanswered. What, precisely, *is* rewarding? Is it usually more rewarding to be with someone who differs from us or someone who is similar to us? to be lavishly flattered or constructively criticized? What factors have fostered *your* close relationships?

PROXIMITY

One of the most powerful predictors of whether any two people are friends is their sheer **proximity** to one another. Proximity can also breed hostility; most assaults and murders involve people living in close proximity. (Guns purchased for self-defense are much more likely to be turned on family members than against intruders.) But far more often, proximity kindles liking. Though it may seem trivial to those pondering the mysterious origins of romantic love, sociologists have found that most people marry someone who lives in the same neighborhood, or works at the same job, or sits in the same class (Bossard, 1932; Burr, 1973; Clarke, 1952; Katz & Hill, 1958). Look around. If you choose to marry, it will likely be to someone who has lived or worked or studied within walking distance.

Interaction

Actually, it is not geographic distance that is critical but "functional distance"—how often people's paths cross. People frequently become friends with those who use the same entrances, parking lots, and recreation areas. Randomly assigned college roommates, who of course can hardly avoid frequent interaction, are far more likely to become good friends than enemies (Newcomb, 1961). Such interaction enables people to explore their similarities, to sense one another's liking, and to perceive themselves as a social unit (Arkin & Burger, 1980).

At the college where I teach, the men and women students once lived on opposite sides of the campus. They understandably bemoaned the dearth of cross-sex friendships. Now that they occupy different areas of the same dormitories and share common sidewalks, lounges, and laundry facilities, cross-sex friendships are far more frequent. So, if you're new in town and want to make friends, try to get an apartment near the mailboxes, an office desk near the coffee pot, a parking spot near the main buildings. Such is the architecture of friendship.

But why does proximity breed liking? One factor is the availability of people nearby; obviously, there are fewer opportunities to get to know someone who attends a different school or lives in another town. But there is more to it than that; most people like their roommates, or those one door away, better than those two doors away. After all, those just a few doors away, or even a floor below, hardly live at an inconvenient distance. Moreover, those close by are potential enemies as well as friends. So why does proximity encourage affection more often than animosity?

Anticipation of Interaction

Already we have noted one answer: Proximity enables people to discover commonalities and exchange rewards. What is more, merely *anticipating* interaction boosts liking. John Darley and Ellen Berscheid (1967) discovered this when they gave University of Minnesota women ambiguous information about two other women, one of whom they expected to converse with intimately. Asked how much they liked each one, the women preferred the person they expected to meet. Expecting to date someone similarly boosts liking (Berscheid & others, 1976). Anticipating interaction stimulates us to perceive the other person as pleasant and compatible, maximizing the chance of a rewarding relationship (Knight & Vallacher, 1981; Kunda, 1990; Miller & Marks, 1982).

The phenomenon is adaptive. Our lives are filled with relationships with people whom we may not have chosen but with whom we need to have continuing interactions—dorm mates, grandparents, teachers, classmates, co-workers. Liking such people is surely conducive to better relationships with them, which in turn makes for happier, more productive living.

Mere Exposure

Proximity leads to liking for yet another reason: More than 200 experiments reveal that, contrary to the old proverb, familiarity does not breed contempt. Rather, it breeds fondness (Bornstein, 1989). **Mere exposure** to all sorts of novel stimuli—nonsense syllables, Chinese characters, musical selections, faces—boosts people's ratings of them. Do the supposed Turkish words *nansoma*, *saricik*, and *afworbu* mean something better or something worse than the words *iktitaf*, *biwojni*, and *kadirga*? University of Michigan students tested by Robert Zajonc (1968, 1970) preferred whichever of these words they had seen most frequently. The more times they had seen a meaningless word or Chinese ideograph, the more likely they were to say it meant something good (Figure 28–1). Or consider: What is your favorite letter of the alphabet? People of differing nationalities, languages, and ages prefer the letters appearing in their own name and those that frequently appear in their own language (Hoorens & others, 1990; Nuttin, 1987). French students rate capital "W," the least frequent letter in French, as their least favorite letter.

When completed in 1889, the Eiffel Tower in Paris was mocked as grotesque. Today it is the beloved symbol of Paris (Harrison, 1977). Such changes make one wonder about people's initial reactions to new things. Do visitors to the Louvre in Paris really adore the *Mona Lisa*, or are they simply delighted to find a familiar face? It might be both: To know her is to like her.

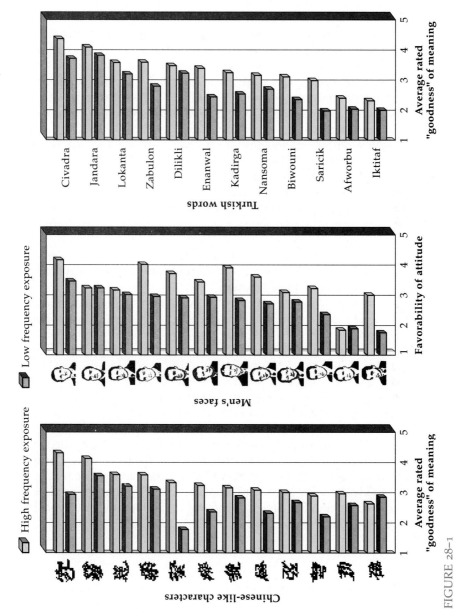

FIGURE 28–1

The mere-exposure effect. Stimuli are rated more positively after being shown repeatedly. (From Zajonc, 1968).

You may object that to become familiar with some people is to *dis*like them, and that some stimuli lose their appeal when *over*exposed. A new song that grows on you becomes wearisome after the hundredth hearing. And given incessant boring or negative stimuli, exposure does not breed liking (Bornstein & others, 1990, Grush, 1976).

Still, as a generalization the principle works, and it colors our evaluations of others. Familiar people we like more (Swap, 1977). We even like ourselves better when we are the way we're used to seeing ourselves. In a delightful experiment, Theodore Mita, Marshall Dermer, and Jeffrey Knight (1977) photographed women students at the University of Wisconsin-Milwaukee and later showed each one her actual picture along with a mirror image of it. Asked which picture they liked better, most preferred the mirror image—the image they were used to seeing. (No wonder our photographs never look quite right.) When close friends of the subjects were shown the same two pictures, they preferred the true picture—the image *they* were used to seeing.

Advertisers and politicians exploit the mere exposure phenomenon. When people don't have strong feelings about a product or a candidate, repetition alone can boost sales or votes (McCullough & Ostrom, 1974; Winter, 1973). If candidates are relatively unknown, as often happens in local elections, those with the most media exposure usually win (Patterson, 1980; Schaffner & others, 1981).

The respected Washington State Supreme Court Chief Justice Keith Callow learned this lesson, after his 1990 loss to a nominal opponent, Charles Johnson. Johnson, an unknown attorney who handled minor criminal cases and divorces, filed for the seat on the principle that judges "need to be challenged." Neither man campaigned, and the media ignored the race. On election day the two candidates' names appeared without any identification—just one name next to the other. The result: a 53 percent to 47 percent Johnson victory. "There are a lot more Johnsons out there than Callows," offered the ousted judge afterward to a stunned legal community. Indeed, a Seattle newspaper counted 27 Charlie Johnsons in Seattle alone. There was Charles Johnson, the King County judge. And down in Tacoma there was television anchorman Charles Johnson, whose broadcasts were seen on statewide cable TV. Forced to choose between two unknown names, many voters apparently preferred the comfortable, familiar name of Charlie Johnson.

*P*HYSICAL ATTRACTIVENESS

What do (or did) you look for in a potential date? Sincerity? Good looks? Character? Conversational ability? Sophisticated, intelligent people are unconcerned with such superficial qualities as good looks; they know that "beauty is only skin deep" and "you can't judge a book by its cover." At least they know that's how they *ought* to feel. As Cicero counseled, "The final good and the supreme duty of the wise man is to resist appearance."

The belief that looks matter little may be another instance of our denying real influences upon us, for there is now a file drawer full of research studies showing that appearance *does* matter. The consistency and pervasiveness of this effect is disconcerting. Good looks are a great asset.

Dating

Like it or not, a young woman's physical attractiveness is a moderately good predictor of how frequently she dates. A young man's attractiveness is slightly less a predictor of how frequently he dates (Berscheid & others, 1971; Krebs & Adinolfi, 1975; Reis & others, 1980, 1982; Walster & others, 1966). Does this imply, as many have surmised, that women are better at following Cicero's advice? Or does it merely reflect the fact that men more often do the inviting? If women were to indicate their preferences among various men, would looks be as important to them as to men? Philosopher Bertrand Russell (1930, p. 139) thought not: "On the whole women tend to love men for their character while men tend to love women for their appearance."

To see whether indeed men are more influenced by looks, researchers provide men and women students with various pieces of information about someone of the other sex, including a picture of the person. Or they briefly introduce a man and a woman and later ask each about their interest in dating the other. In such experiments, men somewhat more than women value opposite-sex physical attractiveness (Feingold, 1990, 1991). Perhaps sensing this, women more than men worry about their appearance and constitute 90 percent of cosmetic surgery patients (Dion & others, 1990). But women, too, respond to a man's looks.

In one ambitious study, Elaine Hatfield and her co-workers (1966) matched 752 University of Minnesota first-year students for a "Welcome Week" computer dance. The researchers gave each individual personality and aptitude tests but then matched the couples randomly. On the night of the dance, the couples danced and talked for two and one-half hours and then took a brief intermission to evaluate their dates. How well did the personality and aptitude tests predict attraction? Did people like better someone who was high in self-esteem, or low in anxiety, or different from themselves in outgoingness? The researchers examined a long list of possibilities, but so far as they could determine, only one thing mattered: how physically attractive the person was. The more attractive a woman was, as rated by the experimenters and, especially, as rated by her date, the more he liked her and wanted to date her again. And the more attractive the man was, the more she liked him and wanted to date him again. Pretty pleases.

To say that attractiveness is important, other things being equal, is not to say that physical appearance always outranks other qualities. Attractiveness probably most affects first impressions. But first impressions are important—and are becoming more so as society becomes increasingly mobile and urbanized and as contacts with people become more fleeting (Berscheid, 1981).

Moreover, though interviewers may deny it, attractiveness and grooming affect first impressions in job interviews (Cash & Janda, 1984; Mack & Rainey, 1990; Marvelle & Green, 1980). This helps explain why attractive people have more prestigious jobs, make more money, and describe themselves as happier (Umberson & Hughes, 1987). Patricia Roszell and her colleagues (1990) looked at the attractiveness of a national sample of Canadians whom interviewers had rated on a 1 (homely) to 5 (strikingly attractive) scale. They found that for each additional scale unit of rated attractiveness, people earned, on average, an additional $1988. Irene Hanson Frieze and her associates (1991) did the same analysis with 737 M.B.A. graduates after rating them on a similar 1 to 5 scale using student picture book photos. For each additional scale unit of rated attractiveness, men earned an added $2600 and women earned an added $2150.

The Matching Phenomenon

But not everyone can end up paired with someone stunningly attractive. So how do people pair off? Judging from research by Bernard Murstein (1986) and others, they pair off with people who are about as attractive as they are. Several studies have found a strong correspondence between the attractiveness of husbands and wives, of dating partners, and even of those within particular fraternities (Feingold, 1988). People tend to select as friends and especially to marry those who are a "good match" not only to their level of intelligence but also to their level of attractiveness.

Experiments confirm this **matching phenomenon**. When choosing whom to approach, knowing the other is free to say yes or no, people usually approach someone whose attractiveness roughly matches their own (Berscheid & others, 1971; Huston, 1973; Stroebe & others, 1971). Good physical matches may also be conducive to good relationships, as Gregory White (1980) found in a study of UCLA dating couples. Those who were most similar in physical attractiveness were most likely, nine months later, to have fallen more deeply in love. So, who might we expect to be most closely matched for attractiveness—married couples or couples casually dating? White found, as have other researchers, that married couples are better matched.

Perhaps this research prompts you to think of happy couples who are not similarly attractive. In such cases, the less attractive person often has compensating qualities. Each partner brings assets to the social marketplace, and the value of the respective assets creates an equitable match. Personal advertisements exhibit this exchange of assets (Koestner & Wheeler, 1988). Men typically offer status and seek attractiveness; women more often do the reverse: "Attractive, bright woman, 38, slender, seeks warm, professional male." The social-exchange process helps explain why beautiful young women often marry older men whose social status exceeds their own (Elder, 1969). Secretary of State Henry Kissinger, though not the handsomest man around, reportedly had plenty of dates with attractive women for whom power was "the ultimate aphrodisiac."

Who Is Attractive?

I have described attractiveness as if it were an objective quality like height, which some people have more of, some less. Strictly speaking, attractiveness is whatever the people of any given place and time find attractive. This, of course, varies. The beauty standards by which Miss Universe is judged hardly apply to the whole planet. Even in a given place and time, people (fortunately) disagree about who's attractive and who's not (Morse & Gruzen, 1976).

But there is also some agreement. Generally, "attractive" facial and bodily features do not deviate too drastically from the average (Beck & others, 1976; Graziano & others, 1978; Symons, 1981). People perceive noses, legs, or statures that are not unusually large or small as relatively attractive. Judith Langlois and Lori Roggman (1990) showed this by digitizing the faces of up to 32 college students and using a computer to average them. Students judged the composite faces as more appealing than 96 percent of the individual faces. So in some respects, perfectly average is strikingly attractive.

What's attractive to you also depends on your comparison standards. Douglas Kenrick and Sara Gutierres (1980) had male confederates interrupt Montana State University men in their dormitory rooms and explain, "We have a friend coming to town this week and we want to fix him up with a date, but we can't decide whether to fix him up with her or not, so we decided to conduct a survey. . . . We want you to give us your vote on how attractive you think she is . . . on a scale of 1 to 7." Shown a picture of an average young woman, those who had just been watching three beautiful women on television's *Charlie's Angels* rated her less attractive than those who hadn't.

Laboratory experiments confirm this "contrast effect." To men who have recently been gazing at centerfolds, average women—or even their own wives—seem less attractive (Kenrick & others, 1989). Viewing pornographic films simulating passionate sex similarly decreases dissatisfaction with one's own partner (Zillmann, 1989). Being sexually aroused may temporarily make a person of the other sex seem more attractive. But the residual effect of exposure to perfect "10s," or of unrealistic sexual depictions, is to make one's own partner seem less appealing—more like a "5" than an "8." It works the same way with our self-perceptions. After viewing a superattractive person of the same sex, people *feel* less attractive than after viewing a homely person (Brown & others, 1992).

We can conclude our discussion of attractiveness on a heartwarming note. Not only do we perceive attractive people as likable, but we also perceive likable people as attractive. Perhaps you can recall individuals who, as you grew to like them, became more attractive, their physical imperfections no longer so noticeable. Alan Gross and Christine Crofton (1977) had University of Missouri–St. Louis students view someone's photograph after reading a favorable or unfavorable description of the person's personality. When portrayed as warm, helpful, and considerate, people *looked* more attractive. Discovering someone's similarities to us also makes the person seem more attractive (Beaman & Klentz, 1983; Klentz & others, 1987). Moreover, love sees loveliness: The more in love a woman is with a man, the more physically attractive she finds him (Price & others, 1974). And the more in love people are, the *less* attractive they find all others of the opposite sex (Johnson & Rusbult, 1989; Simpson & others, 1990). "The grass may be greener on the other side," note Rowland Miller and Jeffry Simpson (1990), "but happy gardeners are less likely to notice." To paraphrase Benjamin Franklin, when Jill's in love, she finds Jack more handsome than his friends.

*S*IMILARITY VERSUS COMPLEMENTARITY

From our discussion so far, one might surmise that Leo Tolstoy was entirely correct: "Love depends . . . on frequent meetings, and on the style in which the hair is done up, and on the color and cut of the dress." However, as people get to know one another, other factors influence whether an acquaintanceship will develop into a friendship. Thus, men's initial liking for one another after the first week of living in the same boardinghouse does *not* predict very well their ultimate liking four months later (Nisbett & Smith, 1989). Their similarity, however, does.

Do Birds of a Feather Flock Together?

Of this much we may be sure: Birds who flock together are of a feather. Friends, engaged couples, and spouses are far more likely than people randomly paired to share common attitudes, beliefs, and values. Further-

more, among married couples, the greater the similarity between husband and wife, the happier they are and the less likely they are to divorce
(Byrne, 1971; Caspi & Herbener, 1990). Such correlational findings are
intriguing. But cause and effect remain an enigma. Does similarity lead to
liking? Or does liking lead to similarity?

Likeness Begets Liking

To discern cause and effect, we experiment. Imagine that at a campus
party Laura gets involved in a long discussion of politics, religion, and
personal likes and dislikes with Les and Larry. She and Les discover that
they agree on almost everything; she and Larry, on few things. Afterward, she reflects: "Les is really intelligent. And he's so likable. I hope we
meet again." In experiments, Donn Byrne (1971) and his colleagues
captured the essence of Laura's experience. Over and over again they
found that the more similar someone's attitudes are to your own, the
more likable you will find the person. This "likeness-leads-to-liking"
relationship holds true not only for college students but also for children
and the elderly, for people of various occupations, and for those in
various nations.

   This agreement effect has been tested in real-life situations by noting
who comes to like whom. At the University of Michigan, Theodore
Newcomb (1961) studied two groups of 17 unacquainted male transfer
students. After 13 weeks of living together in a boardinghouse, those
whose agreement was initially highest were most likely to have formed
close friendships. One group of friends was composed of five liberal arts
students, each a political liberal with strong intellectual interests. Another was made up of three conservative veterans who were all enrolled in
the engineering college.

   William Griffitt and Russell Veitch (1974) compressed the getting-to-
know-you process by confining 13 unacquainted men in a fallout shelter.
(The men were paid volunteers.) Knowing the men's opinions on various
issues, the researchers could predict with better-than-chance accuracy
whom each man would most like and most dislike. As in the boardinghouse, the men liked best those most like themselves. Similarity breeds
content. Surely you have noticed this upon discovering a special someone
who shares your ideas, values, and desires, a soul mate who likes the
same music, the same activities, even the same foods you do.

Do Opposites Attract?

But are we not also attracted to people who are in some ways *different* from
ourselves, different in ways that complement our own characteristics?
Researchers have explored this question by comparing not only the
attitudes and beliefs of friends and spouses but also their age, religion,

race, smoking behavior, economic level, education, height, intelligence, and appearance. In all these ways and more, similarity still prevails (Buss, 1985; Kandel, 1978). Smart birds flock together. So do rich birds, Protestant birds, tall birds, pretty birds.

Still we resist: Are we not attracted to people whose needs and personalities complement our own? Would a gratifying relationship develop from the meeting of a sadist and a masochist? Even the *Reader's Digest* tells us that "opposites attract. . . . Socializers pair with loners, novelty-lovers with those who dislike change, free spenders with scrimpers, risk-takers with the very cautious" (Jacoby, 1986). Sociologist Robert Winch (1958) reasoned that the needs of someone who is outgoing and domineering would naturally complement those of someone who is shy and submissive. The logic seems compelling, and most of us can think of couples who view their differences as complementary: "My husband and I are perfect for each other. I'm Aquarius—a decisive person. He's Libra—can't make decisions. But he's always happy to go along with arrangements I make."

Some **complementarity** may evolve as a relationship progresses (even a relationship between two identical twins). Yet people seem, if anything, slightly more prone to marry those whose needs and personalities are *similar* (Berscheid & Walster, 1978; Buss, 1984; D. Fishbein & Thelen, 1981a, 1981b; Nias, 1979). Perhaps we shall yet discover some ways (other than heterosexuality) in which differences commonly breed liking. But researcher David Buss (1985) doubts it: "The tendency of opposites to marry, or mate . . . has never been reliably demonstrated, with the single exception of sex." So it seems that the "opposites-attract" rule, if it's ever true, is of minuscule importance compared to the powerful tendency of likes to attract.

*L*IKING THOSE WHO LIKE US

With hindsight, the reward principle explains our conclusions so far:

- *Proximity* is rewarding. It costs less time and effort to receive friendship's benefits with someone who lives or works close by.
- We like *attractive* people because we perceive that they offer other desirable traits and because we benefit by associating with them.
- If others have *similar* opinions, we feel rewarded because we presume that they like us in return. Moreover, those who share our views help validate them.

If we like those whose behavior is rewarding, then we ought to adore those who like and admire us. The best friendships should be mutual admiration societies. Do we in fact like those who like us? Indeed, one person's liking for another predicts the other's liking in return (Kenny & Nasby, 1980). Liking is mutual.

But does one person's liking another *cause* the other to return the appreciation? People's reports of how they fell in love suggest yes (Aron & others, 1989). Discovering that an appealing someone really likes you seems to awaken romantic feelings. And experiments confirm it. Those told that certain others like or admire them feel a reciprocal affection (Berscheid & Walster, 1978).

Ellen Berscheid and her colleagues (1969) even found that University of Minnesota students liked better another student who said eight positive things about them than one who said seven positive things and one negative thing. We are sensitive to the slightest hint of criticism. Writer Larry L. King speaks for many in noting, "I have discovered over the years that good reviews strangely fail to make the author feel as good as bad reviews make him feel bad." Whether we are judging ourselves or others, negative information carries more weight because, being less usual, it grabs more attention (Yzerbyt & Leyens, 1991). People's votes are more influenced by their impressions of presidential candidates' weaknesses than by their impressions of strengths (Klein, 1991), a phenomenon that has not been lost on those who design negative campaign tactics.

This principle—that we like and treat warmly those we perceive as liking us—was recognized long before social psychologists confirmed it. Observers from the ancient philosopher Hecate ("If you wish to be loved, love") to Ralph Waldo Emerson ("The only way to have a friend is to be one") to Dale Carnegie ("Dole out praise lavishly") anticipated the findings. What they did not anticipate were the precise conditions under which the principle works.

Self-Esteem and Attraction

The reward principle also implies that another's approval should be especially rewarding after one has been deprived of approval, much as eating is most powerfully rewarding when we are extremely hungry. To test this idea, Elaine Hatfield (Walster, 1965) gave some college women either very favorable or very unfavorable analyses of their personalities, affirming some and wounding others. Then she asked them to evaluate several people, including an attractive male confederate who just before the experiment had struck up a warm conversation with each subject and had asked each for a date. (Not one turned him down.) After the affirmation or criticism, which women do you suppose most liked the man? It was those whose self-esteem had been temporarily shattered and who were presumably hungry for social approval. This helps explain why people sometimes fall in love quickly on the rebound, after an ego-bruising rejection. (After this experiment Dr. Hatfield spent almost an hour explaining the experiment and talking with each woman. She reports that in the end, none remained disturbed by the temporary ego blow or the broken date.)

Proximity, attractiveness, similarity, being liked—these are factors known to influence our friendship formation. Sometimes friendship deepens into the passion and intimacy of love. What is love? And why does it sometimes flourish and sometimes fade? To those questions we turn next.

CONCEPTS TO REMEMBER

Reward theory of attraction   The theory that we like those whose behavior we find rewarding or whom we associate with rewarding events.

Proximity   Geographic nearness. Proximity (more precisely, "functional distance") powerfully predicts liking.

Mere-exposure effect   The tendency for novel stimuli to be liked more or rated more positively after the rater has been repeatedly exposed to them.

Matching phenomenon   The tendency for men and women to choose as partners those who are a "good match" in attractiveness and other traits.

Complementarity   The supposed tendency, in a relationship between two people, for each to complete what is missing in the other. The questionable complementarity hypothesis proposes that people attract those whose needs are different, in ways that complement their own.

The Ups and Downs
of Love

❖

W hat is this thing called "love"? Loving is more complex than liking and
thus more difficult to measure, more perplexing to study. People yearn
for it, live for it, die for it. Yet only in the last few years has loving
become a serious topic in social psychology.

Most attraction researchers have studied what is most easily studied—
responses during brief encounters between strangers. The influences on our
initial liking of another—proximity, attractiveness, similarity, being liked—also
influence our long-term, close relationships. Indeed, if romances in the United
States flourished *randomly*, without regard to proximity and similarity, then most
Catholics (being a minority) would marry Protestants, most Blacks would marry
Whites, and college graduates would be as apt to marry high school dropouts as
fellow graduates.

So first impressions are important. Nevertheless, loving is not merely an
intensification of initial liking. Social psychologists are therefore shifting their
attention from the mild attraction experienced during first encounters to the study
of enduring, close relationships.

One line of investigation compares the nature of love in various close relationships—same-sex friendships, parent-child relationships, and spouses or lovers (Davis, 1985; Maxwell, 1985; Sternberg & Grajek, 1984). These investigations
reveal elements that are common to all loving relationships: mutual understanding, giving and receiving support, valuing and enjoying being with the loved one.
Although such ingredients of love apply equally to love between best friends or
between husband and wife, they are spiced differently depending on the relation-

ship. Passionate love, especially in its initial phase, is distinguished by physical affection, an expectation of exclusiveness, and an intense fascination with the loved one.

PASSIONATE LOVE

The first step in scientifically studying romantic love, as in studying any variable, is to decide how to define and measure it. We have ways to measure aggression, altruism, prejudice, and liking: but how do we measure love? Elizabeth Barrett Browning asked a similar question: "How do I love thee? Let me count the ways." Social scientists have counted various ways. Psychologist Robert Sternberg (1988) views love as a triangle, whose three sides (of varying lengths) are passion, intimacy, and commitment (Figure 29–1). Drawing from ancient philosophy and literature, sociologist John Alan Lee (1988) and psychologists Clyde Hendrick and Susan Hendrick (1993) identify three primary love styles— *eros* (passion), *ludus* (game playing), and *storge* (friendship)—which, like the primary colors, combine to form secondary love styles. Pioneering love researcher Zick Rubin (1970, 1973) discerned somewhat different factors. To tap each, he wrote questionnaire items:

1. *Attachment* (for example, "If I were lonely, my first thought would be to seek _____ out.")

FIGURE 29–1
Robert Sternberg's (1988) conception of kinds of loving as combinations of three basic components of love.

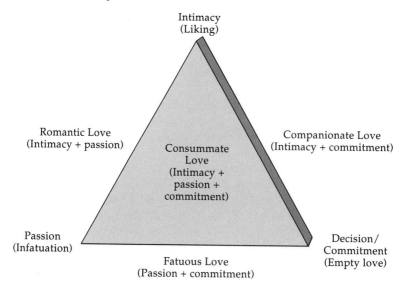

2. *Caring* (for example, "If _____ were feeling bad, my first duty would be to cheer him [her] up.")

3. *Intimacy* (for example, "I feel that I can confide in _____ about virtually everything.")

Rubin gave his Love Scale to hundreds of dating couples at the University of Michigan. He later invited to the laboratory couples whose scores suggested that their relationship was either weak or strong. While each couple awaited the session, observers behind a one-way mirror clocked the time they maintained eye contact. The "weak-love" couples looked at one another less than the "strong-love" couples, who gave themselves away by gazing into one another's eyes.

Passionate love is emotional, exciting, intense. Hatfield (1988) defines it as *"a state of intense longing for union with another"* (p. 193). If reciprocated, one feels fulfilled and joyous; if not, one feels empty or despairing. Like other forms of emotional excitement, passionate love involves a mix of elation and gloom, tingling exhilaration and dejected misery.

A Theory of Passionate Love

To explain passionate love, Hatfield notes that a given state of arousal can be steered into any of several emotions, depending on how we attribute the arousal. An emotion involves both body and mind, both arousal and how we interpret and label the arousal. Imagine yourself with pounding heart and trembling hands: Are you experiencing fear, anxiety, joy? Physiologically, one emotion is quite similar to another. You may therefore experience the arousal as joy if you are in a euphoric situation, anger if your environment is hostile, and passionate love if the situation is romantic. In this view, passionate love is the psychological experience of being biologically aroused by someone we find attractive.

If indeed passion is a revved-up state that's labeled "love," then whatever revs one up should intensify feelings of love. In several experiments, college men aroused sexually by reading or viewing erotic materials had a heightened response to a woman (for example, by scoring much higher on Rubin's Love Scale when describing their girlfriend) (Carducci & others, 1978; Dermer & Pyszczynski, 1978; Stephan & others, 1971). Proponents of the **two-factor theory of emotion** argue that when the revved-up men respond to a woman, they easily misattribute some of their arousal to her.

According to this theory, being aroused by *any* source should intensify one's passionate feelings—providing one's mind is free to attribute some of the arousal to a romantic stimulus. Donald Dutton and Arthur Aron (1974, 1989) invited University of British Columbia men to partici-

Arousal amplified attraction after crossing
the Capilano River bridge.

pate in a learning experiment. After meeting their attractive female partner, some were frightened with the news that they would be suffering
some "quite painful" electric shocks. Before the experiment was to begin,
the researcher gave a brief questionnaire "to get some information on
your present feelings and reactions, since these often influence performance on the learning task." Asked how much they would like to date and
kiss their female partner, the aroused (frightened) men expressed more
intense attraction toward the woman.

Does this phenomenon occur outside the laboratory? Dutton and
Aron (1974) had an attractive young woman approach individual young
men as they crossed a narrow, wobbly 450-foot-long suspension walkway
hanging 230 feet above British Columbia's rocky Capilano River. The
woman asked each man to help her fill out a class questionnaire. When he
had finished, she scribbled her name and phone number and invited him
to call if he wanted to hear more about the project. Most accepted the
phone number, and half who did so called. By contrast, men approached
by the woman on a low, solid bridge, and men approached on the high
bridge by a *male* interviewer, rarely called. Once again, physical arousal
accentuated romantic responses. Adrenaline made the heart grow
fonder.

Variations in Love

Time and Culture

There is always a temptation (called the "false consensus effect") to assume that others share our feelings and ideas. We assume, for example, that love is a precondition for marriage. But this assumption is not shared in cultures that practice arranged marriages. Moreover, until recently in North America, marital choices, especially those by women, were strongly influenced by considerations of economic security, family background, and professional status. But by the mid-1980s, as Figure 29–2 indicates, almost 9 in 10 young adults surveyed indicate that love is essential for marriage. Thus cultures vary in the importance placed upon romantic love. In western cultures today, love generally precedes marriage; in others, it more often follows marriage.

Personality

Within any given place and time, individuals also vary in their approach to heterosexual relationships. Some seek a succession of short involve-

FIGURE 29–2

Passionate love: now, but not always, an essential precondition for marriage in North America. As college women have become freer of economic dependence on men, they have also become more likely to regard love as a prerequisite for marriage. (From Simpson & others, 1986.)

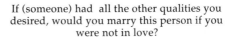

If (someone) had all the other qualities you desired, would you marry this person if you were not in love?

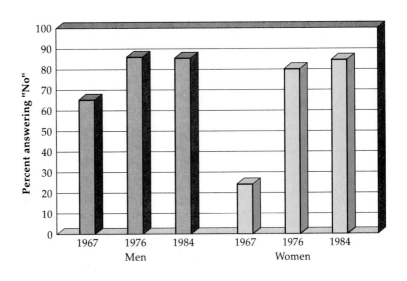

ments; others value the intimacy of an exclusive and enduring relationship. In a series of studies, Mark Snyder and his colleagues (1985, 1988; Snyder & Simpson, 1985) identified a personality difference linked with these two approaches to romance. Some people—those high in **self-monitoring**—skillfully monitor their own behavior to create the desired effect in any given situation. Others—those low in self-monitoring—are more internally guided, more likely to report that they act the same way regardless of the situation.

Which type of person—someone high or low in self-monitoring—would you guess to be more affected by a prospect's physical appearance? to be more willing to end a relationship in favor of a new partner and therefore to date more people for shorter periods of time? to be more sexually promiscuous?

Snyder and Simpson report that in each case the answer is the person high in self-monitoring. Such people are skilled in managing first impressions but tend to be less committed to deep and enduring relationships. Low self-monitors, being less externally focused, are more committed and display more concern for people's inner qualities. When perusing folders to examine potential dates or employees, they place a higher premium on personal attributes than on appearance. Given a choice between someone who shares their attitudes or their preferred activities, low self-monitors (unlike high self-monitors) feel drawn to those with kindred attitudes (Jamieson & others, 1987).

Gender

Do males and females differ in how they experience passionate love? Studies of men and women falling in and out of love reveal some surprises. Most people, including the writer of the following letter to a newspaper advice columnist, suppose that women fall in love more readily:

> Dear Dr. Brothers:
> Do you think it's effeminate for a 19-year-old guy to fall in love so hard it's like the whole world's turned around? I think I'm really crazy because this has happened several times now and love just seems to hit me on the head from nowhere. . . . My father says this is the way girls fall in love and that it doesn't happen this way with guys—at least it's not supposed to. I can't change how I am in this way but it kind of worries me.—P.T. (quoted by Dion & Dion, 1985)

P.T. would be reassured by the repeated finding that it is actually *men* who tend to fall more readily in love. Men also seem to fall out of love more slowly and are less likely than women to break up a premarital romance. However, women in love are typically as emotionally involved as their partners, or more so. They are more likely to report feeling euphoric and "giddy and carefree," as if they were "floating on a cloud." Women are also somewhat more likely than men to focus on the intimacy of the friendship and on their concern for their partner. Men are more likely than women to think about the playful and physical aspects of the relationship (Dion & Dion, 1985; Peplau & Gordon, 1985).

COMPANIONATE LOVE

Although passionate love burns hot, it inevitably simmers down. Much as we develop tolerance for drug-induced highs, so the passionate high we feel for a romantic partner is fated to become more lukewarm as the initial excitement wanes. The longer a relationship endures, the fewer its emotional ups and downs (Berscheid & others, 1989). The high of romance may be sustained for a few months, even a couple of years. But as the "adaptation level phenomenon" reminds us, no high lasts forever. If a close relationship is to endure, it settles to a steadier but still warm afterglow that Hatfield calls **companionate love**.

Unlike the wild emotions of passionate love, companionate love is lower key; it's a deep, affectionate attachment. And it is just as real. Even if one develops tolerance for a drug, withdrawal can be painful. So it is with close relationships. Mutually dependent couples who no longer feel the flame of passionate love will often, upon divorce or death, discover that they have lost more than they expected. Having focused on what was not working, they failed to notice all the things that did work, including hundreds of interdependent activities (Carlson & Hatfield, 1992).

The cooling of passionate love over time and the growing importance of other factors, such as shared values, can be seen in the feelings of those who enter arranged versus love-based marriages in India. Usha Gupta and Pushpa Singh (1982) asked 50 couples in Jaipur, India, to complete Zick Rubin's Love Scale. They found that those who married out of love reported diminishing feelings of love if they had been married more than five years. By contrast, those in arranged marriages reported *more* love if they were not newlyweds (Figure 29-3).

The cooling of intense romantic love often triggers a period of disillusion, especially among those who regard such love as essential both for a marriage (recall Figure 29-2) and for its continuation. Jeffry Simpson, Bruce Campbell, and Ellen Berscheid (1986) suspect that "the sharp rise in the divorce rate in the past two decades is linked, at least in part, to the growing importance of intense positive emotional experiences (e.g., romantic love) in people's lives, experiences that may be particularly diffi-

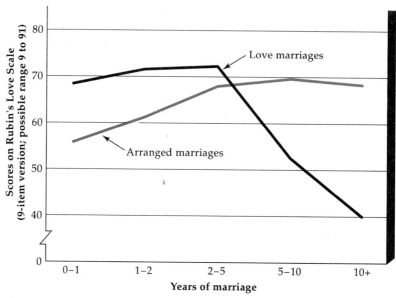

FIGURE 29-3
Romantic love between partners in arranged or love marriages in Jaipur, India. (Data from Gupta & Singh, 1982.)

cult to sustain over time." Compared to North Americans, Asians tend to be less focused on personal feelings, such as passion, and more concerned with the practical aspects of social attachments (Dion & Dion, 1988). Thus, they may be less vulnerable to disillusionment. Asians are also less prone to the self-focused individualism that in the long run can undermine a relationship and lead to divorce (Dion & Dion, 1991; Triandis & others, 1988).

The decline in intense mutual fascination may be natural and adaptive for species survival. The result of passionate love is frequently children, whose survival is aided by the parents' waning obsession with one another (Kenrick & Trost, 1987). Nevertheless, for those married more than 20 years, some of the lost romantic feeling is often renewed as the family nest empties and the parents are once again free to focus their attention on one another (Hatfield & Sprecher, 1986). "No man or woman really knows what love is until they have been married a quarter of a century," said Mark Twain. If the relationship has been intimate and mutually rewarding, companionate love probably still thrives. But what is "intimacy"? And what is "mutually rewarding"?

Self-Disclosure

Deep, companionate relationships are intimate. They enable us to be known as we truly are and feel accepted. We discover this delicious experience in a good marriage or a close friendship—a relationship where trust displaces anxiety and where we are therefore free to open ourselves without fear of losing the other's affection (Holmes & Rempel, 1989). Such relationships are characterized by what the late Sidney Jourard called **self-disclosure**. As their relationship grows, self-disclosing partners reveal more and more; their knowledge of one another penetrates to deeper and deeper levels until it reaches an appropriate depth. Lacking such opportunities for intimacy, we experience the pain of loneliness (Berg & Peplau, 1982; Solano & others, 1982).

Experiments have probed both the *causes* and the *effects* of self-disclosure. Researchers have wondered: When are people most willing to disclose intimate information concerning "what you like and don't like about yourself" or "what you're most ashamed and most proud of"? And what effects do such revelations have upon those who reveal and receive them?

The most reliable finding is the **disclosure reciprocity** effect: Disclosure begets disclosure (Berg, 1987; Miller, 1990; Reis & Shaver, 1988). We reveal more to those who have been open with us. But intimacy is seldom instant. Far more often, it progresses like a dance: I reveal a little, you reveal a little—but not too much. You then reveal more, as do I.

Some people are especially skilled "openers"—people who readily elicit intimate disclosures from others, even from those who normally don't reveal very much of themselves (Miller & others, 1983). Such people tend to be good listeners. During conversation they maintain attentive facial expressions and appear to be comfortably enjoying themselves (Purvis & others, 1984). They may also express interest by uttering supportive phrases while their conversational partner is speaking. They are what psychologist Carl Rogers (1980) called "growth-promoting" listeners—people who are *genuine* in revealing their own feelings, who are *accepting* of others' feelings, and who are *empathic*, sensitive, reflective listeners.

What are the effects of such self-disclosure? Jourard (1964) argued that dropping our masks, letting ourselves be known as we are, nurtures love. He presumed that it is gratifying to open up to another and then to receive the trust another implies by being open with us. For example, having an intimate friend with whom we can discuss threats to our self-image seems to help us comfortably survive such stresses (Swann & Predmore, 1985). A true friendship is a special relationship that helps us cope with our other relationships. "When I am with my friend," reflected the Roman playwright Seneca, "methinks I am alone, and as much at liberty to speak anything as to think it." At its best, marriage is such a friendship, sealed by commitment.

Although intimacy is rewarding, the results of many experiments caution us not to presume that self-disclosure will automatically kindle love. It's just not that simple. It's true that we like best those to whom we've disclosed ourselves (R. L. Archer & others, 1980). But we are not always fond of those who most intimately reveal themselves to us (Archer & Burleson, 1980; Archer & others, 1980). Someone who early in an acquaintanceship rushes to tell us intimate details may seem indiscreet, immature, even unstable (Dion & Dion, 1978; Miell & others, 1979). Usually, though, people prefer an open, self-disclosing person to one who holds back. This is especially so when the disclosure is appropriate to the conversation. We feel pleased when a normally reserved person says that something about us "made me feel like opening up" and shares confidential information (Archer & Cook, 1986; D. Taylor & others, 1981). It's gratifying to be singled out for another's disclosure.

Intimate self-disclosure is one of companionate love's delights. Dating and married couples who most reveal themselves to one another express most satisfaction with their relationship and are more likely to endure in it (Berg & McQuinn, 1986; Hendrick & others, 1988; Sprecher, 1987). In a recent Gallup national marriage survey, 75 percent of those who prayed with their spouse (and 57 percent of those who didn't) reported their marriage as very happy (Greeley, 1991). Among believers, shared prayer from the heart is a humbling, intimate, soulful exposure. Those who pray together also more often say they discuss their marriage together, respect their spouse, and rate their spouse as a skilled lover.

Researchers have also found that women are often more willing to disclose their fears and weaknesses than men (Cunningham, 1981). As Kate Millett (1975) put it, "Women express, men repress." Nevertheless, men today, particularly men with egalitarian gender-role attitudes, seem increasingly willing to reveal intimate feelings and to enjoy the satisfactions that accompany a relationship of mutual trust and self-disclosure.

Equity

In Module 28, "Who Likes Whom?" we noted an equity rule at work in the matching phenomenon: People usually bring equal assets to romantic relationships. Often they are matched for attractiveness, status, and so forth. If they are mismatched in one area, such as attractiveness, they tend to be compensatingly mismatched in some other area, such as status. But in total assets, they are an equitable match. No one says, and few even think, "I'll trade you my good looks for your big income." But especially in relationships that last, equity is the rule.

Those in a relationship that is equitable are more content (Fletcher & others, 1987; Hatfield & others, 1985; Van Yperen & Buunk, 1990). Those who perceive their relationship as inequitable feel discomfort: The one who has the better deal may feel guilty, and the one who senses a raw deal may feel strong irritation. (Given the self-serving bias, the person who is "overbenefited" is less sensitive to the inequity.) Robert Schafer and Patricia Keith (1980) surveyed several hundred married couples of all ages, noting those who felt their marriage was somewhat unfair because one spouse contributed too little to the cooking, housekeeping, parenting, or providing. Inequity took its toll: Those who perceived inequity also felt more distressed and depressed.

Ending or Sustaining a Close Relationship

What do people do when they perceive that a relationship is inequitable? Comparing their seemingly unsatisfying partner with the support and affection they imagine is available elsewhere, some will exit the relationship. Among dating couples, the closer and longer the relationship and the fewer the available alternatives, the more painful the breakup (Simpson, 1987). Surprisingly, Roy Baumeister and Sara Wotman (1992) report that months or years later people recall more pain over spurning someone's love than over having been spurned. Their distress arises from guilt over hurting someone, from upset over the heartbroken lover's persistence, or from uncertainty over how to respond.

Among married couples, the breakup has additional costs: shocked parents and friends, restricted parental rights, guilt over broken vows. Still, each year millions of couples are willing to pay such costs to extricate themselves from what they perceive as the greater costs of continuing a painful, unrewarding relationship. Sociologists and demographers report that divorce is least likely among those who marry after age 20, date for a long while before marrying, are well educated, enjoy a stable income, live in a small town or on a farm, do not cohabit or become pregnant before marrying, and are actively religious (Myers, 1992).

When relationships suffer, there are alternatives to exiting through divorce. Caryl Rusbult and her colleagues (1986, 1987) have explored three other ways of coping with a failing relationship. Some people exhibit *loyalty*—passively but optimistically waiting for conditions to improve. The problems are too painful to speak of and the risks of separation are too great, so the loyal partner grits teeth and perseveres, hoping the good old days will return. Others (especially men) display *neglect*, by passively allowing the relationship to deteriorate. When painful dissatisfactions are ignored, an insidious emotional uncoupling ensues as the partners begin redefining their lives without each other. Still others, however, will *voice* their concerns and take active steps to improve the relationship.

Study after study reveals that unhappy couples disagree, command, criticize, and put down. Happy couples more often agree, approve, assent, and laugh (Noller & Fitzpatrick, 1990). So would relationships brighten if the partners agreed to *act* more as happy couples do—by complaining and criticizing less? by affirming and agreeing more? by setting times aside to voice their concerns? by praying or playing together daily? As attitudes trail behaviors, do affections trail actions?

Joan Kellerman, James Lewis, and James Laird (1989) wondered about this. They knew that among couples passionately in love, eye gazing is typically prolonged and mutual. Would intimate eye gazing similarly stir feelings between those not in love? To find out, they asked unacquainted male-female pairs to gaze intently for two minutes either at one another's hands or in one another's eyes. When they separated, the eye gazers reported a tingle of attraction and affection toward each other. Simulating love had begun to stir it.

By enacting and expressing love, researcher Robert Sternberg (1988) believes that the passion of initial romance can evolve into enduring love:

> "Living happily ever after" need not be a myth, but if it is to be a reality, the happiness must be based upon different configurations of mutual feelings at various times in a relationship. Couples who expect their passion to last forever, or their intimacy to remain unchallenged, are in for disappointment. . . . We must constantly work at understanding, building, and rebuilding our loving relationships. Relationships are constructions, and they decay over time if they are not maintained and improved. We cannot expect a relationship simply to take care of itself, any more than we can expect that of a building. Rather, we must take responsibility for making our relationships the best they can be.

Given the psychological ingredients of marital happiness—kindred minds, social and sexual intimacy, equitable giving and receiving of emotional and material resources—it becomes possible to contest the French saying, "Love makes the time pass and time makes love pass." But it takes effort to stem love's decay. It takes effort to carve out time each day to talk over the day's happenings. It takes effort to forgo nagging and bickering and instead to disclose and hear one another's hurts, concerns, and dreams. It takes time to make a relationship into "a classless utopia of social equality" (Sarnoff & Sarnoff, 1989), in which both partners freely give and receive, share decision making, and enjoy life together.

CONCEPTS TO REMEMBER

Passionate love   A state of intense longing for union with another. Passionate lovers are absorbed in one another, feel ecstatic at attaining their partner's love, and are disconsolate on losing it.

Two-factor theory of emotion   Arousal × label = emotion.

Self-monitoring   Being attuned to the way one presents oneself in social situations and adjusting one's performance to create the desired impression.

Companionate love   The affection we feel for those with whom our lives are deeply intertwined.

Self-disclosure   Revealing intimate aspects of oneself to others.

Disclosure reciprocity   The tendency for one person's intimacy of self-disclosure to match that of a conversational partner.

MODULE

30

When Do People Help?

❖

On March 13, 1964, Kitty Genovese is set upon by a knife-wielding rapist as she returns to her Queens, New York, apartment house at 3 A.M. Her screams of terror and pleas for help—"Oh my God, he stabbed me! Please help me! Please help me!"—arouse 38 of her neighbors. Many come to their windows and watch while, for 35 minutes, she struggles to escape her attacker. Not until her attacker departs does anyone so much as call the police. Soon after, she dies.

Eleanor Bradley trips and breaks her leg while shopping. Dazed and in pain, she pleads for help. For 40 minutes the stream of shoppers simply parts and flows around her. Finally, a cab driver helps her to a doctor (Darley & Latané, 1968).

What is shocking is not that some people failed to help but that almost 100 percent of those involved failed to respond. Why? In the same or similar situations, would you, would I, react as they did? Or would we be heroes, like Everett Sanderson. Hearing the rumble of an approaching New York subway train, Sanderson leapt down onto the tracks and raced toward the approaching headlights to rescue Michelle De Jesus, a four-year-old who had fallen from the platform. Three seconds before the train would have run her over, he flung Michelle into the crowd above. As the train roared in, he himself failed in his first effort to jump back to the platform. At the last instant, bystanders pulled him to safety (Young, 1977).

Or consider the hillside in Jerusalem where 800 trees form a simple line, the Avenue of the Righteous. Beneath each tree is a plaque with the name of a European Christian who gave refuge to one or more Jews during the Nazi Holocaust. These "righteous Gentiles" knew that if the refugees were discovered, Nazi policy dictated that both host and refugee would suffer a common fate. Many did (Hellman, 1980; Wiesel, 1985).

Less dramatic acts of comforting, caring, and helping abound: Without asking anything in return, people offer directions, donate money, give blood. Why, and when, will people perform altruistic acts?

Altruism is selfishness in reverse. An altruistic person is concerned and helpful even when no benefits are offered or expected in return. Jesus' parable of the Good Samaritan provides the classic illustration of altruism:

> A man was going down from Jerusalem to Jericho, and fell into the hands of robbers, who stripped him, beat him, and went away, leaving him half dead. Now by chance a priest was going down that road; and when he saw him, he passed by on the other side. So likewise a Levite, when he came to the place and saw him, passed by on the other side. But a Samaritan while traveling came near him; and when he saw him, he was moved with pity. He went to him and bandaged his wounds, having poured oil and wine on them. Then he put him on his own animal, brought him to an inn, and took care of him. The next day he took out two denarii, gave them to the innkeeper, and said, "Take care of him; and when I come back, I will repay you whatever more you spend." (Luke 10:30–35)

The Samaritan illustrates pure altruism. Filled with compassion, he gives a total stranger time, energy, and money while expecting neither repayment nor appreciation.

WHY DO PEOPLE HELP?

What motivates altruism? One idea, called **social-exchange theory**, is that we help after doing a cost-benefit analysis. As part of an exchange of benefits, helpers aim to maximize their rewards and minimize their costs. When donating blood we weigh the costs (the inconvenience and discomfort) against the benefits (the social approval and noble feeling). If the anticipated rewards exceed the costs, we help.

You may object: Social-exchange theory takes the selflessness out of altruism. It seems to imply that a helpful act is never genuinely altruistic; we merely call it "altruistic" when the rewards are inconspicuous. If we know people are tutoring only to alleviate guilt or gain social approval, we hardly credit them for a good deed. We laud people for their altruism only when we can't otherwise explain it.

From babyhood onward, however, people sometimes exhibit a natural **empathy**, by feeling distress when seeing someone in distress and relief when their suffering ends. Loving parents (unlike child abusers and other perpetrators of cruelty) suffer when their children suffer and rejoice over their children's joys (Miller & Eisenberg, 1988). Although some helpful acts are indeed done to gain rewards or relieve guilt, experiments suggest that other helpful acts aim simply to increase another's welfare, producing satisfaction for oneself merely as a by-product (Batson, 1991). In these experiments, empathy often produces helping only when help-givers believe the other will actually receive the needed help and regardless of whether the recipient knows who helped.

Social norms also motivate helping. They prescribe how we *ought* to behave. We learn the **reciprocity norm**—that we should return help to those who've helped us. Thus we expect that those who receive favors (gifts, invitations, help) should later return them. The reciprocity norm is qualified by our awareness that some people are incapable of reciprocal giving and receiving. Thus we also feel a **social responsibility norm**—that we should help those who really need it, without regard to future exchanges. When we pick up the dropped books for the person on crutches, we expect nothing in return.

These suggested reasons for helping make biological sense. The empathy that parents feel for their children and other relatives promotes the survival of their shared genes. Likewise, say evolutionary psychologists, reciprocal altruism in small groups boosts everyone's survival.

*W*HEN DO PEOPLE HELP?

Social psychologists were curious and concerned about bystanders' lack of involvement during such events as the Kitty Genovese rape-murder. So they undertook experiments to identify when people will help in an emergency. Then they broadened the question to ask: Who is likely to help in nonemergencies—by such deeds as giving money, donating blood, or contributing time (Myers, 1993)? Among their answers: Helping often increases among people who are

- Feeling guilty, thus providing a way to relieve the guilt or restore self-image
- In a good mood
- Deeply religious (evidenced by higher rates of charitable giving and volunteerism)

Social psychologists also study the *circumstances* that enhance helpfulness. The odds of our helping someone increase when

- We have just observed a helpful model
- We are not hurried
- The victim appears to need and deserve help
- The victim is similar to ourselves
- We are in a small town or rural area
- There are few other bystanders

Number of Bystanders

Bystander passivity during emergencies prompted social commentators to lament today's "alienation," "apathy," "indifference," and "unconscious sadistic impulses." These explanations attribute the nonintervention to the bystanders' dispositions. This allows us to reassure ourselves that as caring people, we *would* have helped. But why were the bystanders such dehumanized characters?

Social psychologists Bibb Latané and John Darley (1970) were unconvinced that the bystanders were dehumanized. So Latané and Darley staged ingenious emergencies and found that a single situational factor—the presence of other bystanders—greatly decreased intervention. By 1980 some four dozen experiments compared help given by bystanders who perceived themselves to be either alone or with others. In about 90 percent of these comparisons, involving nearly 6000 people, lone bystanders were more likely to help (Latané & Nida, 1981).

Sometimes, the victim was actually less likely to get help when many people were around. When Latané, James Dabbs (1975), and 145 collaborators "accidentally" dropped coins or pencils during 1497 elevator rides, they were helped 40 percent of the time when one other person was on the elevator and less than 20 percent of the time when there were six passengers. Why? Latané and Darley surmised that as the number of bystanders increases, any given bystander is less likely to *notice* the incident, less likely to *interpret* the incident as a problem or emergency, and less likely to *assume responsibility* for taking action (Figure 30–1).

Noticing

Twenty minutes after Eleanor Bradley has fallen and broken her leg on a crowded city sidewalk, you come along. Your eyes are on the backs of the pedestrians in front of you (it is bad manners to stare at those you pass), and your private thoughts are on the day's events. Would you therefore

FIGURE 30–1

Latané and Darley's decision tree. Only one path up the tree leads to helping. At each fork of the path, the presence of other bystanders may divert a person down a branch toward not helping. (Adapted from Darley & Latané, 1968.)

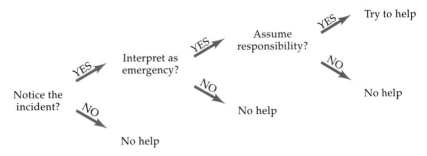

be less likely to notice the injured woman than if the sidewalk were virtually deserted?

To find out, Latané and Darley (1968) had Columbia University men fill out a questionnaire in a room, either by themselves or with two strangers. While they were working (and being observed through a one-way mirror), there was a staged emergency: Smoke poured into the room through a wall vent. Solitary students, who often glanced idly about the room while working, noticed the smoke almost immediately—usually in less than five seconds. Those in groups kept their eyes on their work. It typically took them about 20 seconds to *notice* the smoke.

Interpreting

Once we notice an ambiguous event, we must interpret it. Put yourself in the room filling with smoke. Though worried, you don't want to embarrass yourself by getting flustered. You glance at the others. They look calm, indifferent. Assuming everything must be OK, you shrug it off and go back to work. Then one of the others notices the smoke and, noting your apparent unconcern, reacts similarly. This is yet another example of "informational influence." Each person uses others' behavior as clues to reality.

So it happened in the actual experiment. When those working alone noticed the smoke, they usually hesitated a moment, then got up, walked over to the vent, felt, sniffed, waved at the smoke, hesitated again, and then went to report it. In dramatic contrast, those in groups of three did not move. Among the twenty-four men in eight groups, only one person reported the smoke within the first four minutes (Figure 30-2). By the end of the six-minute experiment, the smoke was so thick it was obscuring the men's vision and they were rubbing their eyes and coughing. Still, in only three of the eight groups did even a single person leave to report the problem.

Equally interesting, the group's passivity affected its members' interpretations. What caused the smoke? "A leak in the air conditioning," "Chemistry labs in the building," "Steam pipes," "Truth gas." They offered many explanations. Not one said, "Fire." The group members, in serving as nonresponsive models, influenced each other's interpretation.

This experimental dilemma parallels dilemmas each of us face. Are the shrieks outside merely playful antics or the desperate screams of someone being assaulted? Is the boys' scuffling a friendly tussle or a vicious fight? Is the woman slumped in the doorway sleeping, or is she seriously ill, perhaps in a diabetic coma?

Assuming Responsibility

Misinterpretation is not the only cause of the **bystander effect**—the inaction among strangers faced with ambiguous emergencies. Sometimes the emergency is obvious. Those who watched Kitty Genovese being attacked and heard her pleas for help correctly interpreted what was

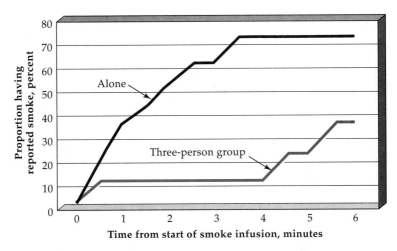

FIGURE 30–2
The smoke-filled room experiment. Smoke pouring into the testing room was much more likely to be reported by individuals working alone than by three-person groups. (Data from Latané & Darley, 1968.)

attacked and heard her pleas for help correctly interpreted what was happening. But the lights and silhouetted figures in neighboring windows told them that others were also watching. This diffused the responsibility for action.

Few of us have observed a murder. But all of us have at times been slower to react to a need when others were present. Passing a stranded motorist, we are much less likely to offer help when on a highway than when on a back country road. To explore further why bystanders inhibit action, Darley and Latané (1968) simulated the Genovese drama. They placed people in separate rooms from which the subjects would hear a victim crying for help. To create this situation, Darley and Latané asked some New York University students to discuss over a laboratory intercom their problems with university life. They told the students that to guarantee their anonymity, no one would be visible, nor would the experimenter eavesdrop. During the ensuing discussion, the participants heard one person, when the experimenter turned his microphone on, lapse into an epileptic seizure. With increasing intensity and speech difficulty, he pleaded for someone to help.

Of those led to believe that they were the only listener, 85 percent left their room to seek help. Of those who believed four others also overheard the victim, only 31 percent went for help. Were those who didn't respond apathetic and indifferent? When the experimenter entered the room to end the experiment, she did not find them so. Most immediately expressed concern. Many had trembling hands and sweating palms. They believed an emergency had occurred but were undecided whether to act.

After the smoke-filled room and the seizure experiments, Latané and Darley asked the participants whether the others' presence had influenced them. We know the other bystanders had a dramatic effect. Yet the participants almost invariably denied the influence. The typical reply? "I was aware of the others, but I would have reacted just the same if they weren't there." This response reinforces a familiar point: We often do not know why we do what we do. And that, of course, is why experiments such as these are revealing. A survey of uninvolved bystanders following a real emergency would have left the bystander effect hidden.

These experiments raise again the issue of research ethics. Were the researchers in the seizure experiment ethical when they forced people to decide whether to abort the discussion to report the problem? Would you object to being in such a study? Note that it would have been impossible to get your "informed consent"; doing so would have destroyed the cover for the experiment.

In defense of the researchers, they were always careful to debrief their laboratory participants. After explaining the seizure experiment, probably the most stressful, the experimenter gave the participants a questionnaire. One hundred percent said the deception was justified and that they would be willing to take part in similar experiments in the future. None of the participants reported feeling angry at the experimenter. Other researchers similarly report that the overwhelming majority of subjects in such experiments say afterward that their participation was both instructive and ethically justified (Schwartz & Gottlieb, 1981). In field experiments, such as one involving a collapsing person in a subway car, an accomplice assisted the victim if no one else did, thus reassuring bystanders that the problem was being dealt with.

Also, remember that the social psychologist has a twofold ethical obligation: to protect the participants and to enhance human welfare by discovering influences upon human behavior. Such discoveries can alert us to unwanted influences and show us how we might exert positive influences. The ethical principle thus seems to be: After protecting participants' welfare, social psychologists fulfill their responsibility to society by doing such research.

Does learning about factors that inhibit altruism indeed reduce their influence? Experiments with University of Montana students by Arthur Beaman and his colleagues (1978) reveal that once people understand why bystanders inhibit helping, they become more likely to help in group situations. The researchers used a lecture to inform some students about how bystander refusal can affect both one's interpretation of an emergency and one's feelings of responsibility. Other students heard either a different lecture or no lecture at all. Two weeks later, as part of a different experiment in a different location, the participants found themselves walking (with an unresponsive confederate) past someone slumped over or past a person sprawled beneath a bicycle. Of those who had not heard the helping lecture, a fourth paused to offer help; twice as many of those "enlightened" did so.

Having read this module, you, too, have perhaps changed. For as you come to understand what influences people's responses—whether hostile, indifferent, or caring—your attitudes, and perhaps your behavior, may never again be the same. Coincidentally, shortly before I wrote the last paragraph, a former student, now living in Washington, D.C., stopped by. She mentioned that she recently found herself part of a stream of pedestrians striding past a man lying unconscious on the sidewalk. "It took my mind back to our social psych class and the accounts of why people fail to help in such situations. Then I thought, well, if I just walk by, too, who's going to help him?" So she made a call to an emergency help number and waited with the victim—and other bystanders who now joined her—until help arrived.

Another student, happening upon a drunk man beating up a street person near midnight in a Vienna subway station, flowed by with the crowd.

> Finally, I was convinced enough of the truth we learned in social psychology to go back and pull the drunk off the street person. Suddenly he was very mad at me and chased me through the subway until police came, arrested him, and got an ambulance for the victim. It was pretty exciting and made me feel good. But the coolest part was how a little insight into social-psychological aspects of our own behavior can help us overcome the power of the situation and change our predicted actions.

So, how will learning about social influences upon good and evil affect you? Will the knowledge you've gained affect your actions? I hope so.

CONCEPTS TO REMEMBER

Altruism Concern and help for others that asks nothing in return; devotion to others without conscious regard for one's self-interests.

Social-exchange theory The theory that human interactions are transactions that aim to maximize one's rewards and minimize one's costs.

Reciprocity norm An expectation that people will help, not hurt, those who have helped them.

Social-responsibility norm An expectation that people will help those dependent upon them.

Empathy The ability to understand and feel what another feels, to put oneself in someone else's shoes.

Bystander effect The finding that a person is less likely to provide help when there are other bystanders (especially when they are strangers and the situation is subject to alternative interpretations).

Epilogue

Big Ideas In Social Psychology and Religion

— ❖ —

In any academic field the results of tens of thousands of studies, the conclusions of thousands of investigators, the insights of hundreds of theorists, can usually be boiled down to a few overriding ideas. Biology offers us principles such as natural selection and adaptation. Sociology builds upon concepts such as social structure, cultural relativity, and societal organization. Music exploits our ideas of rhythm, melody, and harmony.

Which concepts might we include on our short list of social psychology's big ideas? What basic principles are worth remembering long after you have forgotten most of what you learned in this book? And how well do these big ideas about human nature connect with those found in other fields, such as religious studies? Every religious tradition offers answers to some big questions: Who are we? Why are we here? What ought we to do? So let's ask, how do some of social psychology's big ideas connect with those of the Jewish-Christian religious tradition that prevails in Europe and the Americas?[1]

My list of "great ideas we ought never forget" includes four truths, each two-sided. As Pascal reminded us 300 years ago, no single truth is ever sufficient, because the world is not simple. Any truth separated from its complementary truth is a half-truth. It is in the union of partial truths—of what the Chinese call yin and yang (complementary opposites)—that we glimpse the larger reality.

---

[1] One could similarly relate social psychology's view of human nature with ideas derived from other religious traditions. I chose the Judeo-Christian tradition because of its familiarity to me and to most of my readers.

RATIONALITY AND IRRATIONALITY

How "noble in reason!" and "infinite in faculties!" is the human intellect, rhapsodized Shakespeare's Hamlet. In some ways, indeed, *our cognitive capacities are awesome.* The 3-pound tissue in our skulls contains circuitry more complex than all the phone networks on the planet, enabling us to process information either effortfully or automatically, to remember vast quantities of information, and to make snap judgments using rule-of-thumb heuristics. One of the most human of tendencies is our urge to explain behavior, to attribute it to some cause, and therefore to make it seem orderly, predictable, and controllable. As intuitive scientists, we make our attributions efficiently and with enough accuracy for our daily needs.

Yes, echo Jewish and Christian theologians. We are *made in the divine image* and given stewardship for the earth and its creatures. We are the summit of the Creator's work, God's own children.

Yet our explanations are vulnerable to error, insist social psychologists. In ways we are often unaware, *our explanations and social judgments are vulnerable to error.* When observing others we are sometimes too prone to be biased by our preconceptions, to "see" illusory relationships and causes, to treat people in ways that trigger their fulfilling our expectations, to be swayed more by vivid anecdotes than by statistical reality, and to attribute their behavior to their dispositions (for example, to think that someone who acts strangely must *be* strange). Failing to recognize such sources of error in our social thinking, we are prone to overconfidence in our social judgments.

Such conclusions have a familiar ring to theologians, who remind us that *we are finite creatures* of the one who declares "I am God, and there is none like me" and that "as the heavens are higher than the earth, so are my ways higher than your ways and my thoughts than your thoughts" (Isaiah 46:9 and 55:9). As God's children we have dignity, but not deity. Thus we must be skeptical of those who claim for themselves godlike powers of omniscience (reading others' minds, foretelling the future), omnipresence (viewing happenings in remote locations), and omnipotence (creating or altering physical reality with mental power). We should be wary even of those who idolize their religion, presuming their doctrinal fine points to be absolute truth. Always, we see reality through a dim mirror.

SELF-SERVING BIAS AND SELF-ESTEEM

Our views of ourselves are fragile containers of truth. Heeding the ancient admonition to "know thyself," we analyze our behavior, but hardly impartially. Our human tendency to *self-serving bias* appears in our differing explanations for our successes and failures, for our good deeds and bad. On any socially desirable dimension, we commonly view ourselves as relatively superior—as, say, more ethical, socially skilled, and tolerant than our average peer. Moreover, we justify our past behaviors; we have an inflated confidence in the accuracy of our beliefs; we misremember our own past in self-enhancing ways; and we overestimate how virtuously we would behave in situations that draw less-than-virtuous behavior out of most people. Researcher Anthony Greenwald (1984) speaks for dozens of researchers: "People experience life through a self-centered filter."

That conclusion echoes a very old religious idea—that *self-righteous pride is the fundamental sin*, the original sin, the deadliest of the seven deadly sins. Thus the Psalmist could declare that "no one can see his own errors" and the Pharisee could thank God "that I am not like other men" (and you and I can thank God that we are not like the Pharisee). Pride goes before a fall. It corrodes our relations with one another, as in conflicts between partners in marriage, management and labor, nations at war. Each side views its motives alone as pure, its actions beyond reproach. But so does its opposition, continuing the conflict.

Yet *self-esteem pays dividends*. Self-affirmation is often adaptive. It helps maintain our confidence and minimize our depression. To doubt our efficacy and to blame ourselves for our failures is a recipe for failure, loneliness, or dejection. People made to feel secure and valued exhibit less prejudice and contempt for others.

Again, there is a religious parallel in the idea that to sense an *ultimate acceptance* (divine "grace"—the religious parallel to psychology's "unconditional positive regard") is to be liberated from both self-protective pride and self-condemnation. To feel profoundly affirmed, just as I am, lessens my need to define my self-worth in terms of achievements, prestige, or material and physical well-being. It's rather like insecure Pinocchio saying to his maker Geppetto, "Papa, I am not sure who I am. But if I'm all right with you, then I guess I'm all right with me."

A TTITUDES AND BEHAVIOR

Studies during the 1960s shocked social psychologists with revelations that our attitudes sometimes lie dormant, overwhelmed by other influences. But follow-up research was reassuring. *Our attitudes influence our behavior*—when they are relevant and brought to mind. Thus our political attitudes influence our behavior in the voting booth. Our smoking attitudes influence our susceptibility to peer pressures to smoke. Our attitudes toward famine victims influence our contributions. Change the way people think and—whether we call such persuasion "education" or "propaganda"—the impact may be considerable.

If social psychology has taught us anything it is that the reverse is also true: we are as likely to act ourselves into a way of thinking as to think ourselves into action. We are as likely to believe in what we have stood up for as to stand up for what we believe. Especially when we feel responsible for how we have acted, *our attitudes follow our behavior*. This self-persuasion enables all sorts of people—political campaigners, lovers, even terrorists—to believe more strongly in that for which they have witnessed or suffered.

The realization that inner attitude and outer behavior, like chicken and egg, generate one another parallels the Jewish-Christian idea that inner faith and outer action likewise feed one another. Thus, *faith is a source of action*. Elijah is overwhelmed by the Holy as he huddles in a cave. Paul is converted on the Damascus Road. Ezekiel, Isaiah, and Jeremiah undergo an inner transformation. In each case, a new spiritual consciousness produces a new pattern of behavior.

But *faith is also a consequence of action*. Throughout the Old and New Testaments, faith is seen as nurtured by obedient action. For example, in the Old Testament the Hebrew word for *know* is usually a verb, something one does. To *know* love, one must not only know about love, one must *act* lovingly. Philosophers and theologians note how faith grows as people act on what little faith they have. Rather than insist that people believe before they pray, Talmudic scholars would tell rabbis, get them to pray and their belief will grow. "The proof of Christianity really consists in 'following,'" declared Soren Kierkegaard (1851). To attain faith, said Pascal (1670), "follow the way by which [the committed] began; by acting as if they believed, taking the holy water, having masses said, etc. Even this will naturally make you believe. . . ." C. S. Lewis (1960) concurred:

> Believe in God and you will have to face hours when it seems *obvious* that this material world is the only reality; disbelieve in Him and you must face hours when this material world seems to shout at you that it is not all. No conviction, religious or irreligious, will, of itself, end once and for all [these doubts] in the soul. Only the practice of Faith resulting in the habit of Faith will gradually do that.

*P*ERSONS AND SITUATIONS

On this incomplete list of big ideas, my final two-sided truth is that people and situations interact. We see this, first, in the evidence that social influences powerfully affect our behavior. *We are the creatures of our social worlds*.

Recall the studies of conformity, role playing, persuasion, and group influence. The most dramatic findings come from experiments that put well-intentioned people in evil situations to see whether good or evil prevailed. To a dismaying extent, evil pressures overwhelm good intentions, inducing people to conform to falsehoods or capitulate to cruelty. Faced with a powerful situation, nice people often don't behave so nicely. Depending on the social context, most of us are capable of acting kindly or brutally, independently or submissively, wisely or foolishly. In one irony-laden experiment, even most seminary students en route to recording an extemporaneous talk on the Good Samaritan parable failed to stop and give aid to a slumped, groaning person—*if* they had been pressed to hurry (Darley & Batson, 1973). External social forces shape our social behavior.

The social psychological idea that there are powers greater than the individual is paralleled by the religious idea of *transcendent good and evil powers*, symbolized in the creation story as a seductive demonic force. Evil involves not only individual rotten apples here and there. It also is a product of "principalities and powers"—corrosive forces—that can make a whole barrel of apples go bad. And because evil is collective as well as personal, responding to it takes a communal religious life.

Although powerful situations may override people's individual dispositions, social psychologists do not view humans as mere passive tumbleweeds, blown this way and that by the social winds. Facing the same situation, different people may react differently, depending on their personality and culture. Feeling coerced by blatant pressure, they will sometimes react in ways that restore their sense of freedom. In a numerical minority, they will sometimes oppose and sway the majority. When they believe in themselves, maintaining an "internal locus of control," they sometimes work wonders. Moreover, people choose their situations—their college environments, their jobs, their locales. And their social expectations are sometimes self-fulfilling, as when we expect someone to be warm or hostile and they become so. In such ways, *we are the creators of our social worlds*.

To most religious traditions, that rings true. *We are morally responsible*—accountable for how we use whatever freedom we have. What we decide matters. The stream of causation from past to future runs through our choices.

Faced with these pairs of complementary ideas, framed either psychologically or religiously, we are like someone stranded in a deep well with two ropes dangling down. If we grab either one alone we sink deeper into the well. Only when we hold both ropes can we climb out, because at the top, beyond where we can see, they come together around a pulley. Grabbing only the rope of rationality or irrationality, of self-serving pride or self-esteem, of attitudes-first or behavior-first, of personal or situational causation, plunges us to the bottom of a well. So instead we grab both ropes, perhaps without yet fully grasping how they come together. In doing so, we may be comforted that in both science and religion a confused acceptance of complementary principles is sometimes more honest than an over-simplified theory that ignores half the evidence. In the scissors of truth, the cutting edge lies between the blades of yin and yang.

References
for Exploring
Social Psychology

ABELSON, R. P., KINDER, D. R., PETERS, M. D., & FISKE, S. T. (1982). Affective and semantic components in political person perception. *Journal of Personality and Social Psychology, 42,* 619–630.

ABRAMS, D. (1991). AIDS: What young people believe and what they do. Paper presented at the British Association for the Advancement of Science conference.

ABRAMS, D., WETHERELL, M., COCHRANE, S., HOGG, M. A., & TURNER, J. C. (1990). Knowing what to think by knowing who you are: Self-categorization and the nature of norm formation, conformity and group polarization. *British Journal of Social Psychology, 29,* 97–119.

ABRAMSON, L. Y. (Ed.). (1988). *Social cognition and clinical psychology: A synthesis.* New York: Guilford.

ABRAMSON, L. Y., METALSKY, G. I., & ALLOY, L. B. (1989). Hopelessness depression: A theory-based subtype. *Psychological Review, 96,* 358–372.

ADAIR, J. G., DUSHENKO, T. W., & LINDSAY, R. C. L. (1985). Ethical regulations and their impact on research practice. *American Psychologist, 40,* 59–72.

ADAMS, D. (Ed.) (1991). *The Seville statement on violence: Preparing the ground for the constructing of peace.* UNESCO.

ADLER, R. P., LESSER, G. S., MERINGOFF, L. K., ROBERTSON, T. S., & WARD, S. (1980). *The effects of television advertising on children.* Lexington, MA: Lexington.

ADORNO, T., FRENKEL-BRUNSWIK, E., LEVINSON, D., & SANFORD, R. N. (1950). *The authoritarian personality*. New York: Harper.

AIELLO, J. R., THOMPSON, D. E., & BRODZINSKY, D. M. (1983). How funny is crowding anyway? Effects of room size, group size, and the introduction of humor. *Basic and Applied Social Psychology, 4*, 193–207.

ALLEE, W. C., & MASURE, R. M. (1936). A comparison of maze behavior in paired and isolated shell-parakeets (*Melopsittacus undulatus Shaw*) in a two-alley problem box. *Journal of Comparative Psychology, 22*, 131–155.

ALLEN, V. L., & WILDER, D. A. (1979). Group categorization and attribution of belief similarity. *Small Group Behavior, 10*, 73–80.

ALLISON, S. T., JORDAN, M. R., & YEATTS, C. E. (1992). A cluster-analytic approach toward identifying the structure and content of human decision making. *Human Relations, 45*, in press.

ALLISON, S. T., MESSICK, D. M., & GOETHALS, G. R. (1989). On being better but not smarter than others: The Muhammad Ali effect. *Social Cognition, 7*, 275–296.

ALLOY, L. B., & ABRAMSON, L. Y. (1979). Judgment of contingency in depressed and nondepressed students: Sadder but wiser? *Journal of Experimental Psychology: General, 108*, 441–485.

ALLOY, L. B., ALBRIGHT, J. S., ABRAMSON, L. Y., & DYKMAN, B. M. (1990). Depressive realism and nondepressive optimistic illusions: The role of the self. In R. E. Ingram (Ed.), *Contemporary psychological approaches to depression: Theory, research and treatment*. New York: Plenum.

ALLOY, L. B., & CLEMENTS, C. M. (1991). The illusion of control: Invulnerability to negative affect and depressive symptoms following laboratory and natural stressors. *Journal of Abnormal Psychology*, in press.

ALLPORT, F. H. (1920). The influence of the group upon association and thought. *Journal of Experimental Psychology, 3*, 159–182.

ALLPORT, G. W. (1958). *The nature of prejudice* (abridged). Garden City, NY: Anchor.

ALTEMEYER, B. (1988). *Enemies of freedom: Understanding right-wing authoritarianism*. San Francisco: Jossey-Bass.

ALTEMEYER, B. (1992). Six studies of right-wing authoritarianism among American state legislators. Unpublished manuscript, Univ. of Manitoba.

ALWIN, D. F. (1990). Historical changes in parental orientations to children. In N. Mandell (Ed.), *Sociological studies of child development*, Vol. 3. Greenwich, CT: JAI.

AMABILE, T. M., & GLAZEBROOK, A. H. (1982). A negativity bias in interpersonal evaluation. *Journal of Experimental Social Psychology, 18*, 1–22.

American Enterprise (1991, March/April). Women and the use of force, p. 85–86.

American Psychological Association (1981). Ethical principles of psychologists. *American Psychologist, 36*, 633–638.

American Psychological Association (1992). Ethical principles of psychologists. Washington, DC: American Psychological Association, in press.

AMIR, Y. (1969). Contact hypothesis in ethnic relations. *Psychological Bulletin, 71*, 319–342.

ANDERSON, C. A. (1989). Temperature and aggression: Ubiquitous effects of heat on occurrence of human violence. *Psychological Bulletin, 106*, 74–96.

ANDERSON, C. A., & HARVEY, R. J. (1988). Discriminating between problems in living: An examination of measures of depression, loneliness, shyness, and social anxiety. *Journal of Social and Clinical Psychology, 6,* 482–491.

ANDERSON, C. A., HOROWITZ, L. M., & FRENCH, R. D. (1983). Attributional style of lonely and depressed people. *Journal of Personality and Social Psychology, 45,* 127–136.

ANDERSON, C. A., & RIGER, A. L. (1991). A controllability attributional model of problems in living: Dimensional and situational interactions in the prediction of depression and loneliness. *Social Cognition, 9,* 149–181.

ANTHONY, T., COPPER, C., & MULLEN, B. (1992). Cross-racial facial identification: A social cognitive integration. *Personality and Social Psychology Bulletin,* in press.

ANTILL, J. K. (1983). Sex role complementarity versus similarity in married couples. *Journal of Personality and Social Psychology, 45,* 145–155.

ARCHER, D., & GARTNER, R. (1976). Violent acts and violent times: A comparative approach to postwar homicide rates. *American Sociological Review, 41,* 937–963.

ARCHER, D., IRITANI, B., KIMES, D. B., & BARRIOS, M. (1983). Face-ism: Five studies of sex differences in facial prominence. *Journal of Personality and Social Psychology, 45,* 725–735.

ARCHER, J. (1991). The influence of testosterone on human aggression. *British Journal of Psychology, 82,* 1–28.

ARCHER, R. L., BERG, J. M., & BURLESON, J. A. (1980). Self-disclosure and attraction: A self-perception analysis. Unpublished manuscript, Univ. of Texas at Austin.

ARCHER, R. L., BERG, J. M., & RUNGE, T. E. (1980). Active and passive observers' attraction to a self-disclosing other. *Journal of Experimental Social Psychology, 16,* 130–145.

ARCHER, R. L., & BURLESON, J. A. (1980). The effects of timing of self-disclosure on attraction and reciprocity. *Journal of Personality and Social Psychology, 38,* 120–130.

ARCHER, R. L., & COOK, C. E. (1986). Personalistic self-disclosure and attraction: Basis for relationship or scarce resource. *Social Psychology Quarterly, 49,* 268–272.

ARENDT, H. (1963). *Eichmann in Jerusalem: A report on the banality of evil.* New York: Viking.

ARGYLE, M., SHIMODA, K., & LITTLE, B. (1978). Variance due to persons and situations in England and Japan. *British Journal of Social and Clinical Psychology, 17,* 335–337.

ARKES, H. R., FAUST, D., GUILMETTE, T. J., & HART, K. (1988). Eliminating the hindsight bias. *Journal of Applied Psychology, 73,* 305–307.

ARKIN, R. M., & BAUMGARDNER, A. H. (1985). Self-handicapping. In J. H. Harvey & C. Weary (Eds.), *Attribution: Basic issues and applications.* New York: Academic Press.

ARKIN, R. M., & BURGER, J. M. (1980). Effects of unit relation tendencies on interpersonal attraction. *Social Psychology Quarterly, 43,* 380–391.

ARKIN, R. M., COOPER, H., & KOLDITZ, T. (1980). A statistical review of the literature concerning the self-serving attribution bias in interpersonal influence situations. *Journal of Personality, 48,* 435–448.

ARKIN, R. M., LAKE, E. A., & BAUMGARDNER, A. H. (1986). Shyness and self-presentation. In W. H. Jones, J. M. Cheek, & S. R. Briggs (Eds.), *Shyness: Perspectives on research and treatment.* New York: Plenum.

ARKIN, R. M., & MARUYAMA, G. M. (1979). Attribution, affect, and college exam performance. *Journal of Educational Psychology, 71,* 85–93.

ARMS, R. L., RUSSELL, G. W., & SANDILANDS, M. L. (1979). Effects on the hostility of spectators of viewing aggressive sports. *Social Psychology Quarterly, 42,* 275–279.

ARMSTRONG, B. (1981, January). An interview with Herbert Kelman. *APA Monitor,* pp. 4–5, 55.

ARON, A., & ARON, E. (1989). *The heart of social psychology,* 2nd ed. Lexington, MA: Lexington.

ARON, A., DUTTON, D. G., ARON, E. N., & IVERSON, A. (1989). Experiences of falling in love. *Journal of Social and Personal Relationships, 6,* 243–257.

ARONSON, E. (1988). *The social animal.* New York: Freeman.

ARONSON, E., BREWER, M., & CARLSMITH, J. M. (1985). Experimentation in social psychology. In G. Lindzey & E. Aronson (Eds.), *Handbook of social psychology,* vol. 1. Hillsdale, NJ: Erlbaum.

ARONSON, E., & GONZALEZ, A. (1988). Desegregation, jigsaw, and the Mexican-American experience. In P. A. Katz & D. Taylor (Eds.), *Towards the elimination of racism: Profiles in controversy.* New York: Plenum.

ARONSON, E., & MILLS, J. (1959). The effect of severity of initiation on liking for a group. *Journal of Abnormal and Social Psychology, 59,* 177–181.

ASCH, S. E. (1955, November). Opinions and social pressure. *Scientific American,* pp. 31–35.

ASENDORPF, J. B. (1987). Videotape reconstruction of emotions and cognitions related to shyness. *Journal of Personality and Social Psychology, 53,* 541–549.

ASHER, J. (1987, April). Born to be shy? *Psychology Today,* pp. 56–64.

ASHMORE, R. D. (1990). Sex, gender, and the individual. In L. A. Pervin (Ed.), *Handbook of personality: Theory and research.* New York: Guilford.

ASSOCIATED PRESS (1988, July DM). Rain in Iowa. *Grand Rapids Press,* p. 6.

ASTIN, A., & OTHERS (1991). *The American freshman: National norms for Fall 1991.* Los Angeles: American Council on Education and UCLA.

ASTIN, A. W., GREEN, K. C., & KORN, W. S. (1987a). *The American freshman: Twenty year trends.* Los Angeles: Higher Education Research Institute, UCLA.

ASTIN, A. W., GREEN, K. C., KORN, W. S., & SCHALIT, M. (1987b). *The American freshman: National norms for Fall 1987.* Los Angeles: Higher Education Research Institute, UCLA.

ATWELL, R. H. (1986, July 28). Drugs on campus: A perspective. *Higher Education & National Affairs,* p. 5.

AVERILL, J. R. (1983). Studies on anger and aggression: Implications for theories of emotion. *American Psychologist, 38,* 1145–1160.

AXELROD, R., & DION, D. (1988). The further evolution of cooperation. *Science, 242,* 1385–1390.

AXSOM, D., YATES, S., & CHAIKEN, S. (1987). Audience response as a heuristic cue in persuasion. *Journal of Personality and Social Psychology, 53,* 30–40.

AYRES, I. (1991). Fair driving: Gender and race discrimination in retail car negotiations. *Harvard Law Review, 104,* 817–872.

AZRIN, N. H. (1967, May). Pain and aggression. *Psychology Today*, pp. 27–33.

BABAD, E., BERNIERI, F., & ROSENTHAL, R. (1991). Students as judges to teachers' verbal and nonverbal behavior. *American Educational Research Journal, 28,* 211–234.

BACHMAN, J. G., & O'MALLEY, P. M. (1977). Self-esteem in young men: A longitudinal analysis of the impact of educational and occupational attainment. *Journal of Personality and Social Psychology, 35,* 365–380.

BAER, R., HINKLE, S., SMITH, K., & FENTON, M. (1980). Reactance as a function of actual versus projected autonomy. *Journal of Personality and Social Psychology, 38,* 416–422.

BAIRAGI, R. (1987). Food crises and female children in rural Bangladesh. *Social Science, 72,* 48–51.

BANDURA, A. (1979). The social learning perspective: Mechanisms of aggression. In H. Toch (Ed.), *Psychology of crime and criminal justice.* New York: Holt, Rinehart & Winston.

BANDURA, A. (1986). *Social foundations of thought and action: A social cognitive theory.* Englewood Cliffs, NJ: Prentice-Hall.

BANDURA, A., ROSS, D., & ROSS, S. A. (1961). Transmission of aggression through imitation of aggressive models. *Journal of Abnormal and Social Psychology, 63,* 575–582.

BANDURA, A., & WALTERS, R. H. (1959). *Adolescent aggression.* New York: Ronald.

BANDURA, A., & WALTERS, R. H. (1963). *Social learning and personality development.* New York: Holt, Rinehart & Winston.

BARATZ, D. (1983). How justified is the "obvious" reaction. *Dissertation Abstracts International 44/02B,* 644B (Univ. Microfilms No. DA 8314435). Reported by N. L. Gage (1991, January–February). The obviousness of social and educational research results. *Educational Researcher,* pp. 10–16.

BARNETT, P. A., & GOTLIB, I. H. (1988). Psychosocial functioning and depression: Distinguishing among antecedents, concomitants, and consequences. *Psychological Bulletin, 104,* 97–126.

BARON, L., & STRAUS, M. A. (1984). Sexual stratification, pornography, and rape in the United States. In N. M. Malamuth & E. Donnerstein (Eds.), *Pornography and sexual aggression.* New York: Academic Press.

BARON, R. M., MANDEL, D. R., ADAMS, C. A., & GRIFFEN, L. M. (1976). Effects of social density in university residential environments. *Journal of Personality and Social Psychology, 34,* 434–446.

BARON, R. S. (1986). Distraction-conflict theory: Progress and problems. In L. Berkowitz (Ed.), *Advances in experimental social psychology,* Orlando, FL: Academic Press.

BATSON, C. D. (1991). *The altruism question: Toward a social-psychological answer.* Hillsdale, NJ: Erlbaum.

BAUMEISTER, R. F. (1991). *Meanings of life.* New York: Guilford.

BAUMEISTER, R. F., & ILKO, S. A. (1991). Shallow gratitude: Public and private acknowledgement of external help in accounts of success. Unpublished manuscript, Case Western Reserve University.

BAUMEISTER, R. F., & SCHER, S. J. (1988). Self-defeating behavior patterns among normal individuals: Review and analysis of common self-destructive tendencies. *Psychological Bulletin, 104,* 3–22.

BAUMEISTER, R. F., & STEINHILBER, A. (1984). Paradoxical effects of supportive audiences on performance under pressure: The home field disadvantage in sports championships. *Journal of Personality and Social Psychology, 47,* 85–93.

BAUMEISTER, R. F., & WOTMAN, S. R. (1992). *Breaking hearts: The two sides of unrequited love.* New York: Guilford.

BAUMGARDNER, A. H. (1991). Claiming depressive symptoms as a self-handicap: A protective self-presentation strategy. *Basic and Applied Social Psychology, 12,* 97–113.

BAUMGARDNER, A. H., & BROWNLEE, E. A. (1987). Strategic failure in social interaction: Evidence for expectancy disconfirmation process. *Journal of Personality and Social Psychology, 52,* 525–535.

BAUMGARDNER, A. H., KAUFMAN, C. M., & LEVY, P. E. (1989). Regulating affect interpersonally: When low esteem leads to greater enhancement. *Journal of Personality and Social Psychology, 56,* 907–921.

BAUMHART, R. (1968). *An honest profit.* New York: Holt, Rinehart & Winston.

BAXTER, T. L., & GOLDBERG, L. R. (1987). Perceived behavioral consistency underlying trait attributions to oneself and another: An extension of the actor-observer effect. *Personality and Social Psychology Bulletin, 13,* 437–447.

BAYER, E. (1929). Beitrage zur zeikomponenten theorie des hungers. *Zeitschrift fur Psychologie, 112,* 1–54.

BAZERMAN, M. H. (1986, June). Why negotiations go wrong. *Psychology Today,* pp. 54–58.

BEAMAN, A. L., BARNES, P. J., KLENTZ, B., & McQUIRK, B. (1978). Increasing helping rates through information dissemination: Teaching pays. *Personality and Social Psychology Bulletin, 4,* 406–411.

BEAMAN, A. L., & KLENTZ, B. (1983). The supposed physical attractiveness bias against supporters of the women's movement: A meta-analysis. *Personality and Social Psychology Bulletin, 9,* 544–550.

BEAMAN, A. L., KLENTZ, B., DIENER, E., & SVANUM, S. (1979). Self-awareness and transgression in children: Two field studies. *Journal of Personality and Social Psychology, 37,* 1835–1846.

BEAUVOIS, J. L., & DUBOIS, N. (1988). The norm of internality in the explanation of psychological events. *European Journal of Social Psychology, 18,* 299–316.

BECK, A. T., & YOUNG, J. E. (1978, September). College blues. *Psychology Today,* pp. 80–92.

BECK, S. B., WARD-HULL, C. I., & McLEAR, P. M. (1976). Variables related to women's somatic preferences of the male and female body. *Journal of Personality and Social Psychology, 34,* 1200–1210.

BELL, P. A. (1980). Effects of heat, noise, and provocation on retaliatory evaluative behavior. *Journal of Social Psychology, 110,* 97–100.

BELL, R. Q., & CHAPMAN, M. (1986). Child effects in studies using experimental or brief longitudinal approaches to socialization. *Developmental Psychology, 22,* 595–603.

BELSON, W. A. (1978). *Television violence and the adolescent boy.* Westmead, England: Saxon House, Teakfield.

BEM, D. J. (1972). Self-perception theory. In L. Berkowitz (Ed.), *Advances in experimental social psychology,* Vol. 6. New York: Academic Press.

BEM, D. J., & McCONNELL, H. K. (1970). Testing the self-perception explanation of dissonance phenomena: On the salience of premanipulation attitudes. *Journal of Personality and Social Psychology, 14,* 23–31.

BENNIS, W. (1984). Transformative power and leadership. In T. J. Sergiovani & J. E. Corbally (Eds.), *Leadership and organizational culture.* Urbana: Univ. of Illinois Press.

BERG, J. H. (1987). Responsiveness and self-disclosure. In V. J. Derlega & J. H. Berg (Eds.), *Selfdisclosure: Theory, research, and therapy.* New York: Plenum.

BERG, J. H., & McQUINN, R. D. (1986). Attraction and exchange in continuing and noncontinuing dating relationships. *Journal of Personality and Social Psychology, 50,* 942–952.

BERG, J. H., & McQUINN, R. D. (1988). Loneliness and aspects of social support networks. Unpublished manuscript, Univ. of Mississippi.

BERG, J. H., & PEPLAU, L. A. (1982). Loneliness: The relationship of self-disclosure and androgyny. *Personality and Social Psychology Bulletin, 8,* 624–630.

BERGER, P. (1963). *Invitation to sociology: A humanistic perspective.* Garden City, NY: Doubleday Anchor.

BERGLAS, S., & JONES, E. E. (1978). Drug choice as a self-handicapping strategy in response to noncontingent success. *Journal of Personality and Social Psychology, 36,* 405–417.

BERKOWITZ, L. (1954). Group standards, cohesiveness, and productivity. *Human Relations, 7,* 509–519.

BERKOWITZ, L. (1968, September). Impulse, aggression and the gun. *Psychology Today,* pp. 18–22.

BERKOWITZ, L. (1978). Whatever happened to the frustration-aggression hypothesis? *American Behavioral Scientists, 21,* 691–708.

BERKOWITZ, L. (1981, June). How guns control us. *Psychology Today,* pp. 11–12.

BERKOWITZ, L. (1983). Aversively stimulated aggression: Some parallels and differences in research with animals and humans. *American Psychologist, 38,* 1135–1144.

BERKOWITZ, L. (1984). Some effects of thoughts on anti- and prosocial influences of media events: A cognitive-neoassociation analysis. *Psychological Bulletin, 95,* 410–427.

BERKOWITZ, L. (1989). Frustration-aggression hypothesis: Examination and reformulation. *Psychological Bulletin, 106,* 59–73.

BERKOWITZ, L., & GEEN, R. G. (1966). Film violence and the cue properties of available targets. *Journal of Personality and Social Psychology, 3,* 525–530.

BERKOWITZ, L., & LePAGE, A. (1967). Weapons as aggression-eliciting stimuli. *Journal of Personality and Social Psychology, 7,* 202–207.

BERNARD, J. (1976). *Sex differences: An overview.* New York: MSS Modular Publications.

BERSCHEID, E. (1981). An overview of the psychological effects of physical attractiveness and some comments upon the psychological effects of knowledge of the effects of physical attractiveness. In W. Lucker, K. Ribbens, & J. A. McNamera (Eds.), *Logical aspects of facial form (craniofacial growth series).* Ann Arbor: Univ. of Michigan Press.

BERSCHEID, E. (1985). Interpersonal attraction. In G. Lindzey & E. Aronson (Eds.), *The handbook of social psychology.* New York: Random House.

BERSCHEID, E., BOYE, D., & WALSTER (HATFIELD), E. (1968). Retaliation as a means of restoring equity. *Journal of Personality and Social Psychology, 10,* 370–376.

BERSCHEID, E., DION, K., WALSTER (HATFIELD), E., & WALSTER, G. W. (1971). Physical attractiveness and dating choice: A test of the matching hypothesis. *Journal of Experimental Social Psychology, 7,* 173–189.

BERSCHEID, E., GRAZIANO, W., MONSON, T., & DERMER, M. (1976). Outcome dependency: Attention, attribution, and attraction. *Journal of Personality and Social Psychology, 34*, 978–989.

BERSCHEID, E., & PEPLAU, L. A. (1983). The emerging science of relationships. In H. H. Kelley, E. Berscheid, A. Christensen, J. H. Harvey, T. L. Huston, G. Levinger, E. McClintock, L. A. Peplau, & D. R. Peterson (Eds.), *Close relationships*. New York: Freeman.

BERSCHEID, E., SNYDER, M., & OMOTO, A. M. (1989). Issues in studying close relationships: Conceptualizing and measuring closeness. In C. Hendrick (Ed.), *Review of personality and social psychology*, Vol. 10. Newbury Park, CA: Sage.

BERSCHEID, E., & WALSTER (HATFIELD), E. (1978). *Interpersonal attraction*. Reading, MA: Addison-Wesley.

BERSCHEID, E., WALSTER, G. W., & WALSTER (HATFIELD), E. (1969). Effects of accuracy and positivity of evaluation on liking for the evaluator. Unpublished manuscript. Summarized by E. Berscheid and E. Walster (Hatfield) in *Interpersonal attraction*. Reading, MA: Addison-Wesley, 1978.

BIERBRAUER, G. (1979). Why did he do it? Attribution of obedience and the phenomenon of dispositional bias. *European Journal of Social Psychology, 9*, 67–84.

BIERLY, M. M. (1985). Prejudice toward contemporary outgroups as a generalized attitude. *Journal of Applied Social Psychology, 15*, 189–199.

BIERNAT, M. (1991). Gender stereotypes and the relationship between masculinity and femininity: A developmental analysis. *Journal of Personality and Social Psychology, 61*, 351–365.

BIERNAT, M., & WORTMAN, C. B. (1991). Sharing of home responsibilities between professionally employed women and their husbands. *Journal of Personality and Social Psychology, 60*, 844–860.

BILLIG, M., & TAJFEL, H. (1973). Social categorization and similarity in intergroup behaviour. *European Journal of Social Psychology, 3*, 27–52.

BLACKBURN, R. T., PELLINO, G. R., BOBERG, A., & O'CONNELL, C. (1980). Are instructional improvement programs off target? *Current Issues in Higher Education, 1*, 31–48.

BLAKE, R. R., & MOUTON, J. S. (1962). The intergroup dynamics of win-lose conflict and problem-solving collaboration in union-management relations. In M. Sherif (Ed.), *Intergroup relations and leadership*. New York: Wiley.

BLAKE, R. R., & MOUTON, J. S. (1979). Intergroup problem solving in organizations: From theory to practice. In W. G. Austin and S. Worchel (Eds.), *The social psychology of intergroup relations*. Monterey, CA: Brooks/Cole.

BLANCHARD, F. A., & COOK, S. W. (1976). Effects of helping a less competent member of a cooperating interracial group on the development of interpersonal attraction. *Journal of Personality and Social Psychology, 34*, 1245–1255.

BLOCK J., & FUNDER, D. C. (1986). Social roles and social perception: Individual differences in attribution and error. *Journal of Personality and Social Psychology, 51*, 1200–1207.

BODENHAUSEN, G. V. (1990). Stereotypes as judgmental heuristics: Evidence of circadian variations in discrimination. *Psychological Science, 1*, 319–322.

Bolt, M., & Brink, J. (1991, November 1). Personal correspondence.

Bond, C. F., Jr., & Titus, L. J. (1983). Social facilitation: A meta-analysis of 241 studies. *Psychological Bulletin, 94,* 265–292.

Borgida, E., & Brekke, N. (1985). Psycholegal research on rape trials. In A. W. Burgess (Ed.), *Rape and sexual assault: A research handbook.* New York: Garland.

Bornstein, R. F. (1989). Exposure and affect: Overview and meta-analysis of research, 1968–1987. *Psychological Bulletin, 106,* 265–289.

Bornstein, R. F., Kale, A. R., & Cornell, K. R. (1990). Boredom as a limiting condition on the mere exposure effect. *Journal of Personality and Social Psychology, 58,* 791–800.

Bossard, J. H. S. (1932). Residential propinquity as a factor in marriage selection. *American Journal of Sociology, 38,* 219–224.

Bothwell, R. K., Brigham, J. C., & Malpass, R. S. (1989). Cross-racial identification. *Personality and Social Psychology Bulletin, 15,* 19–25.

Bower, G. H. (1987). Commentary on mood and memory. *Behavioral Research and Therapy, 25,* 443–455.

Brehm, S., & Brehm, J. W. (1981). *Psychological reactance: A theory of freedom and control.* New York: Academic Press.

Brehm, S. S., & Smith, T. W. (1986). Social psychological approaches to psychotherapy and behavior change. In S. L. Garfield & A. E. Bergin (Eds.), *Handbook of psychotherapy and behavior change,* 3rd ed. New York: Wiley.

Brenner, S. N., & Molander, E. A. (1977). Is the ethics of business changing? *Harvard Business Review,* January–February, pp. 57–71.

Brewer, M. B. (1987). Collective decisions. *Social Science, 72,* 140–143.

Brewer, M. B., & Miller, N. (1988). Contact and cooperation: When do they work? In P. A. Katz & D. Taylor (Eds.), *Towards the elimination of racism: Profiles in controversy.* New York: Plenum.

Brewer, M. B., & Silver, M. (1978). In-group bias as a function of task characteristics. *European Journal of Social Psychology, 8,* 393–400.

Brickner, M. A., Harkins, S. G., & Ostrom, T. M. (1986). Effects of personal involvement: Thought-provoking implications for social loafing. *Journal of Personality and Social Psychology, 51,* 763–769.

Brigham, J. C., & Malpass, R. S. (1985). The role of experience and contact in the recognition of faces of own- and other-race persons. *Journal of Social Issues, 41,* 139–155.

Brigham, J. C., & Williamson, N. L. (1979). Cross-racial recognition and age: When you're over 60, do they still all look alike? *Personality and Social Psychology Bulletin, 5,* 218–222.

British Psychological Society (1991). *Code of conduct ethical principles & guidelines.* Leicester.

Brockner, J., & Hulton, A. J. B. (1978). How to reverse the vicious cycle of low self-esteem: The importance of attentional focus. *Journal of Experimental Social Psychology, 14,* 564–578.

Brockner, J., Rubin, J. Z., Fine, J., Hamilton, T. P., Thomas, B., & Turetsky, B. (1982). Factors affecting entrapment in escalating conflicts: The importance of timing. *Journal of Research in Personality, 16,* 247–266.

BRODT, S. E., & ZIMBARDO, P. G. (1981). Modifying shyness-related social behavior through symptom misattribution. *Journal of Personality and Social Psychology, 41,* 437–449.

BRONFENBRENNER, U. (1961). The mirror image in Soviet-American relations. *Journal of Social Issues, 17*(3), 45–56.

BROWN, J. D. (1986). Evaluations of self and others: Self-enhancement biases in social judgments. *Social Cognition, 4,* 353–376.

BROWN, J. D. (1991). Accuracy and bias in self-knowledge: Can knowing the truth be hazardous to your health? In C. R. Snyder & D. F. Forsyth (Eds.), *Handbook of social and clinical psychology: The health perspective.* New York: Pergamon.

BROWN, J. D., COLLINS, R. L., & SCHMIDT, G. W. (1988). Self-esteem and direct versus indirect forms of self-enhancement. *Journal of Personality and Social Psychology, 55,* 445–453.

BROWN, J. D., NOVICK, N. J., LORD, K. A., & RICHARDS, J. M. (1992). When Gulliver travels: Social context, psychological closeness, and self-appraisals. *Journal of Personality and Social Psychology, 62,* 717–727.

BROWN, J. D., & SIEGEL, J. M. (1988). Attributions for negative life events and depression: The role of perceived control. *Journal of Personality and Social Psychology, 54,* 316–322.

BROWN, J. D., & TAYLOR, S. E. (1986). Affect and the processing of personal information: Evidence for mood-activated self-schemata. *Journal of Experimental Social Psychology, 22,* 436–452.

BURCHILL, S. A. L., & STILES, W. B. (1988). Interactions of depressed college students with their roommates: Not necessarily negative. *Journal of Personality and Social Psychology, 55,* 410–419.

BURGER, J. M. (1987). Increased performance with increased personal control: A self-presentation interpretation. *Journal of Experimental Social Psychology, 23,* 350–360.

BURGER, J. M. (1991). Changes in attributions over time: The ephemeral fundamental attribution error. *Social Cognition, 9,* 182–193.

BURGER, J. M., & BURNS, L. (1988). The illusion of unique invulnerability and the use of effective contraception. *Personality and Social Psychology Bulletin, 14,* 264–270.

BURGER, J. M., & PALMER, M. L. (1991). Changes in and generalization of unrealistic optimism following experiences with stressful events: Reactions to the 1989 California earthquake. *Personality and Social Psychology Bulletin, 18,* 39–43.

BURGER, J. M., & PAVELICH, J. L. (1991). Attributions for presidential elections: The situational shift over time. Unpublished manuscript, Santa Clara University.

BURNS, D. D. (1980). *Feeling good: The new mood therapy.* New York: Signet.

BURNSTEIN, E., & KITAYAMA, S. (1989). Persuasion in groups. In T. C. Brock & S. Shavitt (Eds.), *The psychology of persuasion.* San Francisco: Freeman.

BURNSTEIN, E., & VINOKUR, A. (1977). Persuasive argumentation and social comparison as determinants of attitude polarization. *Journal of Experimental Social Psychology, 13,* 315–332.

BURNSTEIN, E., & WORCHEL, P. (1962). Arbitrariness of frustration and its consequences for aggression in a social situation. *Journal of Personality, 30,* 528–540.

BURR, W. R. (1973). *Theory construction and the sociology of the family*. New York: Wiley.

BURROS, M. (1988, February 24). Women: Out of the house but not out of the kitchen. *New York Times*.

BURTON, J. W. (1969). *Conflict and communication*. New York: Free Press.

BUSHMAN, B. J., & COOPER, H. M. (1990). Effects of alcohol on human aggression: An integrative research review. *Psychological Review, 107*, 341–354.

BUSHMAN, B. J., & GEEN, R. G. (1990). Role of cognitive-emotional mediators and individual differences in the effects of media violence on aggression. *Journal of Personality and Social Psychology, 58*, 156–163.

BUSS, D. M. (1984). Toward a psychology of person-environment (PE) correlation: The role of spouse selection. *Journal of Personality and Social Psychology, 47*, 361–377.

BUSS, D. M. (1985). Human mate selection. *American Scientist, 73*, 47–51.

BUSS, D. M. (1989). Sex differences in human mate preferences: Evolutionary hypotheses tested in 37 cultures. *Behavioral and Brain Sciences, 12*, 1–49.

BUSS, D. M. (1991). Evolutionary personality psychology. *Annual Review of Psychology*. Palo Alto: CA: Annual Reviews.

BUTCHER, S. H. (1951). *Aristotle's theory of poetry and fine art*. New York: Dover.

BYRNE, D. (1971). *The attraction paradigm*. New York: Academic Press.

BYRNE, D., & WONG, T. J. (1962). Racial prejudice, interpersonal attraction, and assumed dissimilarity of attitudes. *Journal of Abnormal and Social Psychology, 65*, 246–253.

BYTWERK, R. L. (1976). Julius Streicher and the impact of *Der Stürmer*. *Wiener Library Bulletin, 29*, 41–46.

CACIOPPO, J. T., PETTY, R. E., KAO, C. F., & RODRIGUEZ, R. (1986). Central and peripheral routes to persuasion: An individual difference perspective. *Journal of Personality and Social Psychology, 51*, 1032–1043.

CACIOPPO, J. T., PETTY, R. E., & MORRIS, K. J. (1983). Effects of need for cognition on message evaluation, recall, and persuasion. *Journal of Personality and Social Psychology, 45*, 805–818.

CACIOPPO, J. T., UCHINO, B. N., CRITES, S. L., SNYDERSMITH, M. A., SMITH, G., BERNTSON, G. G., & LANG, P. J. (1991). Relationship between facial expressiveness and sympathetic activation in emotion: A critical review, with emphasis on modeling underlying mechanisms and individual differences. *Journal of Personality and Social Psychology, 62*, 110–128.

CALHOUN, J. B. (1962, February). Population density and social pathology. *Scientific American*, pp. 139–148.

CAMPBELL, E. Q., & PETTIGREW, T. F. (1959). Racial and moral crisis: The role of Little Rock ministers. *American Journal of Sociology, 64*, 509–516.

CANTRIL, H., & BUMSTEAD, C. H. (1960). *Reflections on the human venture*. New York: New York Univ. Press.

CARDUCCI, B. J., COSBY, P. C., & WARD, D. D. (1978). Sexual arousal and interpersonal evaluations. *Journal of Experimental Social Psychology, 14*, 449–457.

CARLI, L. L. (1991). Gender, status, and influence. In E. J. Lawler & B. Markovsky (Ed.), *Advances in group processes: Theory and research*, vol. 8. Greenwich, CT: JAI.

CARLI, L. L., COLUMBO, J., DOWLING, S., KULIS, M., & MINALGA, C. (1990). Victim derogation as a function of hindsight and cognitive bolstering. Paper presented at the American Psychological Association convention.

CARLI, L. L., & LEONARD, J. B. (1989). The effect of hindsight on victim derogation. *Journal of Social and Clinical Psychology, 8,* 331–343.

CARLSON, J., & HATFIELD, E. (1992). *The psychology of emotion.* Fort Worth, TX: Holt, Rinehart & Winston.

CARLSON, M., MARCUS-NEWHALL, A., & MILLER, N. (1990). Effects of situational aggression cues: A quantitative review. *Journal of Personality and Social Psychology, 58,* 622–633.

CARLSTON, D. E., & SHOVAR, N. (1983). Effects of performance attributions on others' perceptions of the attributor. *Journal of Personality and Social Psychology, 44,* 515–525.

CARTWRIGHT, D. S. (1975). The nature of gangs. In D. S. Cartwright, B. Tomson, & H. Schwartz (Eds.), *Gang delinquency.* Monterey, CA: Brooks/Cole.

CARVER, C. S., & SCHEIER, M. F. (1986). Analyzing shyness: A specific application of broader self-regulatory principles. In W. H. Jones, J. M. Cheek, & S. R. Briggs (Eds.), *Shyness: Perspectives on research and treatment.* New York: Plenum.

CASH, T. F., & JANDA, L. H. (1984, December). The eye of the beholder. *Psychology Today,* pp. 46–52.

CASPI, A., & HERBENER, E. S. (1990). Continuity and change: Assortative marriage and the consistency of personality in adulthood. *Journal of Personality and Social Psychology, 58,* 250–258.

CASTRO, J. (1990, Fall issue on women). Get set: Here they come. *Time,* p. 50–52.

CENTERWALL, B. S. (1989). Exposure to television as a risk factor for violence. *American Journal of Epidemiology, 129,* 643–652.

CHAIKEN, S. (1979). Communicator physical attractiveness and persuasion. *Journal of Personality and Social Psychology, 37,* 1387–1397.

CHAIKEN, S. (1980). Heuristic versus systematic information processing and the use of source versus message cues in persuasion. *Journal of Personality and Social Psychology, 39,* 752–766.

CHAIKEN, S. (1987). The heuristic model of persuasion. In M. P. Zanna, J. M. Olson, & C. P. Herman (Eds.), *Social influence: The Ontario symposium,* Vol. 5. Hillsdale, NJ: Erlbaum.

CHANCE, J. E. (1985). Faces, folklore, and research hypotheses. Presidential address to the Midwestern Psychological Association convention.

CHANCE, J. E., & GOLDSTEIN, A. G. (1981). Depth of processing in response to own- and other-race faces. *Personality and Social Psychology Bulletin, 7,* 475–480.

CHAPMAN, L. J., & CHAPMAN, J. P. (1969). Genesis of popular but erroneous psychodiagnostic observations. *Journal of Abnormal Psychology, 74,* 272–280.

CHAPMAN, L. J., & CHAPMAN, J. P. (1971, November). Test results are what you think they are. *Psychology Today,* pp. 18–22, 106–107.

CHECK, J., & MALAMUTH, N. (1984). Can there be positive effects of participation in pornography experiments? *Journal of Sex Research, 20,* 14–31.

CHECK, J. M., & MELCHIOR, L. A. (1990). Shyness, self-esteem, and self-consciousness. In H. Leitenberg (Ed.), *Handbook of social and evaluation anxiety.* New York: Plenum.

CHEN, S. C. (1937). Social modification of the activity of ants in nest-building. *Physiological Zoology, 10,* 420–436.

CHICKERING, A. W., & McCORMICK, J. (1973). Personality development and the college experience. *Research in Higher Education,* No. 1, 62–64.

CHODOROW, N. J. (1978). *The reproduction of mother: Psychoanalysis and the sociology of gender*. Berkeley, CA: Univ. of California Press.

CHODOROW, N. J. (1989). *Feminism and psychoanalytic theory*. New Haven, CT: Yale Univ. Press.

CHRISTENSEN, L. (1988). Deception in psychological research: When is its use justified? *Personality and Social Psychology Bulletin, 14,* 664–675.

CHRISTIAN, J. J., FLYGER, V., & DAVIS, D. E. (1960). Factors in the mass mortality of a herd of sika deer, *Cervus Nippon. Chesapeake Science, 1,* 79–95.

CHURCH, G. J. (1986, January 6). China. *Time,* pp. 6–19.

CIALDINI, R. B. (1988). *Influence: Science and practice*. Glenview, IL: Scott, Foresman/ Little, Brown.

CIALDINI, R. B., CACIOPPO, J. T., BASSETT, R., & MILLER, J. A. (1978). Lowball procedure for producing compliance: Commitment then cost. *Journal of Personality and Social Psychology, 36,* 463–476.

CIALDINI, R. B., & RICHARDSON, K. D. (1980). Two indirect tactics of image management: Basking and blasting. *Journal of Personality and Social Psychology, 39,* 406–415.

CLARK, K., & CLARK, M. (1947). Racial identification and preference in Negro children. In T. M. Newcomb & E. L. Hartley (Eds.), *Readings in social psychology*. New York: Holt.

CLARK, M. S., & BENNETT, M. E. (1992). Research on relationships: Implications for mental health. In D. Ruble, P. Costanzo, & M. Oliveri (Eds.), *Basic social psychological processes in mental health*. New York: Guilford.

CLARK, R. D., III, & MAASS, A. (1990). The effects of majority size on minority influence. *European Journal of Social Psychology, 20,* 99–117.

CLARKE, A. C. (1952). An examination of the operation of residual propinquity as a factor in mate selection. *American Sociological Review, 27,* 17–22.

CLORE, G. L., BRAY, R. M., ITKIN, S. M., & MURPHY, P. (1978). Interracial attitudes and behavior at a summer camp. *Journal of Personality and Social Psychology, 36,* 107–116.

COATES, B., PUSSER, H. E., & GOODMAN, I. (1976). The influence of "Sesame Street" and "Mister Rogers' Neighborhood" on children's social behavior in the preschool. *Child Development, 47,* 138–144.

CODOL, J.-P. (1976). On the so-called superior conformity of the self behavior: Twenty experimental investigations. *European Journal of Social Psychology, 5,* 457–501.

COHEN, M., & DAVIS, N. (1981). *Medication errors: Causes and prevention*. Philadelphia: Stickley. Cited by R. B. Cialdini (1989). Agents of influence: Bunglers, smugglers, and sleuths. Paper presented at the American Psychological Association convention.

COHEN, S. (1980). Training to understand TV advertising: Effects and some policy implications. Paper presented at the American Psychological Association convention.

CONWAY, F., & SIEGELMAN, J. (1979). *Snapping: America's epidemic of sudden personality change*. New York: Delta.

CONWAY, M., & ROSS, M. (1985). Remembering one's own past: The construction of personal histories. In R. Sorrentino & E. T. Higgins (Eds.), *Handbook of motivation and cognition*. New York: Guilford.

COOK, T. D., & CURTIN, T. R. (1987). The mainstream and the underclass: Why are the differences so salient and the similarities so unobtrusive? In J. C.

Masters & W. P. Smith (Eds.), *Social comparison, social justice, and relative deprivation: Theoretical, empirical, and policy perspectives*. Hillsdale, NJ: Erlbaum.

COOK, T. D., & FLAY, B. R. (1978). The persistence of experimentally induced attitude change. In L. Berkowitz (Ed.), *Advances in experimental social psychology*, Vol. 11. New York: Academic Press.

COOPER, H. (1983). Teacher expectation effects. In L. Bickman (Ed.), *Applied social psychology annual*, Vol. 4. Beverly Hills, CA: Sage.

COSTA, P. T., JR., McCRAE, R. R., & ZONDERMAN, A. B. (1987). Environmental and dispositional influences on well-being: Longitudinal follow-up of an American national sample. *British Journal of Psychology, 78,* 299–306.

COTA, A. A., & DION, K. L. (1986). Salience of gender and sex composition of ad hoc groups: An experimental test of distinctiveness theory. *Journal of Personality and Social Psychology, 50,* 770–776.

COTTON, J. L. (1981). Ambient temperature and violent crime. Paper presented at the Midwestern Psychological Association convention.

COTTON, J. L. (1986). Ambient temperature and violent crime. *Journal of Applied Social Psychology, 16,* 786–801.

COTTRELL, N. B., WACK, D. L., SEKERAK, G. J., & RITTLE, R. M. (1968). Social facilitation of dominant responses by the presence of an audience and the mere presence of others. *Journal of Personality and Social Psychology, 9,* 245–250.

COURT, J. H. (1984). Sex and violence: A ripple effect. In N. M. Malamuth & E. Donnerstein (Eds.), *Pornography and sexual aggression*. New York: Academic Press.

COUSINS, N. (1989). *Head first: The biology of hope*. New York: Dutton.

COUSINS, S. D. (1989). Culture and self-perception in Japan and the United States. *Journal of Personality and Social Psychology, 56,* 124–131.

COYNE, J. C., BURCHILL, S. A. L., & STILES, W. B. (1991). In C. R. Snyder & D. O. Forsyth (Eds.), *Handbook of social and clinical psychology: The health perspective*. New York: Pergamon.

CRAIG, M. E. (1990). Coercive sexuality in dating relationships: A situational model. *Clinical Psychology Review, 10,* 395–423.

CROCKER, J., & MAJOR, B. (1989). Social stigma and self-esteem: The self-protective properties of stigma. *Psychological Review, 96,* 608–630.

CROCKER, J., & McGRAW, K. M. (1984). What's good for the goose is not good for the gander: Solo status as an obstacle to occupational achievement for males and females. *American Behavioral Scientist, 27,* 357–370.

CROCKER, J., THOMPSON, L. L., McGRAW, K. M., & INGERMAN, C. (1987). Downward comparison, prejudice, and evaluations of others: Effects of self-esteem and threat. *Journal of Personality and Social Psychology, 52,* 907–916.

CROSBY, F., BROMLEY, S., & SAXE, L. (1980). Recent unobtrusive studies of black and white discrimination and prejudice: A literature review. *Psychological Bulletin, 87,* 546–563.

CROSBY, F., PUFALL, A., SNYDER, R. C., O'CONNELL, M., & WHALEN, P. (1989). The denial of personal disadvantage among you, me, and all the other ostriches. In M. Crawford & M. Gentry (Eds.), *Gender and thought*. New York: Springer-Verlag.

CROSS, P. (1977). Not *can* but *will* college teaching be improved? *New Directions for Higher Education*, Spring, No. 17, pp. 1–15.

CROXTON, J. S., & MILLER, A. G. (1987). Behavioral disconfirmation and the observer bias. *Journal of Social Behavior and Personality, 2*, 145–152.

CROXTON, J. S., & MORROW, N. (1984). What does it take to reduce observer bias? *Psychological Reports, 55*, 135–138.

CROYLE, R. T., & COOPER, J. (1983). Dissonance arousal: Physiological evidence. *Journal of Personality and Social Psychology, 45*, 782–791.

CSIKSZENTMIHALYI, M. (1988). The future of flow. In M. Csikszentmihalyi & I. S. Csikszentmihalyi (Eds.), *Optimal experience: Psychological studies of flow in consciousness.* Cambridge: Cambridge Univ. Press.

CSIKSZENTMIHALYI, M., & CSIKSZENTMIHALYI, I. S. (1988). *Optimal experience: Psychological studies of flow in consciousness.* Cambridge: Cambridge Univ. Press.

CUNNINGHAM, J. D. (1981). Self-disclosure intimacy: Sex, sex-of-target, cross-national, and generational differences. *Personality and Social Psychology Bulletin, 7*, 314–319.

DABBS, J. M., & JANIS, I. L. (1965). Why does eating while reading facilitate opinion change? An experimental inquiry. *Journal of Experimental Social Psychology, 1*, 133–144.

DABBS, J. M., JR., & MORRIS, R. (1990). Testosterone, social class, and antisocial behavior in a sample of 4,462 men. *Psychological Science, 1*, 209–211.

DABBS, J. M., JR., RUBACK, R. B., FRADY, R. L., HOPPER, C. H., & SGOUTAS, D. S. (1988). Saliva testosterone and criminal violence among women. *Personality and Individual Differences, 7*, 269–275.

DALLAS, M. E. W., & BARON, R. S. (1985). Do psychotherapists use a confirmatory strategy during interviewing? *Journal of Social and Clinical Psychology, 3*, 106–122.

DARLEY, J. M., & BATSON, C. D. (1973). From Jerusalem to Jericho: A study of situational and dispositional variables in helping behavior. *Journal of Personality and Social Psychology, 27*, 100–108.

DARLEY, J. M., & BERSCHEID, E. (1967). Increased liking as a result of the anticipation of personal contact. *Human Relations, 20*, 29–40.

DARLEY, J. M., & LATANÉ, B. (1968). Bystander intervention in emergencies: Diffusion of responsibility. *Journal of Personality and Social Psychology, 8*, 377–383.

DARLEY, J. M., & LATANÉ, B. (1968, December). When will people help in a crisis? *Psychology Today*, pp. 54–57, 70–71.

DARLEY, S., & COOPER, J. (1972). Cognitive consequences of forced noncompliance. *Journal of Personality and Social Psychology, 24*, 321–326.

DASHIELL, J. F. (1930). An experimental analysis of some group effects. *Journal of Abnormal and Social Psychology, 25*, 190–199.

DAVIS, B. M., & GILBERT, L. A. (1989). Effect of dispositional and situational influences on women's dominance expression in mixed-sex dyads. *Journal of Personality and Social Psychology, 57*, 294–300.

DAVIS, K. E. (1985, February). Near and dear: Friendship and love compared. *Psychology Today*, pp. 22–30.

DAVIS, K. E., & JONES, E. E. (1960). Changes in interpersonal perception as a means of reducing cognitive dissonance. *Journal of Abnormal and Social Psychology, 61*, 402–410.

DAVIS, L., LAYLASEK, L., & PRATT, R. (1984). Teamwork and friendship: Answers to social loafing. Paper presented at the Southwestern Psychological Association, New Orleans.

DAVIS, M. H., & FRANZOI, S. L. (1986). Adolescent loneliness, self-disclosure, and private self-consciousness: A longitudinal investigation. *Journal of Personality and Social Psychology, 51,* 595–608.

DAVIS, M. H., & STEPHAN, W. G. (1980). Attributions for exam performance. *Journal of Applied Social Psychology, 10,* 235–248.

DAWES, R. M. (1976). Shallow psychology. In J. S. Carroll & J. W. Payne (Eds.), *Cognition and social behavior.* Hillsdale, NJ: Erlbaum.

DAWES, R. M. (1980). You can't systematize human judgment: Dyslexia. In R. A. Shweder (Ed.), *New directions for methodology of social and behavioral science: Fallible judgment in behavioral research.* San Francisco: Jossey-Bass.

DAWES, R. M. (1990). The potential nonfalsity of the false consensus effect. In R. M. Hogarth (Ed.), *Insights in decision making: A tribute to Hillel J. Einhorn.* Chicago: Univ. of Chicago Press.

DAWES, R. M. (1991). Social dilemmas, economic self-interest, and evolutionary theory. In D. R. Brown & J. E. Keith Smith (Eds.), *Frontiers of mathematical psychology: Essays in honor of Clyde Coombs.* New York: Springer-Verlag.

DAWES, R. M., FAUST, D., & MEEHL, P. E. (1989). Clinical versus actuarial judgment. *Science, 243,* 1668–1674.

DAWSON, N. V., ARKES, H. R., SICILIANO, C., BLINKHORN, R., LAKSHMANAN, M., & PETRELLI, M. (1988). Hindsight bias: An impediment to accurate probability estimation in clinicopathologic conferences. *Medical Decision Making, 8,* 259–264.

DE VRIES, N. K., & VAN KNIPPENBERG, A. (1987). Biased and unbiased self-evaluations of ability: The effects of further testing. *British Journal of Social Psychology, 26,* 9–15.

DECI, E. L., & RYAN, R. M. (1987). The support of autonomy and the control of behavior. *Journal of Personality and Social Psychology, 53,* 1024–1037.

DEJONG-GIERVELD, J. (1987). Developing and testing a model of loneliness. *Journal of Personality and Social Psychology, 53,* 119–128.

DEMBROSKI, T. M., LASATER, T. M., & RAMIREZ, A. (1978). Communicator similarity, fear arousing communications, and compliance with health care recommendations. *Journal of Applied Social Psychology, 8,* 254–269.

DENGERINK, H. A., & MYERS, J. D. (1977). Three effects of failure and depression on subsequent aggression. *Journal of Personality and Social Psychology, 35,* 88–96.

DEPAULO, B. M., KENNY, D. A., HOOVER, C. W., WEBB, W., & OLIVER, P. V. (1987). Accuracy of person perception: Do people know what kinds of impressions they convey? *Journal of Personality and Social Psychology, 52,* 303–315.

DERMER, M., & PYSZCZYNSKI, T. A. (1978). Effects of erotica upon men's loving and liking responses for women they love. *Journal of Personality and Social Psychology, 36,* 1302–1309.

DESFORGES, D. M., LORD, C. G., RAMSEY, S. L., MASON, J. A., VAN LEEUWEN, M. D., WEST, S. C., & LEPPER, M. R. (1991). Effects of structured cooperative contact on changing negative attitudes toward stigmatized social groups. *Journal of Personality and Social Psychology, 60,* 531–544.

DESMOND, E. W. (1987, November 30). Out in the open. *Time,* pp. 80–90.

DESTEFANO, L., & COLASANTO, D. (1990, February). Unlike 1975, today most Americans think men have it better. *Gallup Poll Monthly,* No. 293, 25–36.

DEUTSCH, M. (1985). *Distributive justice: A social psychological perspective.* New Haven: Yale Univ. Press.

DEUTSCH, M. (1986). Folie à deux: A psychological perspective on Soviet-American relations. In M. P. Kearns (Ed.), *Persistent patterns and emergent structures in a waving century.* New York: Praeger.

DEUTSCH, M. (1991). Educating for a peaceful world. Presidential address to the Division of Peace Psychology, American Psychological Association convention.

DEUTSCH, M., & GERARD, H. B. (1955). A study of normative and informational social influence upon individual judgment. *Journal of Abnormal and Social Psychology, 51,* 629–636.

DEVINE, P. G. (1989). Stereotypes and prejudice: Their automatic and controlled components. *Journal of Personality and Social Psychology, 56,* 5–18.

DEVINE, P. G., HIRT, E. R., & GEHRKE, E. M. (1990). Diagnostic and confirmation strategies in trait hypothesis testing. *Journal of Personality and Social Psychology, 58,* 952–963.

DEVINE, P. G., MONTEITH, M. J., ZUWERINK, J. R., & ELLIOT, A. J. (1991). Prejudice with and without compunction. *Journal of Personality and Social Psychology, 60,* 817–830.

DIENER, E. (1976). Effects of prior destructive behavior, anonymity, and group presence on deindividuation and aggression. *Journal of Personality and Social Psychology, 33,* 497–507.

DIENER, E. (1979). Deindividuation, self-awareness, and disinhibition. *Journal of Personality and Social Psychology, 37,* 1160–1171.

DIENER, E. (1980). Deindividuation: The absence of self-awareness and self-regulation in group members. In P. Paulus (Ed.), *The psychology of group influence.* Hillsdale, NJ: Erlbaum.

DIENER, E., & CRANDALL, R. (1979). An evaluation of the Jamaican anticrime program. *Journal of Applied Social Psychology, 9,* 135–146.

DIENER, E., FRASER, S. C., BEAMAN, A. L., & KELEM, R. T. (1976). Effects of deindividuation variables on stealing among Halloween trick-or-treaters. *Journal of Personality and Social Psychology, 33,* 178–183.

DIENER, E., HORWITZ, J. & EMMONS, R. A. (1985). Happiness of the very wealthy. *Social Indicators, 16,* 263–274.

DIENER, E., & WALLBOM, M. (1976). Effects of self-awareness on antinormative behavior. *Journal of Research in Personality, 10,* 107–111.

DION, K. K. (1979). Physical attractiveness and interpersonal attraction. In M. Cook & G. Wilson (Eds.), *Love and attraction.* New York: Pergamon.

DION, K. K., & DION, K. L. (1978). Defensiveness, intimacy, and heterosexual attraction. *Journal of Research in Personality, 12,* 479–487.

DION, K. K., & DION, K. L. (1985). Personality, gender, and the phenomenology of romantic love. In P. R. Shaver (Ed.), *Review of personality and social psychology,* Vol. 6. Beverly Hills, CA: Sage.

DION, K. K., & DION, K. L. (1991). Psychological individualism and romantic love. *Journal of Social Behavior and Personality, 6,* 17–33.

DION, K. K., PAK, A. W-P., & DION, K. L. (1990). Stereotyping physical attractiveness: A sociocultural perspective. *Journal of Cross-Cultural Psychology, 21,* 378–398.

DION, K. K., & STEIN, S. (1978). Physical attractiveness and interpersonal influence. *Journal of Experimental Social Psychology, 14,* 97–109.

DION, K. L. (1987). What's in a title? The Ms. stereotype and images of women's titles of address. *Psychology of Women Quarterly, 11,* 21–36.

DION, K. L., & COTA, A. A. (1991). The Ms. stereotype: Its domain and the role of explicitness in title preference. *Psychology of Women Quarterly, 15,* 403–410.

DION, K. L., & DION, K. K. (1988). Romantic love: Individual and cultural perspectives. In R. J. Sternberg & M. L. Barnes (Eds.), *The psychology of love.* New Haven, CT: Yale Univ. Press.

DION, K. L., DION, K. K., & KEELAN, J. P. (1990). Appearance anxiety as a dimension of social-evaluative anxiety: Exploring the ugly duckling syndrome. *Contemporary Social Psychology, 14*(4), 220–224.

DION, K. L., & SCHULLER, R. A. (1991). The Ms. stereotype: Its generality and its relation to managerial and marital status stereotypes. *Canadian Journal of Behavioural Science, 23,* 25–40.

DOBSON, K., & FRANCHE, R. L. (1989). A conceptual and empirical review of the depressive realism hypothesis. *Canadian Journal of Behavioural Science, 21,* 419–433.

DOLLARD, J., DOOB, L., MILLER, N., MOWRER, O. H., & SEARS, R. R. (1939). *Frustration and aggression.* New Haven, CT: Yale Univ. Press.

DONNERSTEIN, E. (1980). Aggressive erotica and violence against women. *Journal of Personality and Social Psychology, 39,* 269–277.

DONNERSTEIN, E., & BERKOWITZ, L. (1981). Victim reactions in aggressive erotic films as a factor in violence against women. *Journal of Personality and Social Psychology, 41,* 710–724.

DONNERSTEIN, E., LINZ, D., & PENROD, S. (1987). *The question of pornography.* London: Free Press.

DOOB, A. N., & ROBERTS, J. (1988). Public attitudes toward sentencing in Canada. In N. Walker & M. Hough (Eds.), *Sentencing and the public.* London: Gower.

DOTY, R. M., PETERSON, B. E., & WINTER, D. G. (1991). Threat and authoritarianism in the United States, 1978–1987. *Journal of Personality and Social Psychology, 61,* 629–640.

DUMONT, M. P. (1989, September). An unfolding memoir of community mental health. *Readings: A Journal of Reviews and Commentary in Mental Health,* pp. 4–7.

DUNCAN, B. L. (1976). Differential social perception and attribution of intergroup violence: Testing the lower limits of stereotyping of blacks. *Journal of Personality and Social Psychology, 34,* 590–598.

DUNNING, D., GRIFFIN, D. W., MILOJKOVIC, J. D., & ROSS, L. (1990). The overconfidence effect in social prediction. *Journal of Personality and Social Psychology, 58,* 568–581.

DUNNING, D., & PARPAL, M. (1989). Mental addition versus subtraction in counterfactual reasoning: On assessing the impact of personal actions and life events. *Journal of Personality and Social Psychology, 57,* 5–15.

DUNNING, D., PERIE, M., & STORY, A. L. (1991). Self-serving prototypes of social categories. *Journal of Personality and Social Psychology, 61,* 957–968.

DUTTON, D. G., & ARON, A. (1989). Romantic attraction and generalized liking for others who are sources of conflict-based arousal. *Canadian Journal of Behavioural Science, 21,* 246–257.

DUTTON, D. G., & ARON, A. P. (1974). Some evidence for heightened sexual attraction under conditions of high anxiety. *Journal of Personality and Social Psychology, 30,* 510–517.

DUVAL, S. (1976). Conformity on a visual task as a function of personal novelty on attitudinal dimensions and being reminded of the object status of self. *Journal of Experimental Social Psychology, 12,* 87–98.

EAGLY, A. H. (1986). Some meta-analytic approaches to examining the validity of gender-difference research. In J. S. Hyde & M. C. Linn (Eds.), *The psychology of gender: Advances through meta-analysis.* Baltimore: Johns Hopkins Univ. Press.

EAGLY, A. H. (1987). Sex differences in social behavior: A social-role interpretation. Hillsdale, NJ: Erlbaum.

EAGLY, A. H., ASHMORE, R. D., MAKHIJANI, M. G., & LONGO, L. C. (1991). What is beautiful is good, but . . . : A meta-analytic review of research on the physical attractiveness stereotype. *Psychological Bulletin, 110,* 109–128.

EAGLY, A. H., & CHAIKEN, S. (1992). *The psychology of attitudes.* San Diego: Harcourt Brace Jovanovich.

EAGLY, A. H., & CROWLEY, M. (1986). Gender and helping behavior: A meta-analytic review of the social psychological literature. *Psychological Bulletin, 100,* 283–308.

EAGLY, A. H., & JOHNSON, B. T. (1990). Gender and leadership style: A meta-analysis. *Psychological Bulletin, 108,* 233–256.

EAGLY, A. H., & KARAU, S. J. (1991). Gender and the emergence of leaders: A meta-analysis. *Journal of Personality and Social Psychology, 60,* 685–710.

EAGLY, A. H., & STEFFEN, V. J. (1986). Gender and aggressive behavior: A meta-analytic review of the social psychological literature. *Psychological Bulletin, 100,* 309–330.

EAGLY, A. H., & WOOD, W. (1991). Explaining sex differences in social behavior: A meta-analytic perspective. *Personality and Social Psychology Bulletin, 17,* 306–315.

EARLY, P. C. (1989). Social loafing and collectivism: A comparison of the United States and the People's Republic of China. *Administrative Science Quarterly, 34,* 565–581.

EBBESEN, E. B., DUNCAN, B., & KONECNI, V. J. (1975). Effects of content of verbal aggression on future verbal aggression: A field experiment. *Journal of Experimental Social Psychology, 11,* 192–204.

EDNEY, J. J. (1979). The nuts game: A concise commons dilemma analog. *Environmental Psychology and Nonverbal Behavior, 3,* 252–254.

EDWARDS, C. P. (1991). Behavioral sex differences in children of diverse cultures: The case of nurturance to infants. In M. Pereira & L. Fairbanks (Eds.), *Juveniles: Comparative socioecology.* Oxford: Oxford Univ. Press.

EISENBERG, N., & LENNON, R. (1983). Sex differences in empathy and related capacities. *Psychological Bulletin, 94,* 100–131.

ELDER, G. H., JR. (1969). Appearance and education in marriage mobility. *American Sociological Review, 34,* 519–533.

ELDER, G. H., JR., & CLIPP, E. C. (1988). Wartime losses and social bonding: Influences across 40 years in men's lives. *Psychiatry, 51,* 177–197.

ELLICKSON, P. L., & BELL, R. M. (1990). Drug prevention in junior high: A multisite longitudinal test. *Science, 247,* 1299–1305.

ELLIS, H. D. (1981). Theoretical aspects of face recognition. In G. H. Davies, H. D. Ellis, & J. Shepherd (Eds.), *Perceiving and remembering faces.* London: Academic Press.

ELLYSON, S. L., DOVIDIO, J. F., & BROWN, C. E. (1991). The look of power: Gender differences and similarities in visual dominance behavior. In C. Ridgeway (Ed.), *Gender and interaction: The role of microstructures in inequality.* New York: Springer-Verlag.

ENGS, R., & HANSON, D. J. (1989). Reactance theory: A test with collegiate drinking. *Psychological Reports, 64,* 1083–1086.

ENNIS, B. J., & VERRILLI, D. B., JR. (1989). Motion for leave to file brief amicus curiae and brief of Society for the Scientific Study of Religion, American Sociological Association, and others. U.S. Supreme Court Case No. 88–1600, Holy Spirit Association for the Unification of World Christianity, *et al.,* v. David Molko and Tracy Leal. On petition for write of certiorari to the Supreme Court of California. Washington, DC: Jenner & Block, 21 Dupont Circle N.W.

ENNIS, R., & ZANNA, M. P. (1991). Hockey assault: Constitutive versus normative violations. Paper presented at the Canadian Psychological Association convention.

EPSTEIN, S., & FEIST, G. J. (1988). Relation between self- and other-acceptance and its moderation by identification. *Journal of Personality and Social Psychology, 54,* 309–315.

ERICKSON, B., HOLMES, J. G., FREY, R., WALKER, L., & THIBAUT, J. (1974). Functions of a third party in the resolution of conflict: The role of a judge in pretrial conferences. *Journal of Personality and Social Psychology, 30,* 296–306.

ERNST, J. M., & HEESACKER, M. (1991). Application of the Elaboration Likelihood Model of attitude change to assertion training. Unpublished manuscript, Univ. of Florida.

ERON, L. D. (1987). The development of aggressive behavior from the perspective of a developing behaviorism. *American Psychologist, 42,* 425–442.

ERON, L. D., & HUESMANN, L. R. (1980). Adolescent aggression and television. *Annals of the New York Academy of Sciences, 347,* 319–331.

ERON, L. D., & HUESMANN, L. R. (1984). The control of aggressive behavior by changes in attitudes, values, and the conditions of learning. In R. J. Blanchard & C. Blanchard (Eds.), *Advances in the study of aggression,* Vol. 1. Orlando, FL: Academic Press.

ERON, L. D., & HUESMANN, L. R. (1985). The role of television in the development of prosocial and antisocial behavior. In D. Olweus, M. Radke-Yarrow, and J. Block (Eds.), *Development of antisocial and prosocial behavior.* Orlando, FL: Academic Press.

ESSER, J. K., & LINDOERFER, J. S. (1989). Groupthink and the space shuttle Challenger accident: Toward a quantitative case analysis. *Journal of Behavioral Decision Making, 2,* 167–177.

ETZIONI, A. (1967). The Kennedy experiment. *The Western Political Quarterly, 20,* 361–380.

ETZIONI, A. (1991, May–June). The community in an age of individualism (interview). *The Futurist,* pp. 35–39.

EVANS, C. R., & DION, K. L. (1991). Group cohesion and performance: A meta-analysis. *Small Group Research, 22,* 175–186.

EVANS, G. W. (1979). Behavioral and physiological consequences of crowding in humans. *Journal of Applied Social Psychology, 9,* 27–46.

EVANS, R. I., SMITH, C. K., & RAINES, B. E. (1984). Deterring cigarette smoking in adolescents: A psycho-social-behavioral analysis of an intervention strategy. In A. Baum, J. Singer, & S. Taylor (Eds.), *Handbook of psychology and health: Social psychological aspects of health*, Vol. 4, Hillsdale, NJ: Erlbaum.

FAUST, D., & ZISKIN, J. (1988). The expert witness in psychology and psychiatry. *Science, 241,* 31–35.

FAZIO, R. H. (1990). Multiple processes by which attitudes guide behavior: The mode model as an integrative framework. *Advances in Experimental Social Psychology, 23,* 75–109.

FAZIO, R. H., & ZANNA, M. P. (1981). Direct experience and attitude-behavior consistency. In L. Berkowitz (Ed.), *Advances in experimental social psychology*, Vol. 14. New York: Academic Press.

FEATHER, N. T. (1983a). Causal attributions and beliefs about work and unemployment among adolescents in state and independent secondary schools. *Australian Journal of Psychology, 35,* 211–232.

FEATHER, N. T. (1983b). Causal attributions for good and bad outcomes in achievement and affiliation situations. *Australian Journal of Psychology, 35,* 37–48.

FEIN, S., HILTON, J. L., & MILLER, D. T. (1990). Suspicion of ulterior motivation and the correspondence bias. *Journal of Personality and Social Psychology, 58,* 753–764.

FEINGOLD, A. (1988). Matching for attractiveness in romantic partners and same-sex friends: A meta-analysis and theoretical critique. *Psychological Bulletin, 104,* 226–235.

FEINGOLD, A. (1990). Gender differences in effects of physical attractiveness on romantic attraction: A comparison across five research paradigms. *Journal of Personality and Social Psychology, 59,* 981–993.

FEINGOLD, A. (1991). Sex differences in the effects of similarity and physical attractiveness on opposite-sex attraction. *Basic and Applied Social Psychology, 12,* 357–367.

FELDMAN, K. A., & NEWCOMB, T. M. (1969). *The impact of college on students.* San Francisco: Jossey-Bass.

FELSON, R. B. (1984). The effect of self-appraisals of ability on academic performance. *Journal of Personality and Social Psychology, 47,* 944–952.

FENIGSTEIN, A. (1984). Self-consciousness and the overperception of self as a target. *Journal of Personality and Social Psychology, 47,* 860–870.

FESHBACH, N. D. (1980). The child as "psychologist" and "economist": Two curricula. Paper presented at the American Psychological Association convention.

FESTINGER, L. (1954). A theory of social comparison processes. *Human Relations, 7,* 117–140.

FESTINGER, L. (1957). *A theory of cognitive dissonance.* Stanford: Stanford Univ. Press.

FESTINGER, L., & MACCOBY, N. (1964). On resistance to persuasive communications. *Journal of Abnormal and Social Psychology, 68,* 359–366.

FESTINGER, L., PEPITONE, A., & NEWCOMB, T. (1952). Some consequences of deindividuation in a group. *Journal of Abnormal and Social Psychology, 47,* 382–389.

FIEBERT, M. S. (1990). Men, women and housework: The Roshomon effect. *Men's Studies Review, 8,* 6.

FIEDLER, F. E. (1987, September). When to lead, when to stand back. *Psychology Today*, pp. 26–27.

FIEDLER, K., SEMIN, G. R., & KOPPETSCH, C. (1991). Language use and attributional biases in close personal relationships. *Personality and Social Psychology Bulletin, 17*, 147–155.

FIELDS, J. M., & SCHUMAN, H. (1976). Public beliefs about the beliefs of the public. *Public Opinion Quarterly, 40*, 427–448.

FINCH, J. F., & CIALDINI, R. B. (1989). Another indirect tactic of (self-) image management: Boosting. *Personality and Social Psychology Bulletin, 15*, 222–232.

FINCHAM, F. D., & JASPARS, J. M. (1980). Attribution of responsibility: From man the scientist to man as lawyer. In L. Berkowitz (Ed.), *Advances in experimental social psychology*, Vol. 13. New York: Academic Press.

FINDLEY, M. J., & COOPER, H. M. (1983). Locus of control and academic achievement: A literature review. *Journal of Personality and Social Psychology, 44*, 419–427.

FINEBERG, H. V. (1988). Education to prevent AIDS: Prospects and obstacles. *Science, 239*, 592–596.

FISCHHOFF, B. (1982). Debiasing. In D. Kahneman, P. Slovic, & A. Tversky (Eds.), *Judgment under uncertainty: Heuristics and biases*. New York: Cambridge Univ. Press.

FISCHHOFF, B., SLOVIC, P., & LICHTENSTEIN, S. (1977). Knowing with certainty: The appropriateness of extreme confidence. *Journal of Experimental Psychology: Human Perception and Performance, 3*, 552–564.

FISHBEIN, D., & THELEN, M. H. (1981a). Husband-wife similarity and marital satisfaction: A different approach. Paper presented at the Midwestern Psychological Association convention.

FISHBEIN, D., & THELEN, M. H. (1981b). Psychological factors in mate selection and marital satisfaction: A review (Ms. 2374). *Catalog of Selected Documents in Psychology, 11*, 84.

FLAY, B. R., RYAN, K. B., BEST, J. A., BROWN, K. S., KERSELL, M. W., d'AVERNAS, J. R., & ZANNA, M. P. (1985). Are social-psychological smoking prevention programs effective? The Waterloo study. *Journal of Behavioral Medicine, 8*, 37–59.

FLEMING, I., BAUM, A., & WEISS, L. (1987). Social density and perceived control as mediators of crowding stress in high-density residential neighborhoods. *Journal of Personality and Social Psychology, 52*, 899–906.

FLETCHER, G. J. O., FINCHAM, F. D., CRAMER, L., & HERON, N. (1987). The role of attributions in the development of dating relationships. *Journal of Personality and Social Psychology, 53*, 481–489.

FOLEY, L. A. (1976). Personality and situational influences on changes in prejudice: A replication of Cook's railroad game in a prison setting. *Journal of Personality and Social Psychology, 34*, 846–856.

FOLLETT, M. P. (1940). Constructive conflict. In H. C. Metcalf & L. Urwick (Eds.), *Dynamic administration: The collected papers of Mary Parker Follett*. New York: Harper.

FORGAS, J. P., BOWER, G. H., & KRANTZ, S. E. (1984). The influence of mood on perceptions of social interactions. *Journal of Experimental Social Psychology, 20*, 497–513.

FORGAS, J. P., & MOYLAN, S. (1987). After the movies: Transient mood and social judgments. *Personality and Social Psychology Bulletin, 13*, 467–477.

FÖRSTERLING, F. (1986). Attributional conceptions in clinical psychology. *American Psychologist, 41,* 275–285.

FORSYTH, D. R., BERGER, R. E., & MITCHELL, T. (1981). The effects of self-serving vs. other-serving claims of responsibility on attraction and attribution in groups. *Social Psychology Quarterly, 44,* 59–64.

FRANK, M. G., & GILOVICH, T. (1988). The dark side of self and social perception: Black uniforms and aggression in professional sports. *Journal of Personality and Social Psychology, 54,* 74–85.

FRANK, M. G., & GILOVICH, T. (1989). Effect of memory perspective on retrospective causal attributions. *Journal of Personality and Social Psychology, 57,* 399–403.

FRANKEL, A., & SNYDER, M. L. (1987). Egotism among the depressed: When self-protection becomes self-handicapping. Paper presented at the American Psychological Association convention.

FREEDMAN, J. L. (1988). Television violence and aggression: What the evidence shows. In S. Oskamp (Ed.), *Television as a social issue. Applied social psychology annual,* Vol. 8. Newbury Park, CA: Sage.

FREEDMAN, J. L., BIRSKY, J., & CAVOUKIAN, A. (1980). Environmental determinants of behavioral contagion: Density and number. *Basic and Applied Social Psychology, 1,* 155–161.

FREEDMAN, J. L., & FRASER, S. C. (1966). Compliance without pressure: The foot-in-the-door technique. *Journal of Personality and Social Psychology, 4,* 195–202.

FREEDMAN, J. L., & PERLICK, D. (1979). Crowding, contagion, and laughter. *Journal of Experimental Social Psychology, 15,* 295–303.

FREEDMAN, J. L., & SEARS, D. O. (1965). Warning, distraction, and resistance to influence. *Journal of Personality and Social Psychology, 1,* 262–266.

FREEDMAN, J. S. (1965). Long-term behavioral effects of cognitive dissonance. *Journal of Experimental Social Psychology, 1,* 145–155.

FRENCH, J. R. P. (1968). The conceptualization and the measurement of mental health in terms of self-identity theory. In S. B. Sells (Ed.), The definition and measurement of mental health. Washington, DC: Department of Health, Education, and Welfare. (Cited by M. Rosenberg, 1979, *Conceiving the self.* New York: Basic Books.)

FRIEDRICH, L. K., & STEIN, A. H. (1973). Aggressive and prosocial television programs and the natural behavior of preschool children. *Monographs of the Society of Research in Child Development, 38* (4, Serial No. 151).

FRIEDRICH, L. K., & STEIN, A. H. (1975). Prosocial television and young children: The effects of verbal labeling and role playing on learning and behavior. *Child Development, 46,* 27–38.

FRIEZE, I. H., OLSON, J. E., & RUSSELL, J. (1991). Attractiveness and income for men and women in management. *Journal of Applied Social Psychology, 21,* 1039–1057.

FURNHAM, A. (1982). Explanations for unemployment in Britain. *European Journal of Social Psychology, 12,* 335–352.

FURNHAM, A., & GUNTER. B. (1984). Just world beliefs and attitudes towards the poor. *British Journal of Social Psychology, 23,* 265–269.

GABRENYA, W. K., JR., WANG, Y.-E., & LATANÉ, B. (1985). Social loafing on an optimizing task: Cross-cultural differences among Chinese and Americans. *Journal of Cross-Cultural Psychology, 16,* 223–242.

GAERTNER, S. L., & DOVIDIO, J. F. (1977). The subtlety of white racism, arousal, and helping behavior. *Journal of Personality and Social Psychology, 35,* 691–707.

GAERTNER, S. L., & DOVIDIO, J. F. (1986). The aversive form of racism. In J. F. Dovidio & S. L. Gaertner (Eds.), *Prejudice, discrimination, and racism.* Orlando, FL: Academic Press.

GAERTNER, S. L., & DOVIDIO, J. F. (1991). Reducing bias: The common ingroup identity model. Unpublished manuscript, Univ. of Delaware.

GAERTNER, S. L., MANN, J. A., DOVIDIO, J. F., MURRELL, A. J., & POMARE, M. (1990). How does cooperation reduce intergroup bias? *Journal of Personality and Social Psychology, 59,* 692–704.

GAERTNER, S. L., MANN, J., MURRELL, A., & DOVIDIO, J. F. (1989). Reducing intergroup bias: The benefits of recategorization. *Journal of Personality and Social Psychology, 57,* 239–249.

GALANTER, M. (1989). *Cults: Faith, healing, and coercion.* New York: Oxford Univ. Press.

GALANTER, M. (1990). Cults and zealous self-help movements: A psychiatric perspective. *American Journal of Psychiatry, 147,* 543–551.

GALIZIO, M., & HENDRICK, C. (1972). Effect of musical accompaniment on attitude: The guitar as a prop for persuasion. *Journal of Applied Social Psychology, 2,* 350–359.

GALLUP, G. H. (1972). *The Gallup poll: Public opinion 1935–1971,* Vol. 3. New York: Random House, pp. 551, 1716.

GALLUP, G., JR., & HUGICK, L. (1990, June). Racial tolerance grows, progress on racial equality less evident. *Gallup Poll Monthly,* pp. 23–32.

GALLUP, G., JR., & NEWPORT, F. (1990, December). Americans now drinking less alcohol. *Gallup Poll Monthly,* pp. 2–6.

GALLUP ORGANIZATION (1989, July). Cigarette smoking at 45-year low. *Gallup Poll Monthly,* No. 286, pp. 23–26.

GALLUP ORGANIZATION (1990). April 19–22 survey reported in *American Enterprise,* September/October, 1990, p. 92.

GAMSON, W. A., FIREMAN, B., & RYTINA, S. (1982). *Encounters with unjust authority.* Homewood, IL: Dorsey.

GASTORF, J. W., SULS, J., & SANDERS, G. S. (1980). Type A coronary-prone behavior pattern and social facilitation. *Journal of Personality and Social Psychology, 8,* 773–780.

GATES, M. F., & ALLEE, W. C. (1933). Conditioned behavior of isolated and grouped cockroaches on a simple maze. *Journal of Comparative Psychology, 15,* 331–358.

GECAS, V. (1989). The social psychology of self-efficacy. *Annual Review of Sociology, 15,* 291–316.

GEEN, R. G., & GANGE, J. J. (1983). Social facilitation: Drive theory and beyond. In H. H. Blumberg, A. P. Hare, V. Kent, & M. Davies (Eds.), *Small groups and social interaction,* Vol. 1. London: Wiley.

GEEN, R. G., & QUANTY, M. B. (1977). The catharsis of aggression: An evaluation of a hypothesis. In L. Berkowitz (Ed.), *Advances in experimental social psychology,* Vol. 10. New York: Academic Press.

GEEN, R. G., & THOMAS, S. L. (1986). The immediate effects of media violence on behavior. *Journal of Social Issues, 42*(3), 7–28.

GERARD, H. B., & MATHEWSON, G. C. (1966). The effects of severity of initiation on liking for a group: A replication. *Journal of Experimental Social Psychology, 2,* 278–287.

GERBNER, G., GROSS, L., MORGAN, M., & SIGNORIELLI, N. (1990). Growing up with television: The cultivation perspective. In J. Bryant & D. Zillmann (Eds.), *Media effects: Advances in theory and research.* Hillsdale, NJ: Erlbaum.

GERGEN, K. J., GERGEN, M. M., & BARTON, W. N. (1973, October). Deviance in the dark. *Psychology Today,* pp. 129–130.

GIFFORD, R., & PEACOCK, J. (1979). Crowding: More fearsome than crime-provoking? Comparison of an Asian city and a North American city. *Psychologia, 22,* 79–83.

GILBERT, D. T., & HIXON, J. G. (1991). The trouble of thinking: Activation and application of stereotypic beliefs. *Journal of Personality and Social Psychology, 60,* 509–517.

GILBERT, D. T., PELHAM, B. W., & KRULL, D. S. (1988). On cognitive busyness: When person perceivers meet persons perceived. *Journal of Personality and Social Psychology, 54,* 733–740.

GILLIGAN, C. (1982). *In a different voice: Psychological theory and women's development.* Cambridge, MA: Harvard Univ. Press.

GILLIGAN, C., LYONS, N. P., & HANMER, T. J. (Eds.) (1990). *Making connections: The relational worlds of adolescent girls at Emma Willard School.* Cambridge, MA: Harvard Univ. Press.

GILLIS, J. S., & AVIS, W. E. (1980). The male-taller norm in mate selection. *Personality and Social Psychology Bulletin, 6,* 396–401.

GILMOR, T. M., & REID, D. W. (1979). Locus of control and causal attribution for positive and negative outcomes on university examinations. *Journal of Research in Personality, 13,* 154–160.

GILOVICH, T. (1987). Secondhand information and social judgment. *Journal of Experimental Social Psychology, 23,* 59–74.

GILOVICH, T., & DOUGLAS, C. (1986). Biased evaluations of randomly determined gambling outcomes. *Journal of Experimental Social Psychology, 22,* 228–241.

GINSBURG, B., & ALLEE, W. C. (1942). Some effects of conditioning on social dominance and subordination in inbred strains of mice. *Physiological Zoology, 15,* 485–506.

GLASS, D. C. (1964). Changes in liking as a means of reducing cognitive discrepancies between self-esteem and aggression. *Journal of Personality, 32,* 531–549.

GLENN, N. D. (1980). Aging and attitudinal stability. In O. G. Brim, Jr., & J. Kagan (Eds.), *Constancy and change in human development.* Cambridge, MA: Harvard Univ. Press.

GLENN, N. D. (1981). Personal communication.

GLENN, N. D. (1990). The social and cultural meaning of contemporary marriage. In B. Christensen (Ed.), *The retreat from marriage.* Rockford, IL: Rockford Institute.

GLENN, N. D. (1991). The recent trend in marital success in the United States. *Journal of Marriage and the Family, 53,* 261–270.

GLICK, D., GOTTESMAN, D., & JOLTON, J. (1989). The fault is not in the stars: Susceptibility of skeptics and believers in astrology to the Barnum effect. *Personality and Social Psychology Bulletin, 15,* 572–583.

GOETHALS, G. R., MESSICK, D. M., & ALLISON, S. T. (1991). The uniqueness bias:

Studies of constructive social comparison. In J. Suls & T. A. Wills (Eds.), *Social comparison: Contemporary theory and research*. Hillsdale, NJ: Erlbaum.

GOETHALS, G. R., & ZANNA, M. P. (1979). The role of social comparison in choice shifts. *Journal of Personality and Social Psychology, 37*, 1469–1476.

GOGGIN, W. C., & RANGE, L. M. (1985). The disadvantages of hindsight in the perception of suicide. *Journal of Social and Clinical Psychology, 3*, 232–237.

GOLDBERG, P. (1968, April). Are women prejudiced against women? *Transaction*, pp. 28–30.

GOLDING, W. (1962). *Lord of the flies*. New York: Coward-McCann.

GOLDSTEIN, J. H. (1982). Sports violence. *National Forum, 62*(1), 9–11.

GOLDSTEIN, J. H., & ARMS, R. L. (1971). Effects of observing athletic contests on hostility. *Sociometry, 34*, 83–90.

GOLEMAN, D. (1990, May 29). As bias crime seems to rise, scientists study roots of racism. *New York Times*, pp. C1, C5.

GOODHART, D. E. (1986). The effects of positive and negative thinking on performance in an achievement situation. *Journal of Personality and Social Psychology, 51*, 117–124.

GOTLIB, I. H., & LEE, C. M. (1989). The social functioning of depressed patients: A longitudinal assessment. *Journal of Social and Clinical Psychology, 8*, 223–237.

GOULD, R., BROUNSTEIN, P. J., & SIGALL, H. (1977). Attributing ability to an opponent: Public aggrandizement and private denigration. *Sociometry, 40*, 254–261.

GRAY, J. D., & SILVER, R. C. (1990). Opposite sides of the same coin: Former spouses' divergent perspectives in coping with their divorce. *Journal of Personality and Social Psychology, 59*, 1180–1191.

GRAZIANO, W., BROTHEN, T., & BERSCHEID, E. (1978). Height and attraction: Do men and women see eye-to-eye? *Journal of Personality, 46*, 128–145.

GREELEY, A. M. (1991). *Faithful attraction*. New York: Tor.

GREELEY, A. M., & SHEATSLEY, P. B. (1971). Attitudes toward racial integration. *Scientific American, 225*(6), 13–19.

GREENBERG, J. (1986). Differential intolerance for inequity from organizational and individual agents. *Journal of Applied Social Psychology, 16*, 191–196.

GREENBERG, J., PYSZCZYNSKI, T., SOLOMON, S., ROSENBLATT, A., VEEDER, M., KIRKLAND, S., & LYON, D. (1990). Evidence for terror management theory II: The effects of mortality salience on reactions to those who threaten or bolster the cultural worldview. *Journal of Personality and Social Psychology, 58*, 308–318.

GREENWALD, A. G. (1980). The totalitarian ego: Fabrication and revision of personal history. *American Psychologist, 35*, 603–618.

GREENWALD, A. G. (1984, June 12). Quoted by D. Goleman, A bias puts self at center of everything. *New York Times*, pp. C1, C4.

GREENWALD, A. G. (1990). What cognitive representations underlie prejudice? Presentation to the American Psychological Association convention.

GREENWALD, A. G. (1992). Unconscious cognition reclaimed. *American Psychologist, 47*, 766–779.

GREENWALD, A. G., SPANGENBERG, E. R., PRATKANIS, A. R., & ESKENAZI, J. (1991). Double-blind tests of subliminal self-help audiotapes. *Psychological Science, 2*, 119–122.

GRIFFIN, B. Q., COMBS, A. L., LAND, M. L., & COMBS, N. N. (1983). Attribution of success and failure in college performance. *Journal of Psychology, 114*, 259–266.

GRIFFITT, W. (1970). Environmental effects on interpersonal affective behavior. Ambient effective temperature and attraction. *Journal of Personality and Social Psychology, 15*, 240–244.

GRIFFITT, W. (1987). Females, males, and sexual responses. In K. Kelley (Ed.), *Females, males, and sexuality: Theories and research*. Albany: State Univ. of New York Press.

GRIFFITT, W., & VEITCH, R. (1971). Hot and crowded: Influences of population density and temperature on interpersonal affective behavior. *Journal of Personality and Social Psychology, 17*, 92–98.

GRIFFITT, W., & VEITCH, R. (1974). Preacquaintance attitude similarity and attraction revisited: Ten days in a fallout shelter. *Sociometry, 37*, 163–173.

GROSS, A. E., & CROFTON, C. (1977). What is good is beautiful. *Sociometry, 40*, 85–90.

GROVE, J. R., HANRAHAN, S. J., & McINMAN, A. (1991). Success/failure bias in attributions across involvement categories in sport. *Personality and Social Psychology Bulletin, 17*, 93–97.

GRUDER, C. L., COOK, T. D., HENNIGAN, K. M., FLAY, B., ALESSIS, C., & KALAMAJ, J. (1978). Empirical tests of the absolute sleeper effect predicted from the discounting cue hypothesis. *Journal of Personality and Social Psychology, 36*, 1061–1074.

GRUMAN, J. C., & SLOAN, R. P. (1983). Disease as justice: Perceptions of the victims of physical illness. *Basic and Applied Social Psychology, 4*, 39–46.

GRUNBERGER, R. (1971). *The 12-year-Reich: A social history of Nazi Germany 1933–1945*. New York: Holt, Rinehart & Winston.

GRUSH, J. E. (1976). Attitude formation and mere exposure phenomena: A non-artifactual explanation of empirical findings. *Journal of Personality and Social Psychology, 33*, 281–290.

GRUSH, J. E., & GLIDDEN, M. V. (1987). Power and satisfaction among distressed and nondistressed couples. Paper presented at the Midwestern Psychological Association convention.

GUDYKUNST, W. B. (1989). Culture and intergroup processes. In M. H. Bond (Ed.), *The cross-cultural challenge to social psychology*. Newbury Park, CA: Sage.

GUERIN, B. (1986). Mere presence effects in humans: A review. *Journal of Personality and Social Psychology, 22*, 38–77.

GUERIN, B., & INNES, J. M. (1982). Social facilitation and social monitoring: A new look at Zajonc's mere pesence hypothesis. *British Journal of Social Psychology, 21*, 7–18.

GUPTA, U., & SINGH, P. (1982). Exploratory study of love and liking and type of marriages. *Indian Journal of Applied Psychology, 19*, 92–97.

GUTMANN, D. (1977). The cross-cultural perspective: Notes toward a comparative psychology of aging. In J. E. Birren & K. Warner Schaie (Eds.), *Handbook of the psychology of aging*. New York: Van Nostrand Reinhold.

HACKMAN, J. R. (1986). The design of work teams. In J. Lorsch (Ed.), *Handbook of organizational behavior*. Englewood Cliffs, NJ: Prentice-Hall.

HAEMMERLIE, F. M. (1987). Creating adaptive illusions in counseling and therapy using a self-perception theory perspective. Paper presented at the Midwestern Psychological Association, Chicago.

HAEMMERLIE, F. M., & MONTGOMERY, R. L. (1982). Self-perception theory and unobtrusively biased interactions: A treatment for heterosocial anxiety. *Journal of Counseling Psychology, 29,* 362–370.

HAEMMERLIE, F. M., & MONTGOMERY, R. L. (1984). Purposefully biased interventions: Reducing heterosocial anxiety through self-perception theory. *Journal of Personality and Social Psychology, 47,* 900–908.

HAEMMERLIE, F. M., & MONTGOMERY, R. L. (1986). Self-perception theory and the treatment of shyness. In W. H. Jones, J. M. Cheek, & S. R. Briggs (Eds.), *A sourcebook on shyness: Research and treatment.* New York: Plenum.

HAGIWARA, S. (1983). Role of self-based and sample-based consensus estimates as mediators of responsibility judgments for automobile accidents. *Japanese Psychological Research, 25,* 16–28.

HALBERSTADT, A. G., & SAITTA, M. B. (1987). Gender, nonverbal behavior, and perceived dominance: A test of the theory. *Journal of Personality and Social Psychology, 53,* 257–272.

HALL, J. A. (1984). *Nonverbal sex differences: Communication accuracy and expressive style.* Baltimore: Johns Hopkins Univ. Press.

HALL, T. (1985, June 25). The unconverted: Smoking of cigarettes seems to be becoming a lower-class habit. *Wall Street Journal,* pp. 1, 25.

HALLMARK CARDS (1990). Cited in *Time,* Fall special issue on women.

HAMBLIN, R. L., BUCKHOLDT, D., BUSHELL, D., ELLIS, D., & FERITOR, D. (1969, January). Changing the game from get the teacher to learn. *Transaction,* pp. 20–25, 28–31.

HAMILL, R., WILSON, T. D., & NISBETT, R. E. (1980). Insensitivity to sample bias: Generalizing from atypical cases. *Journal of Personality and Social Psychology, 39,* 578–589.

HANSEN, C. H. (1989). Priming sex-role stereotypic event schemas with rock music videos: Effects on impression favorability, trait inferences, and recall of a subsequent male-female interaction. *Basic and Applied Social Psychology, 10,* 371–391.

HANSEN, C. H., & HANSEN, R. D. (1988). Priming stereotypic appraisal of social interactions: How rock music videos can change what's seen when boy meets girl. *Sex Roles, 19,* 287–316.

HANSEN, C. H., & HANSEN, R. D. (1990). Rock music videos and antisocial behavior. *Basic and Applied Social Psychology, 11,* 357–369.

HARDIN, G. (1968). The tragedy of the commons. *Science, 162,* 1243–1248.

HARDY, C., & LATANÉ, B. (1986). Social loafing on a cheering task. *Social Science, 71,* 165–172.

HARITOS-FATOUROS, M. (1988). The official torturer: A learning model for obedience to the authority of violence. *Journal of Applied Social Psychology, 18,* 1107–1120.

HARKINS, S. G. (1981). Effects of task difficulty and task responsibility on social loafing. Presentation to the First International Conference on Social Processes in Small Groups, Kill Devil Hills, NC.

HARKINS, S. G., & JACKSON, J. M. (1985). The role of evaluation in eliminating social loafing. *Personality and Social Psychology Bulletin, 11,* 457–465.

HARKINS, S. G., LATANÉ, B., & WILLIAMS, K. (1980). Social loafing: Allocating effort or taking it easy? *Journal of Experimental Social Psychology, 16,* 457–465.

HARKINS, S. G., & PETTY, R. E. (1981). Effects of source magnification of cognitive effort on attitudes: An information-processing view. *Journal of Personality and Social Psychology, 40,* 401–413.

HARKINS, S. G., & PETTY, R. E. (1982). Effects of task difficulty and task uniqueness on social loafing. *Journal of Personality and Social Psychology, 43,* 1214–1229.

HARKINS, S. G., & PETTY, R. E. (1987). Information utility and the multiple source effect. *Journal of Personality and Social Psychology, 52,* 260–268.

HARKINS, S. G., & SZYMANSKI, K. (1989). Social loafing and group evaluation. *Journal of Personality and Social Psychology, 56,* 934–941.

HARPER'S MAGAZINE (1989, November). Harper's index, p. 15.

HARRIES, K. D., & STADLER, S. J. (1988). Heat and violence: New findings from Dallas field data, 1980–1981. *Journal of Applied Social Psychology, 18,* 129–138.

HARRIS, M. J., & ROSENTHAL, R. (1985). Mediation of interpersonal expectancy effects: 31 meta-analyses. *Psychological Bulletin, 97,* 363–386.

HARRIS, M. J., & ROSENTHAL, R. (1986). Four factors in the mediation of teacher expectancy effects. In R. S. Feldman (Ed.), *The social psychology of education.* New York: Cambridge Univ. Press.

HARRISON, A. A. (1977). Mere exposure. In L. Berkowitz (Ed.), *Advances in experimental social psychology,* Vol. 10. New York: Academic Press, pp. 39–83.

HARVEY, J. H., TOWN, J. P., & YARKIN, K. L. (1981). How fundamental is the fundamental attribution error? *Journal of Personality and Social Psychology, 40,* 346–349.

HASSAN I. N. (1980). Role and status of women in Pakistan: An empirical research review. *Pakistan Journal of Psychology, 13,* 36–56.

HATFIELD, E. (see also Walster, E.)

HATFIELD, E. (1988). Passionate and compassionate love. In R. J. Sternberg & M. L. Barnes (Eds.), *The psychology of love.* New Haven, CT: Yale Univ. Press.

HATFIELD, E., & SPRECHER, S. (1986). *Mirror, mirror: The importance of looks in everyday life.* Albany, NY: SUNY Press.

HATFIELD, E., TRAUPMANN, J., SPRECHER, S., UTNE, M., & HAY, J. (1985). Equity and intimate relations: Recent research. In W. Ickes (Ed.), *Compatible and incompatible relationships.* New York: Springer-Verlag.

HAWKINS, S. A., & HASTIE, R. (1990). Hindsight: Biased judgments of past events after the outcomes are known. *Psychological Bulletin, 107,* 311–327.

HEADEY, B., & WEARING, A. (1987). The sense of relative superiority—central to well-being. *Social Indicators Research, 20,* 497–516.

HEAROLD, S. (1986). A synthesis of 1043 effects of television on social behavior. In G. Comstock (Ed.), *Public communication and behavior,* Vol. 1. Orlando, FL: Academic Press.

HEATON, A. W., & SIGALL, H. (1989). The "championship choke" revisited: The role of fear of acquiring a negative identity. *Journal of Applied Social Psychology, 19,* 1019–1033.

HEATON, A. W., & SIGALL, H. (1991). Self-consciousness, self-presentation, and performance under pressure: Who chokes, and when? *Journal of Applied Social Psychology, 21,* 175–188.

HEESACKER, M. (1989). Counseling and the elaboration likelihood model of attitude change. In J. F. Cruz, R. A. Goncalves, & P. P. Machado (Eds.), *Psychology and education: Investigations and interventions.* (Proceedings of the International Conference on Interventions in Psychology and Education,

Porto, Portugal, July, 1987.) Porto, Portugal: Portuguese Psychological Association.

HEILMAN, M. E. (1976). Oppositional behavior as a function of influence attempt intensity and retaliation threat. *Journal of Personality and Social Psychology, 33,* 574–578.

HELLMAN, P. (1980). *Avenue of the righteous of nations.* New York: Atheneum.

HENDRICK, C. (1988). Roles and gender in relationships. In S. Duck (Ed.), *Handbook of personal relationships.* Chichester, England: Wiley.

HENDRICK, C., & HENDRICK, S. (1993). *Romantic love.* Newbury Park, CA: Sage.

HENDRICK, S. S., HENDRICK, C., & ADLER, N. L. (1988). Romantic relationships: Love, satisfaction, and staying together. *Journal of Personality and Social Psychology, 54,* 980–988.

HENDRICK, S. S., HENDRICK, C., SLAPION-FOOTE, J., & FOOTE, F. H. (1985). Gender differences in sexual attitudes. *Journal of Personality and Social Psychology, 48,* 1630–1642.

HENLEY, N. (1977). *Body politics: Power, sex, and nonverbal communication.* Englewood Cliffs, NJ: Prentice-Hall.

HENSLIN, M. (1967). Craps and magic. *American Journal of Sociology, 73,* 316–330.

HEPWORTH, J. T., & WEST, S. G. (1988). Lynchings and the economy: A time-series reanalysis of Hovland and Sears (1940). *Journal of Personality and Social Psychology, 55,* 239–247.

HERADSTVEIT, D. (1979). *The Arab-Israeli conflict: Psychological obstacles to peace,* Vol. 28, Oslo, Norway: Universitetsforlaget. Distributed by Columbia Univ. Press. Reviewed by R. K. White, *Contemporary Psychology, 1980, 25,* 11–12.

HEREK, G. M. (1986). The instrumentality of attitudes: Toward a neofunctional theory. *Journal of Social Issues, 42,* 99–114.

HEREK, G. M. (1987). Can functions be measured? A new perspective on the functional approach to attitudes. *Social Psychology Quarterly, 50,* 285–303.

HEREK, G. M. (1990). The context of anti-gay violence: Notes on cultural and psychological heterosexism. *Journal of Interpersonal Violence, 5,* 316–333.

HEWSTONE, M., HANTZI, A., & JOHNSTON, L. (1991). Social categorisation and person memory: The pervasiveness of race as an organizing principle. *European Journal of Social Psychology, 21,* 517–528.

HIGBEE, K. L., MILLARD, R. J., & FOLKMAN, J. R. (1982). Social psychology research during the 1970s: Predominance of experimentation and college students. *Personality and Social Psychology Bulletin, 8,* 180–183.

HIGGINS, E. T., & McCANN, C. D. (1984). Social encoding and subsequent attitudes, impressions and memory: "Context-driven" and motivational aspects of processing. *Journal of Personality and Social Psychology, 47,* 26–39.

HIGGINS, E. T., & RHOLES, W. S. (1978). Saying is believing: Effects of message modification on memory and liking for the person described. *Journal of Experimental Social Psychology, 14,* 363–378.

HILL, T., LEWICKI, P., CZYZEWSKA, M., & BOSS, A. (1989). Self-perpetuating development of encoding biases in person perception. *Journal of Personality and Social Psychology, 57,* 373–387.

HINDE, R. A. (1984). Why do the sexes behave differently in close relationships? *Journal of Social and Personal Relationships, 1,* 471–501.

HINSZ, V. B., & DAVIS, J. H. (1984). Persuasive arguments theory, group polarization, and choice shifts. *Personality and Social Psychology Bulletin, 10,* 260–268.

HIRSCHMAN, R. S., & LEVENTHAL, H. (1989). Preventing smoking behavior in school children: An initial test of a cognitive-development program. *Journal of Applied Social Psychology, 19,* 559–583.

HIRT, E. R. (1990). Do I see only what I expect? Evidence for an expectancy-guided retrieval model. *Journal of Personality and Social Psychology, 58,* 937–951.

HIRT, E. R., & KIMBLE, C. E. (1981). The home-field advantage in sports: Differences and correlates. Paper presented at the Midwestern Psychological Association convention.

HOFFMAN, C., & HURST, N. (1990). Gender stereotypes: Perception or rationalization? *Journal of Personality and Social Psychology, 58,* 197–208.

HOFFMAN, L. W. (1977). Changes in family roles, socialization, and sex differences. *American Psychologist, 32,* 644–657.

HOFLING, C. K., BROTZMAN, E., DAIRYMPLE, S., GRAVES, N., & PIERCE, C. M. (1966). An experimental study in nurse-physician relationships. *Journal of Nervous and Mental Disease, 143,* 171–180.

HOGG, M. A., & ABRAMS, D. (1988). *Social identifications: A social psychology of intergroup relations and group processes.* London: Routledge.

HOGG, M. A., TURNER, J. C., & DAVIDSON, B. (1990). Polarized norms and social frames of reference: A test of the self-categorization theory of group polarization. *Basic and Applied Social Psychology, 11,* 77–100.

HOKANSON, J. E., & EDELMAN, R. (1966). Effects of three social responses on vascular processes. *Journal of Personality and Social Psychology, 3,* 442–447.

HOLMBERG, D., & HOLMES, J. G. (in press). Reconstruction of relationship memories: A mental models approach. In N. Schwarz & S. Sudman (Eds.), *Autobiographical memory and the validity of retrospective reports.* New York: Springer-Verlag.

HOLMES, J. G., & REMPEL, J. K. (1989). Trust in close relationships. In C. Hendrick (Ed.), *Review of personality and social psychology,* Vol. 10. Newbury Park, CA: Sage.

HOLTGRAVES, T., & SRULL, T. K. (1989). The effects of positive self-descriptions on impressions: General principles and individual differences. *Personality and Social Psychology Bulletin, 15,* 452–462.

HOORENS, V., NUTTIN, J. M., HERMAN, I. E., & PAVAKANUN, U. (1990). Mastery pleasure versus mere ownership: A quasi-experimental cross-cultural and cross-alphabetical test of the name letter effect. *European Journal of Social Psychology, 20,* 181–205.

HORMUTH, S. E. (1986). Lack of effort as a result of self-focused attention: An attributional ambiguity analysis. *European Journal of Social Psychology, 16,* 181–192.

HOUSE, R. J., & SINGH, J. V. (1987). Organizational behavior: Some new directions for I/O psychology. *Annual Review of Psychology, 38,* 669–718.

HOVLAND, C. I., LUMSDAINE, A. A., & SHEFFIELD, F. D. (1949). *Experiments on mass communication. Studies in social psychology in World War II,* Vol. III. Princeton, NJ: Princeton Univ. Press.

HOVLAND, C. I., & SEARS, R. (1940). Minor studies of aggression: Correlation of lynchings with economic indices. *Journal of Psychology, 9,* 301–310.

HOWES, M. J., HOKANSON, J. E., & LOEWENSTEIN, D. A. (1985). Induction of depressive affect after prolonged exposure to a mildly depressed individual. *Journal of Personality and Social Psychology, 49,* 1110–1113.

HUESMANN, L. R., LAGERSPETZ, K., & ERON, L. D. (1984). Intervening variables in the TV violence-aggression relation: Evidence from two countries. *Developmental Psychology, 20,* 746–775.

HUI, C. H. (1988). Measurement of individualism-collectivism. *Journal of Research in Personality, 22,* 17–36.

HUI, C. H. (1990). West meets East: Individualism versus collectivism in North America and Asia. Invited address, Hope College.

HULL, J. G., & BOND, C. F., JR., (1986). Social and behavioral consequences of alcohol consumption and expectancy: A meta-analysis. *Psychological Bulletin, 99,* 347–360.

HULL, J. G., LEVENSON, R. W., YOUNG, R. D., & SHER, K. J. (1983). Self-awareness-reducing effects of alcohol consumption. *Journal of Personality and Social Psychology, 44,* 461–473.

HULL, J. G., & YOUNG, R. D. (1983). The self-awareness-reducing effects of alcohol consumption: Evidence and implications. In J. Suls & A. G. Greenwald (Eds.), *Psychological perspectives on the self,* Vol. 2. Hillsdale, NJ: Erlbaum.

HUNT, M. (1990). *The compassionate beast: What science is discovering about the humane side of human kind.* New York: William Morrow.

HUNT, P. J., & HILLERY, J. M. (1973). Social facilitation in a location setting: An examination of the effects over learning trials. *Journal of Experimental Social Psychology, 9,* 563–571.

HUNTER, J. A., STRINGER, M., & WATSON, R. P. (1991). Intergroup violence and intergroup attributions. *British Journal of Social Psychology, 30,* 261–266.

HUSTON, T. L. (1973). Ambiguity of acceptance, social desirability, and dating choice. *Journal of Experimental Social Psychology, 9,* 32–42.

HYDE, J. S. (1986). Gender differences in aggression. In J. S. Hyde & M. C. Linn (Eds.), *The psychology of gender: Advances through meta-analysis.* Baltimore: Johns Hopkins Univ. Press.

HYMAN, H. H., & SHEATSLEY, P. B. (1956 & 1964). Attitudes toward desegregation. *Scientific American, 195*(6), 35–39, and *211*(1), 16–23.

ICKES, B. (1980). On disconfirming our perceptions of others. Paper presented at the American Psychological Association convention.

ICKES, W., & LAYDEN, M. A. (1978). Attributional styles. In J. H. Harvey, W. Ickes, & R. F. Kidd (Eds.), *New directions in attribution research,* Vol. 2. Hillsdale, NJ: Erlbaum.

ICKES, W., LAYDEN, M. A., & BARNES, R. D. (1978). Objective self-awareness and individuation: An empirical link. *Journal of Personality, 46,* 146–161.

ICKES, W., SNYDER, M., & CARCIA, S. (1990). Personality influences on the choice of situations. In S. Briggs, R. Hogan, & W. Jones (Eds.), *Handbook of personality psychology.* New York: Academic Press.

INGHAM, A. G., LEVINGER, G., GRAVES, J., & PECKHAM, V. (1974). The Ringelmann effect: Studies of group size and group performance. *Journal of Experimental Social Psychology, 10,* 371–384.

INGLEHART, R. (1990). *Culture shift in advanced industrial society.* Princeton: Princeton Univ. Press.

ISEN, A. M., & MEANS, B. (1983). The influence of positive affect on decision-making strategy. *Social Cognition, 2,* 28–31.

ISLAM, M. R., & HEWSTONE, M. (1991). Intergroup attributions and affective consequences in majority and minority groups. Unpublished manuscript, Univ. of Bristol.

ISOZAKI, M. (1984). The effect of discussion on polarization of judgments. *Japanese Psychological Research, 26,* 187–193.

ISR NEWSLETTER (1975). Institute for Social Research, Univ. of Michigan, *3*(4), 4–7.

JACKMAN, M. R., & SENTER, M. S. (1981). Beliefs about race, gender, and social class different, therefore unequal: Beliefs about trait differences between groups of unequal status. In D. J. Treiman & R. V. Robinson (Eds.), *Research in stratification and mobility,* Vol. 2. Greenwich, CT: JAI.

JACKSON, J., & WILLIAMS, K. D. (1985). Social loafing on difficult tasks: Working collectively can improve performance. *Journal of Personality and Social Psychology, 49,* 937–942.

JACKSON, J. M., & LATANÉ, B. (1981). All alone in front of all those people: Stage fright as a function of number and type of co-performers and audience. *Journal of Personality and Social Psychology, 40,* 73–85.

JACKSON, J. M., & WILLIAMS, K. D. (1988). Social loafing: A review and theoretical analysis. Unpublished manuscript, Fordham University.

JACKSON, L. A. (1989). Relative deprivation and the gender wage gap. *Journal of Social Issues, 45*(4), 117–133.

JACOBY, S. (1986, December). When opposites attract. *Reader's Digest,* pp. 95–98.

JAIN, U. (1990). Social perspectives on causal attribution. In G. Misra (Ed.), *Applied social psychology in India.* New Delhi: Sage.

JAMIESON, D. W., LYDON, J. E., STEWART, G., & ZANNA, M. P. (1987). Pygmalion revisited: New evidence for student expectancy effects in the classroom. *Journal of Educational Psychology, 79,* 461–466.

JAMIESON, D. W., LYDON, J. E., & ZANNA, M. P. (1987). Attitude and activity preference similarity: Differential bases of interpersonal attraction for low and high self-monitors. *Journal of Personality and Social Psychology, 53,* 1052–1060.

JANIS, I. L. (1971, November). Groupthink. *Psychology Today,* pp. 43–46.

JANIS, I. L. (1982). Counteracting the adverse effects of concurrence-seeking in policy-planning groups: Theory and research perspectives. In H. Brandstatter, J. H. Davis, & G. Stocker-Kreichgauer (Eds.), *Group decision making.* New York: Academic Press.

JANIS, I. L., KAYE, D., & KIRSCHNER, P. (1965). Facilitating effects of eating while reading on responsiveness to persuasive communications. *Journal of Personality and Social Psychology, 1,* 181–186.

JANIS, I. L., & MANN, L. (1977). *Decision-making: A psychological analysis of conflict, choice and commitment.* New York: Free Press.

JEFFERY, R. (1964). The psychologist as an expert witness on the issue of insanity. *American Psychologist, 19,* 838–843.

JELLISON, J. M., & GREEN, J. (1981). A self-presentation approach to the fundamental attribution error: The norm of internality. *Journal of Personality and Social Psychology, 40,* 643–649.

JOHNSON, B. T., & EAGLY, A. H. (1990). Involvement and persuasion: Types, traditions, and the evidence. *Psychological Bulletin, 107,* 375–384.

JOHNSON, D. J., & RUSBULT, C. E. (1989). Resisting temptation: Devaluation of alternative partners as a means of maintaining commitment in close relationships. *Journal of Personality and Social Psychology, 57,* 967–980.

JOHNSON, D. W., MARUYAMA, G., JOHNSON, R., NELSON, D., & SKON, L. (1981). Effects of cooperative, competitive, and individualistic goal structures on achievement: A meta-analysis. *Psychological Bulletin, 89,* 47–62.

JOHNSON, E. J., & TVERSKY, A. (1983). Affect, generalization, and the perception of risk. *Journal of Personality and Social Psychology, 45,* 20–31.

JOHNSON, J. T., JEMMOTT, J. B., III, & PETTIGREW, T. F. (1984). Causal attribution and dispositional inference: Evidence of inconsistent judgments. *Journal of Experimental Social Psychology, 20,* 567–585.

JOHNSON, M. H., & MAGARO, P. A. (1987). Effects of mood and severity on memory processes in depression and mania. *Psychological Bulletin, 101,* 28–40.

JOHNSON, M. K., & SHERMAN, S. J. (1990). Constructing and reconstructing the past and the future in the present. In E. T. Higgins & R. M. Sorrentino (Eds.), *Handbook of motivation and cognition.* New York: Guilford.

JOHNSON, R. D., & DOWNING, L. J. (1979). Deindividuation and valence of cues: Effects of prosocial and antisocial behavior. *Journal of Personality and Social Psychology, 37,* 1532–1538.

JOHNSTON, L. D., BACHMAN, J. G., & O'MALLEY, P. M. (1992, January 27). Press release with accompanying tables. Ann Arbor: Univ. of Michigan News and Information Services.

JONAS, K. (1991). Modeling and suicide: A test of the Werther effect hypothesis. Unpublished manuscript, Univ. of Tubingen.

JONES, E. E. (1976). How do people perceive the causes of behavior? *American Scientist, 64,* 300–305.

JONES, E. E., & HARRIS, V. A. (1967). The attribution of attitudes. *Journal of Experimental Social Psychology, 3,* 2–24.

JONES, E. E., & NISBETT, R. E. (1971). *The actor and the observer: Divergent perceptions of the cases of behavior.* Morristown, NJ: General Learning Press.

JONES, E. E., RHODEWALT, F., BERGLAS, S., & SKELTON, J. A. (1981). Effects of strategic self-presentation on subsequent self-esteem. *Journal of Personality and Social Psychology, 41,* 407–421.

JONES, E. E., & SIGALL, H. (1971). The bogus pipeline: A new paradigm for measuring affect and attitude. *Psychological Bulletin, 76,* 349–364.

JONES, J. M. (1983). The concept of race in social psychology: From color to culture. In L. Wheeler & P. Shaver (Eds.), *Review of personality and social psychology,* Vol. 4. Beverly Hills, CA: Sage.

JONES, W. H., CARPENTER, B. N., & QUINTANA, D. (1985). Personality and interpersonal predictors of loneliness in two cultures. *Journal of Personality and Social Psychology, 48,* 1503–1511.

JONES, W. H., FREEMON, J. E., & GOSWICK, R. A. (1981). The persistence of loneliness: Self and other determinants. *Journal of Personality, 49,* 27–48.

JONES, W. H., HOBBS, S. A., & HOCKENBURY, D. (1982). Loneliness and social skill deficits. *Journal of Personality and Social Psychology, 42,* 682–689.

JOSEPHSON, W. L. (1987). Television violence and children's aggression: Testing the priming, social script, and disinhibition predictions. *Journal of Personality and Social Psychology, 53,* 882–890.

JOURARD, S. M. (1964), *The transparent self.* Princeton, NJ: Van Nostrand.

JUSSIM, L. (1986). Self-fulfilling prophecies: A theoretical and integrative review. *Psychological Review, 93,* 429–445.

JUSSIM, L., & ECCLES, J. (1993). Teacher expectations II: Construction and reflection of student achievement. *Journal of Personality and Social Psychology.*

JUSTER, F. T., & STAFFORD, F. P. (1991). The allocation of time: Empirical findings, behavioral models, and problems of measurement. *Journal of Economic Literature*.

KAGAN, J. (1989). Temperamental contributions to social behavior. *American Psychologist, 44,* 668–674.

KAHN, M. W. (1951). The effect of severe defeat at various age levels on the aggressive behavior of mice. *Journal of Genetic Psychology, 79,* 117–130.

KAHNEMAN, D., & TVERSKY, A. (1979). Intuitive prediction: Biases and corrective procedures. *Management Science, 12,* 313–327.

KAMEN, L. P., SELIGMAN, M. E. P., DWYER, J., & RODIN, J. (1988). Pessimism and cell-mediated immunity. Unpublished manuscript, Univ. of Pennsylvania.

KAMMER, D. (1982). Differences in trait ascriptions to self and friend: Unconfounding intensity from variability. *Psychological Reports, 51,* 99–102.

KANDEL, D. B. (1978). Similarity in real-life adolescent friendship pairs. *Journal of Personality and Social Psychology, 36,* 306–312.

KAPLAN, M. F. (1989). Task, situational, and personal determinants of influence processes in group decision making. In E. J. Lawler (Ed.), *Advances in group processes*, Vol. 6. Greenwich, CT: JAI.

KAPLAN, M. F., WANSHULA, L. T., & ZANNA, M. P. (1992). Time pressure and information integration in social judgment: The effect of need for structure. In O. Svenson & J. Maule (Eds.), *Time pressure and stress in human judgment and decision making*. Cambridge: Cambridge Univ. Press.

KATO, P. S., & RUBLE, D. N. (1992). Toward an understanding of women's experience of menstrual cycle symptoms. In V. Adesso, D. Reddy, & R. Fleming (Eds.), *Psychological perspectives on women's health*. Washington, DC: Hemisphere.

KATZ, A. M., & HILL, R. (1958). Residential propinquity and marital selection: A review of theory, method, and fact. *Marriage and Family Living, 20,* 237–335.

KAUFMAN, J., & ZIGLER, E. (1987). Do abused children become abusive parents? *American Journal of Orthopsychiatry, 57,* 186–192.

KEATING, J. P., & BROCK, T. C. (1974). Acceptance of persuasion and the inhibition of counterargumentation under various distraction tasks. *Journal of Experimental Social Psychology, 10,* 301–309.

KELLERMAN, J., LEWIS, J., & LAIRD, J. D. (1989). Looking and loving: The effects of mutual gaze on feelings of romantic love. *Journal of Research in Personality, 23,* 145–161.

KELLEY, H. H., & STAHELSKI, A. J. (1970). The social interaction basis of cooperators' and competitors' beliefs about others. *Journal of Personality and Social Psychology, 16,* 66–91.

KELMAN, H. C., & COHEN, S. P. (1986). Resolution of international conflict: An interactional approach. In S. Worchel & W. G. Austin (Eds.), *Psychology of intergroup relations* (2nd ed.). Chicago: Nelson-Hall.

KENNY, D. A., & ALBRIGHT, L. (1987). Accuracy in interpersonal perception: A social relations analysis. *Psychology Bulletin, 102,* 390–402.

KENNY, D. A., & NASBY, W. (1980). Splitting the reciprocity correlation. *Journal of Personality and Social Psychology, 38,* 249–256.

KENRICK, D. T. (1987). Gender, genes, and the social environment: A biosocial interactionist perspective. In P. Shaver & C. Hendrick (Eds.), *Sex and gender: Review of personality and social psychology*, Vol. 7. Beverly Hills, CA: Sage.

KENRICK, D. T., & GUTIERRES, S. E. (1980). Contrast effects and judgments of physical attractiveness: When beauty becomes a social problem. *Journal of Personality and Social Psychology, 38,* 131–140.

KENRICK, D. T., GUTIERRES, S. E., & GOLDBERG, L. L. (1989). Influence of popular erotica on judgments of strangers and mates. *Journal of Experimental Social Psychology, 25,* 159–167.

KENRICK, D. T., & MACFARLANE, S. W. (1986). Ambient temperature and horn-honking: A field study of the heat/aggression relationship. *Environment and Behavior, 18,* 179–191.

KENRICK, D. T., & TROST, M. R. (1987). A biosocial theory of heterosexual relationships. In K. Kelly (Ed.), *Females, males, and sexuality.* Albany: State Univ. of New York Press.

KERR, N. L. (1983). Motivation losses in small groups: A social dilemma analysis. *Journal of Personality and Social Psychology, 45,* 819–828.

KERR, N. L. (1989). Illusions of efficacy: The effects of group size on perceived efficacy in social dilemmas. *Journal of Experimental Social Psychology, 25,* 287–313.

KERR, N. L., & BRUUN, S. E. (1981). Ringelmann revisted: Alternative explanations for the social loafing effect. *Personality and Social Psychology Bulletin, 7,* 224–231.

KERR, N. L., & BRUUN, S. E. (1983). Dispensability of member effort and group motivation losses: Free-rider effects. *Journal of Personality and Social Psychology, 44,* 78–94.

KERR, N. L., HARMON, D. L., & GRAVES, J. K. (1982). Independence of multiple verdicts by jurors and juries. *Journal of Applied Social Psychology, 12,* 12–29.

KIDD, J. B., & MORGAN, J. R. (1969). A predictive information system for management. *Operational Research Quarterly, 20,* 149–170.

KIERKEGAARD, S. (1851/1944). *For self-examination and judge for yourself.* Trans. W. Lowrie. Princeton: Princeton Univ. Press.

KIESLER, C. A. (1971). *The psychology of commitment: Experiments linking behavior to belief.* New York: Academic Press.

KIMMEL, M. J., PRUITT, D. G., MAGENAU, J. M., KONAR-GOLDBAND, E., & CARNEVALE, P. J. D. (1980). Effects of trust, aspiration, and gender on negotiation tactics. *Journal of Personality and Social Psychology, 38,* 9–22.

KINDER, D. R., & SEARS, D. O. (1985). Public opinion and political action. In. G. Lindzey & E. Aronson (Eds.), *The handbook of social psychology* (3rd ed.). New York: Random House.

KIRMEYER, S. L. (1978). Urban density and pathology: A review of research. *Environment and Behavior, 10,* 257–269.

KLAAS, E. T. (1978). Psychological effects of immoral actions: The experimental evidence. *Psychological Bulletin, 85,* 756–771.

KLECK, R. E., & STRENTA, A. (1980). Perceptions of the impact of negatively valued physical characteristics on social interaction. *Journal of Personality and Social Psychology, 39,* 861–873.

KLEIN, J. G. (1991). Negative effects in impression formation: A test in the political arena. *Personality and Social Psychology Bulletin, 17,* 412–418.

KLEINKE, C. L. (1977). Compliance to requests made by gazing and touching experimenters in field settings. *Journal of Experimental Social Psychology, 13,* 218–223.

KLENTZ, B., BEAMAN, A. L., MAPELLI, S. D., & ULLRICH, J. R. (1987). Perceived physical attractiveness of supporters and nonsupporters of the women's movement: An attitude-similarity-mediated error (AS-ME). *Personality and Social Psychology Bulletin, 13,* 513–523.

KLOPFER, P. M. (1958). Influence of social interaction on learning rates in birds. *Science, 128,* 903–904.

KNIGHT, J. A., & VALLACHER, R. R. (1981). Interpersonal engagement in social perception: The consequences of getting into the action. *Journal of Personality and Social Psychology, 40,* 990–999.

KNOWLES, E. S. (1983). Social physics and the effects of others: Tests of the effects of audience size and distance on social judgment and behavior. *Journal of Personality and Social Psychology, 45,* 1263–1279.

KNUDSON, R. M., SOMMERS, A. A., & GOLDING, S. L. (1980). Interpersonal perception and mode of resolution in marital conflict. *Journal of Personality and Social Psychology, 38,* 751–763.

KOEHLER, D. J. (1991). Explanation, imagination, and confidence in judgment. *Psychological Bulletin, 110,* 499–519.

KOESTNER, R., & WHEELER, L. (1988). Self-presentation in personal advertisements: The influence of implicit notions of attraction and role expectations. *Journal of Social and Personal Relationships, 5,* 149–160.

KOMORITA, S. S., & BARTH, J. M. (1985). Components of reward in social dilemmas. *Journal of Personality and Social Psychology, 48,* 364–373.

KOOP, C. E. (1987). Report of the Surgeon General's workshop on pornography and public health. *American Psychologist, 42,* 944–945.

KORIAT, A., LICHTENSTEIN, S., & FISCHHOFF, B. (1980). Reasons for confidence. *Journal of Experimental Social Psychology: Human Learning and Memory, 6,* 107–118.

KOSS, M. P. (1990, August 29). Rape incidence: A review and assessment of the data. Testimony on behalf of the American Psychological Association before the U.S. Senate Judiciary Committee.

KOSS, M. P. (1992). The underdetection of rape: Methodological choices influence incidence estimates. *Journal of Social Issues, 48,* 61–75.

KOSS, M. P., & BURKHART, B. R. (1989). A conceptual analysis of rape victimization. *Psychology of Women Quarterly, 13,* 27–40.

KOSS, M. P., DINERO, T. E., SEIBEL, C. A., & COX, S. L. (1988). Stranger and acquaintance rape. *Psychology of Women, 12,* 1–24.

KRAUT, R. E., & POE, D. (1980). Behavioral roots of person perception: The deception judgments of customs inspectors and laymen. *Journal of Personality and Social Psychology, 39,* 784–798.

KRAVITZ, D. A., & MARTIN, B. (1986). Ringelmann rediscovered: The original article. *Journal of Personality and Social Psychology, 50,* 936–941.

KREBS, D., & ADINOLFI, A. A. (1975). Physical attractiveness, social relations, and personality style. *Journal of Personality and Social Psychology, 31,* 245–253.

KROSNICK, J. A., & ALWIN, D. F. (1989). Aging and susceptibility to attitude change. *Journal of Personality and Social Psychology, 57,* 416–425.

KRUGLANSKI, A. W., & WEBSTER, D. M. (1991). Group members' reactions to opinion deviates and conformists at varying degrees of proximity to decision deadline and of environmental noise. *Journal of Personality and Social Psychology, 61,* 212–225.

KUIPER, N. A., & HIGGINS, E. T. (1985). Social cognition and depression: A general integrative perspective. *Social Cognition, 3*, 1–15.

KUNDA, Z. (1990). The case for motivated reasoning. *Psychological Bulletin, 108,* 480–498.

LaFRANCE, M. (1985, Spring). Does your smile reveal your status? *Social Science News Letter, 70,* 15–18.

LAGERSPETZ, K. (1979). Modification of aggressiveness in mice. In S. Feshbach & A. Fraczek (Eds.), *Aggression and behavior change.* New York: Praeger.

LALLJEE, M., LAMB, R., FURNHAM, A., & JASPARS, J. (1984). Explanations and information search: Inductive and hypothesis-testing approaches to arriving at an explanation. *British Journal of Social Psychology, 23,* 201–212.

LAMAL, P. A. (1979). College student common beliefs about psychology. *Teaching of Psychology, 6,* 155–158.

LANDERS, A. (1973, September). Syndicated newspaper column. April 8, 1969. Cited by L. Berkowitz, The case for bottling up rage. *Psychology Today,* pp. 24–31.

LANGER, E. J. (1977). The psychology of chance. *Journal for the Theory of Social Behavior, 7,* 185–208.

LANGER, E. J., & IMBER, L. (1980). The role of mindlessness in the perception of deviance. *Journal of Personality and Social Psychology, 39,* 360–367.

LANGER, E. J., JANIS, I. L., & WOFER, J. A. (1975). Reduction of psychological stress in surgical patients. *Journal of Experimental Social Psychology, 11,* 155–165.

LANGER, E. J., & RODIN, J. (1976). The effects of choice and enhanced personal responsibility for the aged: A field experiment in an institutional setting. *Journal of Personality and Social Psychology, 334,* 191–198.

LANGLOIS, J. H., & ROGGMAN, L. A. (1990). Attractive faces are only average. *Psychological Science, 1,* 115–121.

LANZETTA, J. T. (1955). Group behavior under stress. *Human Relations, 8,* 29–53.

LARSEN, R. J., & DIENER, E. (1987). Affect intensity as an individual difference characteristic: A review. *Journal of Research in Personality, 21,* 1–39.

LARSON, R. J., CSIKSZENTMIHALYI, N., & GRAEF, R. (1982). Time alone in daily experience: Loneliness or renewal? In L. A. Peplau & D. Perlman (Eds.), *Loneliness: A sourcebook of current theory, research and therapy.* New York: Wiley.

LARWOOD, L. (1978). Swine flu: A field study of self-serving biases. *Journal of Applied Social Psychology, 18,* 283–289.

LARWOOD, L., & WHITTAKER, W. (1977). Managerial myopia: Self-serving biases in organizational planning. *Journal of Applied Psychology, 62,* 194–198.

LASSITER, G. D., & DUDLEY, K. A. (1991). The *a priori* value of basic research: The case of videotaped confessions. *Journal of Social Behavior and Personality, 6,* 7–16.

LASSITER, G. D., & IRVINE, A. A. (1986). Videotaped confessions: The impact of camera point of view on judgments of coercion. *Journal of Applied Social Psychology, 16,* 268–276.

LATANÉ, B., & DABBS, J. M., JR. (1975). Sex, group size and helping in three cities. *Sociometry, 38,* 180–194.

LATANÉ, B., & DARLEY, J. M. (1970). *The unresponsive bystander: Why doesn't he help?* New York: Appleton-Century-Crofts.

LATANÉ, B., & DARLEY, J. M. (1968). Group inhibition of bystander intervention in emergencies. *Journal of Personality and Social Psychology, 10,* 215–221.

LATANÉ, B., & NIDA, S. (1981). Ten years of research on group size and helping. *Psychological Bulletin, 89,* 308–324.

LATANÉ, B., WILLIAMS, K., & HARKINS. S. (1979). Many hands make light the work: The causes and consequences of social loafing. *Journal of Personality and Social Psychology, 37,* 822–832.

LAYDEN, M. A. (1982). Attributional therapy. In C. Antaki & C. Brewin (Eds.), *Attributions and psychological change: Applications of attributional theories to clinical and educational practice.* London: Academic Press.

LAZARSFELD, P. F. (1949). *The American soldier*—an expository review. *Public Opinion Quarterly, 13,* 377–404.

LEARY, M. R. (1982). Hindsight distortion and the 1980 presidential election. *Personality and Social Psychology Bulletin, 8,* 257–263.

LEARY, M. R. (1984). *Understanding social anxiety.* Beverly Hills, CA: Sage.

LEARY, M. R. (1986). The impact of interactional impediments on social anxiety and self-presentation. *Journal of Experimental Social Psychology, 22,* 122–135.

LEARY, M. R., & MADDUX, J. E. (1987). Progress toward a viable interface between social and clinical counseling psychology. *American Psychologist, 42,* 904–911.

LEE, J. A. (1988). Love-styles. In R. J. Sternberg & M. L. Barnes (Eds.), *The psychology of love.* New Haven: Yale Univ. Press.

LEFCOURT, H. M. (1982). *Locus of control: Current trends in theory and research.* Hillsdale, NJ: Erlbaum.

LEFEBVRE, L. M. (1979). Causal attributions for basketball outcomes by players and coaches. *Psychological Belgica, 19,* 109–115.

LEHMAN, D. R., & NISBETT, R. E. (1985). Effects of higher education on inductive reasoning. Unpublished manuscript, Univ. of Michigan.

LEIPPE, M. R., & ELKIN, R. A. (1987). Dissonance reduction strategies and accountability to self and others: Ruminations and some initial research. Presentation to the Fifth International Conference on Affect, Motivation, and Cognition, Nags Head Conference Center.

LEMYRE, L., & SMITH, P. M. (1985). Intergroup discrimination and self-esteem in the minimal group paradigm. *Journal of Personality and Social Psychology, 49,* 660–670.

LENIHAN, K. J. (1965). Perceived climates as a barrier to housing desegregation. Unpublished manuscript, Bureau of Applied Social Research, Columbia University.

LEON, D. (1969). *The Kibbutz: A new way of life.* London: Pergamon, 1969. Cited by B. Latané, K. Williams, & S. Harkins, Many hands make light the work: The causes and consequences of social loafing. *Journal of Personality and Social Psychology, 37,* 822–832.

LERNER, M. J. (1980). *The belief in a just world: A fundamental delusion.* New York: Plenum.

LERNER, M. J., & MILLER, D. T. (1978). Just world research and the attribution process: Looking back and ahead. *Psychological Bulletin, 85,* 1030–1051.

LERNER, M. J., & SIMMONS, C. H. (1966). Observer's reaction to the "innocent victim": Compassion or rejection? *Journal of Personality and Social Psychology, 4,* 203–210.

LERNER, M. J., SOMERS, D. G., REID, D., CHIRIBOGA, D., & TIERNEY, M. (1991). Adult children as caregivers: Egocentric biases in judgments of sibling contributions. *Gerontologist, 31,* 746–755.

LEVENTHAL, H. (1970). Findings and theory in the study of fear communications. In L. Berkowitz (Ed.), *Advances in experimental social psychology*, Vol. 5. New York: Academic Press.

LEVER, J. (1978). Sex differences in the complexity of children's play and games. *American Sociological Review, 43*, 471–483.

LEVINE, A. (1990, May 7). America's youthful bigots. *U.S. News and World Report*, pp. 59–60.

LEVINE, J. M. (1989). Reaction to opinion deviance in small groups. In P. Paulus (Ed.), *Psychology of group influence: New perspectives*. Hillsdale, NJ: Erlbaum.

LEVINE, J. M., & MORELAND, R. L. (1985). Innovation and socialization in small groups. In S. Moscovici, G. Mugny, & E. Van Avermaet (Eds.), *Perspectives on minority influence*. Cambridge: Cambridge Univ. Press.

LEVINE, J. M., & RUSSO, E. M. (1987). Majority and minority influence. In C. Hendrick (Ed.), *Group processes: Review of personality and social psychology*, Vol. 8. Newbury Park, CA: Sage.

LEVINE, R., & ULEMAN, J. S. (1979). Perceived locus of control, chronic self-esteem, and attributions to success and failure. *Journal of Personality and Social Psychology, 5*, 69–72.

LEVY, S., LEE, J., BAGLEY, C., & LIPPMAN, M. (1988). Survival hazards analysis in first recurrent breast cancer patients: Seven-year follow-up. *Psychosomatic Medicine, 50*, 520–528.

LEVY-LEBOYER, C. (1988). Success and failure in applying psychology. *American Psychologist, 43*, 779–785.

LEWICKI, P. (1983). Self-image bias in person perception. *Journal of Personality and Social Psychology, 45*, 384–393.

LEWINSOHN, P. M., HOBERMAN, H., TERI, L., & HAUTZINER, M. (1985). An integrative theory of depression. In S. Reiss & R. Bootzin (Eds.), *Theoretical issues in behavior therapy*. New York: Academic Press.

LEWINSOHN, P. M., MISCHEL, W., CHAPLINE, W., & BARTON, R. (1980). Social competence and depression: The role of illusionary self-perceptions. *Journal of Abnormal Psychology, 89*, 203–212.

LEWINSOHN, P. M., & ROSENBAUM, M. (1987). Recall of parental behavior by acute depressives, remitted depressives, and nondepressives. *Journal of Personality and Social Psychology, 52*, 611–619.

LEWIS, C. S. (1960). *Mere Christianity*. New York: Macmillan.

LEWIS, M., & FEIRING, C. (1992). Development as history. *Child Development*.

LEYENS, J. P. (1989). Another look at confirmatory strategies during a real interview. *European Journal of Social Psychology, 19*, 255–262.

LEYENS, J. P., CAMINO, L., PARKE, R. D., & BERKOWITZ, L. (1975). Effects of movie violence on aggression in a field setting as a function of group dominance and cohesion. *Journal of Personality and Social Psychology, 32*, 346–360.

LICHTENSTEIN, S., & FISCHHOFF, B. (1980). Training for calibration. *Organizational Behavior and Human Performance, 26*, 149–171.

LIEBERMAN, S. (1956). The effects of changes in roles on the attitudes of role occupants. *Human Relations, 9*, 385–402.

LIEBERT, R. M., & BARON, R. A. (1972). Some immediate effects of televised violence on children's behavior. *Developmental Psychology, 6*, 469–475.

LIEBRAND, W. B. G., MESSICK, D. M., & WOLTERS, F. J. M. (1986). Why we are fairer than others: A cross-cultural replication and extension. *Journal of Experimental Social Psychology, 22,* 590–604.

Life (1988, Spring). What we believe, pp. 69–70.

LINDSKOLD, S. (1978). Trust development, the GRIT proposal, and the effects of conciliatory acts on conflict and cooperation. *Psychological Bulletin, 85,* 772–793.

LINDSKOLD, S. (1979). Conciliation with simultaneous or sequential interaction: Variations in trustworthiness and vulnerability in the prisoner's dilemma. *Journal of Conflict Resolution, 27,* 704–714.

LINDSKOLD, S. (1979). Managing conflict through announced conciliatory initiatives backed with retaliatory capability. In W. G. Austin and S. Worchel (Eds.), *The social psychology of intergroup relations.* Monterey, CA: Brooks/Cole.

LINDSKOLD, S. (1981). The laboratory evaluation of GRIT: Trust, cooperation, aversion to using conciliation. Paper presented at the American Association for the Advancement of Science convention.

LINDSKOLD, S. (1983). Cooperators, competitors, and response to GRIT. *Journal of Conflict Resolution, 27,* 521–532.

LINDSKOLD, S., & ARONOFF, J. R. (1980). Conciliatory strategies and relative power. *Journal of Experimental Social Psychology, 16,* 187–198.

LINDSKOLD, S., BENNETT, R., & WAYNER, M. (1976). Retaliation level as a foundation for subsequent conciliation. *Behavioral Science, 21,* 13–18.

LINDSKOLD, S., BETZ, B., & WALTERS, P. S. (1986). Transforming competitive or cooperative climate. *Journal of Conflict Resolution, 30,* 99–114.

LINDSKOLD, S., & COLLINS, M. G. (1978). Inducing cooperation by groups and individuals. *Journal of Conflict Resolution, 22,* 679–690.

LINDSKOLD, S., & FINCH, M. L. (1981). Styles of announcing conciliation. *Journal of Conflict Resolution, 25,* 145–155.

LINDSKOLD, S., & HAN, G. (1988). GRIT as a foundation for integrative bargaining. *Personality and Social Psychology Bulletin, 14,* 335–345.

LINDSKOLD, S., HAN, G., & BETZ, B. (1986a). The essential elements of communication in the GRIT strategy. *Personality and Social Psychology Bulletin, 12,* 179–186.

LINDSKOLD, S., HAN, G., & BETZ, B. (1986b). Repeated persuasion in interpersonal conflict. *Journal of Personality and Social Psychology, 51,* 1183–1188.

LINDSKOLD, S., WALTERS, P. S., KOUTSOURAIS, H., & SHAYO, R. (1981). Cooperators, competitors, and response to GRIT. Unpublished manuscript, Ohio University.

LINVILLE, P. W., GISCHER, G. W., & SALOVEY, P. (1989). Perceived distributions of the characteristics of in-group and out-group members: Empirical evidence and a computer simulation. *Journal of Personality and Social Psychology, 57,* 165–188.

LINZ, D. G., DONNERSTEIN, E., & ADAMS, S. M. (1989). Physiological desensitization and judgments about female victims of violence. *Human Communication Research, 15,* 509–522.

LINZ, D. G., DONNERSTEIN, E., & PENROD, S. (1988). Effects of long term exposure to violent and sexually degrading depictions of women. *Journal of Personality and Social Psychology, 55,* 758–768.

LIPSITZ, A., KALLMEYER, K., FERGUSON, M., & ABAS, A. (1989). Counting on blood donors: Increasing the impact of reminder calls. *Journal of Applied Social Psychology, 19*, 1057–1067.

LOCKE, E. A., & LATHAM, G. P. (1990). Work motivation and satisfaction: Light at the end of the tunnel. *Psychological Science, 1*, 240–246.

LOCKSLEY, A., BORGIDA, E., BREKKE, N., & HEPBURN, C. (1980). Sex stereotypes and social judgment. *Journal of Personality and Social Psychology, 39*, 821–831.

LOFLAND, J., & STARK, R. (1965). Becoming a worldsaver: A theory of conversion to a deviant perspective. *American Sociological Review, 30*, 862–864.

LOFTIN, C., McDOWALL, D., WIERSEMA, B., & COTTEY, T. J. (1991). Effects of restrictive licensing of handguns on homicide and suicide in the District of Columbia. *New England Journal of Medicine, 325*, 1615–1620.

LOFTUS, E. F., & KLINGER, M. R. (1992). Is the unconscious smart or dumb? *American Psychologist, 47*, 761–765.

LONNER, W. J. (1989). The introductory psychology text and cross-cultural psychology: Beyond Ekman, Whorf, and biased I.Q. tests. In D. Keats, D. R. Munro, & L. Mann (Eds.), *Heterogeneity in cross-cultural psychology*. Bellingham, WA: Western Washington University.

LORD, C. G., ROSS, L., & LEPPER, M. (1979). Biased assimilation and attitude polarization: The effects of prior theories on subsequently considered evidence. *Journal of Personality and Social Psychology, 37*, 2098–2109.

LOUW-POTGIETER, J. (1988). The authoritarian personality: An inadequate explanation for intergroup conflict in South Africa. *Journal of Social Psychology, 128*, 75–87.

LOWE, R. H., & WITTIG, M. A. (1989). Comparable worth: Individual, interpersonal, and structural considerations. *Journal of Social Issues, 45*, 223–246.

LOWENTHAL, M. F., THURNHER, M., CHIRIBOGA, D., BEEFON, D., GIGY, L., LURIE, E., PIERCE, R., SPENCE, D., & WEISS, L. (1975). *Four stages of life*. San Francisco: Jossey-Bass.

MAASS, A., BRIGHAM, J. C., & WEST, S. G. (1985). Testifying on eyewitness reliability: Expert advice is not always persuasive. *Journal of Applied Social Psychology, 15*, 207–229.

MAASS, A., & CLARK, R. D., III (1984). Hidden impact of minorities: Fifteen years of minority influence research. *Psychological Bulletin, 95*, 428–450.

MAASS, A., & CLARK, R. D., III (1986). Conversion theory and simultaneous majority/minority influence: Can reactance offer an alternative explanation? *European Journal of Social Psychology, 16*, 305–309.

MACK, D., & RAINEY, D. (1990). Female applicants' grooming and personnel selection. *Journal of Social Behavior and Personality, 5*, 399–407.

MACKAY, J. L. (1980). Selfhood: Comment on Brewster Smith. *American Psychologist, 35*, 106–107.

MACKIE, D. M. (1987). Systematic and nonsystematic processing of majority and minority persuasive communications. *Journal of Personality and Social Psychology, 53*, 41–52.

MACKIE, D. M., WORTH, L. T., & ASUNCION, A. G. (1990). Processing of persuasive in-group messages. *Journal of Personality and Social Psychology, 58*, 812–822.

MADDUX, J. E. (1991). Personal efficacy. In V. Derlega, B. Winstead, & W. Jones (Eds.), *Personality: Contemporary theory and research*. Chicago: Nelson-Hall.

MADDUX, J. E., NORTON, L. W., & LEARY, M. R. (1988). Cognitive components of social anxiety: An investigation of the integration of self-presentation theory and self-efficacy theory. *Journal of Social and Clinical Psychology, 6,* 180–190.

MADDUX, J. E., & ROGERS, R. W. (1983). Protection motivation and self-efficacy: A revised theory of fear appeals and attitude change. *Journal of Experimental Social Psychology, 19,* 469–479.

MAGNUSON, E. (1986, March 10). "A serious deficiency": The Rogers Commission faults NASA's "flawed" decision-making process. *Time,* pp. 40–42, international ed.

MAJOR, B. (1989). Gender differences in comparisons and entitlement: Implications for comparable worth. *Journal of Social Issues, 45,* 99–116.

MAJOR, B., SCHMIDLIN, A. M., & WILLIAMS, L. (1990). Gender patterns in social touch: The impact of setting and age. *Journal of Personality and Social Psychology, 58,* 634–643.

MALAMUTH, N. M., & CHECK, J. V. P. (1981). The effects of media exposure on acceptance of violence against women: A field experiment. *Journal of Research in Personality, 15,* 436–446.

MALAMUTH, N. M., & CHECK, J. V. P. (1984). Debriefing effectiveness following exposure to pornographic rape depictions. *Journal of Sex Research, 20,* 1–13.

MALKIEL, B. G. (1985). *A random walk down Wall Street* (4th ed.). New York: W. W. Norton.

MANIS, M. (1977). Cognitive social psychology. *Personality and Social Psychology Bulletin, 3,* 550–566.

MANN, L. (1981). The baiting crowd in episodes of threatened suicide. *Journal of Personality and Social Psychology, 41,* 703–709.

MARCUS, S. (1974, January 13). Review of *Obedience to authority.* New York Times Book Review, pp. 1–2.

MARKS, G., & MILLER, N. (1987). Ten years of research on the false-consensus effect: An empirical and theoretical review. *Psychological Bulletin, 102,* 72–90.

MARKS, G., MILLER, N., & MARUYAMA, G. (1981). Effect of targets' physical attractiveness on assumptions of similarity. *Journal of Personality and Social Psychology, 41,* 198–206.

MARKUS, G. B. (1986). Stability and change in political attitudes: Observe, recall, and "explain." *Political Behavior, 8,* 21–44.

MARKUS, H., & KITAYAMA, S. (1991). Culture and the self: Implications for cognition, emotion, and motivation. *Psychological Review, 98,* 224–253.

MARSHALL, W. L. (1989). Pornography and sex offenders. In D. Zillmann & J. Bryant (Eds.), *Pornography: Research advances and policy considerations.* Hillsdale, NJ: Erlbaum.

MARTIN, C. L. (1987). A ratio measure of sex stereotyping. *Journal of Personality and Social Psychology, 52,* 489–499.

MARUYAMA, G., RUBIN, R. A., & KINGBURY, G. (1981). Self-esteem and educational achievement: Independent constructs with a common cause? *Journal of Personality and Social Psychology, 40,* 962–975.

MARVELLE, K., & GREEN, S. (1980). Physical attractiveness and sex bias in hiring decisions for two types of jobs. *Journal of the National Association of Women Deans, Administrators, and Counselors, 44*(1), 3–6.

MAXWELL, G. M. (1985). Behaviour of lovers: Measuring the closeness of relationships. *Journal of Personality and Social Psychology, 2,* 215–238.

MAYER, J. D., & SALOVEY, P. (1987). Personality moderates the interaction of mood and cognition. In K. Fiedler & J. Forgas (Eds.), *Affect, cognition, and social behavior*. Toronto: Hogrefe.

McALISTER, A., PERRY, C., KILLEN, J., SLINKARD, L. A., & MACCOBY, N. (1980). Pilot study of smoking, alcohol and drug abuse prevention. *American Journal of Public Health, 70,* 719–721.

McCARREY, M., EDWARDS, H. P., & ROZARIO, W. (1982). Ego-relevant feedback, affect, and self-serving attributional bias. *Personality and Social Psychology Bulletin, 8,* 189–194.

McCARTHY, J. D., & HOGE, D. R. (1984). The dynamics of self-esteem and delinquency. *American Journal of Sociology, 90,* 396–410.

McCARTHY, J. F., & KELLY, B. R. (1978a). Aggressive behavior and its effect on performance over time in ice hockey athletes: An archival study. *International Journal of Sport Psychology, 9,* 90–96.

McCARTHY, J. F., & KELLY, B. R. (1978b). Aggression, performance variables, and anger self-report in ice hockey players. *Journal of Psychology, 99,* 97–101.

McCAULEY, C. (1989). The nature of social influence in groupthink: Compliance and internalization. *Journal of Personality and Social Psychology, 57,* 250–260.

McCAULEY, C., & STITT, C. L. (1978). An individual and quantitative measure of stereotypes. *Journal of Personality and Social Psychology, 36,* 929–940.

McCAULEY, C. R., & SEGAL, M. E. (1987). Social psychology of terrorist groups. In C. Hendrick (Ed.), *Group processes and intergroup relations: Review of personality and social psychology*, Vol. 9. Newbury Park, CA: Sage.

McCONAHAY, J. B. (1981). Reducing racial prejudice in desegregated schools. In W. D. Hawley (Ed.), *Effective school desegregation*. Beverly Hills, CA: Sage.

McCULLOUGH, J. L., & OSTROM, T. M. (1974). Repetition of highly similar messages and attitude change. *Journal of Applied Psychology, 59,* 395–397.

McFARLAND, C., & ROSS, M. (1985). The relation between current impressions and memories of self and dating partners. Unpublished manuscript, Univ. of Waterloo.

McFARLAND, C., ROSS, M., & DeCOURVILLE, N. (1989). Women's theories of menstruation and biases in recall of menstrual symptoms. *Journal of Personality and Social Psychology, 57,* 522–531.

McGILLICUDDY, N. B., WELTON, G. L., & PRUITT, D. G. (1987). Third-party intervention: A field experiment comparing three different models. *Journal of Personality and Social Psychology, 53,* 104–112.

McGUIRE, W. J. (1964). Inducing resistance to persuasion: Some contemporary approaches. In L. Berkowitz (Ed.), *Advances in experimental social psychology*, Vol. 1. New York: Academic Press.

McGUIRE, W. J. (1986). The myth of massive media impact: Savagings and salvagings. In G. Comstock (Ed.), *Public communication and behavior*, Vol. 1. Orlando, FL: Academic Press.

McGUIRE, W. J., & McGUIRE, C. V. (1986). Differences in conceptualizing self versus conceptualizing other people as manifested in contrasting verb types used in natural speech. *Journal of Personality and Social Psychology, 51,* 1135–1143.

McGUIRE, W. J., McGUIRE, C. V., CHILD, P., & FUJIOKA, T. (1978). Salience of ethnicity in the spontaneous self-concept as a function of one's ethnic distinctiveness in the social environment. *Journal of Personality and Social Psychology, 36,* 511–520.

McGuire, W. J., McGuire, C. V., & Winton, W. (1979). Effects of household sex composition on the salience of one's gender in the spontaneous self-concept. *Journal of Experimental Social Psychology, 15,* 77–90.

McGuire, W. J., & Padawer-Singer, A. (1978). Trait salience in the spontaneous self-concept. *Journal of Personality and Social Psychology, 33,* 743–754.

McNeel, S. P. (1980). Tripling up: Perceptions and effects of dormitory crowding. Paper presented at the American Psychological Association convention.

McNeill, B. W., & Stoltenberg, C. D. (1988). A test of the elaboration likelihood model for therapy. *Cognitive Therapy and Research, 12,* 69–79.

Meehl, P. E. (1954). *Clinical vs. statistical prediction: A theoretical analysis and a review of evidence.* Minneapolis: Univ. of Minnesota Press.

Meehl, P. E. (1986). Causes and effects of my disturbing little book. *Journal of Personality Assessment, 50,* 370–375.

Meindl, J. R., & Lerner, M. J. (1984). Exacerbation of extreme responses to an outgroup. *Journal of Personality and Social Psychology, 47,* 71–84.

Menand, L. (1991, May 20). Illiberalisms. *New Yorker,* pp. 101–107.

Messé, L. A., & Sivacek, J. M. (1979). Predictions of others' responses in a mixed-motive game: Self-justification or false consensus? *Journal of Personality and Social Psychology, 37,* 602–607.

Messick, D. M., Bloom, S., Boldizar, J. P., & Samuelson, C. D. (1985). Why we are fairer than others. *Journal of Experimental Social Psychology, 21,* 480–500.

Messick, D. M., & Sentis, K. P. (1979). Fairness and preference. *Journal of Experimental Social Psychology, 15,* 418–434.

Michaels, J. W., Blommel, J. M., Brocato, R. M., Linkous, R. A., & Rowe, J. S. (1982). Social facilitation and inhibition in a natural setting. *Replications in Social Psychology, 2,* 21–24.

Miell, E., Duck, S., & La Gaipa, J. (1979). Interactive effects of sex and timing in self disclosure. *British Journal of Social and Clinical Psychology, 18,* 355–362.

Mikula, G. (1984). Justice and fairness in interpersonal relations: Thoughts and suggestions. In H. Taijfel (Ed.), *The social dimension: European developments in social psychology,* Vol. 1, Cambridge: Cambridge Univ. Press.

Milgram, S. (1965). Some conditions of obedience and disobedience to authority. *Human Relations, 18,* 57–76.

Milgram, S. (1974). *Obedience to authority.* New York: Harper & Row.

Milgram, S., & Sabini, J. (1983). On maintaining social norms: A field experiment in the subway. In H. H. Blumberg, A. P. Hare, V. Kent, and M. Davies (Eds.), *Small groups and social interaction,* Vol. 1. London: Wiley.

Miller, A. (trans. H. & H. Hannum) (1990). *For your own good: Hidden cruelty in child-rearing and the roots of violence.* New York: Noonday.

Miller, A. G. (1986). *The obedience experiments: A case study of controversy in social science.* New York: Praeger.

Miller, A. G., Ashton, W., & Mishal, M. (1990). Beliefs concerning the features of constrained behavior: A basis for the fundamental attribution error. *Journal of Personality and Social Psychology, 59,* 635–650.

Miller, A. G., Gillen, G., Schenker, C., & Radlove, S. (1973). Perception of obedience to authority. *Proceedings of the 81st annual convention of the American Psychological Association, 8,* 127–128.

Miller, D. T., Taylor, B., & Buck, M. L. (1991). Gender gaps: Who needs to be explained? *Journal of Personality and Social Psychology, 61,* 5–12.

MILLER, D. T., & TURNBULL, W. (1986). Expectancies and interpersonal processes. In M. R. Rosenzweig & L. W. Porter (Eds.), *Annual review of psychology*, Vol. 37. Palo Alto: Annual Reviews.

MILLER, J. B. (1986). *Toward a new psychology of women* (2nd ed.). Boston, MA:

MILLER, J. G. (1984). Culture and the development of everyday social explanation. *Journal of Personality and Social Psychology, 46*, 961–978.

MILLER, K. I., & MONGE, P. R. (1986). Participation, satisfaction, and productivity: A meta-analytic review. *Academy of Management Journal, 29*, 727–753.

MILLER, L. C., BERG, J. H., & ARCHER, R. L. (1983). Openers: Individuals who elicit intimate self-disclosure. *Journal of Personality and Social Psychology, 44*, 12 34–1244.

MILLER, N., & MARKS, G. (1982). Assumed similarity between self and other: Effect of expectation of future interaction with that other. *Social Psychology Quarterly, 45*, 100–105.

MILLER, N. E. (1941). The frustration-aggression hypothesis. *Psychological Review, 48*, 337–342.

MILLER, N. E., & BUGELSKI, R. (1948). Minor studies of aggression: II. The influence of frustrations imposed by the in-group on attitudes expressed toward out-groups. *Journal of Psychology, 25*, 437–442.

MILLER, P. A., & EISENBERG, N. (1988). The relation of empathy to aggressive and externalizing/antisocial behavior. *Psychological Bulletin, 103*, 324–344.

MILLER, P. C., LEFCOURT, H. M., HOLMES, J. G., WARE, E. E., & SALEY, W. E. (1986). Marital locus of control and marital problem solving. *Journal of Personality and Social Psychology, 51*, 161–169.

MILLER, R. L., BRICKMAN, P., & BOLEN, D. (1975). Attribution versus persuasion as a means for modifying behavior. *Journal of Personality and Social Psychology, 31*, 430–441.

MILLER, R. S., & SCHLENKER, B. R. (1985). Egotism in group members: Public and private attributions of responsibility for group performance. *Social Psychology Quarterly, 48*, 85–89.

MILLER, R. S., & SIMPSON, J. A. (1990). Relationship satisfaction and attentiveness to alternatives. Paper presented at the American Psychological Association convention.

MILLETT, K. (1975, January). The shame is over. *Ms.*, pp. 26–29.

MINARD, R. D. (1952). Race relationships in the Pocohontas coal field. *Journal of Social Issues, 8*(1), 29–44.

MIRELS, H. L., & McPEEK, R. W. (1977). Self-advocacy and self-esteem. *Journal of Consulting and Clinical Psychology, 45*, 1132–1138.

MITA, T. H., DERMER, M., & KNIGHT, J. (1977). Reversed facial images and the mere-exposure hypothesis. *Journal of Personality and Social Psychology, 35*, 597–601.

MONSON, T. C., & SNYDER, M. (1977). Actors, observers, and the attribution process: Toward a reconceptualization. *Journal of Experimental Social Psychology, 13*, 89–111.

MOODY, K. (1980). *Growing up on television: The TV effect*. New York: Times.

MOORE, D. L., & BARON, R. S. (1983). Social facilitation: A physiological analysis. In J. T. Cacioppo & R. Petty (Eds.), *Social psychophysiology*. New York: Guilford.

MORRISON, D. M. (1989). Predicting contraceptive efficacy: A discriminant analysis of three groups of adolescent women. *Journal of Applied Social Psychology,* *19,* 1431–1452.

MORSE, S. J., & GRUZEN, J. (1976). The eye of the beholder: A neglected variable in the study of physical attractiveness. *Journal of Psychology, 44,* 209–225.

MOSCOVICI, S. (1985). Social influence and conformity. In G. Lindzey & E. Aronson (Eds.), *The handbook of social psychology* (3rd ed.). Hillsdale, NJ: Erlbaum.

MOSCOVICI, S., LAGE, S., & NAFFRECHOUX, M. (1969). Influence of a consistent minority on the responses of a majority in a color perception task. *Sociometry, 32,* 365–380.

MOSCOVICI, S., & ZAVALLONI, M. (1969). The group as a polarizer of attitudes. *Journal of Personality and Social Psychology, 12,* 124–135.

MOYER, K. E. (1976). *The psychobiology of aggression.* New York: Harper & Row.

MOYER, K. E. (1983). The physiology of motivation: Aggression as a model. In C. J. Scheier & A. M. Rogers (Eds.), *G. Stanley Hall Lecture Series,* Vol. 3. Washington, DC: American Psychological Association.

MUCCHI-FAINA, A., MAASS, A., & VOLPATO, C. (1991). Social influence: The role of originality. *European Journal of Social Psychology, 21,* 183–197.

MUELLER, C. W., DONNERSTEIN, E., & HALLAM, J. (1983). Violent films and prosocial behavior. *Personality and Social Psychology Bulletin, 9,* 83–89.

MULLEN, B. (1986a). Atrocity as a function of lynch mob composition: A self-attention perspective. *Personality and Social Psychology Bulletin, 12,* 187–197.

MULLEN, B. (1986b). Stuttering, audience size, and the other-total ratio: A self-attention perspective. *Journal of Applied Social Psychology, 16,* 139–149.

MULLEN, B. (1991). Group composition, salience, and cognitive representations: The phenomenology of being in a group. *Journal of Experimental Social psychology, 27,* 297–323.

MULLEN, B., & BAUMEISTER, R. F. (1987). Group effects on self-attention and performance: Social loafing, social facilitation, and social impairment. In C. Hendrick (Ed.), *Group processes and intergroup relations: Review of personality and social psychology,* Vol. 9. Newbury Park, CA: Sage.

MULLEN, B., & GOETHALS, G. R. (1990). Social projection, actual consensus and valence. *British Journal of Social Psychology, 29,* 279–282.

MULLEN, B., & RIORDAN, C. A. (1988). Self-serving attributions for performance in naturalistic settings: A meta-analytic review. *Journal of Applied Social Psychology, 18,* 3–22.

MULLEN, B., SALAS, E., & DRISKELL, J. E. (1989). Salience, motivation, and artifact as contributions to the relation between participation rate and leadership. *Journal of Experimental Social Psychology, 25,* 545–559.

MULLER, S., & JOHNSON, B. T. (1990). Fear and persuasion: A linear relationship? Paper presented to the Eastern Psychological Association convention.

MUMFORD, M. D. (1986). Leadership in the organizational context: A conceptual approach and its applications. *Journal of Applied Social Psychology, 16,* 508–531.

MURPHY, C. (1990). New findings: Hold on to your hat. *The Atlantic, 265*(6), 22–23.

MURPHY-BERMAN, V., & SHARMA, R. (1986). Testing the assumptions of attribution theory in India. *Journal of Social Psychology, 126,* 607–616.

MURRAY, J. P., & LONNBORG, B. (1989). Using TV sensibly. Cooperative Extension Service, Kansas State University.

MURSTEIN, B. L. (1986). *Paths to marriage.* Newbury Park, CA: Sage.

Muson, G. (1978, March). Teenage violence and the telly. *Psychology Today*, pp. 50–54.

Myers, D. G. (1992a). *Psychology* (3rd ed.). New York: Worth.

Myers, D. G. (1992b). *The pursuit of happiness: Who is happy—and why*. New York: William Morrow.

Myers, D. G. (1993). *Social psychology* (4th ed.). New York: McGraw-Hill.

Myers, D. G., & Bach, P. J. (1976). Group discussion effects on conflict behavior and self-justification. *Psychological Reports, 38*, 135–140.

Myers, D. G., & Bishop, G. D. (1970). Discussion effects on racial attitudes. *Science, 169*, 778–789.

Nadler, A., Goldberg, M., & Jaffe, Y. (1982). Effect of self-differentiation and anonymity in group on deindividuation. *Journal of Personality and Social Psychology, 42*, 1127–1136.

Nagar, D., & Pandey, J. (1987). Affect and performance on cognitive task as a function of crowding and noise. *Journal of Applied Social Psychology, 17*, 147–157.

Napolitan, D. A., & Goethals, G. R. (1979). The attribution of friendliness. *Journal of Experimental Social Psychology, 15*, 105–113.

National Safety Council (1991). *Accident facts*. Chicago.

Naylor, T. H. (1990). Redefining corporate motivation, Swedish style. *Christian Century, 107*, 566–570.

NBC News Poll (1977, November 29–30). Cited by *Public Opinion*, January–February, 1979, p. 36.

NCTV (1988). TV and film alcohol research. *NCTV News, 9*(3–4), 4.

Neimeyer, G. J., MacNair, R., Metzler, A. E., & Courchaine, K. (1991). Changing personal beliefs: Effects of forewarning, argument quality, prior bias, and personal exploration. *Journal of Social and Clinical Psychology, 10*, 1–20.

Nemeth, C. (1979). The role of an active minority in intergroup relations. In W. G. Austin and S. Worchel (Eds.), *The social psychology of intergroup relations*. Monterey, CA: Brooks/Cole.

Nemeth, C. (1986). Intergroup relations between majority and minority. In S. Worchel and W. G. Austin (Eds.), *Psychology of intergroup relations*. Chicago: Nelson-Hall.

Nemeth, C., & Wachtler, J. (1974). Creating the perceptions of consistency and confidence: A necessary condition for minority influence. *Sociometry, 37*, 529–540.

Nemeth, C. J. (1992). Minority dissent as a stimulant to group performance. In S. P. Worchel, W. Wood, & Simpson, J. L. (Eds.), *Group process and productivity*. Newbury Park, CA: Sage.

Newcomb, T. M. (1961). *The acquaintance process*. New York: Holt, Rinehart & Winston.

Newman, H. M., & Langer, E. J. (1981). Post-divorce adaptation and the attribution of responsibility. *Sex Roles, 7*, 223–231.

Nias, D. K. B. (1979). Marital choice: Matching or complementation? In M. Cook and G. Wilson (Eds.), *Love and attraction*. Oxford: Pergamon.

Niemi, R. G., Mueller, J., & Smith, T. W. (1989). *Trends in public opinion: A compendium of survey data*. New York: Greenwood.

Nisbett, R. (1988, Fall). The Vincennes incident: Congress hears psychologists. *Science Agenda* (American Psychological Association), p. 4.

NISBETT, R. E., BORGIDA, E., CRANDALL, R., & REED, H. (1976). Popular induction: Information is not necessarily informative. In J. S. Carroll and J. W. Payne (Eds.), *Cognition and social behavior.* Hillsdale, NJ: Erlbaum.

NISBETT, R. E., & ROSS, L. (1991). *The person and the situation.* New York: McGraw-Hill.

NISBETT, R. E., & SCHACHTER, S. (1966). Cognitive manipulation of pain. *Journal of Experimental Social Psychology, 2,* 227–236.

NISBETT, R. E., & SMITH, M. (1989). Predicting interpersonal attraction from small samples: A reanalysis of Newcomb's acquaintance study. *Social Cognition, 7,* 67–73.

NISBETT, R. E., & WILSON, T. D. (1977). Telling more than we can know: Verbal reports on mental processes. *Psychological Review, 84,* 231–259.

NOEL, J. G., FORSYTH, D. R., & KELLEY, K. N. (1987). Improving the performance of failing students by overcoming their self-serving attributional biases. *Basic and Applied Social Psychology, 8,* 151–162.

NOLEN-HOEKSEMA, S., GIRGUS, J. S., & SELIGMAN, M. E. P. (1986). Learned helplessness in children: A longitudinal study of depression, achievement, and explanatory style. *Journal of Personality and Social Psychology, 51,* 435–442.

NOLLER, P., & FITZPATRICK, M. A. (1990). Marital communication in the eighties. *Journal of Marriage and the Family, 52,* 832–843.

NOREM, J. K., & CANTOR, N. (1986). Defensive pessimism: Harnessing anxiety as motivation. *Journal of Personality and Social Psychology, 51,* 1208–1217.

NUTTIN, J. M., JR. (1987). Affective consequences of mere ownership: The name letter effect in twelve European languages. *European Journal of Social Psychology, 17,* 318–402.

O'DEA, T. F. (1968). Sects and cults. In D. L. Sills (Ed.), *International encyclopedia of the social sciences,* Vol. 14. New York: Macmillan.

O'GORMAN, H. J., & GARRY, S. L. (1976). Pluralistic ignorance—A replication and extension. *Public Opinion Quarterly, 40,* 449–458.

OHBUCHI, K., & KAMBARA, T. (1985). Attacker's intent and awareness of outcome, impression management, and retaliation. *Journal of Experimental Social Psychology, 21,* 321–330.

OKUN, M. A., & STOCK, W. A. (1987). Correlates and components of subjective well-being among the elderly. *Journal of Applied Gerontology, 6,* 95–112.

OLSON, J. M., & ZANNA, M. P. (1981, November). Promoting physical activity: A social psychological perspective. Report prepared for the Ministry of Culture and Recreation, Sports and Fitness Branch, 77 Bloor St. West, 8th Floor, Toronto, Ontario M7A 2R9.

OLWEUS, D. (1979). Stability of aggressive reaction patterns in males: A review. *Psychological Bulletin, 86,* 852–875.

OLWEUS, D., MATTSSON, A., SCHALLING, D., & LOW, H. (1988). Circulating testosterone levels and aggression in adolescent males: A causal analysis. *Psychosomatic Medicine, 50,* 261–272.

ORBELL, J. M., VAN DE KRAGT, A. J. C., & DAWES, R. M. (1988). Explaining discussion-induced cooperation. *Journal of Personality and Social Psychology, 54,* 811–819.

ORIVE, R. (1984). Group similarity, public self-awareness, and opinion extremity: A social projection explanation of deindividuation effects. *Journal of Personality and Social Psychology, 47,* 727–737.

ORNSTEIN, R. (1991). *The evolution of consciousness.* New York: Prentice-Hall.

OSBERG, T. M., & SHRAUGER, J. S. (1986). Self-prediction: Exploring the parameters of accuracy. *Journal of Personality and Social Psychology, 51,* 1044–1057.

OSGOOD, C. E. (1962). *An alternative to war or surrender.* Urbana: Univ. of Illinois Press.

OSGOOD, C. E. (1980). GRIT: A strategy for survival in mankind's nuclear age? Paper presented at the Pugwash Conference on New Directions in Disarmament, Racine, Wis.

OSKAMP, S. (1991). Curbside recycling: Knowledge, attitudes, and behavior. Paper presented at the Society for Experimental Social Psychology meeting, Columbus, Ohio.

OSTERHOUSE, R. A., & BROCK, T. C. (1970). Distraction increases yielding to propaganda by inhibiting counterarguing. *Journal of Personality and Social Psychology, 15,* 344–358.

OZER, E. M., & BANDURA, A. (1990). Mechanisms governing empowerment effects: A self-efficacy analysis. *Journal of Personality and Social Psychology, 58,* 472–486.

PADGETT, V. R. (1989). Predicting organizational violence: An application of 11 powerful principles of obedience. Paper presented at the American Psychological Association convention.

PAK, A. W., DION, K. L., & DION, K. K. (1991). Social-psychological correlates of experienced discrimination: Test of the double jeopardy hypothesis. *International Journal of Intercultural Relations, 15,* 243–254.

PALLAK, S. R., MURRONI, E., & KOCH, J. (1983). Communicator attractiveness and expertise, emotional versus rational appeals, and persuasion: A heuristic versus systematic processing interpretation. *Social Cognition, 2,* 122–141.

PALMER, E. L., & DORR, A. (Eds.) (1980). *Children and the faces of television: Teaching, violence, selling.* New York: Academic Press.

PANDEY, J., SINHA, Y., PRAKASH, A., & TRIPATHI, R. C. (1982). Right-left political ideologies and attribution of the causes of poverty. *European Journal of Social Psychology, 12,* 327–331.

PAPASTAMOU, S., & MUGNY, G. (1990). Synchronic consistency and psychologization in minority influence. *European Journal of Social Psychology, 20,* 85–98.

PARKE, R. D., BERKOWITZ, L., LEYENS, J. P., WEST, S. G., & SEBASTIAN, J. (1977). Some effects of violent and nonviolent movies on the behavior of juvenile delinquents. In L. Berkowitz (Ed.), *Advances in experimental social psychology,* Vol. 10. New York: Academic Press.

PASCAL, B. (1670/1965). *Thoughts* (trans. W. F. Trotter). In M. Mack (Ed.), *World masterpieces.* New York: Norton.

PASCARELLA, E. T., & TERENZINI, P. T. (1991). *How college affects students: Findings and insights from twenty years of research.* San Francisco: Jossey-Bass.

PATTERSON, G. R., LITTMAN, R. A., & BRICKER, W. (1967). Assertive behavior in children: A step toward a theory of aggression. *Monographs of the Society of Research in Child Development* (Serial No. 113), *32,* 5.

PATTERSON, T. E. (1980). The role of the mass media in presidential campaigns: The lessons of the 1976 election. *Items, 34,* 25–30. Social Science Research Council, 605 Third Avenue, New York, N.Y. 10016.

PELHAM, B. W. (1991). On the benefits of misery: Self-serving biases in the depressive self-concept. *Journal of Personality and Social Psychology, 61,* 670–681.

PENNEBAKER, J. (1990) *Opening up: The healing power of confiding in others*. New York: William Morrow.

PEPLAU, L. A., & GORDON, S. L. (1985). Women and men in love: Gender differences in close heterosexual relationships. In V. E. O'Leary, R. K. Unger, & B. S. Wallston (Eds.), *Women, gender, and social psychology*. Hillsdale, NJ: Erlbaum.

PERDUE, C. W., DOVIDIO, J. F., GURTMAN, M. B., & TYLER, R. B. (1990). Us and them: Social categorization and the process of intergroup bias. *Journal of Personality and Social Psychology, 59*, 475–486.

PERLOFF, L. S. (1987). Social comparison and illusions of invulnerability. In C. R. Snyder & C. R. Ford (Eds.), *Coping with negative life events: Clinical and social psychological perspectives*. New York: Plenum.

PERLOFF, R. M., & BROCK, T. C. (1980). ". . . And thinking makes it so": Cognitive responses to persuasion. In M. E. Roloff & G. R. Miller (Eds.), *Persuasion: New directions in theory and research*. Beverly Hills, CA: Sage.

PERLS, F. S. (1973, July). *Ego, hunger and aggression: The beginning of Gestalt therapy*. Random House, 1969. Cited by Berkowitz, The case for bottling up rage. *Psychology Today*, pp. 24–30.

PESSIN, J. (1933). The comparative effects of social and mechanical stimulation on memorizing. *American Journal of Psychology, 45*, 263–270.

PESSIN, J., & HUSBAND, R. W. (1933). Effects of social stimulation on human maze learning. *Journal of Abnormal and Social Psychology, 28*, 148–154.

PETERSON, C., & BARRETT, L. C. (1987). Explanatory style and academic performance among university freshmen. *Journal of Personality and Social Psychology, 53*, 603–607.

PETERSON, C., SCHWARTZ, S. M., & SELIGMAN, M. E. P. (1981). Self-blame and depression symptoms. *Journal of Personality and Social Psychology, 41*, 253–259.

PETERSON, C., & SELIGMAN, M. E. P. (1987). Explanatory style and illness. *Journal of Personality, 55*, 237–265.

PETERSON, C., SELIGMAN, M. E. P., & VAILLANT, G. E. (1988). Pessimistic explanatory style is a risk factor for physical illness: A thirty-five-year longitudinal study. *Journal of Personality and Social Psychology, 55*, 23–27.

PETTIGREW, T., & MEERTENS, R. (1991). Relative deprivation and intergroup prejudice. Unpublished manuscript, Univ. of Amsterdam.

PETTIGREW, T. F. (1958). Personality and socio-cultural factors in intergroup attitudes: A cross-national comparison. *Journal of Conflict Resolution, 2*, 29–42.

PETTIGREW, T. F. (1969). Racially separate or together? *Journal of Social Issues, 2*, 43–69.

PETTIGREW, T. F. (1978). Three issues in ethnicity: Boundaries, deprivations, and perceptions. In J. M. Yinger & S. J. Cutler (Eds.), *Major social issues: A multidisciplinary view*. New York: Free Press.

PETTIGREW, T. F. (1986). The intergroup contact hypothesis reconsidered. In M. Hewstone & R. Brown (Eds.), *Contact and conflict in intergroup encounters*. Oxford: Basil Blackwell.

PETTIGREW, T. F. (1987, May 12). "Useful" modes of thought contribute to prejudice. *The New York Times*, pp. 17–20.

PETTIGREW, T. F. (1988). Advancing racial justice: Past lessons for future use. Paper for the Univ. of Alabama Conference: "Opening Doors: An Appraisal of Race Relations in America."

PETTINGALE, K. W., MORRIS, T., GREER, S., & HAYBITTLE, J. L. (1985, March 30). Mental attitudes to cancer: An additional prognostic factor. *Lancet*, p. 750.

PETTY, R. E., & CACIOPPO, J. T. (1977). Forewarning cognitive responding, and resistance to persuasion. *Journal of Personality and Social Psychology, 35*, 645–655.

PETTY, R. E., & CACIOPPO, J. T. (1979a). Effects of forewarning of persuasive intent and involvement on cognitive response and persuasion. *Personality and Social Psychology Bulletin, 5*, 173–176.

PETTY, R. E., & CACIOPPO, J. T. (1979b). Issue involvement can increase or decrease persuasion by enhancing message-relevant cognitive responses. *Journal of Personality and Social Psychology, 37*, 1915–1926.

PETTY, R. E., & CACIOPPO, J. T. (1986). *Communication and persuasion: Central and peripheral routes to attitude change.* New York: Springer-Verlag.

PETTY, R. E., CACIOPPO, J. T., & GOLDMAN, R. (1981). Personal involvement as a determinant of argument-based persuasion. *Journal of Personality and Social Psychology, 41*, 847–855.

PETTY, R. E., GLEICHER, F., & BAKER, S. M. (1991). Multiple roles for affect in persuasion. In J. Forgas (Ed.), *Emotion and social judgments.* London: Pergamon.

PHILLIPS, D. P. (1985). Natural experiments on the effects of mass media violence on fatal aggression: Strengths and weaknesses of a new approach. In L. Berkowitz (Ed.), *Advances in experimental social psychology*, Vol. 19. Orlando, FL: Academic Press.

PHILLIPS, D. P., CARSTENSEN, L. L., & PAIGHT, D. J. (1989). Effects of mass media news stories on suicide, with new evidence on the role of story content. In D. R. Pfeffer (Ed.), *Suicide among youth: Perspectives on risk and prevention.* Washington, DC: American Psychiatric Press.

PLATZ, S. J., & HOSCH, H. M. (1988). Cross-racial/ethnic eyewitness identification: A field study. *Journal of Applied Social Psychology, 18*, 972–984.

PLINER, P., HART, H., KOHL, J., & SAARI, D. (1974). Compliance without pressure: Some further data on the foot-in-the-door technique. *Journal of Experimental Social Psychology, 10*, 17–22.

POMERLEAU, O. F., & RODIN, J. (1986). Behavioral medicine and health psychology. In S. L. Garfield & A. E. Bergin (Eds.), *Handbook of psychotherapy and behavior change* (3rd ed.). New York: Wiley.

PORTER, N., GEIS, F. L., & JENNINGS (WALSTEDT), J. (1983). Are women invisible as leaders? *Sex Roles, 9*, 1035–1049.

POWELL, J. (1989). *Happiness is an inside job.* Valencia, CA: Tabor.

POWELL, J. L. (1988). A test of the knew-it-all-along effect in the 1984 presidential and statewide elections. *Journal of Applied Social Psychology, 18*, 760–773.

POZO, C., CARVER, C. S., WELLENS, A. R., & SCHEIER, M. F. (1991). Social anxiety and social perception: Construing others' reactions to the self. *Personality and Social Psychology Bulletin, 17*, 355–362.

PRAGER, I. G., & CUTLER, B. L. (1990). Attributing traits to oneself and to others: The role of acquaintance level. *Personality and Social Psychology Bulletin, 16*, 309–319.

PRATKANIS, A. R., GREENWALD, A. G., LEIPPE, M. R., & BAUMGARDNER, M. H. (1988). In search of reliable persuasion effects: III. The sleeper effect is dead. Long live the sleeper effect. *Journal of Personality and Social Psychology, 54*, 203–218.

Pratt, M. W., Pancer, M., Hunsberger, B., & Manchester, J. (1990). Reasoning about the self and relationships in maturity: An integrative complexity analysis of individual differences. *Journal of Personality and Social Psychology, 59*, 575–581.

Prentice-Dunn, S., & Rogers, R. W. (1980). Effects of deindividuating situational cues and aggressive models on subjective deindividuation and aggression. *Journal of Personality and Social Psychology, 39*, 104–113.

Prentice-Dunn, S., & Rogers, R. W. (1989). Deindividuation and the self-regulation of behavior. In P. B. Paulus (Ed.), *Psychology of group influence* (2nd ed.). Hillsdale, NJ: Erlbaum.

Price, G. H., Dabbs, J. M., Jr., Clower, B. J., & Resin, R. P. (1974). At first glance—Or, is physical attractiveness more than skin deep? Paper presented at the Eastern Psychological Association convention. Cited by K. L. Dion & K. K. Dion. Personality and behavioral correlates of romantic love. In M. Cook & G. Wilson (Eds.), *Love and attraction.* Oxford: Pergamon, 1979.

Pruitt, D. G. (1981a). Kissinger as a traditional mediator with power. In J. Z. Rubin (Ed.), *Dynamics of third party intervention: Kissinger in the Middle East.* New York: Praeger.

Pruitt, D. G. (1981b). *Negotiation behavior.* New York: Academic Press.

Pruitt, D. G. (1986, July). Trends in the scientific study of negotiation. *Negotiation Journal*, pp. 237–244.

Pruitt, D. G. (1986). Achieving integrative agreements in negotiation. In R. K. White (Ed.), *Psychology and the prevention of nuclear war.* New York: New York Univ. Press.

Pruitt, D. G., & Kimmel, M. J. (1977). Twenty years of experimental gaming: Critique, synthesis, and suggestions for the future. *Annual Review of Psychology, 28*, 363–392.

Pruitt, D. G., & Lewis, S. A. (1975). Development of integrative solutions in bilateral negotiation. *Journal of Personality and Social Psychology, 31*, 621–633.

Pruitt, D. G., & Lewis, S. A. (1977). The psychology of integrative bargaining. In D. Druckman (Ed.), *Negotiations: A social-psychological analysis.* New York: Halsted.

Pruitt, D. G., & Rubin, J. Z. (1986). *Social conflict.* San Francisco: Random House.

Pryor, J. B. (1987). Sexual harassment proclivities in men. *Sex Roles, 17*, 269–290.

Public Opinion (1984, August/September). Need vs. greed (summary of Roper Report 84-1), p. 25.

Public Opinion (1984, August/September). Vanity fare, p. 22.

Purvis, J. A., Dabbs, J. M., Jr., & Hopper, C. H. (1984). The "opener": Skilled user of facial expression and speech pattern. *Personality and Social Psychology Bulletin, 10*, 61–66.

Pyszczynski, T., & Greenberg, J. (1983). Determinants of reduction in intended effort as a strategy for coping with anticipated failure. *Journal of Research in Personality, 17*, 412–422.

Pyszczynski, T., Greenberg, J., & Holt, K. (1985). Maintaining consistency between self-serving beliefs and available data: A bias in information evaluation. *Personality and Social Psychology Bulletin, 11*, 179–190.

Pyszczynski, T., Hamilton, J. C., Greenberg, J., & Becker, S. E. (1991). Self-awareness and psychological dysfunction. In C. R. Snyder & D. O. Forsyth (Eds.), *Handbook of social and clinical psychology: The health perspective.* New York: Pergamon.

QUATTRONE, G. A. (1982). Behavioral consequences of attributional bias. *Social Cognition, 1,* 358–378.

QUATTRONE, G. A., & JONES, E. E. (1980). The perception of variability within in-groups and out-groups: Implications for the law of small numbers. *Journal of Personality and Social Psychology, 38,* 141–152.

RADECKI, T. (1989, February–March). On picking good television and film enter-tainment. *NCTV NEWS, 10*(1–2), pp. 5–6.

RAMIREZ, A. (1988). Racism toward Hispanics: The culturally monolithic society. In P. A. Katz & D. A. Taylor (Eds.) *Eliminating racism: Profiles in controversy.* New York: Plenum.

RANK, S. G., & JACOBSON, C. K. (1977). Hospital nurses' compliance with medica-tion overdose orders: A failure to replicate. *Journal of Health and Social Behavior, 18,* 188–193.

RAPOPORT, A. (1960). *Fights, games, and debates.* Ann Arbor: Univ. of Michigan Press.

RCAGENDA (1979, November–December). P. 11. 475 Riverside Drive, New York, N.Y. 10027.

REEDER, G. D., FLETCHER, G. J., & FURMAN, K. (1989). The role of observers' expectations in attitude attribution. *Journal of Experimental Social Psychology, 25,* 168–188.

REGAN, D. T., & CHENG, J. B. (1973). Distraction and attitude change: A resolu-tion. *Journal of Experimental Social Psychology, 9,* 138–147.

REIFMAN, A. S., LARRICK, R. P., & FEIN, S. (1991). Temper and temperature on the diamond: The heat-aggression relationship in major league baseball. *Per-sonality and Social Psychology Bulletin, 17,* 580–585.

REIS, H. T., NEZLEK, J., & WHEELER, L. (1980). Physical attractiveness in social interaction. *Journal of Personality and Social Psychology, 38,* 604–617.

REIS, H. T., & SHAVER, P. (1988). Intimacy as an interpersonal process. In S. Duck (Ed.), *Handbook of personal relationships: Theory, relationships and interventions.* Chichester, England: Wiley.

REIS, H. T., WHEELER, L., SPIEGEL, N., KERNIS, M. H., NEZLEK, J., & PERRI, M. (1982). Physical attractiveness in social interaction: II. Why does appearance affect social experience? *Journal of Personality and Social Psychology, 43,* 979–996.

REITZES, D. C. (1953). The role of organizational structures: Union versus neigh-borhood in a tension situation. *Journal of Social Issues, 9*(1), 37–44.

REMLEY, A. (1988, October). From obedience to independence. *Psychology Today,* pp. 56–59.

RENAUD, H., & ESTESS, F. (1961). Life history interviews with one hundred normal American males: "Pathogenicity" of childhood. *American Journal of Ortho-psychiatry, 31,* 786–802.

RESSLER, R. K., BURGESS, A. W., & DOUGLAS, J. E. (1988). *Sexual homicide patterns.* Boston: Lexington.

RHODEWALT, F. (1987). Is self-handicapping an effective self-protective attribu-tional strategy? Paper presented at the American Psychological Association convention.

RHODEWALT, F., & AGUSTSDOTTIR, S. (1986). Effects of self-presentation on the phenomenal self. *Journal of Personality and Social Psychology, 50,* 47–55.

RHODEWALT, F., SALTZMAN, A. T., & WITTMER J. (1984). Self-handicapping among competitive athletes: The role of practice in self-esteem protection. *Basic and Applied Social Psychology*, *5*, 197–209.

RHOLES, W. S., NEWMAN, L. S., & RUBLE, D. N. (1990). Understanding self and other: Developmental and motivational aspects of perceiving persons in terms of invariant dispositions. In E. T. Higgins & R. M. Sorrentino (Eds.), *Handbook of motivation and cognition: Foundations of social behavior*, Vol. 2. New York: Guilford.

RICE, B. (1985, September). Performance review: The job nobody likes. *Psychology Today*, pp. 30–36.

RICHARDSON, L. F. (1969). Generalized foreign policy. *British Journal of Psychology Monographs Supplements*, *23*. Cited by A. Rapoport in *Fights, games, and debates*. Ann Arbor: Univ. of Michigan Press, 1960, p. 15.

RIESS, M., ROSENFELD, P., MELBURG, V., & TEDESCHI, J. T. (1981). Self-serving attributions: Biased private perceptions and distorted public descriptions. *Journal of Personality and Social Psychology*, *41*, 224–231.

ROBBERSON, M. R., & ROGERS, R. W. (1988). Beyond fear appeals: Negative and positive persuasive appeals to health and self-esteem. *Journal of Applied Social Psychology*, *18*, 277–287.

ROBINS, L. N., & REGIER, D. A. (Eds.) (1991). *Psychiatric disorders in America*. New York: Free Press.

ROBINSON, C. L., LOCKARD, J. S., & ADAMS, R. M. (1979). Who looks at a baby in public. *Ethology and Sociobiology*, *1*, 87–91.

ROBINSON, J. P. (1988, December). Who's doing the housework? *American Demographics*, pp. 24–28, 63.

ROBINSON, R. J., KELTNER, D., & ROSS, L. (1991). Misconstruing the views of the "other side": Real and perceived differences in three ideological conflicts. Working Paper No. 18, Stanford Center on Conflict and Negotiation, Stanford Univ.

ROGERS, C. R. (1958). Reinhold Niebuhr's *The self and the dramas of history*: A criticism. *Pastoral Psychology*, *9*, 15–17.

ROGERS, C. R. (1980). *A way of being*. Boston: Houghton Mifflin.

ROGERS, R. W., & MEWBORN, C. R. (1976). Fear appeals and attitude change: Effects of a threat's noxiousness, probability of occurrence, and the efficacy of coping responses. *Journal of Personality and Social Psychology*, *34*, 54–61.

ROGERS, R. W., & PRENTICE-DUNN, S. (1981). Deindividuation and anger-mediated interracial aggression: Unmasking regressive racism. *Journal of Personality and Social Psychology*, *41*, 63–73.

ROKEACH, M., & MEZEI, L. (1966). Race and shared beliefs as factors in social choice. *Science*, *151*, 167–172.

ROOK, K. S. (1984). Promoting social bonding: Strategies for helping the lonely and socially isolated. *American Psychologist*, *39*, 1389–1407.

ROSENFELD, D. (1979). The relationship between self-esteem and egotism in males and females. Unpublished manuscript, Southern Methodist University.

ROSENHAN, D. L. (1973). On being sane in insane places. *Science*, *179*, 250–258.

ROSENTHAL, R. (1985). From unconscious experimenter bias to teacher expectancy effects. In J. B. Dusek, V. C. Hall, & W. J. Meyer (Eds.), *Teacher expectancies*. Hillsdale, NJ: Erlbaum.

ROSENTHAL, R. (1991). Teacher expectancy effects: A brief update 25 years after the Pygmalion experiment. *Journal of Research in Education, 1,* 3–12.

ROSENZWEIG, M. R. (1972). Cognitive dissonance. *American Psychologist, 27,* 769.

ROSS, L. D. (1977). The intuitive psychologist and his shortcomings: Distortions in the attribution process. In L. Berkowitz (Ed.), *Advances in experimental social psychology,* Vol. 10. New York: Academic Press.

ROSS, L. D. (1981). The "intuitive scientist" formulation and its developmental implications. In J. H. Havell & L. Ross (Eds.), *Social cognitive development: Frontiers and possible futures.* Cambridge, England: Cambridge Univ. Press.

ROSS, L. D. (1988). Situationist perspectives on the obedience experiments. Review of A. G. Miller's *The obedience experiments. Contemporary Psychology, 33,* 101–104.

ROSS, L. D., AMABILE, T. M., & STEINMETZ, J. L. (1977). Social roles, social control, and biases in social-perception processes. *Journal of Personality and Social Psychology, 35,* 485–494.

ROSS, M., & FLETCHER, G. J. O. (1985). Attribution and social perception. In G. Lindzey & E. Aronson (Eds.), *The handbook of social psychology,* (3rd ed.). New York: Random House.

ROSS, M., McFARLAND, C., & FLETCHER, G. J. O. (1981). The effect of attitude on the recall of personal histories. *Journal of Personality and Social Psychology, 40,* 627–634.

ROSS, M., & SICOLY, F. (1979). Egocentric biases in availability and attribution. *Journal of Personality and Social Psychology, 37,* 322–336.

ROSS, M., THIBAUT, J., & EVENBECK, S. (1971). Some determinants of the intensity of social protest. *Journal of Experimental Social Psychology, 7,* 401–418.

ROSSI, A. (1978, June). The biosocial side of parenthood. *Human Nature,* pp. 72–79.

ROSZELL, P., KENNEDY, D., & GRABB, E. (1990). Physical attractiveness and income attainment among Canadians. *Journal of Psychology, 123,* 547–559.

ROTH, D. L., SNYDER, C. R., & PACE, L. M. (1986). Dimensions of favorable self-presentation. *Journal of Personality and Social Psychology, 51,* 867–874.

ROTHBART, M., & BIRRELL, P. (1977). Attitude and perception of faces. *Journal of Research Personality, 11,* 209–215.

ROTHBART, M., FULERO, S., JENSEN, C., HOWARD, J., & BIRRELL, P. (1978). From individual to group impressions: Availability heuristics in stereotype formation. *Journal of Experimental Social Psychology, 14,* 237–255.

ROTTER, J. (1973). Internal-external locus of control scale. In J. P. Robinson & R. P. Shaver (Eds.), *Measures of social psychological attitudes.* Ann Arbor: Institute for Social Research.

ROTTON, J., & FREY, J. (1985). Air pollution, weather, and violent crimes: Concomitant time-series analysis of archival data. *Journal of Personality and Social Psychology, 49,* 1207–1220.

RUBACK, R. B., CARR, T. S., & HOPER, C. H. (1986). Perceived control in prison: Its relation to reported crowding, stress, and symptoms. *Journal of Applied Social Psychology, 16,* 375–386.

RUBIN, J. Z. (1986). Can we negotiate with terrorists: Some answers from psychology. Paper presented at the American Psychological Association convention.

RUBIN, J. Z. (1989). Some wise and mistaken assumptions about conflict and negotiation. *Journal of Social Issues, 45,* 195–209.

RUBIN, L. B. (1985). *Just friends: The role of friendship in our lives.* New York: Harper & Row.

RUBIN, Z. (1970). Measurement of romantic love. *Journal of Personality and Social Psychology, 16,* 265–273.

RUBIN, Z. (1973). *Liking and loving: An invitation to social psychology.* New York: Holt, Rinehart & Winston.

RULE, B. G., TAYLOR, B. R., & DOBBS, A. R. (1987). Priming effects of heat on aggressive thoughts. *Social Cognition, 5,* 131–143.

RUSBULT, C. E., JOHNSON, D. J., & MORROW, G. D. (1986). Impact of couple patterns of problem solving on distress and nondistress in dating relationships. *Journal of Personality and Social Psychology, 50,* 744–753.

RUSBULT, C. E., MORROW, G. D., & JOHNSON, D. J. (1987). Self-esteem and problem-solving behaviour in close relationships. *British Journal of Social Psychology, 26,* 293–303.

RUSHTON, J. P., FULKER, D. W., NEALE, M. C., NIAS, D. K. B., & EYSENCK, H. J. (1986). Altruism and aggression: The heritability of individual differences. *Journal of Personality and Social Psychology, 50,* 1192–1198.

RUSSELL, B. (1930/1980). *The conquest of happiness.* London: Unwin.

RUSSELL, G. W. (1983). Psychological issues in sports aggression. In J. H. Goldstein (Ed.), *Sports violence.* New York: Springer-Verlag.

RUZZENE, M., & NOLLER, P. (1986). Feedback motivation and reactions to personality interpretations that differ in favorability and accuracy. *Journal of Personality and Social Psychology, 51,* 1293–1299.

SABINI, J., & SILVER, M. (1982). *Moralities of everyday life.* New York: Oxford Univ. Press.

SACCO, W. P., & DUNN, V. K. (1990). Effect of actor depression on observer attributions: Existence and impact of negative attributions toward the depressed. *Journal of Personality and Social Psychology, 59,* 517–524.

SACKS, C. H., & BUGENTAL, D. P. (1987). Attributions as moderators of affective and behavioral responses to social failure. *Journal of Personality and Social Psychology, 53,* 939–947.

SALES, S. M. (1972). Economic threat as a determinant of conversion rates in authoritarian and nonauthoritarian churches. *Journal of Personality and Social Psychology, 23,* 420–428.

SALES, S. M. (1973). Threat as a factor in authoritarianism: An analysis of archival data. *Journal of Personality and Social Psychology, 28,* 44–57.

SALTZMAN, A. (1991, June 17). Trouble at the top. *U.S. News & World Report,* pp. 40–48.

SANDBERG, G. G., JACKSON, T. L., & PETRETIC-JACKSON, P. (1985). Sexual aggression and courtship violence in dating relationships. Paper presented at the Midwestern Psychological Association convention.

SANDE, G. N., GOETHALS, G. R., & RADLOFF, C. E. (1988). Perceiving one's own traits and others': The multifaceted self. *Journal of Personality and Social Psychology, 54,* 13–20.

SANDERS, G. S. (1981a). Driven by distraction: An integrative review of social facilitation and theory and research. *Journal of Experimental Social Psychology, 17,* 227–251.

SANDERS, G. S. (1981b). Toward a comprehensive account of social facilitation: Distraction/conflict does not mean theoretical conflict. *Journal of Experimental Social Psychology, 17,* 262–265.

SANDERS, G. S., & BARON, R. S. (1977). Is social comparison irrelevant for producing choice shifts? *Journal of Experimental Social Psychology, 13,* 303–314.

SANDERS, G. S., BARON, R. S., & MOORE, D. L. (1978). Distraction and social comparison as mediators of social facilitation effects. *Journal of Experimental Social Psychology, 14,* 291–303.

SANISLOW, C. A., III, PERKINS, D. V., & BALOGH, D. W. (1989). Mood induction, interpersonal perceptions, and rejection in the roommates of depressed, nondepressed-disturbed, and normal college students. *Journal of Social and Clinical Psychology, 8,* 345–358.

SAPADIN, L. A. (1988). Friendship and gender: Perspectives of professional men and women. *Journal of Social and Personal Relationships, 5,* 387–403.

SARAWATHI, T. S., & DUTTA, R. (1988). *Invisible boundaries: Grooming for adult roles.* New Delhi: Northern Book Centre. Cited by R. Larson & M. H. Richards (1989). Introduction: The changing life space of early adolescence. *Journal of Youth and Adolescence, 18,* 501–509.

SARNOFF, I., & SARNOFF, S. (1989). *Love-centered marriage in a self-centered world.* New York: Hemisphere.

SCHACHTER, S. (1951). Deviation, rejection and communication. *Journal of Abnormal and Social Psychology, 46,* 190–207.

SCHACHTER, S., & SINGER, J. E. (1962). Cognitive, social and physiological determinants of emotional state. *Psychological Review, 69,* 379–399.

SCHAFER, R. B., & KEITH, P. M. (1980). Equity and depression among married couples. *Social Psychology Quarterly, 43,* 430–435.

SCHAFFNER, P. E., WANDERSMAN, A., & STANG, D. (1981). Candidate name exposure and voting: Two field studies. *Basic and Applied Social Psychology, 2,* 195–203.

SCHEIER, M. F., & CARVER, C. S. (1992). Effects of optimism on psychological and physical well-being: Theoretical overview and empirical update. *Cognitive Therapy and Research,* in press.

SCHEIN, E. H. (1956). The Chinese indoctrination program for prisoners of war: A study of attempted brainwashing. *Psychiatry, 19,* 149–172.

SCHIFFENBAUER, A., & SCHIAVO, R. S. (1976). Physical distance and attraction: An intensification effect. *Journal of Experimental Social Psychology, 12,* 274–282.

SCHLENKER, B. R. (1976). Egocentric perceptions in cooperative groups: A conceptualization and research review. Final Report, Office of Naval Research Grant NR 170-797.

SCHLENKER, B. R., & LEARY, M. R. (1982). Social anxiety and self-presentation: A conceptualization and model. *Psychological Bulletin, 92,* 641–669.

SCHLENKER, B. R., & LEARY, M. R. (1985). Social anxiety and communication about the self. *Journal of Language and Social Psychology, 4,* 171–192.

SCHLENKER, B. R., & MILLER, R. S. (1977a). Group cohesiveness as a determinant of egocentric perceptions in cooperative groups. *Human Relations, 30,* 1039–1055.

SCHLENKER, B. R., & MILLER, R. S. (1977b). Egocentrism in groups: Self-serving biases or logical information processing? *Journal of Personality and Social Psychology, 35,* 755–764.

SCHLENKER, B. R., & WEIGOLD, M. F. (1992). Interpersonal processes involving impression regulation and management. *Annual Review of Psychology, 43.*

SCHLENKER, B. R., WEIGOLD, M. E., & HALLAM, J. R. (1990). Self-serving attributions in social context: Effects of self-esteem and social pressure. *Journal of Personality and Social Psychology, 58,* 855–863.

SCHLESINGER, A., JR. (1949). The statistical soldier. *Partisan Review, 16,* 852–856.

SCHLESINGER, A., JR. (1991, July 8). The cult of ethnicity, good and bad. *Time,* p. 21.

SCHLESINGER, A. M., JR. (1965). *A thousand days.* Boston: Houghton Mifflin. Cited by I. L. Janis, *Victims of groupthink.* Boston: Houghton Mifflin, 1972, p. 40.

SCHOFIELD, J. (1982). *Black and white in school: Trust, tension, or tolerance?* New York: Praeger.

SCHOFIELD, J. W. (1986). Causes and consequences of the colorblind perspective. In J. F. Dovidio & S. L. Gaertner (Eds.), *Prejudice, discrimination, and racism.* Orlando, FL: Academic Press.

SCHULZ, J. W., & PRUITT, D. G. (1978). The effects of mutual concern on joint welfare. *Journal of Experimental Social Psychology, 14,* 480–492.

SCHUMAN, H., & SCOTT, J. (1989). Generations and collective memories. *American Sociological Review, 54,* 359–381.

SCHWARTZ, S. H., & GOTTLIEB, A. (1981). Participants' post-experimental reactions and the ethics of bystander research. *Journal of Experimental Social Psychology, 17,* 396–407.

SCHWARZ, N., BLESS, H., & BOHNER, G. (1991). Mood and persuasion: Affective states influence the processing of persuasive communications. In M. Zanna (Ed.), *Advances in experimental social psychology,* Vol. 24. New York: Academic Press.

SCHWARZ, N., & KURZ, E. (1989). What's in a picture? The impact of face-ism on trait attribution. *European Journal of Social Psychology, 19,* 311–316.

SCHWARZ, N., STRACK, F., KOMMER, D., & WAGNER, D. (1987). Soccer, rooms, and the quality of your life: Mood effects on judgments of satisfaction with life in general and with specific domains. *Journal of Applied Social Psychology, 17,* 69–79.

SCHWARZWALD, J., BIZMAN, A., & RAZ, M. (1983). The foot-in-the-door paradigm: Effects of second request size on donation probability and donor generosity. *Personality and Social Psychology Bulletin, 9,* 443–450.

SCOTT, J. P., & MARSTON, M. V. (1953). Nonadaptive behavior resulting from a series of defeats in fighting mice. *Journal of Abnormal and Social Psychology, 48,* 417–428.

SEARS, D. O. (1979). Life stage effects upon attitude change, especially among the elderly. Manuscript prepared for Workshop on the Elderly of the Future, Committee on Aging, National Research Council, Annapolis, Md., May 3–5.

SEARS, D. O. (1986). College sophomores in the laboratory: Influences of a narrow data base on social psychology's view of human nature. *Journal of Personality and Social Psychology, 51,* 515–530.

SEGAL, H. A. (1954). Initial psychiatric findings of recently repatriated prisoners of war. *American Journal of Psychiatry, 61,* 358–363.

SEGALL, M. H., DASEN, P. R., BERRY, J. W., & POORTINGA, Y. H. (1990). *Human behavior in global perspective: An introduction to cross-cultural psychology.* New York: Pergamon.

SELIGMAN, M. E. P. (1975). *Helplessness: On depression, development and death.* San Francisco: W. H. Freeman.

SELIGMAN, M. E. P. (1988). Why is there so much depression today? The waxing of the individual and the waning of the commons. The G. Stanley Hall Lecture, American Psychological Association convention.

SELIGMAN, M. E. P. (1991). *Learned optimism.* New York: Knopf.

SELIGMAN, M. E. P., NOLEN-HOEKSEMA, S., THORNTON, N., & THORNTON, K. M. (1990). Explanatory style as a mechanism of disappointing athletic performance. *Psychological Science, 1*, 143–146.

SELIGMAN, M. E. P., & SCHULMAN, P. (1986). Explanatory style as a predictor of productivity and quitting among life insurance sales agents. *Journal of Personality and Social Psychology, 50*, 832–838.

SELTZER, L. F. (1983). Influencing the "shape" of resistance: An experimental exploration of paradoxical directives and psychological reactance. *Basic and Applied Social Psychology, 4*, 47–71.

SETA, C. E., & SETA, J. J. (1992). Increments and decrements in mean arterial pressure levels as a function of audience composition: An averaging and summation analysis. *Personality and Social Psychology Bulletin.*

SETA, J. J. (1982). The impact of comparison processes on coactors' task performance. *Journal of Personality and Social Psychology, 42*, 281–291.

SHARMA, N. (1981). Some aspect of attitude and behaviour of mothers. *Indian Psychological Review, 20*, 35–42.

SHEPPERD, J. A., & ARKIN, R. M. (1991). Behavioral other-enhancement: Strategically obscuring the link between performance and evaluation. *Journal of Personality and Social Psychology, 60*, 79–88.

SHEPPERD, J. A., & WRIGHT, R. A. (1989). Individual contributions to a collective effort: An incentive analysis. *Personality and Social Psychology Bulletin, 15*, 141–149.

SHERIF, M. (1966). *In common predicament: Social psychology of intergroup conflict and cooperation.* Boston: Houghton Mifflin.

SHORT, J. F., JR. (ED.) (1969). *Gang delinquency and delinquent subcultures.* New York: Harper & Row.

SHOTLAND, R. L., & CRAIG, J. M. (1988). Can men and women differentiate between friendly and sexually interested behavior? *Social Psychology Quarterly, 51*, 67–73.

SHOWERS, C., & RUBEN, C. (1987). Distinguishing pessimism from depression: Negative expectations and positive coping mechanisms. Paper presented at the American Psychological Association convention.

SHRAUGER, J. S. (1975). Responses to evaluation as a function of initial self-perceptions. *Psychological Bulletin, 82*, 581–596.

SHRAUGER, J. S. (1983). The accuracy of self-prediction: How good are we and why? Paper presented at the Midwestern Psychological Association convention.

SILVER, M., & GELLER, D. (1978). On the irrelevance of evil: The organization and individual action. *Journal of Social Issues, 34*, 125–136.

SIMPSON, J. A. (1987). The dissolution of romantic relationships: Factors involved in relationship stability and emotional distress. *Journal of Personality and Social Psychology, 53*, 683–692.

SIMPSON, J. A., CAMPBELL, B., & BERSCHEID, E. (1986). The association between romantic love and marriage: Kephart (1967) twice revisited. *Personality and Social Psychology Bulletin, 12*, 363–372.

SIMPSON, J. A., GANGESTAD, S. W., & LERMA, M. (1990). Perception of physical attractiveness: Mechanisms involved in the maintenance of romantic relationships. *Journal of Personality and Social Psychology, 59*, 1192–1201.

SINGER, M. (1979a). Cults and cult members. Address to the American Psychological Association convention.

SINGER, M. (1979b, July–August). Interviewed by M. Freeman. Of cults and communication: A conversation with Margaret Singer. *APA Monitor*, pp. 6–7.

SIVARD, R. L. (1991). *World military and social expenditures*. Washington, DC: World Priorities.

SKAALVIK, E. M., & HAGTVET, K. A. (1990). Academic achievement and self-concept: An analysis of causal predominance in a developmental perspective. *Journal of Personality and Social Psychology, 58*, 292–307.

SLAVIN, R. E. (1990, December/January). Research on cooperative learning: Consensus and controversy. *Educational Leadership*, pp. 52–54.

SLOAN, J. H., KELLERMAN, A. L., REAY, D. T., FERRIS, J. A., KOEPSELL, T., RIVARA, F. P., RICE, C., GRAY, L., & LoGERFO, J. (1988). Handgun regulations, crime, assaults, and homicide: A tale of two cities. *New England Journal of Medicine, 319*, 1256–1261.

SLOVIC, P. (1972). From Shakespeare to Simon: Speculations—and some evidence—about man's ability to process information. *Oregon Research Institute Research Bulletin, 12*(2).

SLOVIC, P., & FISCHHOFF, B. (1977). On the psychology of experimental surprises. *Journal of Experimental Psychology: Human Perception and Performance, 3*, 455–551.

SLOWIACZEK, L. M., KLAYMAN, J., SHERMAN, S. J., & SKOV, R. B. (1991). Information selection and use in hypothesis testing: What is a good question, and what is a good answer? Unpublished manuscript, State Univ. of New York at Albany.

SMEDLEY, J. W., & BAYTON, J. A. (1978). Evaluative race-class stereotypes by race and perceived class of subjects. *Journal of Personality and Social Psychology, 3*, 530–535.

SMITH, A. (1976). *The wealth of nations*. Book 1. Chicago: Univ. of Chicago Press. (Originally published, 1776.)

SMITH, D. E., GIER, J. A., & WILLIS, F. N. (1982). Interpersonal touch and compliance with a marketing request. *Basic and Applied Social Psychology, 3*, 35–38.

SMITH, D. S., & STRUBE, M. J. (1991). Self-protective tendencies as moderators of self-handicapping impressions. *Basic and Applied Social Psychology, 12*, 63–80.

SMITH, H. (1976). *The Russians*. New York: Ballantine. Cited by B. Latané, K. Williams, and S. Harkins, Many hands make light the work. *Journal of Personality and Social Psychology*, 1979, *37*, 822–832.

SMITH, P. B., & TAYEB, M. (1989). Organizational structure and processes. In M. Bond (Ed.), *The cross-cultural challenge to social psychology*. Newbury Park, CA: Sage.

SMITH, T. W. (1990, December). Personal communication. Chicago: National Opinion Research Center.

SMITH, W. P. (1987). Conflict and negotiation: Trends and emerging issues. *Journal of Applied Social Psychology, 17*, 641–677.

SNODGRASS, M. A. (1987). The relationships of differential loneliness, intimacy, and characterological attributional style to duration of loneliness. *Journal of Social Behavior and Personality, 2*, 173–186.

SNYDER, C. R. (1978). The "illusion" of uniqueness. *Journal of Humanistic Psychology, 18*, 33–41.

SNYDER, C. R. (1980, March). The uniqueness mystique. *Psychology Today*, pp. 86–90.

SNYDER, C. R., & FROMKIN, H. L. (1980). *Uniqueness: The human pursuit of difference.* New York: Plenum.

SNYDER, C. R., & HIGGINS, R. L. (1988). Excuses: Their effective role in the negotiation of reality. *Psychological Bulletin, 104*, 23–35.

SNYDER, C. R., & SMITH, T. W. (1986). On being "shy like a fox": A self-handicapping analysis. In W. H. Jones et al. (Eds.), *Shyness: Perspectives on research and treatment.* New York: Plenum.

SNYDER, M. (1981). Seek, and ye shall find: Testing hypotheses about other people. In E. T. Higgins, C. P. Herman, & M. P. Zanna (Eds.), *Social cognition: The Ontario symposium on personality and social psychology.* Hillsdale, NJ: Erlbaum.

SNYDER, M. (1983). The influence of individuals on situations: Implications for understanding the links between personality and social behavior. *Journal of Personality, 51*, 497–516.

SNYDER, M. (1984). When belief creates reality. In L. Berkowitz (Ed.), *Advances in experimental social psychology*, Vol. 18. New York: Academic Press.

SNYDER, M. (1991). Selling images versus selling products: Motivational foundations of consumer attitudes and behavior. *Advances in Consumer Research.*

SNYDER, M., BERSCHEID, E., & GLICK, P. (1985). Focusing on the exterior and the interior: Two investigations of the initiation of personal relationships. *Journal of Personality and Social Psychology, 48*, 1427–1439.

SNYDER, M., BERSCHEID, E., & MATWYCHUK, A. (1988). Orientations toward personnel selection: Differential reliance on appearance and personality. *Journal of Personality and Social Psychology, 54*, 972–979.

SNYDER, M., CAMPBELL, B., & PRESTON, E. (1982). Testing hypotheses about human nature: Assessing the accuracy of social stereotypes. *Social Cognition, 1*, 256–272.

SNYDER, M., & DeBONO, K. G. (1987). A functional approach to attitudes and persuasion. In M. P. Zanna, J. M. Olson, & C. P. Herman (Eds.), *Social influence: The Ontario symposium*, Vol. 5. Hillsdale, NJ: Erlbaum.

SNYDER, M., & ICKES, W. (1985). Personality and social behavior. In G. Lindzey & E. Aronson (Eds.), *Handbook of social psychology* (3rd ed.). New York: Random House.

SNYDER, M., & SIMPSON, J. (1985). Orientations toward romantic relationships. In S. Duckk & D. Perlman (Eds.), *Understanding personal relationships.* Beverly Hills, CA: Sage.

SNYDER, M., TANKE, E. D., & BERSCHEID, E. (1977). Social perception and interpersonal behavior: On the self-fulfilling nature of social stereotypes. *Journal of Personality and Social Psychology, 35*, 656–666.

SNYDER, M., & THOMSEN, C. J. (1988). Interactions between therapists and clients: Hypothesis testing and behavioral confirmation. In D. C. Turk & P. Salovey (Eds.), *Reasoning, inference, and judgment in clinical psychology.* New York: Free Press.

SOKOLL, G. R., & MYNATT, C. R. (1984). Arousal and free throw shooting. Paper presented at the Midwestern Psychological Association convention, Chicago.

SOLANO, C. H., BATTEN, P. G., & PARISH, E. A. (1982). Loneliness and patterns of self-disclosure. *Journal of Personality and Social Psychology, 43,* 524–531.

SOLOMON, S., GREENBERG, J., & PYSZCZYNSKI, T. (1991). A terror management theory of social behavior: The psychological functions of self-esteem and cultural worldviews. *Advances in Experimental Social Psychology, 24,* 93–159.

SORENSON, S. B., STEIN, J. A., SIEGEL, J. M., GOLDING, J. M., & BURNAM, M. A. (1987). Prevalence of adult sexual assault: The Los Angeles Epidemiologic Catchment Area Study. *American Journal of Epidemiology, 126,* 1154–1164.

SORRENTINO, R. M., BOBOCEL, D. R., GITTA, M. Z., OLSEN, J. M., & HEWITT, E. C. (1988). Uncertainty orientation and persuasion: Individual differences in the effects of personal relevance on social judgments. *Journal of Personality and Social Psychology, 55,* 357–371.

SPARRELL, J. A., & SHRAUGER, J. S. (1984). Self-confidence and optimism in self-prediction. Paper presented at the American Psychological Association convention.

SPECTOR, P. E. (1986). Perceived control by employees: A meta-analysis of studies concerning autonomy and participation at work. *Human Relations, 39,* 1005–1016.

SPEER, A. (1971). *Inside the Third Reich: Memoirs.* (P. Winston & C. Winston, trans.). New York: Avon.

SPIEGEL, D., BLOOM, J. R., KRAEMER, H. C., & GOTTHEIL, E. (1989, October 14). Effect of psychosocial treatment on survival of patients with metastatic breast cancer. *The Lancet,* 888–891.

SPIEGEL, H. W. (1971). *The growth of economic thought.* Durham, NC: Duke Univ. Press.

SPITZBERG, B. H., & HURT, H. T. (1987). The relationship of interpersonal competence and skills to reported loneliness across time. *Journal of Social Behavior and Personality, 2,* 157–172.

SPIVAK, J. (1979, June 6). *Wall Street Journal.*

SPIVEY, C. B., & PRENTICE-DUNN, S. (1990). Assessing the directionality of deindividuated behavior: Effects of deindividuation, modeling, and private self-consciousness on aggressive and prosocial responses. *Basic and Applied Social Psychology, 11,* 387–403.

SPRECHER, S. (1987). The effects of self-disclosure given and received on affection for an intimate partner and stability of the relationship. *Journal of Personality and Social Psychology, 4,* 115–127.

ST. LAWRENCE, J. S., & JOYNER, D. J. (1991). The effects of sexually violent rock music on males' acceptance of violence against women. *Psychology of Women Quarterly, 15,* 49–63.

STARK, R., & BAINBRIDGE, W. S. (1980). Networks of faith: Interpersonal bonds and recruitment of cults and sects. *American Journal of Sociology, 85,* 1376–1395.

STASSER, G. (1991). Pooling of unshared information during group discussion. In S. Worchel, W. Wood, & J. Simpson (Eds.), *Group process and productivity.* Beverly Hills, CA: Sage.

STAUB, E. (1989). *The roots of evil: The origins of genocide and other group violence.* Cambridge: Cambridge Univ. Press.

STEELE, C. M., & SOUTHWICK, L. (1985). Alcohol and social behavior I: The psychology of drunken excess. *Journal of Personality and Social Psychology, 48,* 18–34.

STEIN, A. H., & FRIEDRICH, L. K. (1972). Television content and young children's behavior. In J. P. Murray, E. A. Rubinstein, & G. A. Comstock (Eds.), *Television and social learning.* Washington, DC: Government Printing Office.

STEIN, D. D., HARDYCK, J. A., & SMITH, M. B. (1965). Race and belief: An open and shut case. *Journal of Personality and Social Psychology, 1,* 281–289.

STEPHAN, W. G. (1986). The effects of school desegregation: An evaluation 30 years after *Brown.* In R. Kidd, L. Saxe, & M. Saks (Eds.), *Advances in applied social psychology.* New York: Erlbaum.

STEPHAN, W. G. (1987). The contact hypothesis in intergroup relations. In C. Hendrick (Ed.), *Group processes and intergroup relations.* Newbury Park, CA: Sage.

STEPHAN, W. G. (1988). School desegregation: Short-term and long-term effects. Paper presented at the national conference, "Opening doors: An appraisal of race relations in America," Univ. of Alabama.

STEPHAN, W. G., BERSCHEID, E., & WALSTER, E. (1971). Sexual arousal and hetero-sexual perception. *Journal of Personality and Social Psychology, 20,* 93–101.

STERNBERG, R. J. (1988). Triangulating love. In R. J. Sternberg & M. L. Barnes (Eds.), *The psychology of love.* New Haven: Yale Univ. Press.

STERNBERG, R. J., & GRAJEK, S. (1984). The nature of love. *Journal of Personality and Social Psychology, 47,* 312–329.

STILLINGER, C., EPELBAUM, M., KELTNER, D., & ROSS, L. (1991). The "reactive devaluation" barrier to conflict resolution. Unpublished manuscript, Stanford University.

STOKES, J., & LEVIN, I. (1986). Gender differences in predicting loneliness from social network characteristics. *Journal of Personality and Social Psychology, 51,* 1069–1074.

STONE, A. A., HEDGES, S. M., NEALE, J. M., & SATIN, M. S. (1985). Prospective and cross-sectional mood reports offer no evidence of a "blue Monday" phenomenon. *Journal of Personality and Social Psychology, 49,* 129–134.

STONE, A. L., & GLASS, C. R. (1986). Cognitive distortion of social feedback in depression. *Journal of Social and Clinical Psychology, 4,* 179–188.

STONER, J. A. F. (1961). A comparison of individual and group decisions involving risk. Unpublished master's thesis, Massachusetts Institute of Technology. Cited by D. G. Marquis in, Individual responsibility and group decisions involving risk. *Industrial Management Review,* 1962, *3,* 8–23.

STORMS, M. D. (1973). Videotape and the attribution process: Reversing actors' and observers' points of view. *Journal of Personality and Social Psychology, 27,* 165–175.

STORMS, M. D., & THOMAS, G. C. (1977). Reactions to physical closeness. *Journal of Personality and Social Psychology, 35,* 412–418.

STOUFFER, S. A., SUCHMAN, E. A., DEVINNEY, L. C., STAR, S. A., & WILLIAMS, R. M., JR. (1949). *The American soldier: Adjustment during army life,* Vol. 1. Princeton, NJ: Princeton Univ. Press.

STRACK, S., & COYNE, J. C. (1983). Social confirmation of dysphoria: Shared and private reactions to depression. *Journal of Personality and Social Psychology, 44,* 798–806.

STRAUSS, M. A., & GELLES, R. J. (1980). *Behind closed doors: Violence in the American family.* New York: Anchor/Doubleday.

STROEBE, W., & INSKO, C. A. (1989). Stereotype, prejudice, and discrimination: Changing conceptions in theory and research. In D. Bar-Tal, C. F. Graumann, A. W. Kruglanski, & W. Stroebe (Eds.), *Stereotyping and prejudice.* New York: Springer-Verlag.

STROEBE, W., INSKO, C. A., THOMPSON, V. D., & LAYTON, B. D. (1971). Effects of physical attractiveness, attitude similarity, and sex on various aspects of interpersonal attraction. *Journal of Personality and Social Psychology, 18,* 79–91.

STROESSNER, S. J., HAMILTON, D. L., & LEPORE, L. (1990). Intergroup categorization and intragroup differentiation: Ingroup-outgroup differences. Paper presented at the American Psychological Association convention.

STRONG, S. R. (1968). Counseling: An interpersonal influence process. *Journal of Counseling Psychology, 17,* 81–87.

STRONG, S. R. (1978). Social psychological approach to psychotherapy research. In S. L. Garfield & A. E. Bergin (Eds.), *Handbook of psychotherapy and behavior change* (2nd ed.). New York: Wiley.

SULS, J., WAN, C. K., & SANDERS, G. S. (1988). False consensus and false uniqueness in estimating the prevalence of health-protective behaviors. *Journal of Applied Social Psychology, 18,* 66–79.

SUMMERS, G., & FELDMAN, N. S. (1984). Blaming the victim versus blaming the perpetrator: An attributional analysis of spouse abuse. *Journal of Social and Clinical Psychology, 2,* 339–347.

SUNDSTROM, E., DE MEUSE, K. P., & FUTRELL, D. (1990). Work teams: Applications and effectiveness. *American Psychologist, 45,* 120–133.

SVENSON, O. (1981). Are we all less risky and more skillful than our fellow drivers? *Acta Psychologica, 47,* 143–148.

SWANN, W. B., JR., & GIULIANO, T. (1987). Confirmatory search strategies in social interaction: How, when, why, and with what consequences. *Journal of Social and Clinical Psychology, 5,* 511–524.

SWANN, W. B., JR., GIULIANO, T., & WEGNER, D. M. (1982). Where leading questions can lead: The power of conjecture in social interaction. *Journal of Personality and Social Psychology, 42,* 1025–1035.

SWANN, W. B., JR., & PREDMORE, S. C. (1985). Intimates as agents of social support: Sources of consolation or despair? *Journal of Personality and Social Psychology, 49,* 1609–1617.

SWANN, W. B., JR., WENZLAFF, R. M., KRULL, D. S., & PELHAM, B. W. (1991). Seeking truth, reaping despair: Depression, self-verification and selection of relationship partners. *Journal of Abnormal Psychology.*

SWAP, W. C. (1977). Interpersonal attraction and repeated exposure to rewarders and punishers. *Personality and Social Psychology Bulletin, 3,* 248–251.

SWEDISH INFORMATION SERVICE (1980, September). *Social change in Sweden,* No. 19, p. 5. (Published by the Swedish Consulate General, 825 Third Avenue, New York, NY 10022.)

SWEENEY, J. (1973). An experimental investigation of the free rider problem. *Social Science Research, 2,* 277–292.

SWEENEY, P. D., ANDERSON, K., & BAILEY, S. (1986). Attributional style in depression: A meta-analytic review. *Journal of Personality and Social Psychology, 50,* 947–991.

SWIM, J., AIKIN, K., HUNTER, B., & HALL, W. (1991). Sexism and racism: Old fashioned and modern prejudices. Unpublished manuscript, Pennsylvania State University.

SWIM, J., BORGIDA, E., MARUYAMA, G., & MYERS, D. G. (1989). Joan McKay vs. John McKay: Do gender stereotypes bias evaluations? *Psychological Bulletin, 105,* 409–429.

SYMONS, D. (INTERVIEWED BY S. KEEN). (1981, February). Eros and alley cop. *Psychology Today,* p. 54.

TAJFEL, H. (1970, November). Experiments in intergroup discrimination. *Scientific American,* pp. 96–102.

TAJFEL, H. (1981). *Human groups and social categories: Studies in social psychology.* London: Cambridge Univ. Press.

TAJFEL, H. (1982). Social psychology of intergroup relations. *Annual Review of Psychology, 33,* 1–39.

TAJFEL, H., & BILLIG, M. (1974). Familiarity and categorization in intergroup behavior. *Journal of Experimental Social Psychology, 10,* 159–170.

TAYLOR, D. A. (1979). Motivational bases. In G. J. Chelune (Ed.), *Self-disclosure: Origins, patterns, and implications of openness in interpersonal relationships.* San Francisco: Jossey-Bass.

TAYLOR, D. A., GOULD, R. J., & BROUNSTEIN, P. J. (1981). Effects of personalistic self-disclosure. *Personality and Social Psychology Bulletin, 7,* 487–492.

TAYLOR, D. M., & DORIA, J. R. (1981). Self-serving and group-serving bias in attribution. *Journal of Social Psychology, 113,* 201–211.

TAYLOR, D. M., WRIGHT, S. C., MOGHADDAM, F. M., & LALONDE, R. N. (1990). The personal/group discrimination discrepancy: Perceiving my group, but not myself, to be a target for discrimination. *Personality and Social Psychology Bulletin, 16,* 254–262.

TAYLOR, S. E. (1981). A categorization approach to stereotyping. In D. L. Hamilton (Ed.), *Cognitive processes in stereotyping and intergroup behavior.* Hillsdale, NJ: Erlbaum.

TAYLOR, S. E. (1989). *Positive illusions: Creative self-deception and the healthy mind.* New York: Basic Books.

TAYLOR, S. E., & BROWN, J. D. (1988). Illusion and well-being: A social psychological perspective on mental health. *Psychological Bulletin, 103,* 193–210.

TAYLOR, S. E., CROCKER, J., FISKE, S. T., SPRINZEN, M., & WINKLER, J. D. (1979). The generalizability of salience effects. *Journal of Personality and Social Psychology, 37,* 357–368.

TAYLOR, S. E., & FISKE, S. T. (1978). Salience, attention, and attribution: Top of the head phenomena. In L. Berkowitz (Ed.), *Advances in experimental social psychology,* Vol. 11. New York: Academic Press.

TAYLOR, S. E., FISKE, S. T., ETCOFF, N. L., & RUDERMAN, A. J. (1978). Categorical and contextual bases of person memory and stereotyping. *Journal of Personality and Social Psychology, 36,* 778–793.

TAYLOR, S. E., KEMENY, M. E., ASPINWALL, L. G., SCHNEIDER, S. G., RODRIQUEZ, R., & HERBERT, M. (1992). Optimism, coping, psychological distress, and high-risk sexual behavior among men at risk for acquired immunodeficiency syndrome (AIDS). *Journal of Personality and Social Psychology, 63,* 460–473.

TAYLOR, S. P., & LEONARD, K. E. (1983). Alcohol and human physical aggression. *Aggression, 2*, 77–101.

TAYLOR, S. P., & PISANO, R. (1971). Physical aggression as a function of frustration and physical attack. *Journal of Social Psychology, 84*, 261–267.

TEGER, A. I. (1980). *Too much invested to quit.* New York: Pergamon.

TEIGEN, K. H. (1986). Old truths or fresh insights? A study of students' evaluations of proverbs. *British Journal of Social Psychology, 25*, 43–50.

TELCH, M. J., KILLEN, J. D., McALISTER, A. L., PERRY, C. L., & MACCOBY, N. (1981). Long-term follow-up of a pilot project on smoking prevention with adolescents. Paper presented at the American Psychological Association convention.

TENNEN, H., & AFFLECK, G. (1987). The costs and benefits of optimistic explanations and dispositional optimism. *Journal of Personality, 55*, 377–393.

TESSER, A. (1988). Toward a self-evaluation maintenance model of social behavior. In L. Berkowitz (Ed.), *Advances in experimental social psychology*, Vol. 21. San Diego, CA: Academic Press.

TESSER, A., & PAULHUS, D. (1983). The definition of self: Private and public self-evaluation management strategies. *Journal of Personality and Social Psychology, 44*, 672–682.

TETLOCK, P. E. (1985). Integrative complexity of American and Soviet foreign policy rhetoric: A time-series analysis. *Journal of Personality and Social Psychology, 49*, 1565–1585.

THOMAS, K. W., & PONDY, L. R. (1977). Toward an "intent" model of conflict management among principal parties. *Human Relations, 30*, 1089–1102.

THOMAS, L. (1978). Hubris in science? *Science, 200*, 1459–1462.

THOMPSON, L. (1990a). An examination of naive and experienced negotiators. *Journal of Personality and Social Psychology, 59*, 82–90.

THOMPSON, L. (1990b). The influence of experience on negotiation performance. *Journal of Experimental Social Psychology, 26*, 528–544.

THOMPSON, L. L., & CROCKER, J. (1985). Prejudice following threat to the self-concept. Effects of performance expectations and attributions. Unpublished manuscript, Northwestern University.

TICE, D. M. (1991). Esteem protection or enhancement? Self-handicapping motives and attributions differ by trait self-esteem. *Journal of Personality and Social Psychology, 60*, 711–725.

Time (1990, Fall issue on women). Asia: Discarding daughters, p. 40.

TIMKO, C., & MOOS, R. H. (1989). Choice, control, and adaptation among elderly residents of sheltered care settings. *Journal of Applied Social Psychology, 19*, 636–655.

Toronto News (1977, July 26).

TRAVIS, L. E. (1925). The effect of a small audience upon eye-hand coordination. *Journal of Abnormal and Social Psychology, 20*, 142–146.

TRIANDIS, H. C., BONTEMPO, R., VILLAREAL, M. J., ASAI, M., & LUCCA, N. (1988). Individualism and collectivism: Cross-cultural perspectives on self-ingroup relationships. *Journal of Personality and Social Psychology, 54*, 323–338.

TRIANDIS, H. C., BRISLIN, R., & HUI, C. H. (1988). Cross-cultural training across the individualism-collectivism divide. *International Journal of Intercultural Relations, 12*, 269–289.

TRIMBLE, J. E. (1988). Stereotypical images, American Indians, and prejudice. In P. A. Katz & D. A. Taylor (Eds.), *Eliminating racism: Profiles in controversy.* New York: Plenum.

TRIPLETT, N. (1898). The dynamogenic factors in pacemaking and competition. *American Journal of Psychology, 9,* 507–533.

TROPE, Y., BASSOK, M., & ALON, E. (1984). The questions lay interviewers ask. *Journal of Personality, 52,* 90–106.

TROST, M. R., MAASS, A., & KENRICK, D. T. (1992). Minority influence: Personal relevance biases cognitive processes and reverses private acceptance. *Journal of Experimental Social Psychology.*

TUMIN, M. M. (1958). Readiness and resistance to desegregation: A social portrait of the hard core. *Social Forces, 36,* 256–273.

TURNER, C. W., HESSE, B. W., & PETERSON-LEWIS, S. (1986). Naturalistic studies of the long-term effects of television violence. *Journal of Social Issues, 42*(3), 51–74.

TURNER, M. E., PRATKANIS, A. R., PROBASCO, P., & LEVE, C. (1992). Threat, cohesion, and group effectiveness: Testing a collective dissonance reduction perspective on groupthink. *Journal of Personality and Social Psychology.*

TV Guide (1977, January 26), pp. 5–10.

TVERKSY, A., & KAHNEMAN, D. (1974). Judgment under uncertainty: Heuristics and biases. *Science, 185,* 1123–1131.

ULEMAN, J. S. (1989). A framework for thinking intentionally about unintended thoughts. In J. S. Uleman & J. A. Bargh (Eds.), *Unintended thought: The limits of awareness, intention, and control.* New York: Guilford.

ULEMAN, J. S., & BARGH, J. A. (EDS.) (1989). *Unintended thought: The limits of awareness, intention, and control.* New York: Guilford.

UMBERSON, D., & HUGHES, M. (1987). The impact of physical attractiveness on achievement and psychological well-being. *Social Psychology Quarterly, 50,* 227–236.

UPI. (1967, September 23). Cited by P. G. Zimbardo, The human choice: Individuation, reason, and order versus deindividuation, impulse, and chaos. In W. J. Arnold & D. Levine (Eds.), *Nebraska symposium on motivation,* 1969. Lincoln: Univ. of Nebraska Press, 1970.

VAILLANT, G. E. (1977). *Adaptation to life.* Boston: Little, Brown.

VALLONE, R. P., GRIFFIN, D. W., LIN, S., & ROSS, L. (1990). Overconfident prediction of future actions and outcomes by self and others. *Journal of Personality and Social Psychology, 58,* 582–592.

VALLONE, R. P., ROSS, L., & LEPPER, M. R. (1985). The hostile media phenomenon: Biased perception and perceptions of media bias in coverage of the "Beirut Massacre." *Journal of Personality and Social Psychology, 49,* 577–585.

VANCOUVER, J. B., RUBIN, B., & KERR, N. L. (1991). Sex composition of groups and member motivation III: Motivational losses at a feminine task. *Basic and Applied Social Psychology, 12,* 133–144.

VANDERSLICE, V. J., RICE, R. W., & JULIAN, J. W. (1987). The effects of participation in decision-making on worker satisfaction and productivity: An organizational simulation. *Journal of Applied Social Psychology, 17,* 158–170.

VAN LANGE, P. A. M. (1991). Being better but not smarter than others: The Muhammad Ali effect at work in interpersonal situations. *Personality and Social Psychology Bulletin, 17,* 689–693.

VAN STADEN, F. J. (1987). White South Africans' attitudes toward the desegregation of public amenities. *Journal of Social Psychology, 127,* 163–173.

VAN YPEREN, N. W., & BUUNK, B. P. (1990). A longitudinal study of equity and satisfaction in intimate relationships. *European Journal of Social Psychology, 20,* 287–309.

VAUX, A. (1988). Social and personal factors in loneliness. *Journal of Social and Clinical Psychology, 6,* 462–471.

VERPLANKEN, B. (1991). Persuasive communication of risk information: A test of cue versus message processing effects in a field experiment. *Personality and Social Psychology Bulletin, 17,* 188–193.

VITELLI, R. (1988). The crisis issue assessed: An empirical analysis. *Basic and Applied Social Psychology, 9,* 301–309.

WACHTEL, P. L. (1989). *The poverty of affluence: A psychological portrait of the American way of life.* Philadelphia: New Society.

WAGSTAFF, G. F. (1983). Attitudes to poverty, the Protestant ethic, and political affiliation: A preliminary investigation. *Social Behavior and Personality, 11,* 45–47.

WALLACE, M. (1969, November 25). *New York Times.*

WALSTER (HATFIELD), E. (1965). The effect of self-esteem on romantic liking. *Journal of Experimental Social Psychology, 1,* 184–197.

WALSTER (HATFIELD), E., ARONSON, V., ABRAHAMS, D., & ROTTMAN, L. (1966). Importance of physical attractiveness in dating behavior. *Journal of Personality and Social Psychology, 4,* 508–516.

WALSTER (HATFIELD), E., & WALSTER, G. W. (1978). *A new look at love.* Reading, MA: Addison-Wesley.

WALSTER (HATFIELD), E., WALSTER, G. W., & BERSCHEID, E. (1978). *Equity: Theory and research.* Boston: Allyn & Bacon.

WARD, W. C., & JENKINS, H. M. (1965). The display of information and the judgment of contingency. *Canadian Journal of Psychology, 19,* 231–241.

WASON, P. C. (1960). On the failure to eliminate hypotheses in a conceptual task. *Quarterly Journal of Experimental Psychology, 12,* 129–140.

WATSON, D. (1982). The actor and the observer: How are their perceptions of causality divergent? *Psychological Bulletin, 92,* 682–700.

WATSON, R. I., JR. (1973). Investigation into deindividuation using a cross-cultural survey technique. *Journal of Personality and Social Psychology, 25,* 342–345.

WEARY, G., HARVEY, J. H., SCHWIEGER, P., OLSON, C. T., PERLOFF, R., & PRITCHARD, S. (1982). Self-presentation and the moderation of self-serving biases. *Social Cognition, 1,* 140–159.

WEHR, P. (1979). *Conflict regulation.* Boulder, CO: Westview.

WEINER, B. (1981). The emotional consequences of causal ascriptions. Unpublished manuscript, UCLA.

WEINSTEIN, N. D. (1980). Unrealistic optimism about future life events. *Journal of Personality and Social Psychology, 39,* 806–820.

WEINSTEIN, N. D. (1982). Unrealistic optimism about susceptibility to health problems. *Journal of Behavioral Medicine, 5,* 441–460.

WEISS, J., & BROWN, P. (1976). Self-insight error in the explanation of mood. Unpublished manuscript, Harvard University.

WENER, R., FRAZIER, W., & FARBSTEIN, J. (1987, June). Building better jails. *Psychology Today,* pp. 40–49.

WHEELER, L., REIS, H. T., & BOND, M. H. (1989). Collectivism-individualism in everyday social life: The middle kingdom and the melting pot. *Journal of Personality and Social Psychology, 57,* 79–86.

WHITE, G. L. (1980). Physical attractiveness and courtship progress. *Journal of Personality and Social Psychology, 39,* 660–668.

WHITE, P. A., & YOUNGER, D. P. (1988). Differences in the ascription of transient internal states to self and other. *Journal of Experimental Social Psychology, 24,* 292–309.

WHITE, R. K. (1977). Misperception in the Arab-Israeli conflict. *Journal of Social Issues, 33*(1), 190–221.

WHITLEY, B. E., JR., & FRIEZE, I. H. (1985). Children's causal attributions for success and failure in achievement settings: A meta-analysis. *Journal of Educational Psychology, 77,* 608–616.

WHITMAN, R. M., KRAMER, M., & BALDRIDGE, B. (1963). Which dream does the patient tell? *Archives of General Psychology, 8,* 277–282.

WHYTE, G. (1992). Escalating commitment in individual and group decision making: A prospect theory approach. *Organizational Behavior and Human Decision Processes.*

WICKER, A. W. (1971). An examination of the "other variables" explanation of attitude-behavior inconsistency. *Journal of Personality and Social Psychology, 19,* 18–30.

WIDOM, C. S. (1989). Does violence beget violence? A critical examination of the literature. *Psychological Bulletin, 106,* 3–28. (p. 80)

WIEGMAN, O. (1985). Two politicians in a realistic experiment: Attraction, discrepancy, intensity of delivery, and attitude change. *Journal of Applied Social Psychology, 15,* 673–686.

WIESEL, E. (1985, April 6). The brave Christians who saved Jews from the Nazis. *TV Guide,* pp. 4–6.

WILDER, D. A. (1978). Perceiving persons as a group: Effect on attributions of causality and beliefs. *Social Psychology, 41,* 13–23.

WILDER, D. A. (1981). Perceiving persons as a group: Categorization and intergroup relations. In D. L. Hamilton (Ed.), *Cognitive processes in stereotyping and intergroup behavior.* Hillsdale, NJ: Erlbaum.

WILDER, D. A. (1990). Some determinants of the persuasive power of in-groups and out-groups: Organization of information and attribution of independence. *Journal of Personality and Social Psychology, 59,* 1202–1213.

WILDER, D. A., & SHAPIRO, P. N. (1984). Role of out-group cues in determining social identity. *Journal of Personality and Social Psychology, 47,* 342–348.

WILEY, M. G., CRITTENDEN, K. S., & BIRG, L. D. (1979). Why a rejection? Causal attribution of a career achievement event. *Social Psychology Quarterly, 42,* 214–222.

WILLIAMS, C. L. (1989). *Gender differences at work: Women and men in nontraditional occupations.* Berkeley: Univ. of California Press.

WILLIAMS, J. E., & BEST, D. L. (1990a). *Measuring sex stereotypes: A multination study.* Newbury Park, CA: Sage.

WILLIAMS, J. E., & BEST, D. L. (1990b). *Sex and psyche: Gender and self viewed cross-culturally.* Newbury Park, CA: Sage.

WILLIAMS, K. D. (1981). The effects of group cohesion on social loafing. Paper presented at the Midwestern Psychological Association convention.

WILLIAMS, K. D., HARKINS, S., & LATANÉ, B. (1981). Identifiability as a deterrent to social loafing: Two cheering experiments. *Journal of Personality and Social Psychology, 40,* 303–311.

WILLIAMS, K. D., & KARAU, S. J. (1991). Social loafing and social compensation: The effects of expectations of coworker performance. *Journal of Personality and Social Psychology, 61,* 570–581.

WILLIAMS, K. D., NIDA, S. A., BACA, L. D., & LATANÉ, B. (1989). Social loafing and swimming: Effects of identifiability on individual and relay performance of intercollegiate swimmers. *Basic and Applied Social Psychology, 10,* 73–81.

WILLIAMS, T. M. (ED.) (1986). *The impact of television: A natural experiment in three communities.* Orlando, FL: Academic Press.

WILLIS, F. N., & HAMM, H. K. (1980). The use of interpersonal touch in securing compliance. *Journal of Nonverbal Behavior, 5,* 49–55.

WILLS, T. A. (1981). Downward comparison principles in social psychology. *Psychological Bulletin, 90,* 245–271.

WILSON, D. K., KAPLAN, R. M., & SCHNEIDERMAN, L. J. (1987). Framing of decisions and selections of alternatives in health care. *Social Behaviour, 2,* 51–59.

WILSON, D. K., PURDON, S. E., & WALLSTON, K. A. (1988). Compliance to health recommendations: A theoretical overview of message framing. *Health Education Research, 3,* 161–171.

WILSON, R. C., GAFT, J. G., DIENST, E. R., WOOD, L., & BAVRY, J. L. (1975). *College professors and their impact on students.* New York: Wiley.

WILSON, R. S., & MATHENY, JR., A. P. (1986). Behavior-genetics research in infant temperament: The Louisville twin study. In R. Plomin & J. Dunn (Eds.), *The study of temperament: Changes, continuities, and challenges.* Hillsdale, NJ: Erlbaum.

WILSON, T. D., LASER, P. S., & STONE, J. I. (1982). Judging the predictors of one's mood: Accuracy and the use of shared theories. *Journal of Experimental Social Psychology, 18,* 537–556.

WINCH, R. F. (1958). *Mate selection: A study of complementary needs.* New York: Harper & Row.

WINTER, F. W. (1973). A laboratory experiment of individual attitude response to advertising exposure. *Journal of Marketing Research, 10,* 130–140.

WITTENBERG, M. T., & REIS, H. T. (1986). Loneliness, social skills, and social perception. *Personality and Social Psychology Bulletin, 12,* 121–130.

WIXON, D. R., & LAIRD, J. D. (1976). Awareness and attitude change in the forced-compliance paradigm: The importance of when. *Journal of Personality and Social Psychology, 34,* 376–384.

WOLF, S. (1987). Majority and minority influence: A social impact analysis. In M. P. Zanna, J. M. Olson, & C. P. Herman (Eds.), *Social influence: The Ontario symposium on personality and social psychology,* Vol. 5. Hillsdale, NJ: Erlbaum.

WOLF, S., & LATANÉ, B. (1985). Conformity, innovation and the psycho-social law. In S. Moscovici, G. Mugny, & E. Van Avermaet (Eds.), *Perspectives on minority influence.* Cambridge: Cambridge Univ. Press.

WOOD, J. V., SALTZBERG, J. A., & GOLDSAMT, L. A. (1990). Does affect induce self-focused attention? *Journal of Personality and Social Psychology, 58,* 899–908.

WOOD, J. V., SALTZBERG, J. A., NEALE, J. M., STONE, A. A., & RACHMIEL, T. B. (1990). Self-focused attention, coping responses, and distressed mood in everyday life. *Journal of Personality and Social Psychology, 58,* 1027–1036.

WOOD, W., & RHODES, N. (1991). Sex differences in interaction style in task groups. In C. Ridgeway (Ed.), *Gender and interaction: The role of microstructures in inequality.* New York: Springer-Verlag.

WORCHEL, S., & BROWN, E. H. (1984). The role of plausibility in influencing environmental attributions. *Journal of Experimental Social Psychology, 20,* 86–96.

WORD, C. O., ZANNA, M. P., & COOPER, J. (1974). The nonverbal mediation of self-fulfilling prophecies in interracial interaction. *Journal of Experimental Social Psychology, 10,* 109–120.

WORRINGHAM, C. J., & MESSICK, D. M. (1983). Social facilitation of running: An unobtrusive study. *Journal of Social Psychology, 121,* 23–29.

WU, D. Y. H., & TSENG, W. S. (1985). Introduction: The characteristics of Chinese culture. In D. Y. H. Wu and W. S. Tseng (Eds.), *Chinese culture and mental health.* San Diego, CA: Academic Press.

WYLIE, R. C. (1979). *The self-concept (Vol. 2): Theory and research on selected topics.* Lincoln: Univ. of Nebraska Press.

YOUNG, W. R. (1977, February). There's a girl on the tracks! *Reader's Digest,* pp. 91–95.

YUKL, G. (1974). Effects of the opponent's initial offer, concession magnitude, and concession frequency on bargaining behavior. *Journal of Personality and Social Psychology, 30,* 323–335.

YZERBYT, V. Y., & LEYENS, J. P. (1991). Requesting information to form an impression: The influence of valence and confirmatory status. *Journal of Experimental Social Psychology, 27,* 337–356.

ZAJONC, R. B. (1965). Social facilitation. *Science, 149,* 269–274.

ZAJONC, R. B. (1968). Attitudinal effects of mere exposure. *Journal of Personality and Social Psychology, 9,* Monograph Suppl. No. 2, part 2.

ZAJONC, R. B. (1970, February). Brainwash: Familiarity breeds comfort. *Psychology Today,* pp. 32–35, 60–62.

ZAJONC, R. B., & SALES, S. M. (1966). Social facilitation of dominant and subordinate responses. *Journal of Experimental Social Psychology, 2,* 160–168.

ZANDER, A. (1969). Students' criteria of satisfaction in a classroom committee project. *Human Relations, 22,* 195–207.

ZANNA, M. P., HADDOCK, G., & ESSES, V. M. (1990). The nature of prejudice. Paper presented at the Nags Head Conference on Stereotypes and Intergroup Relations, Kill Devil Hills, NC.

ZANNA, M. P., & PACK, S. J. (1975). On the self-fulfilling nature of apparent sex differences in behavior. *Journal of Experimental Social Psychology, 11,* 583–591.

ZEBROWITZ-McARTHUR, L. (1988). Person perception in cross-cultural perspective. In M. H. Bond (Ed.), *The cross-cultural challenge to social psychology.* Newbury Park, CA: Sage.

ZIGLER, E. F., & GILMAN, E. P. (1990). An agenda for the 1990s: Supporting families. In D. Blankenhorn, S. Bayme, & J. B. Elshtain (Eds.), *Rebuilding the nest: A new commitment to the American family.* Milwaukee, WI: Family Service America.

ZILLMANN, D. (1989). Aggression and sex: Independent and joint operations. In H. L. Wagner & A. S. R. Manstead (Eds.), *Handbook of psychophysiology: Emotion and social behavior.* Chichester: Wiley.

ZILLMANN, D. (1989). Effects of prolonged consumption of pornography. In D. Zillmann & J. Bryant (Eds.), *Pornography: Research advances and policy considerations*. Hillsdale, NJ: Erlbaum.

ZIMBARDO, P. G. (1970). The human choice: Individuation, reason, and order versus deindividuation, impulse, and chaos. In W. J. Arnold & D. Levine (Eds.), *Nebraska symposium on motivation, 1969*. Lincoln: Univ. of Nebraska Press.

ZIMBARDO, P. G. (1972). The Stanford prison experiment. A slide/tape presentation produced by Philip G. Zimbardo, Inc., P. O. Box 4395, Stanford, Calif. 94305.

ZIMBARDO, P. G., EBBESEN, E. B., & MASLACH, C. (1977). *Influencing attitudes and changing behavior*. Reading, MA: Addison-Wesley.

ZIMBARDO, P. G., WEISENBERG, M., FIRESTONE, I., & LEVY, B. (1965). Communicator effectiveness in producing public conformity and private attitude change. *Journal of Personality, 33*, 233–256.

Permissions Acknowledgments

———— ❖ ————

Figures

Fig. 4-1   After R. P. Vallone, L. D. Ross, and M. R. Lepper, "The Hostile Media Phenomenon: Biased Perception and Perceptions of Media Bias in Coverage of the 'Beruit Massacre' " in *Journal of Personality and Social Psychology*, vol. 49 (1985), pp. 577–585. © 1985. Used by permission of Prof. Lee D. Ross.

Fig. 4-3   After C. McFarland, M. Ross, and N. DeCourville, "Women's Theories of Menstruation and Biases in Recall of Menstrual Symptoms," in *Journal of Personality and Social Psychology*, vol. 57 (1989), pp. 522–531. © 1989 American Psychological Association. Used by permission of Prof. Cathy McFarland.

Fig. 6-1   After E. E. Jones and V. A. Harris, "The Attribution of Attitudes," in *Journal of Experimental Social Psychology*, vol. 3 (1967), pp. 2–24. © 1967. Used by permission of Academic Press and Prof. Edward E. Jones.

Fig. 6-2   After L. D. Ross, T. M. Amabile, and J. L. Steinmetz, "Social Roles, Social Control, and Biases in Social-perception Process," in *Journal of Personality and Social Psychology*, vol. 35 (1977), pp. 485–494. © 1977 American Psychological Association. Used by permission of Prof. Lee D. Roth.

Fig. 10-2   From J. P. Forgas, G. H. Blower, and S. E. Krantz, "The Influence of Mood on Perceptions of Social Interactions," *Journal of Experimental Social Psychology*, vol. 20 (1984), pp. 497–513. Used by permission of Academic Press.

Fig. 13-1   After A. H. Eagley and W. Wood, "Explaining Sex Differences in Social Behavior: A Meta-analytic Perspective," in *Personality and Social Psychology Bulletin*, vol. 17, no. 3 (1991), pp. 306–315. © 1991 by the Society for Personality and Social Psychology, Inc. Used by permission of Sage Publications, Inc.

Fig. 14-1   After S. E. Asch, "Opinions and Social Pressure." Copyright © 1955 by Scientific American, Inc. All rights reserved.

Fig. 14-2   After S. Milgram, "Some Conditions of Obedience and Disobedience to Authority," in *Human Relations*, vol. 18 (1965), pp. 57–76. © 1965. Used by permission of Mrs. Alexandra Milgram.

Fig. 16–1   After A. McAlister, *et al.*, "Pilot Study of Smoking, Alcohol, and Drug-Abuse Prevention," in *American Journal of Public Health*, vol. 70 (1980), pp. 719–721. © 1980. Used by permission of American Public Health Association.

Fig. 17–1   After R. B. Zajonc and S. M. Sales, "Social Facilitation of Dominant and Subordinate Responses," in *Journal of Experimental and Social Psychology*, vol. 2 (1966), pp. 160–166. © 1966. Used by permission of Academic Press and Prof. R. B. Zajonc.

Fig. 18–2   From J. M. Jackson and K. D. Williams, "Social Loafing: A Review and Theoretical Analysis," Fordham University, unpublished.

Fig. 19–2   After E. Diener, *et al.*, "Effects of Deindividuation Variables on Stealing among Halloween Trick-or-Treaters," in *Journal of Personality and Social Psychology*, vol. 33 (1976), pp. 178–183. © 1976 American Psychology Association. Used by permission of Prof. Edward F. Diener.

Fig. 20–2   After D. A. Myers and G. D. Bishop, "Discussion Effects on Racial Attitudes," in *Science*, vol. 221 (August 21, 1970), p. 770. Copyright 1970 by the AAAS. Used by permission of the AAAS.

Fig. 20–3   Adapted with the permission of the Free Press, a Division of Macmillan, Inc., from *Decision Making*: A Psychological Analysis of Conflict, Choice, and Commitment by Irving L. Janis and Leon Mann. Copyright © 1977 by The Free Press.

Fig. 21–1   After G. Gallup, Jr., and L. Hugick, "Racial Tolerance Grows, Progress on Racial Equality Less Evident," in *Gallup Poll Monthly*, June 23, 1990. Used by permission of the Gallup Organization.
    After R. G. Niemi, J. Mueller, and T. W. Smith, *Trends in Public Opinion: A Compendium of Survey Data*. Copyright © 1989 Greenwood Press, an imprint of Greenwood Publishing Group, Inc., Westport, CT Used with permission.
    After a personal communication of the author with Tom W. Smith, Director, General Social Survey, National Opinion Research Center. Used with his permission.

Fig. 22–2   After R. W. Rogers and S. Prentice-Dunn, "Deindividuation and Anger-mediated Racial Aggression: Unmasking Regressive Racism," in *Journal of Personality and Social Psychology*, vol. 14 (1981), pp. 554–563. © 1981. Used by permission of Prof. Ronald W. Rogers.

Fig. 22–4   After R. G. Niemi, J. Mueller, and T. W. Smith, *Trends in Public Opinion: A Compendium of Survey Data*. Copyright © 1989 Greenwood Press, an imprint of Greenwood Publishing Group, Inc., Westport, CT. Used with permission.
    After a personal communication of the author with Tom W. Smith, Director, General Social Survey, National Opinion Research Center. Used with his permission.
    After P. G. Devine and R. S. Malpass, "Orienting Strategies in Differential Face Recognition," in *Personality and Social Psychology Bulletin*, vol. 11, no. 1 (1985), pp. 33–40. © 1985 by the Society for Personality and Social Psychology, Inc. Reprinted by permission of Sage Publications, Inc.

Fig. 24–2   After A. Bandura, "The Social Learning Perspective: Mechanisms of Aggression," in H. Toch, ed., *Psychology of Crime and Criminal Justice*. © 1979. Used by permission of Prof. Albert Bandura.

Fig. 25–1   After L. D. Eron and L. R. Huesmann, "The Control of Aggressive Behavior by Changes in Attitude," in R. J. Blanchard and C. Blanchard, eds., *Advances in the Study of Aggression*, vol. 1. © 1984. Used by permission of Academic Press and Dr. Leonard D. Eron.

Fig. 25–2   After E. Donnerstein, "Aggressive Erotica and Violence against Women," in *Journal of Personality and Social Psychology*. © 1980. Used by permission of Prof. Edward I. Donnerstein.

Fig. 28–1   After R. B. Zajonc, "Attitudinal Effects of Mere Exposure," in *Journal of Personality and Social Psychology*, vol. 9, pt. 9 (1968), Monograph Supplement no. 2, pt. 2. © 1968 American Psychological Association. Used by permission of R. B. Zajonc.

Fig. 29–1   From R. J. Sternberg and M. L. Barnes, eds., *The Psychology of Love*, © 1988. Used by permission of Yale University Press.

Fig. 29–2   After U. Gupta and P. Singh, "Exploratory Study of Love and Liking and Type of Marriage," in *Indian Journal of Applied Psychology*, vol. 19 (1982), pp. 92–97.

After J. A. Simpson, B. Campbell, and E. Bersheid, "The Association Between Love and Marriage," in *Personality and Social Psychology Bulletin*, vol. 12, no. 3 (1986), pp. 367–372. Copyright © 1986 by the Society for Personality and Social Psychology, Inc. Reprinted by permission of Sage Publications, Inc.

Fig. 30–2   After B. Latane and M. N. Darley, "Group Inhibition of Bystander Intervention in Emergencies," in *Journal of Personality and Social Psychology*, vol. 10 (1968), pp. 215–221. Copyright © 1968 American Psychological Association. Used by permission of Prof. Bibb Latane.

Table

Table 15–1   From L. DeStefano and D. Colasanto, "Unlike 1975, Today Most Americans Think They Have It Better," in *Gallup Poll Monthly*, no. 293 (1990), pp. EH–26. Used by permission of The Gallup Organization.

Text

Chap. 29   Reprinted with special permission of King Features Syndicate.

Name Index

❖

Subject Index